The French Worker

The French Worker

Autobiographies from the Early Industrial Era

Edited, Translated, and with an Introduction by

MARK TRAUGOTT

University of California Press

BERKELEY   LOS ANGELES   OXFORD

University of California Press
Berkeley and Los Angeles, California

University of California Press, Ltd.
Oxford, England

© 1993 by
The Regents of the University of California

Library of Congress Cataloging-in-Publication Data

The French worker : autobiographies from the early industrial era /
  edited, translated, and with an introduction by Mark Traugott.
    p.   cm.
  Includes bibliographical references.
  ISBN 0-520-07931-0 (alk. paper). — ISBN 0-520-07932-9 (alk.
paper : pbk.)
    1. Working class—France—Biography.   2. Working class—
France—History—19th century.   3. Occupations—France—
History—19th century.   I. Traugott, Mark.
HD8433.A1F74   1993
331.7′00944—dc20   92-6310
                                                              CIP

Printed in the United States of America
9 8 7 6 5 4 3 2 1

Contents

Illustrations

Preface and Acknowledgments

Much of the challenge of putting together a volume of this kind comes from the fact that the sources date from another era, are the product of another culture, and were written in another language than our own. These overlays of difference are what make the life stories of nineteenth-century French workers both intriguing and instructive. They also raise continual questions about the meaning these authors intended to convey and about what sense we, as inhabitants of another place and time, are able to make of their words.

Fortunately, the task of translation is made easier by the fact that these worker-authors relate their stories with few stylistic pretensions. Still, as spare and simple as their prose may be, there are a few conventions that are likely to prove discordant to the modern ear. The tendency to repeat key words, phrases, and even whole incidents (most apparent in the texts by Bédé and Truquin) is at times reminiscent of the use of the refrain in popular songs or poems. I have tried to omit redundant passages, particularly when they seemed to interrupt the flow of the narrative, without eliminating altogether an element of style that suggests how closely the writing of working-class authors remained tied to an essentially oral tradition.

My most difficult task has been to pare down the stories so as to keep this anthology to a manageable length. This required cutting out a great deal of valuable material, sometimes at the expense of the continuity of the author's narrative. In deciding what to exclude, I have been guided by a desire to give this collection a clear focus on the everyday activities, work life, and popular politics of the nineteenth-century working class. The result is, however, a very personalized selection, and by no means the only one that could be made. Wherever possible, my practice has been to remove whole passages rather than separate snippets. To ensure that the reader would know whenever something has been removed, I have marked the spot by inserting ellipsis points in brackets, thus: [. . .]. When the excised passage was substantial, I have sometimes inserted a summary of what it contained.

Problems of a more concrete nature arose in translating specialized vocabulary, such as the popular slang or the occupational cant of the nineteenth century. When comment seemed called for, I have usually indicated the French term and added a brief explanatory note. More frequently, I have used footnotes to clarify or contextualize statements in the texts. I see this volume as serving the needs of a mixed audience with widely varying familiarity with French history and culture; however, the notes are aimed at a reader with limited background.

Certain of these authors were in the habit of italicizing words or phrases, presumably for emphasis, though their choices sometimes make little sense to the contemporary reader. I have retained the authors' italics, except in a few cases where they seemed confusing or distracting. I have felt free to make other minor changes to the text to clarify its meaning; for example, I have sometimes added missing punctuation or placed in separate paragraphs the statements and rejoinders in a conversation that are run together in the French.

In attempting to interpret the authors' words, I have often found my own knowledge of the culture, period, and language insufficient, and have turned to others more expert than myself for assistance and advice. In the process, I have contracted a heavy debt to a number of people which I would like to take this opportunity to acknowledge.

Four individuals stand out for the special contributions they have made over a period of several years. First, I have Victoria Bonnell to thank for initially encouraging me to undertake this work, knowing from her own experience with this anthology's companion volume, *The Russian Worker,* that the fascination of the material would draw me in.

Over a five-year period, my editor Sheila Levine provided the practical guidance that made it possible for this project to see completion. Her sure hand as well as her patience and flexibility when it came to deadlines—but above all her willingness to respect what I saw as the larger purpose such a book might serve—never wavered.

Jonathan Beecher has always made me the gift of his vast knowledge of and enthusiasm for French history. I could ask for no more helpful or supportive colleague.

Finally, Susanna Barrows's insight into French popular culture (to say nothing of her mastery of colloquial speech and gesture!) has been a constant source of amazement and delight, whether I was trying to puzzle out the meaning of some tantalizingly ambiguous passage in these memoirs or grappling with the many-layered meanings of the social interactions typical of the working-class café.

There is a much larger group of individuals who have made material contributions to this project, and though I cannot mention them all, I wish at least to acknowledge the combination of kind words of encouragement and the no less valued—and well-deserved—critical appraisals, both of the translations and of the introduction, that I received from Mary Jo Maynes, Bill Reddy, Bill Sewell, George Sheridan, Chuck Tilly, the members of the Berkeley History Seminar, and the anonymous reviewers of this project at its various stages of completion.

What began for me as a casual foray into a new way of looking at the nineteenth century grew to become a long-term project. It has taken far longer than I originally anticipated, and it is with a certain relief that I am able to bring it to a conclusion. Yet there is a small twinge of regret as well, for never again do I expect to work with materials in which the presence and individuality of the authors is as vividly defined as in the stories told in these pages.

Boulder Creek
October 1991

Introduction

In presenting excerpts from the autobiographies of seven nineteenth-century French workers, this volume invites the reader to enter a world to which direct access is difficult to obtain in any other way. The limited body of memoirs written by wage-earning men and women, many of them self-educated, is remarkable for the evocative quality of the narratives they present. This collection includes some of the finest examples to have survived from the early industrial age in France. Taken individually, each of these texts highlights the fascinating testimony of a person whose dual status as both worker and author gives voice to the sentiments of those who more often lived in anonymity. Taken collectively, these memoirs become a window on the world of the working class at a crucial moment in its transformation into an independent economic and political force in French society.

These authors offer a perspective on their era that is unique in at least two respects. First, drawing upon their own experience, they describe in great detail the everyday activities of ordinary workers. Second, they add a subjective dimension to the information they impart, conveying their private thoughts and often passionate reactions to the events that marked their lives. The autobiographer's act of reconstructing what his or her existence has meant lends it the coherence of a "life lived whole."[1] To be sure, this coherence is achieved in part through the selective embellishment or excision of certain life experiences. The result is an apparently seamless raiment of just the sort that we each weave to clothe ourselves before others. For just this reason—that it is a very human creation much

1. The phrase is borrowed from Charles Lemert, "Whole Life Theory," *Theory and Society* 15, no. 3 (1986): 431–42.

1

like the ones we ourselves continually fabricate and mend—the auto-biographical account offers a privileged point of access, allowing us to don the apron and step into the shoes of a worker who inhabited a period and a culture both like and unlike our own. Because we meet the protagonists on a personal footing, we are better able to discern and appreciate the blend of similarities and differences.

For those who read them (as for those who write them), autobiographies may serve quite different purposes. From a literary or "discourse" perspective, memoirs may constitute ends in themselves, texts worthy of study for what they reveal of cultural conventions. In this introduction, however, as in the task of editing the original book-length texts for this anthology, I have chosen to view these sources as a vehicle for deepening and completing our knowledge of how French workers of the previous century lived and labored.[2] The seven texts are described in summary terms in table 1 (pp. 4–5), and the map (opposite) shows places mentioned in each. Some of these texts are acknowledged classics of the literature on nineteenth-century workers; others have only recently been published or reprinted in French. Virtually all have, of course, long been available to specialists in the history of France, but this is the first time, to my knowledge, that extensive segments of any have been translated into English. For this reason, the present volume both opens these texts to a broader audience and creates the opportunity for new perspectives to emerge. Used in combination with the collections published by Burnett, Bonnell, and Kelly, the present work will be particularly useful to those who wish to undertake the comparative study of class formation in Europe by weighing the direct testimony of British, French, German, and Russian workers.[3]

---

2. The distinction between texts as means and as ends is adapted from an observation made by Philippe Lejeune, *Je est un autre: L'Autobiographie de la littérature aux médias* (Paris, 1980), p. 273. It is, of course, impossible to separate the two perspectives completely, since the form and content of a text and the conditions in which it is produced are inextricably linked. Though these issues are discussed in the third part of this introduction, mention of the particularizing circumstances under which the manuscripts were written is largely confined to the brief introductory notes to each chapter.

3. John Burnett, ed., *The Annals of Labour: Autobiographies of British Working-Class People, 1820–1920* (Bloomington, 1974), and *Destiny Obscure: Autobiographies of Childhood, Education, and Family from the 1820s to the 1920s* (London, 1982); Victoria E. Bonnell, ed., *The Russian Worker: Life and Labor under the Tsarist Regime* (Berkeley, 1983); and Alfred Kelly, ed., *The German Worker: Working-Class Autobiographies from the Age of Industrialization* (Berkeley, 1987). A useful bibliography of British working-class autobiographies can be found in David Vincent, *Bread, Knowledge, and Freedom: A Study of Nineteenth-Century Working-Class Autobiography* (London, 1981).

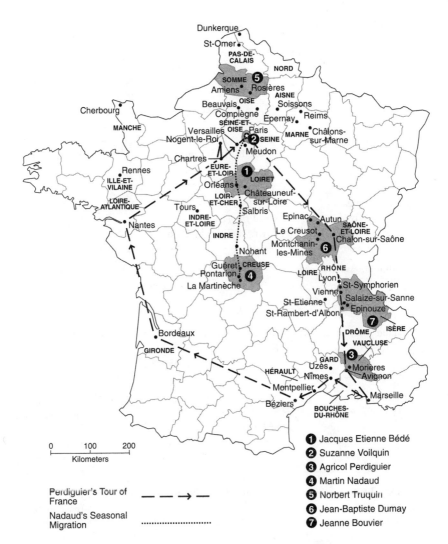

Dunkerque

St-Omer

PAS-DE-CALAIS

NORD

SOMME **5**

Amiens Rosières

AISNE

Beauvais OISE Soissons

Cherbourg Compiègne Epernay Reims

SEINE-ET-OISE

MANCHE

Versailles Paris MARNE Châlons-sur-Marne

Nogent-le-Roi SEINE **2**

Chartres Meudon

Rennes EURE-ET-LOIR **1** LOIRET

ILLE-ET-VILAINE Orléans

LOIRE-ATLANTIQUE LOIR-ET-CHER Châteauneuf-sur-Loire

Tours Salbris

INDRE-ET-LOIRE Epinac Autun

Nantes Le Creusot SAÔNE-ET-LOIRE

INDRE Montchanin-les-Mines **6** Chalon-sur-Saône

Nohant

Guéret CREUSE RHÔNE

Pontarion LOIRE Lyon St-Symphorien

La Martinèche **4** Vienne Salaize-sur-Sanne

St-Etienne Epinouze

St-Rambert-d'Albon **7** ISÈRE

Bordeaux DRÔME

GIRONDE VAUCLUSE

GARD **3**

HÉRAULT Uzès Morières

Nîmes Avignon

Montpellier Marseille

Béziers BOUCHES-DU-RHÔNE

0   100   200
Kilometers

Perdiguier's Tour of France — — → —

Nadaud's Seasonal Migration ....

1 Jacques Etienne Bédé
2 Suzanne Voilquin
3 Agricol Perdiguier
4 Martin Nadaud
5 Norbert Truquin
6 Jean-Baptiste Dumay
7 Jeanne Bouvier

Nineteenth-Century France. The shaded areas are the departments where the authors were born or raised; the numbers correspond to the chapter numbers.

This collection will also enable the reader to form a clearer picture of working-class life during France's turbulent nineteenth century.[4] To provide a context for interpreting the authors' autobiographical accounts, this introductory essay begins with an overview of the forces at work in French society in the age of industrialization, and goes on to sketch what daily life

4. I have chosen to regard the nineteenth century as beginning with the demise of the Old Regime around 1789. This slightly elongated nineteenth century roughly

Table 1. The Authors and Their Texts

Author	Sex	Text	Period covered in these excerpts	Author's Occupation (Sector)
Bédé, Jacques Etienne 1775–1830 +	M	*A Worker in 1820* wr. 1821–36; pub. 1984	1784– 1820	Wood turner (furniture)
Voilquin, Suzanne c. 1798–1865 +	F	*Recollections of a Daughter of the People* wr. 1865; pub. 1866	1807–32	Embroiderer (textiles)
Perdiguier, Agricol 1805–75	M	*Memoirs of a Compagnon* wr. 1852–53; pub. 1854	1805–28	Joiner (construction)
Nadaud, Martin 1815–98	M	*Memoirs of Léonard, a Former Mason's Assistant* wr. 1891; pub. 1895	1815–48	Mason (construction)
Truquin, Norbert 1833–87 +	M	*Memoirs and Adventures of a Proletarian in Times of Revolution* wr. 1887; pub. 1888	1833–67	Silk weaver (textiles); also various unskilled occupations
Dumay, Jean-Baptiste 1841–1926	M	*Memoirs of a Militant Worker from Le Creusot* wr. 1902–26; pub. 1976	1841–68	Metalworker (base metals); also railroad worker
Bouvier, Jeanne 1865–1964	F	*My Memoirs* wr. 1914; pub. 1936	1865–99	Seamstress (clothing); also hatmaker; domestic; silk winder

| Occupation of | | | Region or City of | | |
| | | | | | Adult |
Father	Mother	Spouse	Birth	Training	Residence
Miller	—	Chair seat maker*	Châteauneuf-sur-Loire (Loiret)	Tours (Indre-et-Loire)	Paris
Hatter	—	*Architecte***	Paris (Seine)	Paris	Paris
Joiner	Seamstress	Seamstress	Morières-les-Avignon (Vaucluse)	[Tour of France]	Paris
Mason	—	—	La Martinèche (Creuse)	Paris	Paris
Workshop owner	—	Weaver	Rozières (Somme)	Reims, Amiens, Paris	Lyon (Rhône)
Miner	Seamstress	—	Le Creusot (Saône-et-Loire)	[Tour of France]	Le Creusot
Cooper	—	—	Salaize-sur-Sanne (Isère)	Epinouze (Drôme)	Paris

*Bédé says that his wife worked in the chairmaking shop with him; presumably she was a chair seat maker like Bédé's aunt.

**Voilquin's husband worked in a firm of architects, but the precise nature of his position is not specified.

was like for nineteenth-century French workers. It then discusses the criteria and strategy employed in selecting these autobiographies, before going on to show how such sources can be used to interpret the patterns of economic and political change that took place in the period.

FRENCH SOCIETY IN THE AGE OF INDUSTRIALIZATION

On the eve of the Revolution of 1789–94, the members of French society had little inkling of the momentous changes in the offing. The overthrow and execution of Louis XVI represented no more than the initial phase of a century-long period of civil strife. Though the country would ultimately emerge with a heightened sense of national and cultural unity, traditional social relations were upset by new and dynamic forms of economic activity. These eventually increased the wealth of the society as a whole, but they were often introduced at the expense of the security and well-being of ordinary workers. To understand the experiences of those who lived in this eventful period, we need to examine the interrelated demographic, economic, and political influences which shaped them.

Demographic Dislocation

At the fall of the Old Regime, the size of the population of France was rivaled, among European nations, only by that of Russia. A century and a quarter later, the French population had increased from 27.5 to 40 million inhabitants. Despite this substantial increase in absolute numbers, France lagged so far behind its neighbors in its rate of growth that it had been dwarfed by Russia and surpassed by both Germany and the United Kingdom, where the population had more than tripled in the interim (see table 2).

In the 1830s, a newborn child had slightly higher than a one in six chance of dying before its first birthday, a statistic that changed little before the end of the century.[5] Yet French rates of infant mortality, however high

---

corresponds to the period in which French society witnessed the accelerated capitalist expansion associated with early industrialization. The seven workers chosen for this book make up a group whose members were economically active across the entire period in question. My interest in the interrelationship between the realms of work and collective action led me to focus on the authors' years of childhood, adolescence, and early adulthood, corresponding to the periods in which their socialization, training, and identity formation as workers took place.

5. According to Brian R. Mitchell, there were 176.5 infant deaths per 1,000 live births in the 1830s. The comparable figure for the 1890s was 165.7 deaths. See *European Historical Statistics, 1750–1970* (London, 1981), pp. 137–38.

Table 2. European Population in 1789 and 1914

	1789	1914
European Russia	28 million	140 million
France	27.5	40
Germany	20	68
Austria-Hungary	20	51
Italy	16	36
United Kingdom	14	45

Source: Adapted from Jacques Dupâquier et al., *Histoire de la population française*, vol. 3, *De 1789 à 1914* (Paris, 1988), pp. 2–3. For purposes of comparison, the territory covered (rather than the political entity) has been held constant, since Germany and Italy did not exist in unified form in 1789, and Austria (subsequently Austria-Hungary) lost some territories and acquired others.

by today's standard, do not explain the difference in population growth, for they were similar to those of other European nations. In fact, the relative demographic stagnation of France was largely the result of a rate of birth (just over 25 per year per 1,000 population, on average, during the nineteenth century) that was roughly half that of Russia and consistently remained the lowest in Europe.[6] France saw itself being outdistanced by its European neighbors but was unable to reverse this unfavorable demographic trend.[7]

Just as consequential as changes in the total population were currents of migration within the borders of France. By midcentury, with the construction of railroads, the digging of canals, and improvements in the speed and reliability of the mails, not just the number of French citizens but also the rate at which they were brought into mutual contact was rapidly increasing. Many were drawn from rural areas to the cities, where they expected to earn higher wages and take part in the brawling, vital social life of Paris,

6. Ibid., pp. 116ff. Scholarly debates over the causes of the declining birth rate have pointed to factors as diverse as the French Revolution's promulgation of inheritance laws prescribing the equal division of property among heirs, and the changing family structures associated with industrialization. Even a simple summary of this literature lies far beyond what can be attempted in this introduction.

7. Rates of emigration abroad, primarily to the New World, provide an indirect indication of the demographic pressure in various European countries. During the second half of the nineteenth century, emigrants from Germany numbered just under four million, and those from the United Kingdom (including Ireland) exceeded ten million. In the same period, just 300,000 French citizens emigrated. See Mitchell, *European Historical Statistics*, p. 145.

Lyon, Marseille, and other centers of commercial and cultural activity. The actual number of people living in the countryside remained fairly constant at about twenty million between 1789 and 1914; but whereas at the beginning of this period the rural sector represented 82 percent of the French population, it accounted for just 56 percent at the end.[8] Thus, virtually the entire net increase was experienced in urban areas.

The displacement of the population took various forms. A mason like Martin Nadaud fitted the pattern of seasonal migrants, workers who came to the city for several months at a time, typically at the height of the construction cycle when their skills were much in demand. During the slack season, they would usually return home to join their families in agricultural labors. Other workers made a permanent jump from the countryside to a large metropolitan area in a single move; but more frequent were chain migrations, which took the rural resident from the farm to a small town and then perhaps to a regional center, before he or she ventured on to one of France's leading cities. In a corresponding fashion, a family's transition to urban life might be undertaken in stages, with first the husband, then an older and employable son, and finally the wife and younger children arriving over a period of months or years. Disappointed hopes caused a small fraction to return home almost immediately, and a few eventually realized their long-term ambition of retiring to the village in which they had grown up; but these were merely eddies in a flow that could not be stemmed. Though many of the newly arrived city dwellers would long maintain their ties with the earth from which they sprang, thus bringing even the most isolated regions increasingly within the city's sphere of influence, the migratory currents continued virtually unchecked throughout the nineteenth century.

Those who participated in the great rural exodus, especially during the middle years of the century, commonly encountered new living conditions which we might think appalling. Because the stock of urban housing was inadequate to accommodate the flood of new residents, dense overcrowding was the rule in working-class quarters. Sanitation practices were often primitive, with no consistent provision for street cleaning, garbage disposal, or the removal of human waste. Such conditions encouraged the spread of a number of diseases—malaria, diphtheria, typhoid, smallpox, even dysentery and croup—that claimed lives on a regular basis. An epidemic of cholera in 1832, for example, killed 100,000 people in France, including 18,000 in the poorer districts of Paris alone; the disease returned

8. See Jean-Claude Gegot, *La Population française aux XIXᵉ et XXᵉ siècles* (Paris, 1989), p. 25. He uses the traditional but relatively conservative definition of the rural sector as comprising communes of less than 2,000 inhabitants.

in still more virulent form in 1849. The public health facilities available in most cities, though superior to what was found in rural areas, were incapable of attending to the medical needs of so many impoverished people. Yet the influx continued virtually without interruption throughout the nineteenth century.

It is important to appreciate the role of Paris as the primate city, one which dominated all aspects of French society. In 1811, some 623,000 people lived within the city limits, a population nearly six times greater than that of France's second largest city, Lyon. By 1851, there were one million residents of Paris proper, a figure that exceeded the combined total of the nine next largest cities of France. By the end of the nineteenth century, the greater Paris region had a population of three and a half million and accounted for over 28 percent of the urban, and 9 percent of the total population of France.[9] To translate the numerical preponderance of Paris into terms that fit the contemporary United States, we would have to imagine a metropolitan area of roughly twenty-five million persons. In actuality, there has never been anything comparable in the American experience to the hegemony which Paris exercised—and exercises still—in France. In addition to being by far the largest city, it was also the seat of government, the locus of all administrative and judicial control, the hub of commerce, the site of origination for most important artistic and creative activities, the focal point of the country's system of transport and communication, and the home of the nation's principal cultural and educational institutions. For all these reasons, Paris exerted a powerful attractive influence, making it the end destination for a sizable proportion of all rural migrants and ensuring that through most of the nineteenth century, persons born in the capital constituted only a minority of its population. Changes in other French cities differed mainly in degree, with the result that the urban working class, most of whose members were no more than one generation removed from their rural village of origin, underwent a phenomenal increase in size in the course of the nineteenth century.

Economic Expansion

Between the time of the French Revolution and the last years of the nineteenth century, the French economy underwent a gradual but cumulatively far-reaching transformation. Impediments to the spread of capitalist relations, such as internal tariff barriers and the paternalist regulation of trades, were swept away; new domestic markets for manufactured goods

9. Georges Dupeux, *Atlas historique de l'urbanisation de la France, 1811–1975* (Paris, 1981).

were developed; and the productive capacity of the economy as a whole increased significantly. The labor force in the cities grew at the expense of a slowly contracting agricultural sector, as migrants from the countryside, including an increasing proportion of women, took jobs in workshops and factories.

France blazed its own path in pursuit of economic development. The commercialization of agriculture, the adoption of power-driven machinery, and the shift to an economy of mass production all occurred at a more deliberate pace than in England, the first nation to undergo industrialization. And unlike Germany and Russia, which would overtake it toward the end of the period in question, France relied to a very limited extent on large factories employing masses of unskilled workers.

In fact, factories in France were long restricted to a handful of industrial towns, located for the most part in the north. Skilled artisans formed the backbone of the economy, dominating the labor force in the first half of the nineteenth century and continuing to outnumber factory workers through the turn of the twentieth. Pockets of large-scale industrial production did arise in economic sectors where competition from foreign producers forced the conversion to factory organization, notably in the spinning of cotton and the weaving of some woolen goods. Yet even in textiles, small-scale manufacture like the silk-weaving trade survived into the late nineteenth century, though it ceased to dominate the economy of Lyon after 1850. Indeed, the competition engendered by industrial innovations often produced a proliferation or intensification of more traditional modes of production, especially in the countryside. Aside from Paris and a few regional centers, whose highly skilled labor forces produced luxury goods much in demand abroad, most of the French economy was oriented to domestic (and often local) markets. These and other factors led many earlier analysts to view the French pattern as backward compared to the British model of industrialization. Today, however, the French experience tends to be seen as a differentiated strategy of economic development which by 1900 had succeeded in producing a per capita income comparable to that of England, the standard by which material progress in the industrial age has traditionally been measured.[10]

Growth was, however, very uneven, throwing the lives of workers into frequent disruption. Real wages made halting progress, rising to an early peak in the 1820s, only to decline by 10 to 15 percent through the 1840s

---

10. See Patrick O'Brien and Caglar Keyder, *Economic Growth in Britain and France, 1780–1914: Two Paths to the Twentieth Century* (London, 1978).

before resuming their upward climb for much of the rest of the century.[11] Over the long term, the relatively privileged status of skilled workers faced a serious threat. Competitive pressure from new forms of factory organization began to render the economic prospects of artisans more and more uncertain. The introduction of power-driven machinery in certain sectors increased productivity, but at the cost of displacing workers whose skills were no longer useful. These workers were forced onto a job market which offered an increasing proportion of semiskilled and unskilled positions that required little training and paid low wages.

In industries that became mechanized, workers could no longer hope to own the equipment necessary to do their jobs. They therefore lost some of the independence that craftsmen in many skilled trades had had when they carried both the tools and the knowledge necessary to earn a livelihood with them at all times. Mechanization implied an enlarged scale of production that vastly increased the minimum investment required for efficient operation. This concentration of capital widened the gulf between employer and employee, most obviously in the factory, but even in small shops where egalitarian relations between master and journeymen had been the rule. Where large-scale manufacture was introduced, the division of labor was intensified. The need for coordination among workers performing increasingly specialized tasks reinforced the move toward stricter discipline in the workplace. This translated into a lessening of the control over the pace of work, the taking of breaks, and the patterns of sociability that elite craftsmen had formerly enjoyed. Consequently, there was a decline in the sense of autonomy that had been so central to the craftsman's self-conception.

Thus, the privileged status of highly skilled workers was under continual challenge even when the economy was in an expansive phase. In times of economic contraction, a variety of strategies for reducing labor costs—including sweated labor, putting out, and subcontracting—helped compound the effects of these long-term trends.[12] Most skilled journey-

---

11. See William H. Sewell, Jr., *Work and Revolution in France: The Language of Labor from the Old Regime to 1848* (Cambridge, 1980), p. 160.

12. "Sweated labor" refers to the practice of forcing poorly paid laborers to work exceptionally long hours to earn a meager livelihood. "Putting out" was a system of production in which an entrepreneur would furnish, either on consignment or by outright sale, raw materials like unspun cotton or unwoven wool to individuals who typically worked in their own homes. When these raw materials had been transformed into a more finished product, the entrepreneur would repurchase the product, paying a modest sum for the labor invested. "Subcontracting" was an arrangement under which a lead worker or foreman assumed responsibility for the

men continued to cling to aspirations of upward mobility, but increasing capital requirements and the devaluing of skills in many trades meant that the chances of achieving master's status became more remote as the century wore on. To protect their essential skills against dilution, artisans were forced into a defensive posture. The modest success they were able to achieve can be attributed in part to the demographic and economic circumstances previously discussed, but also to the constant struggles they waged to win the rights of political expression and association that made it possible to organize in pursuit of their collective interests.

A Century of Revolution

During the long nineteenth century, France experienced a level of internal conflict greater than any country of comparable size and international significance before or since. Four times in that period—in 1789, 1830, 1848, and 1871—the government of France was challenged by major revolutionary upsurges, and many additional insurrectionary events of more limited scope were interspersed between those dates. Changes of regime were so frequent that the nation was ruled by three distinct monarchies, three republics, and two empires within a one-hundred-year span.[13] It is little wonder that France has become the benchmark by which the contentiousness of modern politics has been judged.

The revolutionary upheavals in France were closely linked to the more active participation of the urban working class in politics. If the French Revolution of 1789 is seen as marking a watershed in world history, it is in part because the direct intervention of the Parisian crowd significantly altered the course of events at several crucial junctures, thus ending the monopoly that traditional elites had formerly exercised over the conduct of public affairs. Barely more than a half-century later, in the February Revolution of 1848, a worker was included in the provisional government that declared universal manhood suffrage and gave France the most broadly

---

completion of a specified task for an agreed-upon price. That subcontractor, or "jobber," was expected to pay the workers from the proceeds, retaining any balance as his personal profit. It was therefore in the jobber's interest to use all possible means of keeping labor costs low. In general, the intended result of these practices was not only to effect labor savings but also to shift a portion of the entrepreneur's risk to the workers themselves.

13. The monarchies were the Old Regime (to 1792), the Bourbon Restoration (1814 or 1815 to 1830), and the Orleanist Monarchy (1830 to 1848). Three republics were declared: the first lasted from 1792 to 1804, the second from 1848 to 1852, and the third from 1870 through the end of the period that concerns us here. The two empires were those of Napoléon Bonaparte (1804 to 1814 or 1815) and Louis-Napoléon (1852 to 1870).

defined electorate any nation had ever possessed. Yet the progress made by the working class in its quest for political rights and economic betterment was highly uneven. Certain changes of regime—particularly the Bourbon Restoration and the Second Empire—affected workers adversely because they were accompanied by a sudden contraction of economic opportunity or by repressive social control.

Ironically, even those governments that sought to end the hegemony of the rich and powerful sometimes enacted legislation whose unintended consequences proved disastrous for many ordinary citizens. The Le Chapelier law, passed in 1791, is the most often cited example.[14] Consistent with the revolutionaries' objective of striking down privilege in the name of liberty—most obviously in the case of the monopolies and exemptions enjoyed by the aristocracy and the clergy—the National Assembly also abolished "corporations." These organizations, vestiges of the ancient guild system, united the practitioners of a trade for the purpose of maintaining acceptable standards of workmanship, managing relations between journeymen and masters, and limiting the entry of apprentices so as to protect the economic and social status of members. The Revolution declared these corporations to be an illegal restraint on the individual's right freely to choose an occupation. The 1791 law prohibited such groups from naming officers, maintaining records, or adopting regulations, and prohibited any attempt to impose collective agreements on a trade. The Penal Code of 1810 went further by prohibiting the formation of "coalitions" that might attempt to reassert exclusive privileges, whether those of masters or of journeymen.

As a result of this legislation, the individual French worker immediately gained the abstract right to practice any trade at will, but in the longer term, French workers collectively lost the concrete right to organize in pursuit of their common interests. The fact that masters were similarly constrained was small consolation to the majority of workers, as masters were never scrutinized as closely and their smaller numbers and strategic position permitted them to coordinate their activities even in the absence of formal organization. The only workers' associations to survive were those that the authorities judged innocuous—mutual aid societies and compagnonnages—or those that operated clandestinely. Mutual aid societies were voluntary associations of workers, most often in a single trade, who made regular payments into a common fund. By thus pooling resources, workers were able to insure themselves against the unforeseeable expenses

14. On this statute and its predecessor, the d'Allarde law, as well as on the whole subject of working-class organization in the first half of the nineteenth century, see Sewell, *Work and Revolution*.

associated with the illness, injury, or death of a family breadwinner. These organizations can be seen as the distant precursors of such twentieth-century innovations as public unemployment compensation and health insurance. A compagnonnage, or workers' brotherhood, recruited young, unmarried journeymen (compagnons), most of whom had embarked on a Tour of France as a way of acquiring or polishing the skills of their trade. Such organizations helped to regulate supply and demand in skilled labor as well as to order the lives of these itinerant craftsmen-in-training by placing them in jobs, seeing to their subsistence needs, and serving as guarantor of their prudent conduct during their sojourn in some unfamiliar town. Mutual aid societies and compagnonnages were tolerated by public officials as long as they confined their activities to practical welfare considerations and steered clear of all "political" initiatives, explicitly defined to include any attempt to control wage levels or work conditions through labor organization or collective bargaining.[15]

Though it took some time for the full implications of these legal changes to become apparent, the working class soon found itself locked in a protracted struggle to win back the right to organize. During the period in which this campaign was waged, French political opinion was divided among at least four major currents: monarchism, Bonapartism, republicanism, and socialism. The politics of the monarchist camp were complicated by the existence of two distinct and sometimes bitterly opposed factions, the Legitimists loyal to the Bourbon kings, and the Orleanist supporters of the rival dynasty which had acceded to the throne in the person of Louis-Philippe as a result of the popular revolution of 1830. Neither could claim widespread and active support among workers beyond the general acquiescence it enjoyed while actually in power. Bonapartism, on the contrary, inspired enthusiastic, even fanatical adherence in a sizable segment of the working class as well as among most French peasants, at least through the first half of the century. Among its supporters were those who had served in Napoléon's conquering armies as well as the larger

---

15. Cooperative associations, which united either producers or consumers in an effort to increase their combined leverage over markets in labor, commodities, or credit, tended to be viewed less favorably, in part because their impact on the economy was more direct and in part because they were closely associated with certain forms of utopian socialist philosophy that flourished in the middle of the century. Political clubs, intermediate between debating societies and electoral campaign organizations, were prohibited by law except for brief interludes like the short-lived Second Republic. Political parties and labor unions were severely repressed until the Third Republic redefined the nature of civil society in France during the last quarter of the nineteenth century. Under this more liberal regime, trade unionist and Syndicalist movements attempted to secure workers' control and even ownership of key industries through general strikes and direct action.

number who simply remembered with longing the days of glory when France had dominated a continent. The Emperor's legacy proved sufficiently enduring to assure a landslide electoral victory nearly half a century later for his nephew, whose primary qualification for the office of president of France's Second Republic was his last name. Louis-Napoléon went on to overthrow the republican constitution under which he had been elected and to found France's Second Empire. However, the fierce repression of workers' causes which took place in the early years of his rule brought to a rapid end the groundswell of Bonapartist sentiment within the urban working class.

Republicanism was the political strain most clearly in the ascendant during the course of the nineteenth century. At least through 1830, it remained a tendency embraced exclusively by the more progressive segments of the working class; but because its proponents were so actively engaged, they were able to exert an influence far greater than their sheer numbers would suggest. Republican opinion was never unified, however. During the Revolution of 1848, for example, a distinction was drawn between those who had fought for the "democratic republic," whose concerns were focused primarily on the extension of popular political rights, and those who favored the "democratic *and social* republic," which would have effected a sweeping overhaul of the productive system and of property relations in general. The latter camp, critical of the laissez-faire individualism that had led to unrestrained competition and exploitation, overlapped with the small and eclectic group of followers of such visionary Socialist thinkers as Saint-Simon, Fourier, Proudhon, Cabet, and Blanc. Most advocated workers' rights, the reorganization of the economy either along cooperativist lines or with the state assuming greater responsibility for the regulation of production, and certain limited provisions for social welfare. Despite the setback they suffered in the immediate aftermath of the insurrection of June 1848, the progressive republican and socialist factions gradually regained their strength within the working class, partly in reaction to the politics of the Second Empire. In the final quarter of the century, France turned definitively in the direction of republican government.

This equation of political forces was, in sum, an indirect reflection of the economic transformation that France was undergoing. In both the political and the economic realm, the working class had assumed a more prominent role. Yet, despite their acquisition of important individual rights, the situation of workers remained precarious through much of the nineteenth century. A brief sketch of the practical conditions which the French worker confronted on a daily basis will help relate the general trends just outlined to the experiences described in the workers' autobiographies.

THE WORLD OF NINETEENTH-CENTURY
FRENCH WORKERS

To characterize population growth in France as stagnant makes sense only relative to the acceleration observed in other European nations of that era. The birthrate was substantially higher than today's, in part as a response to the high incidence of childhood disease. Jeanne Bouvier begins her autobiography with her earliest childhood memory, the baptism of her younger brother in 1868. Sixteen months later, he would die of measles, an illness which carried off many children in those days. Suzanne Voilquin comments almost matter-of-factly on her mother's loss of three children in infancy. Rearing several offspring was a hedge against the uncertainties that went with a high rate of infant mortality. For the many working-class households that had so recently left behind their parents' rural smallholding, each pair of hands and sturdy back continued to be welcomed for the contribution it would make to the family's well-being. In the urban context as in the rural, children often proved to be a valuable resource, for their earning power could be tapped as early as the age of ten or twelve.

More than it is today, the family in the nineteenth century was a unit of economic production. This was most obviously true in the system of domestic putting out, or cottage industry, where the spouse and children of a weaver like Norbert Truquin might all work side by side in a home that also served as workshop. Especially in small towns and rural areas, the material foundations of the institution of marriage never lay far beneath the surface. Though a tradition of romantic love was well established, the joining of two partners in matrimony was also likely to be seen as the joining of the economic fortunes of two families. Although the prospective bride and groom exercised an ultimate power of veto, their parents often assumed an active role in initiating and negotiating a marital settlement. Through the first half of the nineteenth century at least, the custom of providing a dowry for a daughter offered in matrimony remained widespread among rural families that owned real property, though it had largely died out in the cities. Nadaud's account of successive failed attempts to strike a marriage contract shows to what lengths a young woman's family might go to ensure a favorable match for its daughter, or the young man's to bring in precious resources that might help free itself from debt.

In a substantial proportion of urban workers' families—perhaps half of all those living in midcentury Paris, for example[16]—the wife worked

16. This rough estimate is based on the ratio of male to female workers in the Paris Chamber of Commerce's 1848 survey of the capital's labor force. Due to the limitations of that study (which does not, for example, include domestic service), to

outside the home, as child-rearing responsibilities permitted and as the household's degree of economic need required, and many more women were likely to have worked for wages before getting married. Women's jobs were concentrated in a few sectors of the economy, especially textiles, clothing, and domestic service. Skill levels in these sectors were generally low, and wages even lower. Though rates of divorce were minuscule by comparison to today, the likelihood of a child losing one or both parents to disease or accidental death was far higher; and problematic relations with relatives and stepparents is a theme that recurs in several of the auto-biographies.

The conditions in which nineteenth-century workers were housed and fed contrast sharply with those of our own era. Crowded dwellings and a lack of basic sanitation were the frequent lot of urban workers, though those newly arrived from the countryside, where the peasant family often shared its quarters with the livestock, probably considered their accom-modations in the city a distinct improvement, even when they might seem to us to offer few comforts and minimal privacy. The recent migrant might take up residence in a boarding house (*maison garnie*), which rented furnished rooms by the month, week, or night. The furnishings often consisted of nothing more than simple plank beds, arranged dormitory-style in rooms that might be shared by a dozen or more workers, some-times assigned two per bed. Rents consumed what we might see as a modest share—from 15 to 20 percent—of workers' monthly earnings.[17] Most workers new to the city gravitated to one of the boarding houses frequented by migrants from their own native region, for there they could hope to receive a friendly welcome as well as assistance in their initial orientation.

Established workers and their families were more likely to live in an apartment, consisting of one or perhaps two rooms. This too might be shared by more than one family or more than one generation of the same family and, as circumstances required, might serve as a place of work as well as living space. The large stone buildings that were common in that era were poorly lighted and ventilated, and it was exceptional for workers to live in apartments equipped with a fireplace (much less any form of

---

the fact that it was carried out at a moment of acute economic crisis, and above all to the absence of information on marital status, this general statement should be taken as no more than a crude approximation. It does not, of course, include women engaged in casual employment or those working outside the cash economy. See Chambre de commerce de Paris, *Statistique de l'industrie à Paris, résultant de l'enquête faite par la chambre de commerce pour les années 1847–1848* (Paris, 1851).
17. M. Halbwachs, "Genre de vie," *Revue d'économie politique* 53 (1939): 439–55.

central heating) to blunt the winter's cold.[18] In rural areas, indoor plumbing was almost surely lacking, whereas a well-equipped city dwelling might offer shared water and toilet facilities either on each landing or in the courtyard.

The need to carry water and all provisions to their rooms was quite literally a special burden for members of the working class, who usually lived on the top stories of their buildings. At street level, retail shops and small businesses faced outward to pedestrian traffic, while accommodations which opened onto the building's inner courtyard were likely to be occupied by workshops. The ability of middle-class tenants to pay premium rents allocated to them the choice apartments on the second and third floors. Members of the working class or domestics employed in the apartments of the bourgeois below were forced to make the long climb, sometimes to the sixth or seventh floor, in search of cheaper rents. This inverse relationship between class position and the height above the street at which one lived was among the most consistent patterns of physical and social stratification in the city. As a result, although predominantly working-class quarters existed, there was more mixing of the different socioeconomic strata within neighborhoods than there is in most contemporary American cities.

The worker's diet provides an even more stark contrast between that era and our own. A workday of twelve hours or more of grueling physical labor was frequently sustained on a meager caloric intake which we would today find lacking in both variety and allure.[19] The rich foods in which our present diet abounds, sometimes to the peril of our health, were virtually unknown to many members of the nineteenth-century working class. Only those fresh fruits, like apples, when they were briefly in season in the immediately surrounding area, or vegetables that stored well, like potatoes and cabbage, were likely to be within the means of ordinary people. Without the complex system of worldwide transport and distribution we

18. The lack of light and ventilation was encouraged by a tax assessed on real property according to the number of doors and windows in each habitable structure. (As a National Representative in the 1880s, Nadaud would be instrumental in efforts to repeal this tax.) Data cited in Eugen Weber, *Peasants into Frenchmen: The Modernization of Rural France, 1870–1914* (Stanford, 1976), p. 156, indicate that in 1831–32, one-third of all taxable buildings in France had one window or, particularly in rural areas, none. This kind of practical detail (with which Weber's wonderful book is filled) further explains why cities were relatively attractive.

19. The daily intake of the average French citizen hovered around 2,000 calories in the 1830s, but it rose steadily until by about 1880 it approximated the level of 2,800 to 3,000 calories consumed in twentieth-century industrialized societies. See J.-C. Toutain, "La Consommation alimentaire en France," *Economies et sociétés* 5 (November 1971): 1909ff.

know today, a food as exotic as an orange might be a once-in-a-lifetime treat for many French workers, while one as perishable as a banana was altogether unknown. A cup of hot chocolate each Sunday was the height of luxury for Bouvier when she was a young textile worker. A very few widely cultivated staples constituted the great bulk of the food eaten, day in and day out. Primarily for reasons of diet, the average Frenchman was some four inches shorter than his counterpart today.[20] In general, the daily fare consumed by the working and middle classes respectively was more distinct than it is now, and food represented a much larger share of the typical working-class family's budget, more than one-half of its total yearly expenditures. Bouvier provides the most detailed accounting of such expenditures. As her weekly budget indicates, even late in the nineteenth century the proportion of income spent on food remained high (see table 3).[21]

In most regions of France, a family's largest single expenditure was for bread.[22] Even in the best of times, the worker struggled to maintain a tenuous financial equilibrium. At least through the midcentury, the agricultural sector proved susceptible to periodic crises that might drive the price of the common one-pound loaf up by as much as 50 percent. When this happened, a greater share of the average family budget had to be used to buy basic foodstuffs, and less could be allocated to the purchase of

20. This figure is based on a comparison of contemporary United Nations data for France and the average height of Parisian Mobile Guard recruits in 1848. The evidence cited by Weber, *Peasants into Frenchmen*, p. 150, suggests that the difference would have been even greater in the rural districts.

21. Bouvier specifies expenditures of 15.15 francs; she notes that at the time she was earning more than this, but unfortunately she does not reveal her total income, saying only that she was saving additional money to buy furniture. Elsewhere she indicates that her earnings could rise as high as thirty or even forty francs during the busy season or drop as low as twelve when work was slack. The figures given tend to exaggerate the importance of the midday meal because, she tells us, having recently moved from her cousins' house following a dispute over the amount of money spent on food, she made it the principal meal of her day for fear that word would otherwise get back to her relatives that she was scrimping on meals. Her expenditures on clothes may also have been unusually high because at that time she was trying to build up a stock of underwear. Obviously, these figures can be no more than suggestive of the general proportions among various broad categories of expenditure.

22. For rural workers, the staple grain might vary from region to region; but most urban workers ate white bread made from wheat flour. Even in rural districts, where subsistence production might be expected to supply a larger share of the family's diet, the cost of bread purchases accounted for nearly 40 percent of the family budget in 1800 and 20 percent in 1850, according to figures cited in Weber, *Peasants into Frenchmen*, pp. 138 and 523 n. 25. Throughout the nineteenth century, bread accounted for more than half of the entire caloric intake of the urban population of France.

Table 3. Jeanne Bouvier's Weekly Budget

Daily Expenditure	Weekly Total
Food	Fr 8.40
Morning: bread 5c, milk 5c	
Midday: bread 15c, cheese 15c,	
beef and broth 50c, wine 20c	
Evening: bread 10c	
Rent	3.00
Clothes	3.75
Total	Fr 15.15

manufactured goods. This reduction in the demand for the products of the industrial economy soon resulted in widespread unemployment in the cities. Agriculturally driven crises of this kind, common under the Old Regime, persisted through the first half of the nineteenth century and recurred in particularly acute form between 1846 and 1848, when the Parisian working class, squeezed between the rising cost of living and the declining prospects of earning even a subsistence wage, rose in revolt.

Except when crises threatened, workers ate three meals a day. Breakfast, taken after two or more hours of work, was likely to consist of little more than plain bread accompanied by tea or coffee. (Though part of the working-class diet, sugar and coffee remained minor luxuries, with levels of consumption varying widely according to economic fortunes until late in the century.) Workers ate a second meal in the early afternoon, returning to their place of residence if convenient, purchasing food and drink in a nearby café or wine merchant's shop if this fell within their means, or bringing along simple provisions that they could consume on the spot at work. The principal meal of the day might be eaten either at midday or, more often, in the late evening after work was done. It might take the form of a thin soup or broth in which vegetables and a small quantity of meat had been cooked, and which was usually poured over stale bread to give it bulk and substance. The menu for the other daily meal was likely to be as simple as bread, cooked vegetables, and wine, supplemented by a bit of meat or cheese as circumstances permitted. Meat thus constituted a modest and at times irregular part of workers' diets.[23]

Though deficiencies of diet were one major factor, they were by no

23. Nevertheless, urban workers ate three to four times more meat than peasants. Figures cited in Weber, *Peasants into Frenchmen*, p. 142, give the average yearly consumption of meat as 79.31 kilograms for Paris, 60.39 kilograms for other French cities, and just 21.89 kilograms for the countryside.

means the sole contributor to workers' increased risk of illness. Outbreaks of cholera, a disease spread by a waterborne microbe, were concentrated in (though not limited to) urban areas, where facilities for the purification of drinking water were inadequate. Techniques of sewage disposal remained quite primitive, and raw human waste often coursed in the open gutters of city streets. The reader may be appalled to learn, via the accounts of Nadaud and Bouvier, how rare might be the opportunity for members of the working class to sleep in clean sheets, to bathe, or just to wash their hands and face. All this is a reminder of how recent and how unusual are the standards of hygiene and public health observed in late twentieth-century America.

For many manual workers, the chance of injuries or accidents on the job was a source of genuine anxiety. The risks incurred by Parisian chair turners while performing tasks like storing wood, for which they were not even being paid, figured among the complaints that motivated Jacques-Etienne Bédé and his fellow workers to mount in 1820 what was undoubtedly the first major "strike" to be chronicled by an actual participant since the passage of the law against coalitions.[24] Work-related injuries are a central concern in the accounts of Voilquin, Nadaud, and Dumay. The high incidence of industrial accidents did gradually give rise to governmental regulations, but even those which applied to women and children remained poorly enforced. Because most workers lived close to the margin, even slight injury to one of the family's breadwinners represented a major reverse, and any lingering disability could condemn the family to slow starvation. No form of governmental assistance or public insurance against such risks was available to the working class. In a few cases, large employers might provide a limited plan of protection like the one which paid Dumay and his mother regular stipends after his father was killed in a mining accident. The only recourse for the great majority of workers not covered by such an arrangement was membership in the voluntary mutual aid societies set up in certain trades, though these were usually intended only to meet one-time or short-term costs like funeral expenses or loss of wages due to temporary illness.

Above all, it was the inability to pay that restricted the urban worker's access to medical care. Nadaud recalls that in his native village the local midwife's knowledge of herbs was the only resource available; but, had it not been for his father's insistence, he might have fared no better in the

---

24. Technically, the 1820 action was not a strike at all but a lockout undertaken by employers after workers refused to do unpaid tasks. Note that Bédé also describes an earlier and less protracted work stoppage of 1814 that was due to a dispute between workers and certain masters over the price paid per dozen chairs.

capital. Twice, when injured on construction sites in Paris he had to be shamed or coerced into accepting treatment. Private medical care was simply beyond the reach of most family budgets, and too often the worker would wait so long to consult a physician that all chance of remediation was lost.

One alternative was for the worker to seek admission to a hospital. In nineteenth-century France these institutions, generally operated by a religious order of the Catholic Church, specifically ministered to the health needs of those too poor to pay for private medical care. At least through the 1850s or 1860s this was an option which the self-respecting worker would act on only as a last resort. One reason was the stigma attached to accepting any form of charity; another was the belief among many workers that once admitted to the hospital, it was a rare patient who walked out alive. Such concerns were not entirely groundless. Given the state of medical knowledge in the early part of the century, and the difficult circumstances in which the healing art was practiced, the hospital at times helped spread the very conditions it sought to cure. Only with a certain lag did popular attitudes assimilate the great advances which the midcentury brought to our understanding of the sources of infection and disease, and only in the last three decades of the nineteenth century did many workers come to view hospitals in a more positive light, as places where one might expect to be comforted and healed.

It is in the study of evolving popular attitudes that works of autobiography come into their own, for they directly represent the sentiments of workers. Of course, we should not expect greater unanimity in working-class authors' evaluations of the century in which they lived than in those of other segments of the population. One extreme is here represented by Truquin, whose assessment of his chances of securing a decent life for himself and his family in France was so bleak that he decided to emigrate before the drudgery of his daily toil, the lack of opportunity, and the greed of the possessing classes finally ground him down. We may be tempted to share Truquin's dismal view of life in the nineteenth century, because its material conditions compare unfavorably with those of the present day. The bulk of the evidence shows, however, that despite occasional reversals, the standard of well-being of the working class steadily improved, especially in the second half of the century. Moreover, the greater part of the working class, despite some reservations about the distribution of society's resources, appears to have been convinced that progress was the order of the day. This view is exemplified in Nadaud's calm assurance that, despite all the difficulties he himself had faced, the lot of the average worker was rapidly improving.

In illustration of his point, Nadaud cites the changes introduced by the rapid expansion of the French railroad system. In the late eighteenth century, most members of French society led comparatively insular lives. Unless, like Bédé, a worker were drafted into the army and swept up in the events of the Napoleonic period, he was unlikely to see much of the world. Indeed, aside from visits to nearby markets, he might rarely travel farther from home than the city limits or, in the case of the rural resident, the valley in which his native village was situated.

To be sure, an intrepid minority were prodded by economic circumstance or drawn by a thirst for adventure to journey further afield. Such travelers made use of horse-drawn carts, coaches, and even boats when their meager finances permitted, but they mainly relied on the surest and least expensive of all expedients, travel by foot. This meant that a seasonal migration like Nadaud's from the department of Creuse to Paris required four days of strenuous walking just to reach the two-thirds point in Orléans, while Perdiguier's four-and-a-half-year Tour of France required that he periodically spend several days at a time on the road. [25]

The great boom in railroad construction that began in the 1840s placed new possibilities within the grasp of the working class. Though it would long remain too costly for merely casual use, rail transport gradually knit together the many regional centers of France, creating national markets in labor and commodities and exerting a homogenizing influence that extended far beyond the economic sphere alone. For example, the locomotive helped change the way people spoke, by hastening the eclipse of the local *patois* that had been the nearly exclusive medium of communication in many rural communities. These local dialects, sometimes specific to the vicinity of a single small village, were still common in the nineteenth century. [26] Perdiguier recalls that his first schoolbooks were all in Latin— no special hardship, since he and his schoolmates spoke French little better than the language of the Romans. Nadaud observes that his mother never

25. As described in chapter 3, the Tour of France was the trip often undertaken by young journeymen as a way of finishing their training in a skilled trade. The French *département* is the second-order political-administrative unit, analogous in certain respects to an American state.
26. According to statistics presented in Weber, *Peasants into Frenchmen*, pp. 67–69, 310, and 498–501, roughly 20 percent of the population did not speak French in 1863. Most of these dialect speakers were residents of rural districts. In the cities, the use of French was general, if only as a lingua franca; but given the rate at which provincials constantly arrived, there was a nearly daily need to deal with persons whose mother tongue was some regional dialect. The rivalries Nadaud describes on the work site between *brulas* and *bigaros* (residents of different districts of the Creuse department), make it clear that enclaves of regional population, regional speech, and regional antagonisms persisted in the city.

spoke a word of French in her life. Bouvier tells how, upon returning to her native village as an adult, she encountered difficulty finding her way because she was given directions that referred in French to places she had, as a young girl in the 1870s, known only by their names in dialect. Even more indicative of the tension between the traditional village setting and the more cosmopolitan culture that had grown up in the cities is Bouvier's pretense of understanding the chatter of neighbors who gathered at her mother's home to welcome her back. She was afraid that a frank confession that she had forgotten the local *patois* would make them think she was putting on airs.

For all the hardships of urban life, few workers ever returned to their region of birth for more than brief visits with relatives and childhood friends. They were held in place partly by the prospect of employment, uncertain though it might be, but also by their attachment to a thriving popular culture. With good reason, our own society might envy the strong and vital sense of community which that culture fostered, for this was one of the most remarkable collective achievements of the millions who streamed into the working-class districts of the great cities. A few forms of professional and commercial entertainment were accessible to the working class. Bouvier, for instance, tells how she would scrimp to set aside the price of admission to the popular theaters of Paris, attending light comedies and, on at least one occasion, the opera. But most forms of distraction for workers were more participatory. In these texts we learn of the parties of *boules* (the Provençal bowling game) in which Perdiguier engaged with his fellow compagnons, and the informal martial arts competitions which took place in Nadaud's boarding house as well as in the "academies" where these skills were taught. The celebration of saints' feast days frequently became the occasion for the assemblies and parades in which Bédé and Perdiguier took part as members of their trades. And whether at work, at home, or in their local café, workers were always prepared to provide their own entertainment by joining voices in spirited collective renditions of traditional airs and popular ballads.

Although these few, haphazard examples cannot hope to capture the flavor of the culture workers recreated in the cities, there is one setting which, more than any other, suggests how the different elements of workers' lives were integrated. The café was by all accounts the key institution of working-class culture.[27] Its clientele, like the community in which it was

27. For the sake of simplicity, I have used here the blanket term *café*, ignoring the useful distinctions that might be made among inns (*auberges*), taverns (*tavernes* or *cabarets*), the shops of wine merchants (*marchands de vins*), bistrots, pubs (*brasseries*), coffee houses (*estaminets*), and singing societies and dance halls (*goguettes*

embedded, was composed of loose groupings of workers united by bonds of common regional origin, occupation, or neighboring relations. Since the typical city quarter was likely to host concentrations of various trades within the space of a few city blocks, there might exist an informally designated spot where the members of each occupational group took their breaks or shared their midday meal. As the only public space where it was possible to assemble in any numbers, the café was the site from which workers launched whatever labor organization and protest the laws and police repression made possible. It was not by chance, therefore, that Bédé and two of his fellow workers drew up plans for a mutual aid society to benefit Parisian chair turners while sitting in the shop of a wine merchant, nor that the members of the trade later returned there to deliberate a proposal that they refuse to carry out the unpaid tasks which their masters had imposed. Through much of the century, the affairs of the working class were conducted in such settings, a pattern of which the authorities were sufficiently aware to create a special branch of the police force charged solely with the surveillance of drinking establishments.

After a long and trying day, most workers returned to rooms that were cramped and unheated. Candles or lanterns, the only sources of illumination, were used sparingly in the working-class household. Little wonder, therefore, that many men would head for the neighborhood café in search of what their own lodgings rarely afforded: a warm, inviting spot where entertainment and companionship could be enjoyed over a glass of wine, beer, or spirits. Most such establishments attracted a core of regulars along with a sprinkling of occasional customers, all drawn from similar backgrounds.[28] During the evening hours, these were largely male preserves. Respectable women were likely to shun them except in the company of family or close friends, on special occasions, or when the establishment was

---

and *guinguettes*), as well as variations of these basic types. My intention is to emphasize what all had in common, as sites for the consumption of alcohol and the sharing of good fellowship. On the culture of the café and especially on its patterns of sociability, I have relied heavily on the research of Susanna Barrows, especially "Parliaments of the People," in Susanna Barrows and Robin Room, eds., *Drinking: Behavior and Belief in Modern History* (Berkeley, 1991), and an earlier, unpublished paper, "Arenas of Eloquence: The Café and Popular Political Culture in Nineteenth-Century France" (Berkeley, 1987).

28. Cafés or taverns serving a mixed clientele were the exception, according to research based on eighteenth-century judicial records. See Thomas Edward Brennan, *Public Drinking and Popular Culture in Eighteenth-Century Paris* (Princeton, 1988). His findings indicate that most customers were men drinking in the company of regular associates who might vary widely in age but tended to be of the same social level, same guild, and same neighborhood as themselves. If there was a significant change in such patterns during the nineteenth century, it was toward an increase in contact across trade lines.

one of the dance halls, located on the outskirts of the city, whose very function made the presence of women appropriate.

Alcoholic beverages, formerly a luxury for ordinary workers, steadily dropped in price during the nineteenth century, resulting in a sharp rise in working-class consumption. By the turn of the twentieth century, France led all nations in per capita intake of alcohol, a distinction it has yet to relinquish. Wine remained the standard drink of the working class (as it was not for the peasantry, at least through the midcentury), but the rising incidence of public drunkenness can be traced to the increase in the consumption of distilled spirits, primarily brandy. Activities associated with drinking—particularly gambling, womanizing, and the general squandering of the family's precious resources—all contributed to the café's shady reputation. Most of these authors comment on the excessive drinking habits of some fellow worker who would no sooner collect his Saturday afternoon pay than start on a binge that would sometimes lead to the celebration of "Holy Monday" instead of showing up for work. The toll in lives wasted or destroyed by the abuse of alcohol was considerable.

Yet the café was not merely a place to drink; it was the point of contact and information exchange for a richly varied working-class community. The recently arrived male worker might come there in search of friends who had preceded him in migrating to the city, paying for his welcome with the news and personal messages he brought from their native region. In return, he might obtain advice as to where a cheap room could be rented. It was here that word was first passed of fresh job openings, and here too that the newly employed journeyman would return to buy the customary round of drinks for his fellow workers as part of the ritual of hiring. Pamphlets and tracts were circulated in the café, spreading word of public events and entertainments as well as all manner of political causes. For the benefit of those who were illiterate, a well-spoken worker like Nadaud would be called upon to read aloud from a people's newspaper. Indeed, the corner wine merchant's shop was the principal (and in times when restrictions on assembly and speech were tightened, perhaps the only) public space where discussion of current affairs could take place among workers. Jules Vinçard, another early-nineteenth-century worker who published his autobiography, aptly refers to cafés as "powerful schools of patriotic education," for it was in such venues that the working class acquired its initiation into civic affairs.[29] However, cafés could serve so effectively as sites of political socialization only because workers were already drawn to them as

29. Jules Vinçard, *Mémoires épisodiques d'un vieux chansonnier Saint-Simonien* (Paris, 1878), p. 26.

entertainment centers, informal housing bureaus, assembly halls, employment clearing houses, and all-purpose havens where workers were in the habit of gathering.

These observations evoke the theme around which this collection of memoirs has been organized: the links that existed between the everyday politics of the working class (including the protest and collective action in which it participated) and the predisposing material and cultural influences that gave the nineteenth century its distinctive character. Before examining this connection, however, we must first confront the interpretive dilemmas raised by the use of autobiographical sources in attempts to generalize about the working-class experience.

THE USE OF AUTOBIOGRAPHICAL EVIDENCE IN HISTORICAL INQUIRY

For conveying the ambiance of life in the nineteenth century and documenting workers' impressions of this period of tumultuous change, memoirs constitute a peerless source. However, when we attempt to use them to understand the systematic processes that give social life a semblance of order, we confront an apparent contradiction. Autobiography is a distinctive and useful form of evidence precisely because it captures those elements that are decisive—often unique—in the unfolding of an individual life. Even if we set aside the extreme case in which a worker's memoirs constitute virtually the only surviving record of his or her existence, there are likely to be few opportunities to verify the personal recollections the author offers. There are, moreover, few points of comparison to help separate those elements of the story that are merely idiosyncratic from those that speak faithfully to the experience of an occupational group, a social milieu, or a style of life, especially when they may have since disappeared.

A further difficulty is that the information imparted by such texts is typically framed within a set of conventions that influence whether and how various aspects of the worker's existence are portrayed. These narrative strategies help the author to assemble the disparate events of a lifetime into a seemingly coherent whole. But like any managed form of self-presentation, they inevitably privilege certain bits of information and lead to the concealment of others.[30] Among the most common conventional forms adopted in such works are those we might call (a) the legacy to

30. In the discussion of these issues, I have borrowed freely from M. J. Maynes, "Autobiography and Class Formation in Nineteenth-Century Europe: Methodological Considerations," forthcoming in *Social Science History*; and from the always illuminating comments of my colleague, Jon Beecher.

posterity, in which the author passes on a personal and family history nominally addressed to his or her heirs; (*b*) the picaresque adventure, in which the author comments on the curious quality of human nature and of life in general by stringing together a series of loosely connected vignettes or episodes; (*c*) the success story, detailing the worker's climb within the social hierarchy and his or her conquest of social respectability (often signifying acceptance by or even ascension into the middle class, the principal audience for most working-class autobiographies); (*d*) the plea for the defense (*plaidoyer*), in which an author such as Bédé, who feels he has been unfairly judged, attempts to vindicate his conduct and character as if before a jury of his peers; and (*e*) the conversion experience, in which the author relates his or her awakening after being exposed to a novel world view that reveals a new meaning in life and the potential for personal or social transformation, usually through militant activism.

One additional genre—that of the representative life—deserves special mention because it is so frequent among working-class autobiographies and so pertinent to the methodological issues raised here. All seven of these authors aggressively assert their working-class status by referring to themselves in the titles or subtitles of their memoirs as a worker (Bédé), daughter of the people (Voilquin), compagnon (Perdiguier), mason's assistant (Nadaud), proletarian (Truquin), militant worker (Dumay), or working woman (Bouvier).[31] In so doing, they implicitly claim to be just like others of their class—an interesting inversion of the practice in the autobiographies of members of the elite, where the value of the narrative is established by the distinctiveness of the author's role as a key actor in the events recounted. A rhetoric of authenticity pervades the genre, leading most authors to affirm the unerring truth and candor of their testimony— even when the claim involves a self-evident naiveté and is little more than a ploy for introducing views on how people should live or society should be organized. This stance leads to statements like this one by Perdiguier:

> I am initiating my reader into my entire past. I am showing
> myself just as I was, just as I am. My life is linked to the lives
> of workers in general. When I speak of myself, I speak of
> them.[32]

31. The title is, of course, particularly subject to an editor's or publisher's influence. In each of these cases, however, the text makes it clear that the identification as a worker is the author's own. It would be possible to cite another dozen cases of autobiographies of nineteenth-century French workers, in the titles of which the authors refer to themselves as *compagnon*, *travailleur*, *ouvrier*, *militant*, etc.
32. Agricol Perdiguier, *Mémoires d'un compagnon* (Moulins, 1914), p. 215.

Though it may be valid as a statement of intention, Perdiguier's self-evaluation cannot be accepted at face value.[33] We might weigh it against the following highly critical assessment which Amédée Saint-Ferréol (Perdiguier's fellow Deputy in the 1849 Legislative Assembly and fellow exile in 1855) offered after reading a portion of his autobiography:

> Perdiguier claims to have portrayed the worker in his memoirs. In reality, all he has portrayed is himself. Gazing into the mirror of his memories, our former colleague sees himself in the best possible light and describes himself as seen, believing that everyone must be interested in the petty details of his life, even in *the tears in his pants.* The framework within which the author of *Memoirs of a Compagnon* was working was quite broad and therefore would have lent itself to the propagation of useful truths, precious information, socialist theories concerning the lives of workers or the organization of work. Perdiguier has completely failed in his task. Basically, he only talks about himself.[34]

In taking issue with what he saw as Perdiguier's self-absorption and obsession with detail, Saint-Ferréol believed he had isolated a crucial flaw. Yet, had Perdiguier followed Saint-Ferréol's advice, the result would doubtless have been one more abstract, prescriptive treatise (no less conventionalized or subject to the author's personal predilections), and the literature on nineteenth-century workers would have been deprived of the classic account of the Tour of France and journeymen's associations that Perdiguier was uniquely qualified to write. Distorted though it may be by

33. To state only the most obvious objections: The literal attempt to record any person's entire past would be an overwhelming and impossible task; autobiographies are necessarily selective. As to Perdiguier's claim to show himself just as he was, the level of self-knowledge that this assumes is not given to us all. The author of an autobiography may be best placed to inventory the subject's attributes, but he or she also has the strongest motives to conceal certain facets of personality or dissemble any less than admirable aspects of personal history. Moreover, Perdiguier's statement implies that the person he was when he lived the events and the person he is when he writes about them are continuous if not identical—a problematic assertion for anyone to make, but especially so for one who had undergone the dramatic changes that Perdiguier experienced in the interim. Finally, while it is surely true that his life was linked to the lives of workers in general, the link was convoluted and operated in part through the contrasts and oppositions that were inevitable in one whose personal odyssey took him so far from the workshops where he began.

34. Amédée Saint-Ferréol, *Impressions d'exil à Genève*, quoted in Jean Briquet, *Agricol Perdiguier, compagnon du tour de France et représentant du peuple, 1805–1875* (Paris, 1981), p. 331.

his foibles and preoccupations, Perdiguier's insider's view of the shoproom floor, the compagnons' assembly hall, and the corner café has instructed as well as delighted generations of readers, in large part because it tells us in an authoritative voice about not only the "tears in his pants" but a thousand other particulars of the worker's daily life. It is Saint-Ferréol's vision, not Perdiguier's, that seems short-sighted today, for it fails to recognize that the very traits he criticizes are those that have caused these reminiscences to be treasured by so many.

From the point of view of the social historian, narrative conventions can be a problematic influence when their effect is to filter out information that is inconsistent with the organizing principle which the author has adopted for making sense of his or her life. Yet such biases are not different in kind from those inherent in other forms of evidence. Official statistics, for example, apply universal categories that shape and channel information, giving it the appearance of consistency and comparability.[35] In the process of aggregating individual cases and arriving at a manageably simple version of an irreducibly complex human reality, experiential and contextual information may be jettisoned. Yet if, in reaction to these shortcomings of summary statistics, one seeks to restore the subjective dimension through reliance on, for example, literary sources, the methodological difficulties may merely be compounded. Rarely do fictionalized accounts provide a clear sense of the evidence on which their representation is based or any acknowledgment that such factual information as they present has been filtered through the sensibility of an author whose experience of the reality described is indirect and whose artistic or aesthetic preoccupations are potentially distorting.

One potentially distorting influence that frequently intervenes between the experience as lived and the experience as recounted is the retrospective bias that results when autobiographies are written long after the events described. In addition to suffering from the author's lapses of memory, such accounts tend to present the views of an older person, writing about the experiences of the younger person he or she once was, and adding many elements (of information, of opinion, of moral judgment) that were not actually present at the time. The narrative acquires an orderliness that has been superimposed on the circumstances of the author's life only long after the fact. Yet accounts written contemporaneously with the events in question, especially in the form of a diary or journal, are just as problematic. Insofar as these experiences are still unfolding at the moment they are

35. Compare John I. Kitsuse and Aaron V. Cicourel, "A Note on the Uses of Official Statistics," *Social Problems* 11 (Fall 1963): 131–39.

recorded, the author's initial impressions or spur-of-the-moment reactions may prove inaccurate or misleading in the light of subsequent events or ripe reflection.

Retrospective embellishments tend, however, to be easier to recognize and discount than the purposeful omissions that just as frequently occur. To take one obvious example, the broad outlines of courtship and marriage are commonly related in these texts, from the awkward stages of match-making and first encounters through the actual decision to marry. We may learn a few details concerning the wedding ceremony or the establishment of the new household, but rarely are we offered insight into the private or sentimental side of the married couple's relationship, much less the practical details of sexual mores or any considerations of family planning.[36] Typically, the next allusion to the author's family life is the announcement of the names and dates of birth of children.

Such reticence may seem hardly surprising in an age of greater modesty than our own. More curious is the fact that while most authors recount their childhoods, whether happy or miserable, in lavish detail—including their relations with parents and siblings, the trials they had to overcome, their moments of decision, the influence of role models, and much more—they rarely have much to say about interactions with their own children.[37] Our knowledge of the nineteenth century suffers from this lack of parents' testimony about their children's socialization and occupational training.

Jacques Rancière has remarked on another pointed omission in the autobiographies of nineteenth-century workers, perhaps in part a function of their assertive identification with the working class. He finds that they present a somewhat idealized image of the life of the worker and the redeeming potential of manual labor. The tedium, risk of injury, and cumulative physical toll exacted by many of these occupations are often

36. Voilquin's memoirs teach us a great deal about the realm of private behavior and feelings, but not much about sex or marriage. She mentions such details as the delay in her sister's first menstrual period ("the healthy crisis that makes a child into a young woman") and reproduces, as if verbatim, her mother's revealing account of the emotional bonds that tied her to her husband; but she says little about her own premarital affair or her failed marriage. Similarly, the male authors are much more forthcoming about their mothers than their wives.

37. Nadaud, for example, alludes to what can only be called discussions of strategy between his father and mother concerning how best to keep him—and his growing earning power—from deserting the family before its debts had all been paid off. (He never makes clear when and how he learned of these conversations, from which he presumably was shielded at the time they occurred.) Not one of these authors offers a report of such an exchange with his or her spouse concerning the character and conduct of their own sons and daughters, the dilemmas of parenthood, or the dynamics of family solidarity.

understated or unvoiced. Thus, the reassuring picture of the skilled artisan's sense of competence and fulfillment that emerges from Perdiguier's *Memoirs of a Compagnon* has a dark side that is disclosed only if one chances upon the same author's far less often read *Biographie de l'auteur du livre du compagnonnage* (Paris, 1846), which dwells in considerable detail on "the splinters that have entered his body, the falling wood that has injured him, the lung diseases caught breathing sawdust and, finally, his suicidal thoughts."[38] Rancière sees these as expressions of hatred for manual labor felt even by the author considered the greatest eulogist of the nineteenth-century artisanal tradition.[39] Here, as so often in such works, the matter-of-fact stoicism that was so strong an element in the character of the nineteenth-century worker is often indicated only by what has been left out.

Perhaps the most important source of bias in an anthology such as this is the set of criteria applied in selecting and editing the texts. In this case, consideration has deliberately been restricted to the first-person accounts of authentic workers who spent their years of childhood and early adulthood in France during the long nineteenth century which ran from the demise of the Old Regime, around 1789, to 1899. By "authentic workers" I mean those whose livelihood was primarily derived from manual labor in the production of nonagricultural goods and services. The autobiographies themselves, however, show how difficult or misleading it can be to apply such an abstract definition. Throughout the nineteenth century, most members of the working class were no more than a single generation removed from the soil, and a considerable number maintained ties with their villages of origin long after moving away. Especially among residents of provincial towns, or those in transitional categories, like Nadaud's

38. Jacques Rancière, "The Myth of the Artisan: Critical Reflections on a Category of Social History," *International Labor and Working Class History*, no. 24 (Fall 1983): 6.
39. Ibid. *Memoirs of a Compagnon* actually seems less one-sided than Rancière implies, especially in the sections dealing with Perdiguier's illnesses and injuries; his abrasive, stingy, incompetent, or quirky employers (starting with his overly demanding father); and fellow workers who were incompetent, lazy, drunk, or larcenous. It is surely the case that some aspects of working-class existence—and typically those which the authors themselves perceive to be most negative—are self-censored from specific accounts; but the complement to Perdiguier's upbeat view is in any event to be found in such texts as Bédé's *A Worker in 1820*, which, though also positive in tone, relates skilled workers' failed attempts to obtain relief from their masters' exploitation; or in Truquin's *Memoirs and Adventures*, which retraces a series of degrading, unrewarding, and stultifying jobs and presents an almost unrelievedly negative vista of the fate of the unskilled or semiskilled worker. Although the lack of balance is an important defect of individual works, the genre as a whole does present a multifaceted picture of working-class life.

seasonal migrants who returned home each fall to help with the harvest, it might be difficult to tell peasant from worker.

In similar fashion, the demarcation between skilled artisan and petty bourgeois was often blurred, since the successful master or entrepreneur had almost surely started out as a journeyman and often continued to put in his hours at the workbench or on the construction site alongside his employees. Moreover, the working class remained so internally diverse with respect to source of livelihood, level of skill, standard of living, and sector of economic activity that it is difficult to arrive at a consistent definition capable of embracing domestic servants, elite craftsmen, carters, common laborers, factory operatives, and all the seemingly endless variations the category comprised. It is in dealing with such diversity that autobiographical sources display their special virtues, for they have the capacity to reveal the textures of working-class life, which the convenient categorical shorthand robs of its intrinsic vitality and complexity.

The total number of French workers' memoirs is quite restricted: perhaps forty such texts have survived.[40] They are rare because key resources—education, leisure, and the social connections to get a book published—were themselves rare among nineteenth-century workers. As a result, the intrinsic likelihood of a skilled artisan recording his life story for posterity was so remote that on a priori grounds alone one would have to question whether those who did so could ever be considered representative. And if circumstances proved so limiting even for the skilled elite of the working class, how much more powerfully must they have acted on women or the unskilled?

But however real these obstacles, there were also circumstances that fostered the impulse to write one's autobiography, even within the working class. First, there was the individual's active involvement in some organization. For the seven authors presented here, the organizations in question were variously utilitarian (the mutual aid society that Bédé helped found), professional (Perdiguier's compagnonnage), political (the republican clubs and the precursors of political parties and labor unions with which Nadaud, Dumay, and Bouvier were associated), or social-reformist and philosophical (the circle of Saint-Simonians to which Voilquin belonged). Membership in such an organized group appears to have made resources available

40. This number, though small, continues slowly to grow. Jacques Etienne Bédé's *A Worker in 1820*, completed around 1830, was not published until 1984, nearly four decades after it had resurfaced in manuscript form in the hands of a Paris bookseller. Of course, any estimate of the number of working-class autobiographies is somewhat arbitrary because it depends on how one defines the category; the texts differ markedly in length, content, and intended audience.

and provided practical and psychological support. It also seems to have been a key factor in convincing the author that he or she had a story of more than personal significance, to which a larger audience might be receptive.

A second spur to recording one's life history appears to have been the experience of exceptional social and geographical mobility. It is no accident that much of what we know of the daily lives of manual workers has been told by individuals who began but did not end their lives in that status. Of the seven authors represented here, all spent their early adulthood as members of the working class, yet all but Bédé were led by circumstance to suspend or abandon their careers as workers.[41] The dramatic upward mobility which most of these authors experienced seems, on the one hand, to have convinced them of the exemplary character of their personal histories and, on the other, to have enhanced the appeal of those lives to publishers and public alike. The changes of status which, almost without exception, they underwent again raise questions about the representative character of the testimony these memoirs provide.

Sources of these kinds are invaluable for illustrating relationships or trends that have been independently established through the use of more systematic forms of evidence. Because autobiographies convey their information with greater immediacy and power, they are ideal complements to those analytical works in which historians and social scientists have demonstrated causal relationships with the help of sources of documentation less accessible to nonspecialists, such as administrative statistics, demographic compilations, and archival records. The use of multiple sources can

41. Both Perdiguier and Nadaud were elected to the National Assembly under the short-lived Second Republic, only to be forced into exile after Louis-Napoléon's coup d'état. Perdiguier subsequently earned his living as a bookseller and teacher as much as in woodworking. Nadaud would later resume his political career, serving briefly in 1870–71 as prefect of his native department of Creuse, and for thirteen years as a Deputy to the National Assembly. After his own return from exile, Dumay was elected Conseiller Municipal for Paris and subsequently Deputy to the National Assembly under the early Third Republic. Voilquin became a midwife and traveled to both Egypt and Russia before departing for the United States in 1848. Truquin definitively left France after the Paris Commune and eventually settled in Paraguay, where he tried his hand at farming, with mixed success. Bouvier, through her involvement in the syndicalist and feminist movements and her work in the French Office du Travail à Domicile, became a historian of women and work, publishing three books in addition to her memoirs. As for Bédé, we simply know nothing of his later life.

In an age when travel was either difficult or expensive for a member of the working class, this group of authors moved about a great deal. Every one of them saw Paris, virtually all traveled extensively throughout their native country, and at least four lived for a time outside France.

help bring our historical vision into focus because it allows us to effect small shifts of overall perspective. This process of triangulation is still more effective when the historical sources are diverse, so that their mutually corrective influence is compounded.

The life stories of workers may also suggest hypotheses worthy of systematic investigation. To take just one example, the late-twentieth-century reader will likely be struck by how many of these seven authors lost one or both parents in childhood or adolescence.[42] Not only in the texts collected here but in the literature of nineteenth-century workers' autobiographies generally, such loss is so frequent as to raise the suspicion that it gave rise to a sense of marginality that predisposed these individuals to take up their pens, perhaps as a means of asserting or restoring their sense of who they were. Fortunately, the exacting research required to explore the nature of this association between loss of a parent and authorship has been undertaken by the historian M. J. Maynes. Working from a set of fifty-eight nineteenth- and twentieth-century autobiographies written by French and German workers, she compiled data on the survival of authors' parents. She then compared these data with the parents' expected survival, calculated from the rates of mortality observed in the general population. Twenty-eight percent of those included in her subsample of French authors were found to have lost one or both parents by the age of fourteen.[43] This is actually less than the 40 percent one would expect from what we know of life expectancy in the period.[44] In this case at least, the systematic relationship initially suggested by the texts is disconfirmed; yet the demonstration is instructive in another respect—it emphasizes the fragility of the family unit and the tenuousness of life itself in this period and lends a certain historical perspective to our contemporary concept of the single-parent family.

Finally, the observant reader will glean from autobiographical sources insights that it would be difficult to obtain in any other way. What, for

42. Bédé's father died when he was nine, Truquin's mother died when he was six, and Dumay's father perished in a mining accident before he was born. If we include instances of a parent absent due to abandonment or the breakup of a marriage, then we must also add Bouvier. Voilquin was nearly twenty-one when her mother died.
43. The proportion rises to 34 percent if one counts parental abandonment as parental loss.
44. Maynes made a comparable calculation for a subsample of German workers' memoirs; in this population, the rate of parental loss was somewhat greater than that predicted by actuarial tables. See M. J. Maynes, "The Contours of Childhood: Demography, Strategy, and Mythology of Childhood in French and German Lower-Class Autobiographies," in Louise Tilly, John Gillis, and David Levine, eds., *The Quiet Revolution: Western Europeans in the Era of Declining Fertility* (forthcoming).

example, seems more improbable than to recover the firsthand, written testimony of an illiterate worker living in the mid–nineteenth century? Yet that is, after a fashion, just what we find in the narrative of Truquin, who learned to read and write only in his middle age. In reviewing his life, he therefore includes vignettes that are all the more precious because, by their very nature, they are among the least likely ever to have been documented. Through these memoirs, we share his feelings of helplessness and dependency when, after his employer granted him time off to attend classes in preparation for his First Communion, he was forced to beg his often reluctant fellow workers to help him master the catechism he was unable to read for himself. We are caught up in the mix of reticence and defiance he felt in declaring his illiteracy to the students who had engaged him in heated political debate at the school of silk manufacture where he was employed. And we begin to appreciate the sense of vulnerability of the illiterate as we observe him, as a child, before a house on the door of which was mounted a sign he was unable to decipher. Upon entering to ask for a scrap of bread, he discovers that he has blundered into the home of the local mayor, who threatens to lock him up in the house of correction for having violated the laws against begging.

In such passages, the adaptive strategies (including prodigious feats of memory) with which the unlettered managed to compensate for their disability can be communicated only because the genre of autobiography imposes a longitudinal perspective on the author's life and thus can capture a state of being, illiteracy, from which he had to escape in order to record his experiences. Since most sources of historical data seriously underrepresent that substantial segment of the working class which could not read,[45] in this instance the autobiographical genre has helped complete our picture of nineteenth-century life by documenting experiences otherwise unlikely to be preserved. It is *because* the individual autobiography is unique, in form as well as content, that it can round out our picture of the working

---

45. According to the 1848 survey of the Paris Chamber of Commerce, 87 percent of the male, 79 percent of the female, and 84 percent of the total labor force of the capital was literate. The figure is misleading, however, for at least two reasons. First, the elite corps of skilled workers that was concentrated in Paris contained a smaller proportion of illiterates than the French working class in general. Second, the standard of literacy used in the survey was whether an individual could sign his or her own name—the most common but also the most limited measure of mastery over the written word. See Chambre de commerce de Paris, *Statistique de l'industrie à Paris*. It should also be noted that the ability to read and the ability to write were far more distinct in the nineteenth century than today, and many people were capable of one but not the other.

class by conveying information systematically excluded from other forms of evidence.

Autobiographical sources were presented at the outset of this introduction as a window on the world of the French working class. On closer examination, they have turned out more nearly to resemble the panes of glass still sometimes found in houses that date from the nineteenth century: the traditional techniques of manufacture leave them flawed by irregularities, so that they transmit a somewhat deformed image of what lies beyond. These memoirs likewise show signs of having been hand crafted, for they bear the marks of their authors' individuality. Yet even memoirs which can make no claim to being representative perform two further, vital functions when considered as a group. First, they suggest the range of variations that existed within the working class, variations which more systematic sources, because they frequently present their evidence in aggregated form, tend to truncate or obscure. Second, they allow us to discern gradually emerging trends that could never be detected through consideration of single sources. To see how a strategy of selection and interpretation can elevate autobiographical sources, initially fascinating for the insights they offer into the subjective world of a particular individual, into a tool for understanding large-scale changes which affected the lives of the great mass of society's population over time, let us turn our attention to the transformation of popular collective action which occurred in the course of the nineteenth century.

CHANGING PATTERNS OF WORK AND PROTEST

The seven autobiographies in this anthology have been selected to achieve as balanced a distribution in terms of gender, skill level, occupational sector, region of origin, and degree of urbanization, as the limited array of sources permits. But above all, these worker-authors were chosen as members of successive cohorts, so that their active careers span the entire length of the nineteenth century. With such a chronological spread, we are able to observe the processes set in motion by industrialization. We can begin to distinguish those tendencies that shaped the experience of the working class as a whole from the more ephemeral forces responsible for the contours of the individual authors' lives.

By reference to such large-scale processes we are able to place in context, for example, the fact that just two of these memoirs were written by working women. This underrepresentation of women relative to their proportion in the general population is the combined result of the scarcity of such texts and the requirement that the manuscripts included here deal centrally with issues of occupational socialization, in a period when female participation in the labor force was relatively restricted.[46] Note, however, that the authors' reports of their mothers' or spouses' efforts to supplement the family income help complete our image of the contribution made by women, particularly through activities outside the formal economy (activities that other, more frequently consulted sources typically ignore).

Similarly, these seven authors' primary occupations represent only five sectors within the thirteen-sector scheme frequently used to describe the mid-nineteenth-century French economy. This coverage appears the more limited because the standard classification system considers only the production of goods and leaves out agriculture, transportation, mining, and service occupations of all kinds. But because these seven texts have been selected for their coverage of the authors' years of childhood and young adulthood, some introduce bits of their parents' occupational histories while others detail the authors' protracted search for an occupational niche, during which they tried a number of different jobs. If we include the early or secondary occupations of the authors as well as the mentions made of their fathers' and mothers', ten of the thirteen standard categories are accounted for, as well as occupations not covered by the standard classification scheme—such as maid, miner, miller, navvy, railroad worker, and salesclerk.

By reading these texts in chronological order, we glimpse the changes taking place in the organization of work during the age of industrialization. Neither the statistical summaries generated by the government's periodic surveys of industry nor the bare facts of the authors' lives as displayed in table 1 can convey with such immediacy the gulf that separated the tiny chair-turning shops in which Bédé, the earliest of these authors, perfected his skills, from the huge Schneider ironworks in which Dumay, nearly the last of the seven to live and write, was employed. In Bédé's account we are introduced to an intimate assembly of a half-dozen of the most skillful practitioners of the craft that France had to offer. They lived and worked in an informal community which, though it was threatened by the spread of more highly rationalized capitalist relations, they still viewed as their collective creation and sought actively to protect. In Dumay's memoir, we encounter a vast industrial establishment in which single departments might number workers in the hundreds, relations between employers and

46. It could be argued that for the specific purpose of examining the link between political participation and work life outside the household, equal numbers of male and female authors would amount to an overrepresentation of women, who constituted perhaps one-third of the urban labor force, with the proportion gradually rising as the century advanced.

employees had become distant and based exclusively on the exchange of labor for wages, and the strong sense of identification with one's trade had become secondary to a relatively undifferentiated self-conception as a worker.

Opportunities for training, as well as the form which it might take, changed significantly over the course of the nineteenth century. Perdiguier recounts the four-year tour of French towns he undertook in the 1820s to polish his skills as a joiner and master regional variations of technique. By the midcentury, the compagnonnage system had fallen into disrepair. Even a highly qualified worker like Dumay, attempting his Tour of France in 1860, was often forced to rely on relatives or on the informal networks of those who came from the same native region in order to find jobs, most of which did little to advance his knowledge of the trade. As for unskilled and semiskilled workers, especially those living in the second half of the century, the situation was significantly worse. A formal apprenticeship was rarely required. Bouvier's career as seamstress required practical training, but her initial probationary period was measured in weeks rather than months or years, even though she was hired with no previous experience. Of her earlier stint in a silk-throwing factory in 1876, she tells us that she learned the essentials necessary to perform her duties in the span of her first morning's work. Even if we make allowance for the powerful forces which shunted women into less skilled and lower-paying jobs, the contrast indicates the general direction in which the industrial economy was evolving.

I do not mean to suggest with these few examples that the pattern of changes taking place in the productive process in the course of the nineteenth century was simple and unilinear, nor that it could be faithfully distilled from the experiences related in these or any seven individual workers' autobiographies. Though a number of crucial transformations were already under way, most did not become fully apparent until well into the twentieth century, and it is only thanks to our privileged vantage point one hundred years later that we are able to discern them clearly. During the nineteenth century, the changes were less visible, in part because the artisanal economy which predominated in the first half of that century persisted with considerable vigor through the second half, despite the challenge from a growing industrial sector. Nevertheless, the picture drawn by historians of the economic development of the period is consistent with the workers' narratives anthologized here: gradual, though uneven, erosion of traditional skills; an increase in the scale and capital requirements of production that closed off avenues of mobility for workers, distancing them from their employers and depriving them of ownership of or control over the means of production; and the consequent loss of artisanal autonomy in favor of new forms and higher levels of work discipline in the factory.

These changes in work life can be related to changes in popular protest. Here again, the contrast between the first and second halves of the nineteenth century is imperfect. Our frame of comparison would need to be extended into the twentieth century in order to show that contrast more clearly. But the testimony of these seven authors, most of whom participated actively in the political movements of their day, is illuminating. Let us consider first the four authors who wrote about the earlier part of the century. Bédé led the chair turners of the Rue de Cléry in a collective refusal to perform the unpaid tasks which their masters had imposed. This effort remained highly local and, despite some initial success, was quickly isolated, its organizational base dismembered, and its leaders jailed. Perdiguier's memoirs celebrated the bonds uniting the members of workers' brotherhoods, even as he called attention to the intense and often violent conflicts that pitted different trades or different brotherhoods of compagnons against one another. Voilquin formed such strong ties with a group organized around the communitarian ideals of Saint-Simon that her entire adult life was powerfully redirected as a consequence. Nadaud, a ringleader in an 1840 attempt to mount a strike among construction workers, saw the efforts of its organizing committee collapse the first time workers were challenged by the authorities, who sent troops to break up the initial public meeting. He notes how strongly public opinion was biased against striking workers. Each of these earlier authors, in short, was an energetic participant in a relatively small-scale and homogeneous community of workers whose members interacted on a familiar, firsthand basis and whose outlook was shaped by strong personal bonds of solidarity.[47]

For the three later authors, on the other hand—those whose work years were situated mainly in the second half of the century—the pace, the tone, and the tenor of working-class life had started to change. Truquin was involved in an 1867 wage dispute organized citywide by Lyon silk workers in a variety of related trades. The dispute was settled in the workers' favor and brought real relief to a variety of job categories in the industry— though the lack of improvement in his personal economic position, coupled with the disillusionment he felt at the failure of the short-lived Commune

47. Though faithful to the way these particular authors lived (or wished to portray their lives), this statement may exaggerate the extent to which skilled artisans formed vital and stable communities, as the work of Michael Sonenscher and Jacques Rancière reminds us. There is nonetheless a discernible difference of degree between the experiences of skilled and of semiskilled workers, especially in the later part of the nineteenth century.

of Lyon, convinced Truquin a few years later that his only hopeful prospect lay in emigration to South America. Dumay assumed a prominent role in organizing efforts in his native Le Creusot and went on to a career in politics, punctuated by participation in the 1871 Commune and subsequent exile to Switzerland. His experiences appear to parallel those of an earlier generation, to which Perdiguier and Nadaud belonged; but with the difference that Dumay was motivated by the ideal of a classwide and even cross-national alliance of workers. Nadaud, though later active in politics at the national level, even then identified with the interests and outlook of his native department of Creuse and with the informally organized but densely integrated networks of seasonally migrant masons that he depicted in his autobiography. Dumay, by contrast, ran for election as a workers' candidate in three different regions of France and was identified with a set of labor issues that were truly national in scope. Dumay's affiliation with the Syndicalist movement was shared by Bouvier. It is true that the daily experiences she relates in part 1 of her autobiography, covering the period through 1900, were confined to her largely individualistic efforts to achieve what modest mobility and security her situation permitted. However, she went on to become active in the trade unionist and protofeminist movements in France and abroad. All these later authors differed, if only in degree, from the earlier four because they associated themselves with groups in which dense networks of personal contact were less salient than an organizational style emphasizing inclusiveness of membership and large-scale mobilization.

At the risk of overstating the degree of discontinuity between them, it is possible to discern two styles of collective action that began to diverge in the course of the nineteenth century. In the earlier decades, protest in the work arena was likely to involve relatively small numbers of highly skilled workers, who saw themselves as members of a closed community defined in terms of trade or subtrade groupings and not as members of an economic class. Often their objective was to resist, in the name of communitarian or corporatist ideals, the advance of impersonal market relations. These artisans tended to see their economic concerns as inseparable not only from the organization of work but also from larger social issues like the right of non-elites to participate in political affairs through voting, association, and public debate. When economic and political preoccupations converged, as they did in each of the four major revolutionary events of the period, the mixture could prove highly volatile. The essentially defensive stance adopted by these artisans, premised on a rejection of many elements of the rising capitalist order, made their spontaneously mobilized actions appear capable of effecting a radical break with existing institutions. It succeeded in introducing a new vocabulary of political protest and liberation; but precisely because they were opposing the powerful forces of economic and social rationalization that have broadly defined the modern era, the gains achieved often proved short-lived or illusory.

By comparison, the styles of collective action that began to emerge in the later part of the nineteenth century and firmly took hold only in the twentieth, involved a higher degree of formal organization, exhibited greater continuity, and typically operated on a more than local scale, even when they adopted a narrower economistic focus. Once rights of popular participation had been guaranteed by the Third Republic's more open and stable constitutional regime, the politics of insurrection began to give way to the politics of the ballot box, and protest was aimed increasingly at swaying public opinion. The revolutionary barricade all but disappeared in the last three decades of the century, the general strike and the demonstration were introduced, and social movements gradually took on the form with which we are familiar today.[48] Though continuing to rely on the leadership of highly skilled workers to a degree disproportionate to their numbers, this new style of protest came to be associated with the industrialized segment of the French labor force, which figured more and more prominently in such actions. The dominant ideologies—whether generically Socialist, Marxist, Syndicalist, or other—framed their appeals in terms of class and sought to unite all workers regardless of distinctions based on trade, skill level, regional origin, or even nationality. Rather than reacting to crises, workers' movements became more proactive and aimed at preemptively shaping social policy in directions that would serve the interests of the working class. Despite an often defiant rhetoric of revolution, most of the actions in which large numbers of workers participated adopted pragmatic goals and stopped short of challenging the industrial order itself. They aimed instead at capturing an increased share of power and influence within the existing institutional structures. The Paris Commune of 1871 may have been the last serious attempt to overthrow the government of France by popular insurrection—but this by no means implies that the last quarter of the nineteenth century saw fewer meaningful changes. On the contrary, if we measure its achievements in terms of lasting improvements in the material well-being of the working class, this

48. Charles Tilly has introduced the concept of "repertoire" to characterize the relatively stable and well-defined set of practices on which participants in collective action in any given time and place typically rely. In his view, during the nineteenth century a more traditional repertoire with roots deep in the Old Regime was displaced by a newer one that has persisted into our own era. The argument is most comprehensively stated in *The Contentious French* (Cambridge, 1986).

period of strident but less overtly insurrectionary action produced important cumulative gains in the conditions of work and life and in this respect might be judged more successful than the revolutionary outbursts that had dominated the earlier period in such spectacular fashion.

It is unlikely, of course, that any of the authors represented in this volume would have recognized these shifts in just the terms described. Each lived to see only a segment of this more than century-long progression, and all were denied the benefit of the retrospective point of view that allows us today to interpret the early age of industrialization in the light of late-twentieth-century understanding. In any event, these author-workers, as self-evidently astute and perceptive as they were, have not been chosen for their command of the abstract issues of political economy or the theory of collective action. They were chosen for the detailed and circumstantial accounts they provide of the trades they plied and the events they witnessed. Their testimony concerning the attitudes, beliefs, and values as well as the everyday activities of ordinary laborers is invaluable because it constitutes as direct and unmediated an account of the life experiences of the French worker as any we possess. In their own words, the epochal transformations which social historians and social scientists continue to debate are concretized as the personal recollections of individuals who were not just the products of those changes but their active agents. The following pages offer the reader the rare opportunity to see the world in which these workers lived, as if through their own eyes.

The French Worker

1 Jacques Etienne Bédé

A Worker in 1820

Bédé alone, of all the authors collected in this volume, lived under the Old Regime. He was born in 1775, one year after Louis XVI ascended the throne of France. He experienced the French Revolution in his adolescence, enlisted in Napoléon's army as a young man, and settled into maturity as a worker under the Bourbon Restoration.

Bédé first ventured outside his native region of the Loire River as a soldier, but deserted after six years of military service. Despite being liable to arrest, he returned home and established himself as a wood turner specializing in fine furniture. Within a few years, he had married and begun a family. In time, the need to secure a better livelihood prompted him to migrate to Tours. After a three-year stay, he moved on, like so many others, to Paris. There he joined the community of highly skilled chair turners who were concentrated in the capital.

These memoirs were initially drafted in April 1821, while the author was serving the first month of a two-year sentence in Sainte-Pélagie prison for his role in the labor dispute between masters and journeymen in the chair-turning trade. The original manuscript was recopied sometime between 1826 and 1830, and the last supplemental material was added in 1836. Only two handwritten copies of the text existed. The first was entrusted to Marie Bicheux, the benefactor to whom this work was dedicated. The author intended that the second be buried in his coffin, so that it might be discovered in "future centuries" and serve to honor his memory.

There is no way to be certain which of the two copies survived to resurface in the hands of a Parisian bookseller in the late 1940s. It was eventually acquired by the Bibliothèque Nationale and was published in 1984. Thus, the first of all these texts to be written was the last to appear in print, after a delay of almost precisely a century and a half. Permission to translate these excerpts has been graciously provided by the Presses Universitaires de France, which published the French edition of Un Ouvrier en

1820 *with a foreword by Louis Girard and an introduction and notes by Rémi Gossez.*

BOOK I: SUMMARY OF THE PRIVATE LIFE AND MILITARY CAREER OF J. E. BÉDÉ, WRITTEN BY HIMSELF

A SON OF THE PEOPLE IN CHÂTEAUNEUF AND ORLÉANS (1775–1792)

The place of my birth and the cradle of my misfortunes was a small town named Châteauneuf-sur-Loire, situated on the banks of the Loire river in the department of Loiret, six leagues from Orléans.[1] My father, Jacques Bédé, had also been born there and had lost his father as a young child. [. . .]

When he was a bit older, my father took up the trade of miller and became an apprentice in the mill of a young widow whom he later married, though she had two children in her charge. My father, who had no money of his own, immediately seized this opportunity, since this young widow owned a small house and a windmill that she had acquired with her first husband.

My father's first child was a girl. I was the next to be born, on 27 June 1775. I was given my father's name along with that of my godfather, Etienne. I suffered the misfortune that many children from big families experience: as I was the fourth child overall, I was not loved by my mother. She favored the two girls from her first marriage. My father was as loving to them as to his own children, but by the time I was old enough to be aware of it, I realized with sorrow that my mother only cared for my older sisters, the first of whom was so jealous that she could hardly stand anyone but herself in the household. My mother, who was completely indifferent as far as I was concerned, gave this eldest daughter considerable authority over the rest of us. This produced daily quarrels when my father was not at home, which was often, since he was usually off working at the mill.

---

1. The league was an ancient unit of measurement used originally by the Gauls. Its length has varied, in different times and places, from less than 2.5 to more than 4.5 miles. As employed here and in most of these texts (notably Perdiguier's *Memoirs*), one league was equal to just under four kilometers or about 2.4 miles. Despite the introduction of the metric system during the French Revolution and an 1837 law imposing penalties for the use of nonmetric units, most people continued to use traditional measures like the pound, the foot, and the league virtually through the end of the century. Concerning Bédé's place of birth, Rémi Gossez indicates in the 1984 edition that the population of Châteauneuf-sur-Loire was 3,141 inhabitants in 1818.

He would often take me there in his cart just so I would not have to suffer the mistreatment of my mother and sisters, about which my father always spoke to me with tears in his eyes. When I answered the various questions he asked me, he would sigh, give me a hug and say, "Poor child!" I was touched by his tears but did not know what to make of them and did not dare to ask him their cause. He always made me promise to work hard in school and learn my lessons well. He understood the importance of doing so, for he himself did not know how to read or write. I loved my father very much and was happy when I was with him, even though he did not say very much. He earned people's respect for his upright conduct and his calm demeanor. My father was not rich, but he was courageous, peaceful, and honest. He had a great deal of refinement according to what I have been told by his friends, for I did not have the good fortune to get to know his character inasmuch as I was still too young when I had the bad luck to lose him. I was just nine years old at the time, and he loved me very much.

My Father's Death

One day in 1784, as I was leaving school, I noticed people running as if to go see something extraordinary. I noticed my uncle in the crowd, though he usually never left his home except on important business. I was so surprised to see him mixing with the curiosity seekers that I decided I would join in the general movement that was heading toward my father's mill. I asked several people what there was to see, but no one told me anything. I thought to myself, "My father will tell me; I'll go find him." But suddenly I was astonished to see that the windmill was not turning and that its door was open. I quickly realized that the mill was damaged and I began to fear that some accident had happened to my father and that this was what had attracted so many people to the area.

I do not know who had alerted my uncle, but he must not have been told what had happened, for I would like to think that he would never have gone to that fatal place, any more than I would have, if he had known.

The operation of a windmill is a very dangerous occupation when the weather brings storms and lightning. The day that I am now describing gave me such resounding proof of this fact that I renounced the profession of miller forever. [. . .]

Those lightning bolts struck my family a terrible blow by dislodging one vane of my father's windmill. It fell with a crash and broke apart, slamming into the ground with such force that the shock unsettled the entire frame of the windmill. This terrible catastrophe snapped the thread of my father's life. This was why the curious had come running. I arrived at this baleful spot to see my poor father's corpse being administered useless efforts at first aid. At this sight my uncle fell unconscious and nearly lost his own life. [. . .]

I Learn a Trade

I suffered cruelly from the loss I had just sustained and from seeing that, despite my goodwill and my efforts to make the best of it, I was detested by my unhappy mother and mistreated by my older sister. As a result, I looked forward to the time when, once I had fulfilled my religious obligation, I could leave. I asked my mother's permission to go see my uncle in Orléans to find out if he would consent to take me in apprenticeship as a turner.[2] My mother replied that I could not only go there but stay, for she did not have the means to teach me a trade or even to feed me. She told me I could make whatever arrangements with my uncle I was able to negotiate, but that she could give me nothing toward my apprenticeship. Having received my mother's consent, I left immediately for Orléans.

Once arrived at my uncle's, I no sooner uttered my greetings and gave news of my family than I announced that I had come with the intention of staying on to learn a trade. My uncle asked if I had my mother's consent. I told him that my mother had given me full powers to negotiate with him as he saw fit, telling me simply that she could give me nothing toward my apprenticeship nor toward the cost of my food or upkeep. My uncle, who was no better off than my mother, raised no objection to keeping me with him on those terms. He promised me that he would write my mother. In the end I moved into his home and began work the very next day. My uncle worked with his brother and never hired other workers. My aunt worked with them, making the straw bottoms of chairs.

That is how I came to live at my uncle's. I began to breathe a little easier, seeing that I was at a distance from the place that held such cruel memories for me. Since there were no other youngsters at my uncle's, I no longer heard those childish rows and quarrels that had so long been my cradle

---

2. A turner (*tourneur*) fashioned round or cylindrical objects on a lathe. The lathe was usually turned by the artisan or by an assistant who operated a treadle, though it might occasionally be power driven. The objects produced ranged from simple pegs, bungs, and spools to complex machine parts and delicate ornamental furniture. Although Bédé's text mentions only wood turners, others might work in such materials as metal, ivory, bone, and horn. Most turners were highly skilled and commanded relatively handsome salaries in urban centers, where the demand for their goods was high; this was notably true of the elite chair turners whom Bédé would join after moving to Paris. The religious obligation that Bédé mentions is presumably his First Communion.

song. I felt myself reborn through the inner tranquillity that reigned in my uncle's home and that let me reflect at leisure on the private thoughts that preoccupied me day and night. I was just fine at my uncle's, even though we lacked the barest necessities. It was for me a place of great delights because it was so far from my mother's house. Because my uncle had not written her, I was always afraid he would send me back there, but I no longer dared speak to him about it.

In the end, my uncle did not write to my mother, and she paid me no further attention. She did not come to see whether or not I was at my uncle's or whether she and my uncle needed to arrive at an arrangement or strike a deal. I was no longer around the house, so the matter was closed.

I know that my mother's misfortune was great and that this affected her a great deal. I was very sensitive to this fact and gladly forgave her for ignoring me, knowing that she still had more children living with her than she could afford to raise. Because I was aware of and appreciated her difficulties, I respected her misfortune. I saw her very rarely: she would occasionally come to Orléans to visit one of my half-sisters who was working as a maid there, but she never came to my uncle's. As soon as I learned that she was in Orléans, I would go running to pay her a visit, and as time went on I could see that she received me with less indifference. However, I never asked her to come visit me, knowing that she was not fond of my aunt nor of any of my relatives on my father's side. She had always treated them coldly. In the end I stayed on with my uncle even though no formal arrangement was ever drawn up between him and my mother.

Unsettling Events

Some time after I arrived at my uncle's, the French Revolution began. As I was young and curious, I witnessed the revolt which took place at Orléans on the Rue Dauphine in the Saint-Marceau district. That is where I first saw men die by weapons fire. Young and curious, my friends and I would go wherever we could watch the troops engaging in maneuvers. As they arrived at the bridge, they placed themselves in battle array to confront the rural inhabitants who arrived in a crowd, equipped with every description of firearm and sword. The crowd's objective was to get the price of grain and flour reduced. Seeing the inhabitants arrive in such numbers, the troops marched forward to meet them. Once within range, they fired. The first volley stunned all the curiosity seekers and dispersed most of them. I stayed on as a spectator of this bloody scene and saw several unfortunate inhabitants, fathers with children at home, fall at my feet. [. . .]

I went three years without having my mother inquire how I was doing. This is what made my uncle's brother say that I was an abandoned child. I instantly asked him never to talk that way again, saying that I was not abandoned but just unfortunate. My aunt also asked him not to speak to me about my misfortunes.

After about three years, my aunt fell ill and died. Her death affected me a great deal and caused me many tears. I was again at risk of being called abandoned. During my aunt's lifetime, no one ever spoke to me about my father's death, but soon after this my uncle's brother asked me several questions on the subject. I told him in a firm and determined tone that I knew nothing about it and I begged him to leave me alone. But these questions struck me such a terrible blow that I immediately decided no longer to remain in my uncle's house. What distressed me most was that I was not prepared to find work. But hope and courage soon decided me to seek out another place where I could finish my apprenticeship and prepare myself to go off traveling, for that was still my true intention. I found work with a master in a nearby quarter, and I immediately signed on with him. Though my wage was very low, at least I was earning money.

The change of scene was a distraction from my afflictions. It was just what I needed, and I more than willingly set to work. After changing workshops a few times, I decided to leave. I went to the town hall to obtain a passport for Bordeaux.[3] Wishing to get still further away from my place of birth, my intention was to take a ship to foreign lands. I was very surprised when I was told at the town hall that the city of Bordeaux was in a state of rebellion and that the issuance of passports had been indefinitely suspended. I therefore had to stay a while longer. Soon the Revolution broke out on all sides. The entire National Guard was activated and volunteers were being accepted everywhere, in all government offices and on the public squares. Every man capable of carrying a rifle was leaving for the borders. [. . .]

3. Under the Old Regime and through much of the nineteenth century, a resident who wished to travel within France was first obliged to obtain an internal passport. Workers were, in addition, required to carry a *livret ouvrier* or labor passport in which notations of previous employment were recorded. These documents served both as personal identification and as a means of regulating the movements of the population among areas that were affected by labor shortages or surpluses. They also allowed the authorities to check whether the new arrival was a vagrant. One of the worker's first responsibilities upon reaching a new destination was to proceed to the town hall or the nearest police station to register and be issued a residence permit. In many ways, more restrictive control was exercised over domestic than international movements in the nineteenth century, in part because travel abroad was for the most part limited to a small and privileged elite.

Shall I Travel?

The state of rebellion that had put a halt to the movements of travelers further added to my problems by alerting me to the great difficulty I would have in getting away from those places I had grown to hate. One day, as I was reflecting on all my troubles, three of my friends came to find me, announcing that they had just enlisted in the army and inviting me to follow their example. I told them that although I thought very highly of the military, the only problem was that one did not have freedom of movement, and that I preferred to travel as a worker. They insisted that if I did not enlist I would later be forced to join up, since the war was in full swing and the Netherlands were beginning to rebel. They argued that there would probably be mass conscriptions and that I would certainly be drafted. All my friends' sound arguments caused me to do some serious thinking. I was consumed by grief as well as the tedium of not being free to leave for far-away lands. The deplorable deaths of my relatives led me to foresee that fate doubtless had reserved for me, as for them, a tragic end. This conviction led me to resolve to seek death in battle.

So I informed my friends that I had decided to enlist. "Come," they told me, "we'll all travel together." And we went at once to the town hall, where I enrolled in the first battalion of the department of Loiret. Knowing my mother's indifference where I was concerned, I did not even go to say my good-byes. I did not wish to revive her grief on seeing me, or mine on returning to those most distressing sites of my existence.

I asked one of my older sisters, who was working as a maid in Orléans, to inform my mother that I was leaving for the army and to convey my apologies for not having gone to tell her in person, because I had to leave right away. The one to whom I entrusted this mission was only my half-sister, but she nonetheless had some regard for me and, touched by the unhappy fate that pursued me, she could not keep from crying when she saw me in uniform, so young, yet so determined to leave everything behind—home, family, and friends. She urged me not to abandon my mother and to write to her often, saying that perhaps my absence would cause my mother some reflection.

I told my sister that I could never abandon my mother and that, as soon as I arrived at my destination, I would prove it to her. And in fact, the love in my heart has always overcome all else. Neither my mother's mistreatment nor her indifference prevented me from respecting and cherishing her. I attribute all the sorrow she caused me through her indifference to her great misfortunes, and I would have liked to alleviate them with all my heart. [. . .]

I VOLUNTEER TO DEFEND OUR BORDERS [. . .]

Paris in August 1793

The six of us were to leave together. A few days later, we went to get our marching orders, which directed us to go to Paris. I was pleased, for I had long desired to see this great city. We were slated to take six days of marching to get to Paris, but we pressed on and arrived in two so as to have the pleasure of seeing the sights of this beautiful capital.

Once arrived, I was disoriented at seeing so many people bustling about. I never tired of admiring all the beauty the city contained. I was so enthusiastic that I soon forgot that I was a soldier and in transit. The city of Paris perfectly suited my needs at the time, for all I asked was for the kind of distractions that would help me forget, if possible, all those horrors that had been weighing me down with grief and poisoning my youth.

We stayed a long time in Paris, though we were not even supposed to stop there. Since we were already late, I joined one of my friends, who had confided to me that he also wished to remain, in looking for work. When we found some, we resolved to stay on in Paris. Our other friends did not want to hear of it.

As soon as they had spent all their money, they felt it was time to go sign our marching orders and leave to join our units. I told them that I was staying in Paris. Having remained absent without leave for so long, I was afraid that when we went to sign our marching orders at the office of the war commissioner, he would have us arrested and conducted under escort to the garrison. This, I told them, did not suit me at all. I preferred to remain, since nothing worse was likely to happen. My friend agreed with me, but the others continued to insist that we follow them. They pointed out the public disturbances that were sowing unrest in Paris. And in fact, at just that moment, as we were walking along the boulevards, we heard the sounding of the call to arms. Next we saw the Saint-Antoine district parade by in a body on its way to the Convention.[4] Everywhere people were displaying the red flag, declaring that the country was in danger. Our friends pointed out the risks we were running by staying behind, telling us that we would no doubt soon be arrested and perhaps obliged to face a court martial.

4. The National Convention was the revolutionary assembly that governed France from 21 September 1792 until 26 October 1795, a period which corresponded to the high point of radicalism and popular participation under the French Revolution. With respect to domestic policy, the Convention was responsible for declaring the First French Republic and promoting its democratic reforms, for trying and executing Louis XVI, and for instituting the Terror. In foreign affairs, the Convention successfully defended France against a coalition of hostile European monarchies.

When they saw we were not going to change our minds, they gave up and went off to the war commissioner's to sign their marching orders. They were sent on their way without being admonished in any way. Seeing their signed marching orders, and hearing the rumors that continued to circulate in Paris, I recalled the disturbances in Orléans which had made such an impression on me. I decided to leave so as not to be in violation of the law. I hoped that the sight of armies, the sounds of battle, and the tumult of the camps would offer sufficient distraction to help get rid of the frightening phantom that was pursuing me.

We therefore left the superb city of Paris, to my deep regret. I promised her that, if fate allowed me to return from the army, it was there in her bosom that I would take up residence.

[Bédé's account of his exploits as a soldier in the French army has not been included in the excerpts collected here. In two chapters, he describes his participation in campaigns on the Sambre, Rhine, and Danube rivers and his preparation for a military expedition to Egypt that did not take place. This portion of his memoirs covers the period from 1793, when he enlisted, to 1799, when he deserted and returned to his native region, a fugitive from justice.]

CIVILIAN LIFE IN AN UNLAWFUL STATUS
(1800–1801)

Working in a Trade

My mother received me with tears in her eyes, as did my sisters and all my relatives and friends. This touching scene made me shed tears of joy at seeing my mother again, after being estranged for so long. I made a vow to maintain my relations with her and with the rest of my family on the best of terms, as I intended to remain in the area. But my precarious situation required that I leave the place where my mother lived. Since it was my native district, I could not stay there without feeling anxious and perhaps causing trouble for my mother through the inquiries and legal proceedings that would probably be directed against me. Prudence required that I leave my mother's house after three days. I went to Orléans, where I found work as a turner. I thus abandoned my military status and turned to civilian occupations. I also had to accept being separated from my mother and renouncing the sweet pleasures of going to visit her, so as not to arouse suspicion and to escape the attention of the authorities of Châteauneuf.

I had not been in Orléans very long before I learned that orders had arrived to round up all the soldiers who had returned home. Searches were made of all the workshops and the rooming houses where workers lodged.

These searches made me somewhat uneasy, even though I was not living in one of those houses. I was mainly worried about searches of workshops and denunciations. I confided my concern to the master in whose shop I was working and told him that, as a way of getting around these measures, I had decided to go to Paris, where I thought it would be safer.

The master, who thought a good deal of me and had known me before I left for the army, pointed out that I would be running the risk of being arrested on my way there. He said that if I wanted to work in the countryside while waiting for things to calm down in Orléans, he would protect me while I went to work in the shop of one of his friends, where I would be well taken care of. I answered that I did not care about the terms or conditions of work as long as I could feel at ease and remain outside the orbit of the inhabitants and authorities of Châteauneuf. My master told me that the place he had in mind was in the village of Sandillon, three leagues from Orléans along the banks of the Loire, but on the opposite side from Châteauneuf, so that the gendarmes had no contact with it whatsoever. The job was perfect for me, so I departed on the following Sunday with a note of introduction. Once I arrived in Sandillon, I gave my new master the note I was carrying. He welcomed me enthusiastically and told me that, since I came on the recommendation of his friend, he had work for me. Once we had settled on terms, I promised him I would begin in two days, and I set off once again for Orléans with the intention of attending a show that evening. But I ran across my brother-in-law just as I arrived in Orléans. He was about to take a walk with his friends in the Saint-Marceau district and invited me to join them. I decided on the spot to accompany them and gave up the idea of seeing the performance. This was extremely fortunate, because the theater was surrounded that very evening by troops, who took up positions on both sides of the theater, forming a cordon that led to the town hall opposite and forcing all men leaving the theater to enter it. Those with papers were set free; the others were detained.

That same night, troops were posted at the doors of all rooming houses, all masons' lodgings, and all public places. At daybreak, they entered and made a thorough search, arresting all those whose papers were not in order and taking them off to jail. Happily, I was not sleeping in any of these public lodgings. When my work for my original master was finished, I withdrew to the countryside, where I hoped to be safe, at least for a time.

In my new job, I worked at the rear of the building, which suited my situation very well, for I saw only one neighbor, who lived in the courtyard with his wife and niece. Along with the parish priest and his niece, these were the only people I had contact with. They were all discreet folks who knew my situation and took every precaution to ward off the dangers that threatened me. I was soon fast friends with all these fine people, whose respect I managed to earn by my upright conduct and proper manners. [. . .]

Maria-Julia

One day, while out walking alone, I passed by a house and noticed Maria (for that turned out to be the name of my latest conquest). She was seated by her doorway, reading. She raised her eyes just as I was passing by. I offered a greeting and spoke a few words to her. She answered politely and invited me to sit down. We struck up a conversation. Maria-Julia seemed likable, witty, and uncommonly well-bred for someone who lived in the countryside.

Since the coolness of night was approaching, Maria prepared to go in and invited me to join her. I obeyed without hesitation and we resumed our conversation. I soon came to recognize that Maria was better suited to me than [my previous girlfriend] Theresa in every respect. The truth is, she was old enough to be more serious-minded and had a more fully developed personality. Everything about her spoke of refined sentiments and delicacy.

As I was saying goodbye, Maria invited me to come see her whenever I wanted. This invitation flattered me a great deal, and I did not hesitate to respond. Maria was very fond of reading and indulged in this activity as much as her time permitted. [. . .]

Marriage; We Establish a Household; Amnesty

My situation prevented me from undertaking any serious commitment. Moreover, experience has long provided ample proof that most of the supposedly sacred vows that are exchanged represent just the opposite: the disintegration of all feeling of friendship and the disappearance of all the charm and pleasure in life. Instead, the marriage vows ignite the flame of discord between two hearts that had formerly been united by genuine feelings of love. This day of wedlock—once so intently desired, anticipated with such joy, prepared with such pomp and gaiety, and appearing to portend a happy future—is often nothing more than a contradictory act that poisons the time spent under these happy auspices and engulfs the newlyweds in a horrible morass of constantly renewed sorrows and regrets. These reflections stood between me and any thought of undertaking an act so blindly desired and yet so necessary to society. [. . .]

My love for Maria, as well as the entreaties of my family and friends, enveloped me in a veil of illusion and led me to consent to the vows of marriage. Suddenly I was faced with new anxieties! We had to present ourselves before the authorities to give our first and last names, age, place of birth, and so on. I anticipated that in the course of these preliminaries, I might be arrested.

If destiny were reserving for me this sort of unpleasant catastrophe, I prayed that it would happen before I had pronounced the fatal "I do." I took care of all the preliminary steps quite successfully and without encountering any obstacles. A day was chosen for the celebration of the marriage, and the two families were notified. Maria and I both preferred that the ceremony not take place during the daytime. Her desires were in perfect accord with my situation. At last, the day chosen for our union—7 September 1801—arrived. We had arranged with the mayor and the priest the respective hours at which we would present ourselves before them. The agreement was that we would be married in a civil ceremony at 7 PM, followed by a family dinner, after which we would all go to the chapel to receive the nuptial benediction.

Everything went without a hitch. My mother was present at our marriage and appeared satisfied. She even made me some attractive offers, which gave me pleasure even though I could not take advantage of them at the time without assuming an obvious risk. My mother owned a little house in Châteauneuf-sur-Loire, my village of birth. She proposed that I come live with her and set up my own shop. I told her that I was afraid of the questions that the local officials and the district military authorities might ask me and that I would not be able to answer. All of my relatives and friends encouraged me to follow my mother's advice and take advantage of her offer. Maria also went along. It was a bold course to attempt. Everyone led me to hope for a favorable outcome, arguing that in Châteauneuf there was no one practicing my trade who could cater to the tastes of the bourgeois, who were obliged to make their purchases in Orléans. They also pointed out that someone was liable any day to come live in the local castle, which was quite substantial. This would have been very much to the advantage of all the workers in the area.[5]

Full of such ideas, I resolved to risk this daring undertaking. I moved to Châteauneuf on the strength of my mother's repeated promises. When I arrived at her home, I announced that I had decided to take her up on her offer and had come to join her. When my mother saw that I had decided to move to Châteauneuf, she changed her mind, pointing out several houses that were for rent and about which she had already made inquiries on my

5. Recall that Bédé is speaking of the year 1801. Many of the nobles who had fled France in the wake of the Revolution and the Terror were keeping a close but wary eye on political developments in their homeland in an effort to gauge whether a return was prudent.

behalf. Seeing that my mother no longer intended to put me up in her home, I decided not even to look elsewhere, so sharply was I struck by my mother's sudden change of heart, for it would have pained me to have to explain to my wife, who inevitably would ask me lots of questions. As I was dead set against telling my wife about the hatred that my mother had once had for me and about all my mother's faults, I went to tell my troubles to my aunt, who said that none of this surprised her. She told me that my mother was still the same, but that I should endure her caprices and rent elsewhere if I and my wife wanted to stay. So I went with my aunt to see the house that my mother had indicated. I negotiated terms and returned that very evening to see my wife and tell her that I had rented a place to work, since my mother had changed her mind.

Maria told me that she was just as happy things had worked out that way, for though she had not dared to make her thoughts known, for fear of annoying me and my mother, in her heart she foresaw that we would not have gotten along with my mother and sisters, especially those from my mother's first marriage.

At last the date of my departure arrived and my wife and I moved our household to Châteauneuf. I set up my shop and worked in peace, without having the authorities ask me any questions. Soon after this, a law was passed granting full and complete amnesty to deserters from all branches of the military who could prove that they had been absent from their units for more than three months. I immediately went to see the local mayor to make my declaration as a deserter. He was astonished and told me frankly that he had no idea I was in violation of the law. At the same time, he told me that he could not accept my declaration as a deserter because I had been in his commune less than three months, and he did not know whether, when I arrived in Châteauneuf, I was coming directly from the army or from elsewhere. He said I had to go before the mayor of the commune where I had previously been employed and make my declaration to him. I immediately acted on the advice of the mayor of Châteauneuf and went to present myself before the mayor of Sandillon, who sent me off at once with instructions to take the document that he prepared to the army headquarters in Orléans to obtain my discharge. I received it that very day. I felt reborn when I heard the general say those words, though he said them only after he had urged me to reenlist, promising that I could have my rank and seniority back. When I gave him my definite answer—explaining that I was married and would therefore remain a civilian—and he saw that I was determined, the general told me: "My friend, you're free now; do your duty as an honest man and no one has any right to bother you." The general told me to have my papers signed at the police station in the place where I was living. After thanking him, I left to return that very evening to my wife, to whom I announced the happy news of my discharge.

The next day I went to the police station to present my papers and make everything legal. The sergeant, who already knew who I was, told a gendarme who was there and who knew me personally, being a local, "Before the amnesty law was passed, you reported that there were no deserters in the commune. Now they are coming in droves every day to take advantage of the law that allows them to get their discharge."

The gendarme did not know what to say and remained dumbfounded. Then he responded that he never suspected that deserters would thumb their noses at the military in that way. "I was well aware," he said, "that Bédé had been a soldier, since he was a member of my son's regiment. But when I saw him arrive here with his wife and household belongings, how could I think he was a deserter? I admit that I was wrong not to check and to take it on faith that he had been discharged, but I have every reason to be astonished at the declaration he is now making."

The sergeant signed my papers, and I returned home perfectly satisfied.

Births and Deaths

Soon after my discharge, my wife gave birth to a son who was the crowning grace of our family, but heaven took him from us thirteen months after his birth. Joy at my amnesty soon gave way to other sorrows. My mother fell dangerously ill and expressed the desire to see those of her children who were living in Orléans. I wrote immediately to tell them of their mother's illness and her request. Upon receiving my letter, they hastened to satisfy their mother's deathbed wish. When they came, all eight children were assembled at one time, something that had not happened since my father's death. Our unfortunate mother appeared to be waiting for this gathering of all her children to say her last farewell. The evening of their arrival, my sisters wanted to spend the night at my mother's side, for she was in a very bad state. I invited them to go rest, saying that I would stay with my mother all night long. My brother, who was also living nearby, made the same suggestion to my sisters and offered to join me in my nighttime vigil.

Everyone went to bed except my brother and I, who stayed to watch over my mother. Around midnight, I realized that my mother was getting worse. She was gripped by a faintness that brought her to a desperate state, in which she remained speechless and unconscious. Seeing her alarming condition, I woke my sisters and their husbands, informing them of my mother's lamentable state. They soon were up and came to join us. My mother revived from her collapse and asked for her children. I told her, "We are all gathered near you, mother. What do you want?"

"My son," she told me with complete composure, "your uncle and I have long been trying to straighten out accounts without arriving at any agreement. You'll find in the account book a separate sheet on which I have written everything I've received from him and everything I've paid him back. This is the unpleasant truth that I'm confessing to you before I die."

"Mother," I told her, "don't worry about such things just now; when you're better, we can settle accounts between you and my uncle."

My mother answered me abruptly, "It's you, my son, who will settle them with your uncle, for I sense that I won't see the daylight and I bid you all, my dear children, a last farewell."

At that very instant, she lost consciousness for the last time. She breathed her last in the presence of all her children and was perfectly alert until the final moment. Never has a death made such an impression upon me as that of my mother. I was not prepared for how hard it hit me. Long accustomed to seeing thousands of bodies on the battlefield, I thought my heart was hardened against these emotional and shocking scenes. But because this was my own mother, my sensitivity was awakened. I was taken aback, my heart swelled and I was unable to say a word. My sisters rushed to my aid, and I was soon revived. Once brought back to my senses, I shed a flood of tears, which was a great relief. Once I was myself again, I saw to it that my mother was paid the last honors.

After the funeral, we took care of the customary family business. Because two of the children were minors, I was named their guardian. Because we were the children of two separate marriages, the result in our family, as in so many others, was a split among all the brothers and sisters. After the catastrophe of my mother's death, I experienced another great sorrow: my son fell dangerously ill and died at the age of thirteen months. His loss was a blow to us, and my wife could not be consoled. But as if to make up for this loss, heaven gave us a little girl, born on 10 May 1804, whom we named Caroline Julie.

On 17 March 1806, my wife gave birth to a son whom we named Charles Napoléon. On 24 August 1807, my wife delivered a girl whom we named Sophie Euphrosine. The last of our four surviving children was a girl, born in the city of Tours on 24 June 1810, whom we named Antoinette. [. . .]

AT WORK IN TOURS AND PARIS (1809–1818)

During the time we resided in Châteauneuf, we were hard-pressed to live on what our labor brought in, for there was little money in circulation in the area since the castle had been abandoned. The hope that it would be reinhabited had caused me, like many other workers, to wait patiently. But when we suddenly saw the new owner hire workmen to demolish it, I lost all hope, and decided once again to leave my native region and perhaps bid it farewell forever.

My intention was still to go to Paris, but, upon reflecting that in all my time in Châteauneuf, I had only done work requiring little technique, I thought it appropriate to go work in a big city for a time in order to regain my skills. So I set off on the road to Nantes.

As I was passing through Tours, I stopped to inquire about the state of the local economy. I asked in an inn commonly known as the Compagnons' Mother.[6] There I met compagnon joiners, members of a joint association with compagnon turners. These workers asked if I wanted a job in their city. I answered that if there was employment, I would stay on for a time. The compagnon joiners immediately sent word to a turner they knew, telling him that a worker had arrived looking for a job in their city. The turner soon arrived with the master in whose workshop he was employed. The master asked me if I wanted work, and I told him yes. He said he had room for me and proposed that I work in his shop. We agreed to terms, and I remained in Tours.

When I saw that work was plentiful and that I could provide for my family's needs, I advised the master who had hired me that I intended to send for my wife. When he learned she was a worker, he urged me to have her come and said that he would hire her. When I heard this, I immediately wrote my wife to tell her of my plan. She replied that I could come get her whenever I thought best and that she was ready to follow me wherever necessary. I took advantage of the marriage celebration of two young women from my place of work to make the trip to Orléans and bring back my wife and children. We took a boat down the Loire as far as Tours, where we set up our household on a temporary basis, for my intention was still to settle in Paris.

6. The name in French was *La Mère des compagnons*. The inn to which Bédé refers was the local headquarters of a workers' brotherhood or compagnonnage. The fact that this particular brotherhood admitted both turners and joiners (skilled woodworkers) identifies it as the *Devoir de liberté*, the same organization to which Agricol Perdiguier belonged. For a more complete description of this working-class institution, see the excerpts from his *Memoirs of a Compagnon* in chapter 3. Bédé's contact with this association of turners appears to have been strictly as a nonmember, since he does not indicate having previously been admitted to any workers' brotherhood and would in any event have been expected to resign at the time of his marriage.

We stayed three years in Tours. The third year was marked by a commercial collapse caused by a terrible drought, which frightened the entire working class.[7] The price of bread rose to an exorbitant level. The master for whom we were working, seeing his shelves filled with goods there was no prospect of being able to sell for some time, proposed that I produce only half what I usually turned out, and my wife the same. I realized that this proposal was fair on his part, that he respected me and was trying not to leave me entirely without work. Still, I could not agree to his proposal, as it was impossible to support my family with half our usual income. It was therefore utterly impossible to remain under those circumstances.

I still had enough money to make the journey to Paris. I informed my wife, who wavered a bit before deciding to undertake so long a voyage to go to live in a city she held in awe because of its size and the high cost of all the necessities of life. I told my wife that she should not make the capital into a monster, that people lived in Paris the same way they lived everywhere else: by working. In any event, necessity forced us to leave. The cost of living was rising day by day, and it was impossible to find work. According to the news I heard from my friends in Paris, there was a fair amount of work available there. From this I concluded that I could go there in complete confidence. So I prepared to leave on my own to secure work and see how the employment situation was in the capital, as well as to find a place for my family to live.

Upon arriving in that great city, I immediately found a job and soon I was able to send for my wife and children. So there I was, living in that superb city that I had long promised to make my place of residence.

I worked in the Marais district on the Rue Neuve-Sainte-Catherine, and my home was at 123 Rue Saint-Antoine.[8] I set about providing for my children the education appropriate to our circumstances. Although burdened with four children, my wife and I managed, by dint of hard work and thrift, to give them each a trade that assured them, as well as us, a

7. A commercial and industrial crisis, precipitated by the British naval blockade of France, had reached serious proportions by 1810. Napoléon's Continental System was only partially successful in promoting self-sufficiency among the nations of continental Europe, and the French economy suffered from the lack of access to foreign raw materials and markets. Rémi Gossez, in his notes to the 1984 edition, indicates that the situation was exacerbated in 1811–12 by the effects of a regional drought.
8. The Marais district, located on the right bank of the Seine, to the north and east of Notre Dame and the Ile de la Cité, is among the oldest sections of Paris. It has traditionally housed a large working-class population, particularly in the neighborhoods along the Rue Saint-Antoine.

livelihood. It is terribly difficult for workers, who have no resources except their labor, to raise a large family. But I thank heavens, for if I have suffered to raise my children, I have been more than rewarded by their upright conduct and worthy lives.

Customs in the Trade and Masters' Abuses

Because I lived in a quiet quarter of Paris, the only workers I saw were a few friends I knew from Orléans. They helped acquaint me with the style of work being manufactured in Paris. Through them I soon got to know some of the workers from the Rue de Cléry.[9] I soon learned from them about the various abuses that workers were obliged to suffer, notably with regard to buying the tools necessary to get a job.

For some time, the master chair turners of the city of Paris had been gradually doing away with the custom, as ancient as the trade itself, of furnishing tools to the workers employed in their shops. They even went so far as to do away with the lighting they formerly supplied to their employees for working during the winter.

Although the workers found that they were disadvantaged and burdened by the discontinuation of various practices, they nonetheless put up with these changes, maintaining their moderation and not making any outcry. But further problems arose to compound the workers' burden. It is really the techniques involved—both the number of different styles and the high degree of perfection frequently required—that increase the time it takes the worker to make a product. Yet, even though the work was becoming more complicated, the masters never showed the slightest intention of providing a raise proportional to the additional effort, so that the worker could make an honest living and support his family by the fruit of his labor.

Such generous sentiments have never been expressed by the master turners of the Rue de Cléry. I name that street in particular because the workshops located there have long been the compass point toward which all chair turners of the capital are oriented, for it is in that street that a great quantity of chairs are manufactured by the best craftsmen of Paris.

At the end of 1813 and the beginning of 1814, a series of unfortunate

9. The Rue de Cléry figures prominently in Bédé's narrative as a center of the chair-turning trade, where many of the elite workers of the capital were concentrated. It is located in what today is the second ward of Paris, but at the time of which Bédé is speaking it lay on the northern outskirts of the city proper, just beyond its administrative limits. He therefore contrasts it with the workshops of the "interior," by which he means primarily the Marais district, another focal point of wood-turning activity.

events brought work to a halt and reduced a prodigious number of workers to the direst straits, depriving them of any means of providing for their families. But during the year 1814, business expanded in an extraordinarily satisfactory way and soon raised the price of chairs by twenty to twenty-four francs per dozen above what they usually cost.[10] The masters, however, said nothing about raising workers' wages to compensate them for the discontinuation of certain practices or for the hard times they had just experienced. The chair turners, still calm and peaceful, waited in hopeful anticipation. They met with and consulted one another concerning the measures to adopt as a way of easing their situation without, however, compromising the interests of the masters. [. . .]

The Workers' Moderate Conduct

[. . .] It was proposed that the workers ask for an increase of three francs for every dozen chairs crafted by the worker. This proposal was adopted by an absolute majority, who informed the masters of the Rue de Cléry of their decision. The masters replied that they would not submit to any increase on the part of their journeymen, and that they would sooner turn all the workers out of their shops than accept these demands. That was the decision taken by the first assembly of the masters of the Rue de Cléry. In every shop, the journeymen received the order to finish what they were working on and then find work elsewhere if they were not willing to continue working at the existing rate.

The workers made no outcry and quietly left the Rue de Cléry, finding jobs in all the workshops of the center of Paris and of the suburbs, for the masters in those areas were not so foolish as to refuse the chance to sign on the best workers of the capital. They hired them all and took full advantage of the favorable market that then existed. Meanwhile, the masters of the Rue de Cléry found their shops stripped of both workers and goods. [. . .]

The masters of the Rue de Cléry were seized with jealousy at the sight of their colleagues from the central districts producing unusually large quantities of chairs and selling them at such favorable prices, since these chairs were crafted by the workers who had previously been employed in their own shops. They also saw that the masters of the central districts were putting together workshops very much like those of the Rue de Cléry which might attract the same renown. They began to open their eyes and ponder. They were puzzled at seeing the masters of the central districts and suburbs employing so many of the best workers of the capital, and this

10. The basic denomination of French currency was the *franc*, equal to one hundred *centimes* or cents. A *sou* was a copper coin worth five centimes.

made them give the matter serious thought. What crowned their sense of uneasiness was the fact that one of the masters of the central districts, whose shop was in the Rue Saint-Louis in the Marais, was employing nearly fifty workers all by himself just to fill a long-term government contract for several thousand chairs and armchairs. His workers reaped much greater benefits from their day's work than they had previously earned in the workshops of the Rue de Cléry. Seeing all this, the masters of the Rue de Cléry decided to recall the workers to their shops and pay them the price that they had demanded.

Here the workers gave careful thought to the masters' request and to this large contract for chairs and armchairs, which, they assumed, could not last much longer and would probably slacken off. So they decided that a number of workers would return to the workshops in the Rue de Cléry and that some would stay in the workshops of the central districts so as not to forsake them. A certain number, in fact, stayed in the workshop in the Rue Saint-Louis which, ever since, has been the strongest workshop in Paris for the manufacture of chairs.

I Join the Ranks of Elite Workers[11]

[. . .] Certain small difficulties that I experienced with one of the workers employed in the workshop in the Rue de la Verrerie led me to decide, though with some regret, to look for work in the Rue de Cléry. This had been my intention ever since I had come to Paris, but since the opportunity had never arisen, I had long remained in the Rue de la Verrerie, where I was quite happy. But the desire to work alongside the best craftsmen of the capital and to make friends with them led me to leave the Rue de la Verrerie. The opportunity presented itself when I took part in the ceremony of escort held on behalf of a worker who was leaving the Rue de la Verrerie to go work at the Golden Chair workshop in the Rue de Cléry.[12] I found myself next to his new master, and we struck up a conversation. He asked where I was employed. I told him and added that I would be happy to

11. Bédé employs the term *sublime* to designate the restricted group of elite workers, distinguished even among Parisian artisans by their high levels of skill. The term was revived and repopularized with ironic overtones in the 1870 tract *Le Sublime* by Denis Poulot.

12. When a journeyman was about to leave town to continue his Tour of France or, as here, to move from one place of employment to another, his fellow workers would participate in the ritual or ceremony of escort (*la conduite*). Its purpose was to convey the respect and friendship of fellow workers to an individual about to embark on the next stage of his professional development. Escorting was one of the principal rites observed by the brotherhoods of workers that remained active in the first half of the nineteenth century. For a more detailed description of this practice, see the account by Perdiguier in chapter 3.

work in the Rue de Cléry. He proposed on the spot that I join his workshop. Pleased with this offer, I agreed to do so, and the arrangement was concluded then and there. I was the third person to join his shop at the rate demanded by the workers.

The Golden Chair was one of the best workshops in the Rue de Cléry, and jobs there were advantageous in every respect. Perfection in workmanship was required there in the highest degree. The master was a man whom you could reason with, for he possessed intelligence, experience, and common sense. Yet he had been just as unreasonable as all his fellow masters and, in the recent dispute, had imitated them by turning out all his workers, even though he ran one of the strongest shops of chair turners in the Rue de Cléry. This proves that a person's interests are not always well served when pride takes hold and is allowed to triumph over reason. I use the term "pride," since that is what was in the minds of the masters who refused the workers' request, thinking that any agreement represented a surrender on their part, just because the initiative had come from workers. This seemed to me rather senseless, since a proposal must necessarily originate with one party or the other. Why take offense when you are presented with a request? The customary practice is to respond, not to treat it with contempt, as long as one's honor is not under attack. The party that assumed the initiative did not think that it was humiliating itself any more than it thought it was humiliating the group to which the request was addressed. It can therefore only be presumptuousness that gives rise to such reasoning. [. . .]

Salary Reductions and Occupational Risks

After some time, business began to fall off, and the storerooms were soon filled with previously manufactured goods. The workers had in any event been anticipating the masters' next move. They soon announced and made us increasingly aware of the fact that they were no longer selling their merchandise at the same price as before and could no longer offer the same rates of pay. The masters began by immediately taking back the three francs per dozen chairs that they had granted us so reluctantly, leaving us to hope, nonetheless, that as soon as business improved somewhat, they would restore our rates.

The workers endured this first reduction calmly. Still guided by reason and by a fair and moderate sense of their interests, they managed to bend to these new circumstances with prudence and wisdom. They never did anything to justify being reproached for self-interest or insubordination. It was their judicious and peaceful conduct that subsequently made them victims of the many evils and reverses that the majority of masters visited upon them. It was the masters of the Rue de Cléry, whose conduct proved them to be insensitive to every humane sentiment, who enticed a large share of the other masters of the capital into their conspiracy.

Business remained flat for quite some time, and sales did not improve at all. The modest rate of sales barely sufficed to clear the stores of what was being produced in the workshops, without, however, resulting in any further reduction in the sales price.

The workers labored away, calmly and peacefully. The masters of the Rue de Cléry, counting on the prudent conduct of the chair turners, made yet another attempt to put their good nature to the test. They reduced by three francs the price paid to workers for the manufacture of a dozen chairs. Yet the circumstances required no such reduction, since chairs were still selling at the same price. The masters' policy left us to hope that this was only a temporary measure and that they would manage to compensate us once business expanded on more favorable terms and brought back happier times for all concerned.

The chair turners, still patient and still well behaved, endured this second reduction without any outburst and without raising any clamor against the masters. They were mindful, to be sure, that this way of acting on the part of the masters was unfair, but they felt they had to bend with the circumstances. The workers consoled themselves by saying that it was necessary to accept what one could not prevent, which has always been the motto of the weak against the strong.

These were the main events affecting journeyman turners in 1814 and 1815. Business continued at a slackened pace and goods continued to sell at about the same price, with everything remaining perfectly peaceful on both sides. Still, the worker barely managed to live from the fruit of his labor, and neither the times nor business conditions gave him an opening with the masters to try to improve his lot. Whenever workers happened to assemble, the conversation would turn to this subject. Several times they talked about protesting to the masters, but these plans vanished as soon as the workers dispersed. Once they returned to their workshops, they gave no further thought to protests and quietly resumed their work as usual.

In this way three years passed without any change in business conditions that might have held out to workers some hope of a happier future. Storerooms remained packed with previously manufactured goods; those in the Golden Chair, where I was employed, were also quite full of goods, and far less was sold than was being produced. The master who owned the shop, seeing that business was not getting any better and that his storerooms were choked with merchandise, decided to let go several workers from his shop. I was among them.

So I set my sights on the workshop called the Two Columns, which had just opened in the Rue de Cléry and which promised to become one of the strongest workshops in that street. As soon as I had been laid off, I went straight to see the master and asked to join the workers employed in his shop. My request was granted, and as soon as my work was completed at the Golden Chair I moved over. My new shop brought together a fine group of workers, who vied with one another in terms of craftsmanship, upright conduct, honor, and self-reliance.

These honest workers were outspoken and fair-minded. They were as unhappy as I about the fate that had overwhelmed us. I got to be particularly close friends with two of the workers who had been in the shop the longest and whose conduct and character were beyond reproach. They told me what they thought of the wretched situation of chair turners who were daily exposed to the risk of serious illness due to the cold and heat they experienced as they traipsed from one end of the capital to the other, loaded down with goods manufactured in the workshop that they had to deliver wherever the customer lived. Another and no less dangerous source of annoyance was the workers' exposure to terrible injuries, including broken arms and legs, as they dragged in the enormous hunks of wood, often consisting of entire tree trunks and enormous beams. To do all this, turners were required to leave what they were working on and transport goods to whatever quarter the purchaser lived in, or to store in the cellar the wood for making chairs. If an accident occurred, the worker received no other compensation from the masters than the advice to seek admission to the hospital, since the masters require all these forms of forced labor without offering the slightest remuneration.

The Founding of the Mutual Aid Society

Realizing the dangers to which we were exposed, the three of us talked over the measures we could take to lighten the burden that we and our fellow workers faced. After much discussion and reflection on the subject, we decided to propose the formation of a mutual aid society, open to all the wood turners and long-sawyers of Paris, in order to provide each other support in case of sickness or injury.[13] My friends promised to support me with all the powers they possessed if I would promise in turn to make a

---

13. A long-sawyer, pit sawyer, or ripsawyer (*refendeur*) prepared the wood for the chair turners. Using a saw specially made to cut with the grain, he would "rip" a large piece of unfinished timber to the right proportions. It could then be cut to length and given a roughly cylindrical shape on the lathe. On mutual aid societies, see the introduction, pages 13–14. Michael Sonenscher, in a review of *Un Ouvrier en 1820, Manuscrit inédit de Jacques Etienne Bédé*, ed. Rémi Gossez, *History Workshop Journal* 21 (Summer 1986): 173–79, has noted that there were over one hundred mutual aid societies in Paris in 1820 and that there was "nothing remarkable about the one established by the turners" (177).

serious attempt at running such a useful institution. I made this promise, which they received in a spirit of warm friendship, declaring that they trusted to my diligent efforts for the success of this noble enterprise. Once the three of us had arrived at this decision, we agreed immediately to inform the most sensible and thoughtful of our fellow workers so as to form the kernel of the Society on a solid and lasting foundation. To this end, we announced our proposal to those of our friends who were most devoted to assisting their brothers in case of need and most favorably disposed by their spirit of goodwill to helping found an association of such utility for the working class, which is always vulnerable to a thousand different dangers. Having at last informed our friends of our intentions and received their commitment, I set the date when we would gather and make final decisions in the matter.

It was on Sunday, 18 October 1818, at seven o'clock in the morning, that this first meeting took place in the Golden Sun, located at 1 Rue du Faubourg Poissonnière. The nine persons who assembled were subsequently granted the honorary title of Charter Members of the Society. The three of us—Bédé, Jonel, and Jaffier—were recognized as the Founders of the Society for having had the idea in the first place. We were judged worthy of continuing the project that we had begun. [. . .]

BOOK II: CONFLICT IN THE TRADE

THE ESTABLISHMENT OF A SOCIAL ORDER AMONG ALL TURNERS AND LONG-SAWYERS

Changing Practices

[. . .] Journeyman chair turners had long been accustomed to delivering the chairs manufactured in their workshops wherever the buyer lived and to carrying into the storerooms the wood used for the manufacture of those chairs. I should point out that these practices were established at a time when most workers were paid by the day and very few worked for piece rates.[14] But the old masters had also established the practice of asking the

---

14. Bédé uses the phrase *à la tâche* ("by the task") to refer to the system of payment per unit of output as opposed to a flat daily or hourly rate. Elsewhere he refers to workers employed *aux pièces*, a now obsolete phrase that closely approximates the English-language concepts of "piecework" and "piece rates." In such passages, Bédé implies that payment by the day was a custom of the past that had all but disappeared from the workshops of the capital. In a note to the 1984 edition (p. 156 n. 4), Gossez contends that, contrary to Bédé's assertions, day wages persisted in Parisian wood turning. To further complicate matters, Sonenscher indicates that payment by the day had not, as Bédé claims, generally been the rule in the distant past. He notes that in 1749, "chairmakers (joiners, rather than turners) on and

buyers to pay an extra charge as compensation for this kind of supplemental service. They were also careful not to trouble their workers unless there was a certain quantity of chairs to be delivered. When there were just a few, it was the master and his apprentice who took them. The journeyman working for a piece rate was rarely disturbed.

The practice of working for piece rates was only established subsequently. Though workers continued to deliver chairs and store wood, they received some compensation for their trouble and thus the custom persisted.

Storing wood was no great inconvenience in those days, since the master turners of that period used only finished wood for the construction of chairs, and it could quickly be tossed into the cellar through a basement window. In such cases, the master offered the courtesy of feeding both piece-rate workers and those paid by the day at his table. This is why the workers continued to perform these unpaid tasks.[15] But as the younger masters subsequently began to abuse these arrangements, the result was serious difficulties between masters and workers.

First, the new masters of the Rue de Cléry eliminated the practice of providing meals to workers on days when they helped store wood. They did this even though the turners' job became more demanding and more unpleasant as the use of finished wood was eliminated on the ground that it was not suitable for the manufacture of the new styles of products. These required the use of rough timber that had to be cut into lengths by pit sawyers and reduced to boards and planks. It was these boards and planks that we had to carry down to the storeroom. They represented an enormous weight that had to be taken, using sheer muscle power, down twisting staircases, exposing the workers to frightful dangers.

---

around the Rue de Cléry walked out to obtain a higher price for the chairs they made, demanding an extra 5 sous for cane chairs and 10 sous more for each framed chair (*fauteuil à chassis*). They too presented their claim as an appeal to justice: arguing that a change in the design of chairs meant that they were unable to produce as many in the accustomed time. As is obvious, they were not paid by the day" (Sonenscher, review of *Un Ouvrier en 1820*, 178). As Bédé uses the term, employment "by the task" appears to have been a subcategory of employment at piece rates, under the terms of which turners worked for an agreed-upon price per dozen chairs.

15. The French word here translated as "unpaid tasks" is *corvée*. The term originally referred to the serf's obligation to provide unpaid labor for his feudal lord. In contemporary French, the same term is used to refer to the forced labor of prison inmates. Since the time of the French Revolution, practices of this kind, associated with the hierarchical structure of the Old Regime, had repeatedly been the focus of popular protests. The original French term thus emphasizes the irksome and demeaning character of unremunerated labor that has been imposed even though it is not properly part of the job for which the workers were hired.

The workshops of the Rue de Cléry were the biggest in Paris. They used wood at a rate proportional to their size, with the result that it was not just an hour or two that the workers had to sacrifice to this task but entire days, and often a part of the night. The masters of the Rue de Cléry were so generous as to offer a glass of wine to each worker who had thus spent his time (and perhaps been maimed in the process). Their injuries were their only compensation if they happened to finish at night when all the wine shops were closed. In that case everyone just went home. The workers were exhausted from dragging in enormous timbers and beams, after which they had to join together, five or six workers at a time, and run the risk of lowering them down into the cellar. After all this strenuous, unpaid labor, workers were often obliged to rest up for two or three days at their own expense. We have seen some of our less fortunate fellow workers crippled while doing this sort of demanding labor. They might be forced to enter the hospital, leaving their poor families in dire need and without hope of help from the employers in whose shops such accidents occur. And if someone happened to express pity for these poor injured workers, we were forced to listen to the masters respond that they were just clumsy and always getting themselves hurt. That was the only consolation and compensation that we received from the new masters of the Rue de Cléry. My readers will note that I am always careful to specify "the new masters," because they are the ones who eliminated all those provisions that helped alleviate the workers' suffering and who proliferated all the abuses I will be talking about, whereas the old masters of the central districts have always maintained the practices that helped compensate the workers or ameliorate their fate.

The old masters of the Rue de Cléry were so weak as to let themselves be led along by their younger colleagues. Abandoning all concern for justice or humanity, they adopted new methods that were as unfair in the eyes of God as in the eyes of men. If I use such words, it is because they are justified. And I am going to inform the masters of the central districts about all the abuses that exist in the Rue de Cléry of which they are unaware. I am convinced that if they had only known about them, then certain events that were distressing for all concerned would never have happened.

It was the new masters who initiated and proliferated a whole set of abuses in the work conditions of piece-rate workers. These were the same men who, when they were still journeymen, refused to do anything for their masters that interfered with their ordinary work. Now everything is different. Now that they have changed classes, their characters—or at least their whims—have changed as well. Now they want to force their workers to do the same things they so violently and rightly refused to do when they themselves were piece-rate workers, for now it is their self-interest that is compromised. Where do they get such ideas? How can the simple act of opening up a store or setting up a workshop and employing other workers so change the character of a man that he forgets what he once was?[16] [. . .]

[Our] Honor Is at Stake: The Abolition of Unpaid Tasks

[. . .] The journeymen employed in the workshops of the Rue de Cléry were more than aware of all these abuses and difficulties. Because they saw both their interests and their health compromised to such an extent, they met to discuss what measures to take to eliminate all these abuses, if possible, in a prudent and fair way. Whenever they happened to assemble, whether at mealtimes or in the places they went to relax, the conversation always turned to those miserable unpaid tasks. Even in the workshops, they would discuss the subject with the masters. And the masters agreed with us and advised us to arrive at an understanding among ourselves in order to bring an end to these abuses. The master for whom I was then working told us several times in his workshop that he would himself prefer to have his chairs delivered and his wood brought in by errand boys or common laborers rather than always having unpleasant disputes with his workers. Thus, as far as conversations between masters and journeymen were concerned, we seemed to be in agreement, although what happened subsequently proved that this agreement was more apparent than real on the part of the masters.

The journeymen were clearly in agreement, but their understanding existed only as long as they were actually assembled. Once they returned to their workshops, they would soon be asked to deliver chairs and start discussing whose turn it was to go, forgetting all about the agreement they had previously made. Eventually, one of them would set off as usual, without saying a word. [. . .]

---

16. Bédé's complaint incidentally reveals that many of the master chair turners in 1820 had started out as workers and managed, through some combination of hard work and good fortune, to acquire shops of their own. This degree of social mobility, which Bédé himself refers to as a change of class, was still common enough in the artisanal economy of the capital in the early years of the nineteenth century to represent a realistic aspiration for many members of the working class. It would become less so with time. By the midcentury, though the aspiration remained, the objective probability of a worker achieving the status of master had significantly diminished. By the end of the century, when capital requirements as well as competitive pressures from mechanized, unskilled labor had increased, the worker of humble origins who realized his dream of setting himself up as an independent craftsman had become the great exception.

SAINT MICHAEL'S FEAST DAY

Here is how the explosion among chair turners came about: Once the Mutual Aid Society had been organized, a proposal was made before the general assembly of January 1820 that we adopt a feast day. I put the question up for discussion, and the result was a unanimous vote of those assembled that the Society recognize the observance of the Appearance of Saint Michael as its feast day by holding a celebration each year on 8 May. It was further agreed that the festivities would be open to all workers, whether members of the Society or not, who wanted to participate in the banquet that would immediately follow the service; and that women would be admitted. Once this had been decided, announcements were sent to all the journeyman turners of the capital. Upon receipt of these letters, many workers signed up to participate and some of the younger folk told us they wanted to hold a ball after the banquet. Their wish was realized and musicians were asked to put together an orchestra. We also wrote to all the master chair turners of the capital to invite them to attend the mass to be celebrated in the church of Notre Dame de Bonne Nouvelle. When the masters received this letter, several said they would attend, and it was the workers' pleasure to welcome them.

All the turners and long-sawyers of Paris as well as their ladies were looking forward to the eighth of May, when they would all gather and have such fun together, for our trade had never before held such a celebration in Paris. [. . .]

I had been careful to prepare the seating arrangements in advance, placing the guests near their friends, according to the information I had obtained from most members of the Society so that everyone could have a good time without disturbance or interruption. I took the precaution of informing the authorities so that we would be protected and in no way disturbed by troublemakers.

[On the evening of Saint Michael's feast day, the celebration took place. A midday mass was followed by a sumptuous banquet held in a garden restaurant in Les Prés Saint-Gervais, a suburb of the capital. This meal was punctuated by toasts and speeches and followed by the recitation of poems and songs composed by the guests especially for the occasion. The room was then rearranged for dancing, which lasted, with time out for an intermission and more songs, until six in the morning. This gathering was a great success, and Parisian turners continued to talk about it for several days afterward. A number of workers failed to return to their workshops the next day, and some extended the celebration for as much as three or four days.]

During those days of celebration, the workshops remained nearly deserted. One young master from the Rue de Cléry decided to bring in several loads of wood to be placed in his storeroom. We know that this young master had long been hatching a scheme that would sow dissension, so it is reasonable to conclude that he intentionally had his wood delivered on a day when the journeymen were not at work. The fact is that only two of the nine workers he employed were in the workshop when the wood arrived. It was lunchtime, and the two workers left to go eat. This was on 10 May, two days after the celebration, and the workers had not yet returned to work. It so happened that this was also a day when several workers were due to change shops, and their colleagues therefore conducted "apron checks," a customary ceremony in which a fellow worker is escorted to his new place of employment. This ritual took place once we had all settled into a wine merchant's shop to empty a few bottles. As it happened, several changes of workshops and an apron check took place on that same day, 10 May 1820. What was unusual was that they took place at the same wine merchant's shop in the Rue Poissonnière, opposite the Rue Beauregard. Since this was near the Rue de Cléry, everyone went off to find his fellow workers, as usually occurs.

That is how nearly one hundred chair turners and long-sawyers came to be gathered in an impromptu assembly of workers in a single trade, one that was perhaps as large as any that had ever been seen in Paris. The two journeymen who, as I mentioned above, had left for lunch were met by fellow workers who invited them to come have a glass of wine, informing them that a great many workers had gathered in the Rue Poissonnière. They went along, and soon the presence of so many of their colleagues as well as the divine juice of the grape made them forget that they had a disagreeable and unpaid task waiting for them at their workshop. The result was that all the employees of that workshop benefited, except for the master, who was forced to have his wood brought in by hired help, who were paid for their efforts, instead of by workers who would have run the risks without hope of consolation or assistance on the part of the master. The journeymen rested and enjoyed themselves, but there is no way of convincing them that, because they were not working, they had missed the chance to make some money, since ordinarily they received no compensation whatever for this kind of labor, which is more difficult and dangerous than any other in the trade. [. . .]

The masters acknowledged the injustice they were doing us and the harm it represented to our interests, but they had no intention of improving our situation by ending these abuses. The workers, weary of making useless protests, resolved to refuse to carry out these unpaid tasks, since despite their longstanding complaints they had no hope of a satisfactory outcome and, on the contrary, abuses had been on the increase as new masters set up shops in the Rue de Cléry. At last, rebuffed in their attempts at negotiation and even more tired of enduring this kind of burden, the explosion occurred on 10 May 1820 in the shop of the wine merchant in the Rue Poissonnière where so many chair turners had assembled. They did not fail to discuss those wretched unpaid tasks that weighed so heavily upon the workers, and they ended up by declaring, "Today is the day to decide how we must tell the master chair turners of the Rue de Cléry that we are fed up with these unpaid tasks. Now that we are assembled in such numbers is the time to agree on the steps to be taken in the present circumstances." There was general discussion of this issue, and all the workers agreed to demand the elimination of these tasks. It was assumed that as soon as the master chair turners of the Rue de Cléry learned of this decision, they would meet to confer. It was therefore decided to name one or more workers to appear before their assembly, if, that is, they decided to hear us out. The individuals named were therefore to be empowered to negotiate with the masters in the name of the workers of the capital.

THE DELEGATE OF THE MUTUAL AID SOCIETY IS SENT ON A MISSION TO THE MASTERS[17]

I was not present at this great assembly and was not even aware of it, as I had not at all foreseen so large a gathering. Yet in my absence, all the votes were cast for me, and it was decided that if the masters asked to enter into discussions with the workers, I would be the one to appear before their

17. The delegate in question is, of course, the author himself. In book II of his memoir, Bédé occasionally refers to himself in the third person, as a way of maintaining a separation between his roles as author and as a prominent actor in the events he is recounting. Note that in referring to himself as "delegate," Bédé introduces a potential confusion. On the one hand, he had been named "delegate for life" by the mutual aid society he had helped to found. On the other hand, he now describes how he came to be "delegated" by an informal assembly of workers to speak before the masters on the subject of the unpaid tasks. The conflict with the masters would soon lead to the threat of a walkout by workers and an actual lockout by employers. Bédé is careful to deny that the mutual aid society played any organizational role in the turners' action; however, Bédé might well have been tempted to conceal such a connection, since any such involvement was strictly prohibited by law. Bédé himself says later on that he was not at that time employed in the Rue de Cléry and that his own workshop was therefore not directly affected by the objectionable practices. If we are to accept his version of events, then it must simply have been the visibility he had achieved by promoting the interests of the mutual aid society among Parisian chair turners that led to his being selected to handle negotiations with the masters. The point was potentially significant in the legal actions that followed.

assembly. The workers entrusted me with responsibility for taking these matters in hand. Several asked that I be sent for immediately and informed of their decision so I could undertake whatever measures the circumstances demanded. Some of my fellow workers pointed out that it was quite possible that I would not be able to come, since I was foreman in the shop in the Rue Saint-Louis in the Marais. They said it was pointless to disturb me and would be far better to name a delegation of workers to inform me of their decision and charge me with my mission. When this proposal was accepted, a few workers volunteered to be part of a deputation and undertook to let me know immediately what had just taken place in the Rue Poissonnière. The workers then dispersed in all directions in perfect calm, without any fuss or outburst, relying entirely on the deputation and on me to carry out this important enterprise. [. . .]

AN AFFAIR THAT CONCERNED THE ENTIRE TRADE

[. . .] When he learned of the workers' decision, Mr. Deck senior, in whose shop I was then employed, came at once to find me on the shop floor. I could see from what he told me that he had been misinformed and that the facts had already been distorted. These are the precise words that he said to me: "Mr. Bédé, how many workers are there in your Society?" (At first I thought that he was asking me the total number of members in the Mutual Aid Society. I had no idea he was speaking of matters that had nothing to do with the Society.)

In complete innocence, I replied, "There are about forty of us." He said that was not what he wanted to know but rather how many members were employed in his workshop. I told him there were three of us. He asked which three. I named them for him, myself included. "Well," he told me, "if you carry chairs, you'll be subject to a fine."[18] I told him that I did not

18. Deck's statement, based on what he had been told by other masters, is an accusation of conspiracy (*coalition*), as defined in Article 415 of the Penal Code of 1810, the statute under which the workers were later to be tried. Conspiracy consisted of the act of association plus the imposition of fines to compel members' compliance. The intention of such laws was to remove barriers to the individual's freedom to practice the occupation of his choice. Their practical effect was to do away with most forms of association among workers—mutual aid societies and compagnonnages being the principal exceptions which enjoyed a certain tolerance on the part of the authorities—and seriously to weaken the bargaining position of those whose only economic leverage was concerted action. For a discussion of the labor legislation that issued from the Revolution, see William H. Sewell, Jr., *Work and Revolution in France: The Language of Labor from the Old Regime to 1848* (Cambridge, 1980) and "Artisans, Factory Workers, and the Formation of the French Working Class, 1789–1848," in Ira Katznelson and Aristide R. Zolberg, eds., *Working-Class Formation: Nineteenth-Century Patterns in Western Europe and the United States* (Princeton, 1986).

know what he meant, that the Society was not concerned with such matters, and that what he was talking about had nothing to do with mutual aid. I pointed out that if it were so, I would surely have known about it. "But," he told me, "the other masters assured me that it was true." I replied that these other masters were mistaken, that there was absolutely no question of the Mutual Aid Society levying a fine for such things, which fell completely outside its jurisdiction, and that consequently it could not be involved. "I want to believe you," he told me, "but I also think that there's something of the kind going on, for where there's smoke, there's fire."

I told him, "Yes, sir, there is an uproar among workers from the Rue de Cléry that is connected to what you are talking about. But it's not the Mutual Aid Society; it's workers in general who are protesting against the abuses that the masters are subjecting them to." [. . .]

Mr. Deck senior asked me these questions on 12 May 1820, two days after the gathering in the Rue Poissonnière. That very day, someone came to tell me that Mr. Deslandes, a young master turner from the Rue de Cléry, had got in an argument with his workers and that they were all walking out of his shop.

The details of the precipitating incident are as follows: Young Mr. Deslandes's workers were not present in his shop on the tenth, the day the great assembly in the Rue Poissonnière had taken place, and also the day that Deslandes had arranged for wood to be delivered to his storerooms. That is why he was forced to have his wood brought in by helpers whom he had to pay. He found this rather hard to take, since he was not used to it, but hired hands are no more accustomed than other workers, even common laborers, to working for nothing. It is only the chair turners of the Rue de Cléry who are so good as to do that.

Dismissals for Refusing to Do Unpaid Tasks

Young Mr. Deslandes was so furious at having to pay to have his wood placed in his storerooms that as soon as his workers arrived at the shop— which only happened on the twelfth, as shops were closed on the eleventh for the feast of the Ascension—he began by addressing his foreman, blaming him because the workers had not been present to bring in his wood. Deslandes claimed it was this foreman who had prevented them and that, once he had finished what he was working on, he would begin no new projects in that shop. This worker, who was innocent of everything the master accused him of, calmly answered that he was in no way responsible if the workers were not there to bring in the wood. He pointed out, moreover, that it was hardly surprising that such a thing should happen, since Deslandes never made a point of warning his workers that he was having wood delivered.

"And that," he told him, "is why you're firing me. If I have to leave your shop, I'll leave, since that is your wish. I'm well aware that for some time you've been looking for a pretext to fire me, but pretexts are unnecessary. When a master wants a worker to go, all he has to do is thank him for his services without looking for poor excuses. That's hardly a civil way of acting."

All the workers who witnessed this scene were outraged and told the master he was wrong to blame their colleague for having prevented them from being there to bring in his wood. They said that they had not discussed the matter among themselves and that if they had been absent it was because they were all out celebrating the new hirings.

"Since you insist on firing our friend unfairly," they told him, "we're quitting too. We'd rather all leave your shop than put up with this kind of injustice being imposed on a fellow worker."

When they had all declared that they shared this view, they were ordered to finish their current projects and then look for work elsewhere. This presented no great difficulty because young Mr. Deslandes's workers were among the finest, as much for the quality of their work as for their integrity and conduct. This news quickly spread to all the chair turners' workshops throughout the capital. It caused a great uproar among the workers to see someone fired for not being present to bring in his master's wood. [. . .]

Workers' Assembly of 15 May 1820

[At this meeting, the workers in attendance informed Bédé that they still wished to seek the elimination of unpaid tasks and that they were relying on him to negotiate with the masters.]

I explained that they had to expect that, as in 1814, the masters' first response would be to dismiss everyone employed in their workshops.

The workers replied that they anticipated this response and were prepared for it. They said that not only would they leave the workshops on the masters' orders but that all those in a position to do so were determined to leave the capital so as to leave jobs in the central districts of Paris for workers who could not travel because they had families to support. They declared that they were ready to make any sacrifice, rather than put up any longer with practices that compromised their interests and their health. [. . .]

Letter to the Masters

I then read the assembly a draft version of a letter to be sent to the masters as a way of declaring the workers' intentions. It was also agreed that we would verbally inform the masters that workers had been delegated to attend their assembly and negotiate, if that is what they wished. Because we were in no doubt that upon receiving the workers' letter, the masters would convene an assembly to discuss the matter, we agreed to write only to those masters whose workers were present at our meeting. [. . .]

The draft letter took the following form:

Paris, 15 May 1820

Dear Sir,

In former times, when turners were employed by the day, the customs of delivering chairs in town and bringing in wood were established by agreement among the masters. The workers were not opposed to it, because when they delivered chairs, a small bonus was added to their daily earnings and, on days when they carried in wood, the masters fed the workers, thus compensating them for all their trouble.

Now that we are paid a piece rate, Sir, we do not believe that we are obligated to do this. If we have maintained the custom since we have shifted to piece rates, it has been an act of goodwill on our part. But the abuses that most of the masters have made us suffer for some years by forcing us to deliver a single chair and then taking for themselves the paltry compensation that the customers intended for the delivery-man, along with the elimination of the meal on days when wood is carried in, force us to declare to you that as of 16 May 1820 we will cease to carry out these unpaid tasks.

We will show no less respect for you, Sir, nor any less energy in the fulfillment of our duties or the quality of our work.

Sincerely,
Your Workers

When this initial draft was read, all the workers responded that it was just what they wanted and that it should immediately be copied out and sent to the masters. Seeing that the first version was adopted, I did not even go into the others, for the rain was still coming down in buckets and being blown into the room through a casement window that was being cut into the roof but had not been finished, so that the table and all the papers on it were getting soaked.

So one worker from each shop was sent into the other room and began writing on behalf of all fellow workers employed in the same shop, just as it had been agreed. While this copying was taking place, I was busy with several of my peers working what out we owed the wine merchant in whose establishment the meeting had taken place. [. . .]

The masters received their letters the next day, 16 May. The first thing they did was to let their workers know and ask them if they really intended to stand by what they had stated in their letters. When they received an affirmative reply, they presumed that all their fellow masters had received the same letter. But how were they to be sure? The exchange of information among masters was quite poor, as they did not regularly associate among themselves. It was a difficult problem. [. . .]

Assemblies of the Master Turners

Young Deslandes, the individual with the most at stake because of the wrong he had done to his workers, placed himself in charge of the entire affair. He began by sending word by special messenger from the masters of the Rue de Cléry to every quarter of Paris, announcing the workers' declaration to all Parisian masters. He notified them that a general assembly of all master chair turners of the capital would take place the next day, 17 May, at the Harvest of Burgundy in the Faubourg du Temple. [. . .]

Many of the masters from the central districts did not want to join this cartel and responded to the masters of the Rue de Cléry that they were quite capable of coming to terms with their own workers.[19] They said, moreover, that their workers had not lodged any protest with them, so that there was nothing they needed to negotiate. [. . .]

Despite the absence of many of the masters from the central districts, the assembly nonetheless took place, and the question of recognizing the workers' delegates, hearing them out, and negotiating with them was never seriously considered. It was decided not to listen to the workers and instead to dismiss them all and impose a fine of one hundred francs on any master who kept a worker employed. The weaker masters were intimidated by the stronger ones, believing that they had to respect this decision in order to maintain themselves on an equal footing with their colleagues. They fell in with this arrangement without bothering to consider that they were completely forsaking their own interests just to please colleagues who sought only their destruction, as we shall see from what follows. [. . .]

So the workers were not called upon to speak or discuss the issue at the masters' assembly. The next morning, all workers employed in the shops in

---

19. Bédé's use of the word "cartel" implicitly reminds the reader that conspiracies on the part of masters were just as illegal as those among workers.

the Rue de Cléry received the order to finish eighteen chairs each and then leave the workshop as soon as they were done. Those who had been working on two or three dozen, as was commonly the case, were forced to leave behind all but eighteen and be paid on the basis of an expert's appraisal. The assembly had also forbidden masters from buying chairs from turners working out of their homes. [. . .]

Those masters commonly known as the bigwigs had encouraged vain illusions and made poorly kept promises just in order to cast a veil before their colleagues' eyes and obscure from their view, if possible, the immensity of their own storerooms. These were filled with a prodigious quantity of previously manufactured chairs that placed them in a position to get along without the workers for several months without having to suspend sales, while the other, smaller masters could rely only on goods produced from day to day. Since the latter did not have well-stocked storerooms on which to draw, they were entirely unable to dispense with workers without causing major defections among their clients. That is just what happened. The small chair manufacturers had to watch as their colleagues made brisk sales while they remained idle for lack of workers to produce their goods. [. . .]

In a conversation with workers, one of the masters of the Rue de Cléry went so far as to insult them by saying they could never hold out, since they lacked the resources. A few replied in kind, saying that if there were workers whose means would not permit them to hold fast, there might also be masters who would experience the same fate. "Well," replied the master, "those who can't hold out will come to work for the rest of us." Such was the frank and naive response of the bigwig turners of the Rue de Cléry. Such was their declaration of goodwill for their colleagues. This declaration held no surprise for me, for I knew their way of thinking and acting. I firmly believed that they would stick to this declaration more closely than to the oath they swore to support one another. [. . .]

I took it upon myself to write a note to the police commissioner to let him know the outcome of the workers' assembly and ask his opinion on what course of action we should follow under the circumstances, so as not to be in violation of the laws and ordinances of the higher authorities. [. . .]

I learned from certain masters that there was some talk of asking the administration of the Prefecture of Police to refuse to issue passports to chair turners so that they would not be able to leave Paris. In addition, the masters were going to write to all the major cities in France asking that all workers located there be sent to Paris. One of the masters was also supposed to write to his country of birth, the Netherlands, to have sixty chair turners sent to take our places in the workshops of the Rue de Cléry.

What ambitious projects, Gentlemen! Will they be carried out? I doubt it, and I find these plans a little vague and lacking in substance. If their purpose is to frighten us, I can assure you that you are wasting your time. Workers like those you so rashly banished from your workshops cannot be frightened by such threats. They have on their side their hard work, their skill, and their courage, together with good character and integrity. These qualities will always assure their livelihood and that of their families. [. . .]

THE REFUGE

In that moment of concern over workers' prospects of employment, I received word that a woman from Paris, who already ran a chair turners' workshop in the neighborhood of the Rue de Cléry, was prepared to take advantage of this opportunity to increase the number of workers in her shop. She was complying with the elimination of the unpaid tasks against which the workers were protesting. This news soon spread among the workers, and several who presented themselves at her shop were hired on those conditions.

This woman had a son who also ran a chair store in the Rue de Cléry and employed ten or twelve workers to manufacture his goods. His establishment was in its first year. His mother advised him not to get involved in the dispute and to keep his workers. But the son was full of pride and would not listen to his mother. He fired all his workers in order to make common cause with the other masters of the Rue de Cléry. Because I was friendly with him, I wanted to speak to him personally to let him know of my intentions. The opportunity came a few days later when I met him as he came to visit his mother. I explained to him the mistake he was making by firing his workers and allying with the masters of the Rue de Cléry, an alliance that could prove fatal to him. He could, on the other hand, ally with his mother and maintain production, for he owned a shop that could employ at least twenty workers and put them comfortably to work. I told him the moment was right, and he could put together a workshop from among the finest workers who were leaving the Rue de Cléry. These circumstances promised a highly advantageous expansion of business. He answered that he had given his word to his colleagues and that he would stand by it; that he was not concerned about being made a dupe, since all the masters had promised to support one another. I observed that these were vain hopes, for in this affair the masters only cared about their individual interests, and all the fine promises would vanish if misfortune willed that one of their number should succumb. I said that a casual statement made by one of the masters in the Rue de Cléry made me certain of what I was telling him. But all of my arguments were useless. He repeated that he had given his word and considered himself honor bound. We parted without settling anything, and I wished him a happier outcome than what I foresaw.

Let us now return to his mother, who could truly be said to be a courageous and enterprising woman. The previously mentioned workshop that she managed was located in the Rue Notre-Dame-de-Recouvrance. Mrs. Cornil hired all her son's workers and told them that if they had friends who were leaving the Rue de Cléry and found themselves without work, they could come to her shop. She said she would employ them until they were able to locate work in another shop or find something more to their liking, if indeed she was not able to keep them on herself. As workers finished up projects in the Rue de Cléry and had no new shop to go to, they came to Mrs. Cornil's. All were hired on the understanding that there would be no unpaid tasks and the pay would be the same as in the workshops of the Rue de Cléry, so that Mrs. Cornil's workshop soon had more turners than any other. Before all this happened, Mrs. Cornil had employed very few workers. One of them, remarking on how few they were in so vast a space, jokingly told his buddies that they resembled fugitives who had withdrawn to a place of sanctuary and compared Mrs. Cornil's workshop to the Refuge that existed at that time in Texas.[20] This spontaneously derived name was soon forgotten, but in the period when workers were being banished from the Rue de Cléry and taking refuge in that place, the name "the Refuge" was revived and adopted by the workers. This great workshop and this great multitude were led by a woman whose

20. The reference is to the *Champ d'asile* (the Field of Refuge), a small "republic" founded in 1817 by a group of veterans of Napoléon's armies. This community, located between the Del Norte and Trinity rivers in what would later become the state of Texas, was just one of a number of settlements attempted in the New World during the first half of the nineteenth century. Most were inspired by the teachings of visionary, utopian philosophers and were intended to demonstrate the viability of their economic or political theories. The Refuge, however, attracted staunch Bonapartists unable or unwilling to go on living in France after the restoration of the Bourbon monarchy in 1815. The colony faced many practical difficulties as well as direct conflict with the Spanish government, which claimed the territory on which the community had settled without permission. By the fall of 1818, the members of the community had been forced to abandon their settlement and retreat to New Orleans. On this and other French settlements in the New World, see Ronald Creagh, *Nos cousins d'Amérique: Histoire des français aux Etats-Unis* (Paris, 1988).

courage and energy are beyond imagination and, without speaking ill of anyone, there is perhaps not another master turner in the city of Paris who would have dared such an undertaking unless he had received an extraordinary and substantial order that provided a guarantee of success.

Bédé Is Banished from the Capital

[. . .] It was at an assembly held on 25 or 26 May 1820 that the masters engaged in deliberations concerning what they should do. It was decided that all master turners of the city of Paris would be notified that they should not hire Mr. Bédé on penalty of a fine of one hundred francs, and that Mr. Bédé would be banished from the capital for six months. The president of that assembly explained that once Mr. Bédé was out of the city, all the workers would abandon their cause and would return to the workshops in the Rue de Cléry. I replied to the master who gave me this report that the masters' deliberations surprised but did not frighten me and that they were vague and without force. What seemed amazing was that in a general assembly of most of the master turners of the capital, they would go to the extreme of promulgating an act of banishment. [. . .]

What I did not tell him was that for several days my place had already been reserved at the Refuge, that my friend Bicheux, who was foreman there, had already put the word out, and that I was expected from one day to the next in that great workshop.

[The masters soon began to work on Bédé's employer, Mr. Deck. One day, two of them arrived to speak with Deck in private. The workers heard only voices raised in argument. Soon, the three masters left the shop to continue their dispute elsewhere.]

That very evening—Monday, 27 May 1820—as Mr. Baillache, Mr. Fromont, and I were chatting in the courtyard, Mr. Deck arrived. He greeted us, talked for a moment, and then proposed that we go drink a bottle of wine together. We headed for the wine merchant's in the Rue Neuve-Saint-Gilles. Mr. Deck was in the center and Mr. Fromont walked alongside, holding his son by the hand. As we made our way along, Mr. Deck said to me:

"Mr. Bédé, do you know what's new?"

"No, sir," I replied, "I haven't heard anything today."

"Well," he told me, "I can tell you that the masters of the Rue de Cléry have notified me that if in two days you're still working in my shop, I'll be fined one hundred francs."

To this I answered, "Frankly, sir, if that worries you, you needn't jeopardize yourself on my behalf. I'm quite prepared to leave your shop."

Seeing that I replied without guile or fear, he took me by the hand and said, "Mr. Bédé, I'm more courageous than that. I give you two weeks to see to your needs, and in two weeks I'll ask if you have work. If you don't, I'll give you another week. I have too much respect for you, and far be it from me to fire you in this way. And if, contrary to my wishes, you leave my shop for this reason, I hope that when this business is straightened out, we can get back together. There," he said to me, "don't worry."

I thanked Mr. Deck for his honorable proposition without, however, trusting his word, for I was sure that it would soon be broken. I assured him that I was not angry with him for being swept along in the torrent created by his colleagues of the Rue de Cléry and that up to that point I had reason only to praise his establishment. I told him that nothing stood in the way of my returning there in the future, or at least I presumed not. When the bottle of wine was finished, we parted very peaceably. [. . .]

The news that Mr. Deck had let me go soon made the rounds of all the chair turners of the capital. On Monday morning, 5 June 1820, all my fellow workers who were part of Mrs. Cornil's great workshop, hereafter referred to as the Refuge, were waiting to welcome me. Though this name was coined by chance, it proved entirely appropriate at a time when the chair turners of the Rue de Cléry were being banished, for they found in this vast workshop their field of refuge. [. . .]

All the workers who had decided to leave for the provinces came to pay tribute to the Refuge before their departure, and most of them made one or two dozen chairs there before they left. It was as if this was a duty that they had to fulfill for their friends before leaving them, so that they could announce to all the workers they might encounter in cities all across France that they had worked in the Refuge in Paris with all these old friends, the most highly skilled workers of the capital.

The Refuge became more and more crowded by the day. There was perpetual commotion, as each day some workers left and new ones arrived. Soon the total reached fifty-seven. When they saw what an important workshop it had become, the masters of the Rue de Cléry became worried and did not know what to think. [. . .]

The main workshop of the Refuge, located at 8 Rue Notre-Dame-de-Recouvrance, consisted of a courtyard that had been covered with a glassed-in roof. In this part of the ground floor there were eight veneering vises, all of them well lit; a lathe on which two men could work continuously; and a workbench where two long-sawyers worked. The workshop used for assembling and polishing was on the second floor. The third floor was devoted to applying trim and finishing the chairs, and the fourth was used to spread out lumber so it could dry. All these spaces were very well lit and properly set up for working.

There was a tall and wide fireplace on the ground floor, and next to it stood a large basin containing a quantity of lime for staining wood, as well as a great copper pot filled with water and mahogany sawdust that was always on the fire. There was an old worker who had been crippled while performing the kind of unpaid tasks that we were asking to have eliminated and who in his misfortune had been rejected by the masters and left without a job. This poor man came to the Refuge and explained to us his distressing situation. He offered his services, if he could be useful. Touched by his misfortune, I assembled all the workers of the Refuge and informed them of our old friend's story. Knowing him to be incapable of making chairs due to his infirmity, I proposed that he be set to work staining and polishing wood when required. This proposition was accepted, and an appropriate price per dozen chairs was agreed upon. [. . .]

When the Refuge welcomed workers who came to take a job or for a visit, the pleasure of seeing them always produced a new outburst of joy. All the workers gathered on the ground floor. A couplet about the Refuge was sung by one of its authors, and all the workers joined in the refrain. If a worker had to leave the Refuge, the same ceremony took place, after which we would go to the wine merchant's in the Rue Poissonnière where the workers had held their assemblies. Because this place was enormous, comfortable, and quite near the Refuge, it had been adopted by the workers and dubbed the Soup Kitchen of the Refuge. The workers of the Refuge would always go to the canteen when they wanted a bit of refreshment or to celebrate arrivals or departures. Forty or fifty of them would sometimes assemble at once. One of the first to arrive would stand at the door to count the number present and order enough wine and glasses. The custom we established was never to drink more than one glass of wine or brandy and then to return to the Refuge, or continue the escort if a worker was taking his leave. This practice was maintained as long as the Refuge continued operating on this expanded scale, and there was never any trouble either at the canteen or in the Refuge itself. [. . .]

The Renown of the Refuge

[. . .] The blows of axes, the whistling of planes, the scraping of saws, the whirring of lathes, and the songs of workers made a pleasant and industrious hubbub that stimulated and enlivened all the gallant workers of the Refuge. All the turners and long-sawyers of the city of Paris came there to hear the latest news or add whatever they might have learned. When something new happened, a word was sufficient to bring all the workers downstairs to assemble on the ground floor and hear about it. Nothing took place without the workers being informed and their collective opinion being solicited concerning anything that was being planned. One after another, the young workers voluntarily carried out their plans to go off to the provinces, leaving behind their confidence in their elders to conduct the matter in hand.

The Prefect's Decision and How the Masters Got Around It

At that time a rumor was circulating that the masters of the Rue de Cléry planned to give notice to all the master turners of the central districts that they must fire all the workers they employed in their workshops. They believed this was the only way to make the workers return to the shops in the Rue de Cléry, where the workers, seeing themselves without employment, would be forced to perform the unpaid tasks whose elimination they were calling for. Young Mr. Deslandes had already managed to have some men fired from their workshops and had prevented several others from being hired. [. . .]

Several days had passed since we had sent our petition to His Excellency the Minister of State and Prefect of Police, so I suggested going to the prefecture to see if there was any response. [. . .]

Mr. Huvet and Mr. Dubois were delegated to go to the police commissioner's office, near the covered market, and asked him for news concerning the petition that the chair turners had presented to His Excellency the Minister of State regarding the unpaid tasks whose elimination they were requesting.

"Lads," the commissioner told them, "your request is legitimate and His Excellency's decision is as follows: Because these unpaid tasks represent a loss, pure and simple, and since you're being paid by the task, you are not required to carry them out."

Satisfied with this frank and fair response, Huvet and Dubois thanked the commissioner, who asked them several questions about the conduct of the masters and workers in this affair, in particular whether the workers who had left the workshops in the Rue de Cléry were employed. They answered that all were working and that a portion of the young men had decided to travel in the provinces, thus creating openings in the workshops of the central districts that had been filled by workers from the Rue de Cléry. They also said that the masters of the Rue de Cléry were spreading a rumor that they were going to have them fired. The commissioner made this reply to the workers: "If the masters take it upon themselves to carry out such a plan, tell those of your friends who may be affected to come let me know, and we'll set things right. Farewell, lads; go on working and stay calm."

Book III: The Main Engagement

OUR DAY IN COURT: "A SIMPLE MATTER OF
WORKERS DEFENDING THEIR INTERESTS"

Judgment and Reversal on Appeal

[*The masters next attempted to force the chair turners back to work by initiating a suit claiming that the workers had violated the laws against conspiracy by coercing their fellows into joining their action and thereby threatening the masters' livelihood. After five hearings, a judgment favorable to the workers was rendered. It rejected the assertion that the turners had acted illegally and specifically exonerated Bédé for his role in the events in question.*]

After this judgment was handed down, the workers thought that the matter was ended. It never occurred to us that the masters would have as little respect for the court's judgment as they had shown for the decision of His Excellency the Minister of State and Prefect of Police, who had responded so straightforwardly to the two petitions, one presented to him by the masters and the other by the workers, in concluding that since the tasks represented an uncompensated loss and the workers were being paid by the task, they did not have to do them.

We relied implicitly on this decision, not merely because it was to our advantage but because it was fair. But the masters did not stop with the judgment rendered by the court of first instance. They lodged an appeal before the Royal Court, and we were summoned to appear on 29 January 1821.

The Royal Appeals Court did not arrive at any decision at its first hearing. The court wished to hear the police commissioners who were involved in this affair and adjourned the hearing to Wednesday, January 31.

The reversal that the workers experienced under the Royal Court's decision caused them as much surprise as it produced pleasure in young Mr. Deslandes and Mr. Deck senior who, since the beginning of the affair, had let it be known through their colleagues that they wanted the head of the Mutual Aid Society locked up. Mr. Deck senior himself told me as much in front of witnesses and added with irony that he would have tools and wood delivered to the prison at Bicêtre so I would be able to work and that he would supply me with a cutlet and a bottle of wine every day for lunch. These men carried spitefulness to the point of wanting to have prosecution witnesses appear, but since these witnesses had not been subpoenaed, the court refused to hear them.

The attorney general, in his summation, accused the workers of being "anarchists guilty of conspiracy." At the same time, he declared that he was aware that the workers had been the object of harassment on the part of the masters concerning the matter of unpaid tasks. He said that the court could not allow the masters to force journeymen to work without paying them and that the workers were perfectly within their rights to refuse these tasks, since they were employed by the task and were not being paid for doing them.

Finally, the Royal Court handed down its decision and, after reversing the first judgment, condemned Mr. Bédé to two years of prison. Mr. Chapuis, Mr. Fouchet, Mr. Lebon, and Mr. Baillache received sentences of one month. Mr. Bicheux, Mr. Maillard, Mr. Planquoi, Mr. Gilbert, and Mr. Veaux were sentenced to one day. Mr. George Dumont was acquitted.

So unexpected a reversal overwhelmed the workers with consternation, but it never made them lose their courage. They immediately took steps to ease the fate of their fellow workers who were victims of the treachery of a few masters obstinately determined to do as much harm as they could to men who were doing nothing more than making legitimate protests.

I am placing the judgment of the Royal Court before my readers' eyes so that they may judge for themselves the contrast that exists between the two decisions:

Judgment of 31 January 1821 against Bédé:
Extract from the Minutes of the Clerk of the
Royal Court of Paris

Upon appeal, lodged by the king's prosecutor before the court of first instance of Paris, of a judgment rendered on 21 December 1820 to the said court of petty sessions, according to which Jacques Etienne Bédé, forty-five years of age, a turner, residing in Paris at 123 Rue Saint-Antoine, was released from custody imposed on him for having, in May 1820, formed a conspiracy for the purpose of abolishing unpaid tasks and preventing journeyman turners from working.

The Royal Court of Paris, chamber of petty sessions, by the decree of 31 January 1821, has ruled as follows:

Whereas examination and testimony have shown that meetings of journeyman turners were held on the premises of the wine merchant Tranchant, having as their object the elimination of what they call the unpaid tasks required of workers over and above their normal work and concerning which they had not obtained permission from the authorities to deliberate;

Whereas, as a result of these meetings, circulars were addressed to the master turners warning them that if they did not eliminate these unpaid tasks the workers would cease to work in their shops;

Whereas the demand for the elimination of these unpaid tasks, which from time immemorial have been part of their work, whether paid for by the day or by the task, constitutes a true conspiracy on the part of the workers for the purpose of increasing the price of their labor and obtaining a raise in pay, and this action therefore presents all those characteristics specified by law;

Whereas documents and testimony have shown that Bédé was the leader and initiator of this conspiracy;

For these reasons, the Court annuls both the appeal and the judgment being appealed, and renders a new judgment, declaring Bédé guilty of the offense specified by Article 445 of the Penal Code.[21]

In consequence, and under the terms of the said article, the Court condemns Bédé to serve two years of imprisonment and to pay court costs along with his fellow defendants.

Soon after this, Bédé began serving his two-year sentence in Sainte-Pélagie prison, where these memoirs were originally drafted. Fellow workers sentenced to lesser terms were allowed to stagger their time in jail so as to provide company for Bédé. But thanks to the intervention of the wife of one of his colleagues—the Maria to whom Bédé's memoir is dedicated—a wealthy and politically influential nobleman was persuaded to intercede on his behalf. After serving two months of his sentence, Bédé received a royal pardon. The memoir concludes on a triumphant note, with Bédé's account of the gala celebration held by the Parisian chair turners shortly after his release from prison in April 1821. Virtually nothing is known of his life from the time when his autobiography leaves off.

21. "Article 445" is presumably a typographical error in Bédé's book and should read "Article 415."

2   Suzanne Voilquin

Recollections of a
Daughter of the People

Voilquin's Recollections *were written at the age of sixty-seven, as she looked back upon a life full of movement and change. Parisian born, she traveled the globe and lived abroad to an extent exceptional for a French citizen of her time, of her gender, and of her modest origins.*

Though she can legitimately claim to be a daughter of the people, she was not of typical working-class background. Her father was a producer and small-time entrepreneur in the hat-making trade. He appears to have made a comfortable living until a combination of overconfidence, unwise business decisions, and cyclical downturns of the economy brought him to ruin. This and other texts in this anthology reveal that the experience of financial failure and debt were a remarkably common feature of nineteenth-century life. Because of the reversals her family suffered, Voilquin gradually slipped into the working class, and by her midtwenties she was forced to take jobs with small firms producing embroidered goods. Her career as a manual worker was only temporary, however, and after 1837 she earned her livelihood for the most part as a certified midwife.

The passages collected here tell not only her own life story but that of her parents as well, especially through the revelations that Suzanne's mother made during the long bout with cancer that would eventually lead to her death. These excerpts, drawn entirely from the first five chapters of Voilquin's forty-chapter autobiography, focus on her family and occupational life to the age of thirty-four. Her memoirs were written in 1865 and published in France in 1866.

SKETCH OF THE FIRST TWELVE YEARS OF MY LIFE

If you are to understand my life, dear child,[1] I will need to take a few pages to explain my early years, for the past begets the future; logic makes it so.

---

1. Voilquin's memoir is addressed to her niece and namesake, the child of her deceased brother, whom she refers to in her dedication as her "adopted daughter."

In thinking back on that bygone era, the first thing I become aware of is the gentle countenance of your forebear, my beloved mother. Though she has been dead for more than forty years, she remains as living in me as at the moment of our separation. It was due to her that the years of my youth were devoted to the impassioned practice of Christian worship.

My father, though very much a revolutionary, left our moral upbringing to her, smiling at our extreme devotion and treating it as one of those childhood illnesses without serious consequence for the future.

My mother, who had a big heart but whose intellect had been sharply diminished by her education, never disputed anything the Church laid down. She believed it all, and I followed her example. In my eyes, nothing was as beautiful as the ceremonies of the Catholic Church. I cannot even remember at what age your father and I acquired the habit of going each day to our ancient church, Saint-Merri, to hear the first mass.[2] This mass, our mother told us, had a greater value for our souls than those that followed, for Father Malmaison, my future spiritual director, would intone in a tremulous voice the beautiful hymn *Pange lingua*, before giving the faithful the blessing of the Holy Sacrament. To attend in summertime, we had to get up at five in the morning. For two young chatterboxes, this was nothing more than a joyful promenade. You realize, of course, that in winter our mother's inspiration was a very powerful influence in getting us to leave our beds at six o'clock—that is to say, before daylight—to brave snow and ice to kneel on the cold and damp stone floor. But upon our return we would receive as our reward a very tender kiss and a bowl of very hot soup. The truth is that the first gave me at least as much pleasure as the second.

Continuing in the application of her ultrareligious system, my mother sent me to confession when I was about seven. The Church maintains that at that age the child is responsible. Your father, who was nearly ten years old, was told to introduce me to Father Malmaison. He was a chubby little man, quite plump, who was always smiling and giving children holy pictures and friendly little pats on the cheek, as a result of which they all liked him. He was my spiritual director for several years, even though my father could not stand him because of his ultramontane opinions.[3] For,

2. The cloister of Saint-Merri is situated in the Marais district, just northwest of the Paris city hall and in the heart of a neighborhood which, throughout the nineteenth century, was a center of working-class militancy. The church itself was the site of the last stand of a group of republicans who led the unsuccessful insurrection of 1832.
3. The term *ultramontane* (literally "beyond the mountains," that is, the Alps), refers to those within the Catholic Church who believed in the doctrine of papal

although he was a good priest—or rather, because he was—Father Mal-maison frequently thundered on about the revolution and revolutionaries in a way that was not terribly evangelical. At the time, all of that mattered very little to me. The parish adored him, and I followed the parish's example.

From the time I reached the age of seven, I would go to confession once every month. I admit that the difficulty of pulling together the elements of a suitable confession made this a somewhat distressing undertaking for me. I was a poor, small child with an unblemished conscience who never knew how to answer that formula, spoken in a sleepy tone: "What next, my child?" And so, one month when I found myself well stocked, I decided to save for my next confession one or two enormities like inattention in my prayers, the sin of gluttony, pilfering my mother's provisions, and so on. Pleased with my ingenious idea, I happily brought the balance sheet of my faults before my indulgent spiritual director, and the dreaded quarter hour went by quite satisfactorily.

In this same period, my mother was taking me to the convent of the Saint-Merri cloister, to the school run by the Sisters of Saint-Vincent. Nothing could have been more simplified than the program of study established in that holy abode. First we would pray, then sing hymns, listen to pious and humdrum admonishments, learn to read and write a bit, and on Saturday recite the day's gospel, which we had learned by heart.

These undemanding exercises were still too much for my memory, which had atrophied as the result of an accident the preceding year. One day, as I was deeply involved in playing with some other young girls, one of them—an older girl of ten—turned quickly, without letting go of the racket she was holding in her hand. Unfortunately, this plaything connected with my poor little six-year-old face and broke my nose. Blood spurted with such force that the neighbors did not dare take me up to my mother's for some hours.

This accident was of some gravity for both my body and my mind. I nearly lost my sight and only got rid of my intense headaches toward the age of eight. My mother, whose devotion was sometimes more sincere than enlightened and more concerned with the soul than the body, did not call a doctor, who might have been able, right at the outset and by ordinary means, to fix the broken nose. To the worldly, who would reproach her for it while they pitied me, she would say, "Bah! My daughter will always be

---

supremacy and looked to the Vatican for guidance. A spiritual director was a priest who assumed responsibility for advising an adolescent and guiding his or her moral and religious development.

pretty enough if she remains chaste and pious." She no doubt wanted to nip in the bud the sentiment of vanity that Sterne maintains is too vigorous to eradicate completely.[4]

So, as I said, it was as if my brain was partially paralyzed. Despite a strength of will uncommon in a child, my memory proved resistant to retaining the briefest sentence. My martyrdom would begin each Saturday morning. When it came my turn to recite the gospel, I might just as well have said, like Petit-Jean, "What I know best is the beginning."[5] In fact, I cannot remember ever having gotten past the first line. So once I had said, "And at that time, Jesus said to his disciples . . . ," I would suddenly stop. It was no use racking my poor and unfaithful memory, for I was incapable of finding in it what Jesus might have said to his disciples. At first I was reprimanded and punished, but in the end, at school and in my family, it was recognized that, as I was a pious and timid child, the cause of these failures to perform must lie beyond my control. I was then left to seek in peace the rest of the gentle and divine Jesus's symbolic exchanges with his apostles. [. . .]

MY FAMILY

When my mother brought her last child into the world, we were allowed, a few hours after the delivery, to go kiss the newborn. That is when my mother, in presenting me with this charming little creature, said to me, "It is not a sister that I am giving you but a daughter. From this moment on, she belongs to you." I was barely nine years old. The rather solemn gift of this tiny being, made before the entire family, brought me immense joy. I took it so seriously that from then on I just barely permitted my mother the right to nurse her. [. . .]

This precocious motherhood which, like all sentiments based on exclusivity, caused me both joy and sorrow, became a healthy stimulus in my youth and a source of nourishment for my soul. It was this intensely pure emotion that helped me understand the concept of duty. Still later, in very painful circumstances, it saved me from suicide by forcing me to live for this child. Thus, until her marriage, she never left me, whether for school or apprenticeship. And everything that the hard times of my youth allowed me to assimilate—which, alas, was all too little—I learned in order to share it with this dear adoptive daughter.

So there I was, having just concluded my childhood and beginning my

4. Voilquin probably refers to the English writer Laurence Sterne (1713–68), best known as the author of *Tristram Shandy*.
5. Petit-Jean is a character in *Les Plaideurs*, the only comedy written by Jean Racine (1639–99).

youth under the influence of that painful era that witnessed our French nation diminished, her children dispersed by death and exile, immediately after she had been so great, so feared, under a hero acclaimed by the people.[6]

It is in the family setting that the nuances of children's characters are shaped. My mother, through her tenderness, held sway over the first years of my life, for my exaggerated devoutness was in part her handiwork. But my youth was grafted, so to speak, onto the strong will of my father, with his intelligent nature and openness to generous ideas. It is to him that I owe the first practical awareness of life in the broader sense.

You loved your kind grandfather and you were a witness, dear child, to his peaceful death, a year after our arrival in Louisiana.[7] It was in our arms that the soul of this ardent patriot expired, without pain or agony. Until the age of eighty-four, this philosophical proletarian was never heard to complain of the fate that had constantly kept him in the lower ranks of society, despite his courage and the extraordinary efforts he made to escape. Continue then, my child, to revere his memory. Place flowers on his grave, which must, alas, remain on foreign soil, far from the France he loved so much.

Here is the place to say a few words about his youth. You are aware that before our great revolution, the right of primogeniture was part of our legal system and was imposed even in rural families.[8] The oldest son alone enjoyed the privilege of learning to read and write. For this reason my father, who was the youngest son of a large peasant family, had to resign himself to tending the family flock. Later, when he was strong enough, he went to help his brothers labor in the fields, with only the great book of nature before his eyes to complete his education.

6. Though she does not provide exact dates in her text, Voilquin gives sufficient indications to establish that she was born in 1798 or soon after. This would make her about sixteen at the time of the fall of Napoléon and the First French Empire, which she describes in this passage.

7. In September 1848, Voilquin set out for the United States. She eventually settled in Louisiana, where her sister had gone fifteen years earlier. Voilquin had already lived extensively abroad, first as a member of a Saint-Simonian community established in Egypt (1833–36) and subsequently for seven years in Russia (1839–46), where she worked as a midwife. In the first half of the nineteenth century, her wide-ranging travels were highly unusual for any individual of humble origins, and particularly so for a woman.

8. Primogeniture is the legal requirement, dating from medieval times, that the eldest son inherit the entirety of his father's estate. It ensured that a family's agricultural holdings would not be split up into parcels too small to support a household. By extension, the term refers to the unequal distribution of property and privilege according to birth order.

When he was about eighteen, the love of independence stole him away from a life too calm for his constitution. The ideal of freedom, so much in the air at the end of the eighteenth century, attracted him and made him leave everything behind, his village and his family. First he went off to Nîmes, where he learned the trade of hatter.[9] His goal was to complete his Tour of France.[10] This complement of practical education was necessary in that period to round out the training of a competent compagnon.[11] I shall not undertake to tell you of his travels through the principal cities of France. I would only be repeating very badly what Perdiguier and George Sand have said so well in speaking of these rival brotherhoods.[12]

After several years, these excursions led young Mr. Monnier, my father, to Flanders, which he also traversed. But at last the little town of Malines brought his peregrinations to an end. There he met a young girl—rather pretty, gentle, timid, and devout—whom he made his wife and who became our worthy and pious mother.

Although of a sometimes exuberant nature, my father suffered the effects of his years of isolation. He had spent his first twelve years completely alone in his beautiful mountains of Vivarais, confronting the great scenes of nature. Often I saw him among us, plunged, as he put it so well, in infinite dreams and reveries that recalled to him that sweet period of his youth.

Our revolution, which came along to free the people by destroying all

9. Hatters (*chapeliers*) made headwear of all kinds; they worked primarily in felt, silk, wool, and fur. Hatters were skilled workers whose earnings exceeded the average daily wage of artisans in general. For a recent, detailed study of hatters in the period when Voilquin's father would have been learning his trade, see Michael Sonenscher, *The Hatters of Eighteenth-Century France* (Berkeley, 1987).
10. The Tour of France was the journey made by novice craftsmen to complete their training, master the range of regional variations in the trade, and polish their personal skills. The tour generally consisted of a circuit of provincial towns that might take from one to several years to complete. See the introduction, pages 22 and 39 and chapter 3.
11. The term refers to a journeyman in a skilled trade who belonged to one of the workers' brotherhoods (compagnonnages) which flourished during the eighteenth century and survived with varying degrees of success into the nineteenth. The most important contemporary sources on the purpose, structure, and activities of these organizations are Agricol Perdiguier's *Le Livre du compagnonnage* (Marseille, 1878) and his *Memoirs of a Compagnon*, which is excerpted in chapter 3.
12. George Sand was the pseudonym of Aurore Dupin, the Baroness Dudevant (1804–76), who published a number of popular and influential romantic novels in the mid–nineteenth century. She was, moreover, a woman of strong political conviction who took an active role in the social issues of her day. Among her works dealing with the life of the working class was one entitled *Le Compagnon du tour de France* (Paris, 1861), inspired in part through her acquaintance with Agricol Perdiguier.

outdated and corrupt practices, found my father in the prime of life and happy to see the privileges of masters and feudal rights of every sort fall along with the Bastille.[13] He came to Paris with his wife and two sons. The time for studying was past, for he had to see to the needs of his young family. The youthful Raymond Monnier therefore remained, to his great regret, in his original state of ignorance. Even had his financial means permitted, moreover, how would he have found the time to study in the course of those exciting years? It was for everyone a time of action. The yearning for social intercourse was so intense that individuality was forgotten in favor of collective life.

Oh, to be sure, to take part in the different stages of a social renovation (at times, alas, quite grim but always grand in its objectives), to devote one's free time to attending political clubs, to fraternize every *décadi* with warm and energetic comrades—all this was far more involving and spoke more to the heart than all the books in the world.[14]

The popular festivals on the Champ de Mars were a powerful stimulant for my father.[15] How enthusiastically he would run to them, holding his oldest son by the hand and carrying the youngest on his robust shoulders! In his view, this initiation would make them true and ardent patriots.

My gentle mother was, in every way, the opposite of her husband. Timid and fearful before the emotion and uproar of social life, whose principles moreover offended all her religious beliefs, she effaced herself in complete self-sacrifice. In order to reconcile her feelings and her responsibilities, she made herself silent and submissive. She was, in a word, the Christian spouse of the Middle Ages. Raised in a small town by an inflexible and unresponsive mother, she came to marriage with her spirit numbed by the most complete ignorance of all matters, practical as well as intellectual. For this reason, she had vague aspirations but no initiative. Given the way circumstance had formed her, this Christian mother was hardly prepared to see to our intellectual development, but I always saw her towering above all others by virtue of her courage. It was the radiance of her angelic goodness that constantly illuminated the difficult path that I had to travel and that kept my heart from freezing as a result of contact with the egoism and false friendships of worldly life. [. . .]

13. The effects of the French Revolution on workers' rights is discussed in the introduction, pages 13–14.
14. The republican calendar, in force from 1792 to 1805, had a ten-day week. *Décadi* was the tenth day, the day of rest and relaxation.
15. Voilquin refers to the festivals held in celebration of the spirit and achievements of the Revolution. Perhaps the most famous were those dedicated to the Cult of the Supreme Being, which tried to substitute for traditional Catholicism a secularized form of worship organized around revolutionary principles.

When I was about fifteen, my character underwent spontaneous development. That love of independence and feminine dignity which constantly manifested itself was by no means inspired in me by the theories of Saint-Simon.[16] No, it was part of my being. Let me cite just one example. One day, my father addressed a few brusque and disdainful words to his wife on the subject of religion. This made my brothers smile. I was outraged. "The truth is," I said to my mother, shedding a tear of anger, "you are altogether too patient. Dear mother, why do you let yourself be treated this way?"

"Ah, my daughter, peace is worth its weight in gold."

"Then it costs too much," I said defiantly.

"Oh, my little logician, never forget this proverb: The goat must browse where it is tethered."

But there was no holding me back, and I boldly replied: "No, no, the goat can break its tether and go browse somewhere else."

Although I could not sense its full significance, my mother was frightened by this rejoinder on the part of a child of fifteen. She made me be silent and forced me to go give my father a kiss.

From the time of this altercation, our roles changed. My mother relied on me to demand respect for her gentle and weak nature, and often my intervention served to reestablish the sometimes troubled moral equilibrium between her sons and her husband.

From that time on, I sensed the human spirit coming to life in me and transforming my mind, which had too long been choked by the mysticism of my childhood years. My personality became gay and extroverted. Everything attracted my interest and assumed a cheerful aspect in my eyes. But as my parents occupied an extremely lowly rank in society, I remained, despite my aspirations toward the beautiful, a poor child of the people, quite naive and quite ignorant.

I was not the only one, to be sure, who cried out to God: "Supreme

16. From the time of her initiation in 1830, Suzanne Voilquin was a lifelong devotee of the circle of Saint-Simonians initially led by Prosper "Father" Enfantin, and the bulk of her autobiography is concerned with her experiences as a member of this group. Claude-Henri Saint-Simon (1760–1825) was a key originator of the divergent traditions of French socialism and positivism. A colorful figure who had fought in the American War of Independence, he proposed a scheme to join the Atlantic and Pacific oceans with a Central American canal. Saint-Simon amassed an early fortune, only to die in poverty after exhausting his resources in support of his many experimental ideas. He was also a prolific, if unsystematic, writer; but his ideas attracted a broad audience only after his death. His philosophy, in addition to its emphasis on meritocracy, the equality of the sexes, and the preeminent role of science, also stressed the need for society and organized groups of producers to assume responsibility for directing economic affairs.

intelligence, give me nourishment for my mind, for, alas, my parents can barely give me bread for my body."

Within the restricted circle in which I lived, if an unknown word happened to strike my ear, I would quickly resort to my brother's dictionary in order to learn its meaning and be able to assimilate it. Many times in public concerts and in museums, I would feel my tears flow. In these tears were mixed the joy of aspiring to the unknown and despair at never being able to attain it. "Oh how very fortunate," I would say, "are the children of the rich who can wander at their leisure through this immense garden of human knowledge and pick the fruits of these sacred trees!"

Thank God that our era wants to bring an end to pariah status of whatever sort. The inner pangs of ignorance, aspiring to the life of the intellect, will soon disappear. This century will not reach its conclusion before the last of the children of the people are placed in a position to develop their native talents. Before long, the right of all to receive this opportunity free of charge, and the duty on the part of every government to provide it, will be recognized.

My desire to learn received some satisfaction within my family. Philippe, my younger brother, had wanted, in the period of our extreme devoutness, to become a priest. With that intention, he had taken classes at the seminary of Saint-Merri until the age of seventeen. He then threw away his frock, telling my mother, to console her, that he would rather be an honest worker than a mediocre priest. This young scholar, who never got beyond the initial steps toward the priesthood, was therefore the best-educated member of the family. It was he who initiated me into Greek and Roman history and a bit of contemporary history as well. There before me was the path, but I lacked the time and books to follow it.

I loved reading with a passion. I was allowed to surrender to this enthusiasm each evening in my mother's company on condition that I read to her, while she worked, the entire stock of the neighborhood lending library. In place of that solid instruction that young girls are now beginning to receive, I would draw upon novels for false notions about real life.

When I was able to reflect back on the singular course in literature that I took each evening in my pious mother's presence, I was rather amazed. I could only explain this apparent contradiction on her part by ascribing it to her mixed nature, half Flemish, half Spanish—which is to say, ignorant of worldly affairs and living only through the heart and the imagination. What is more, following her example, this mixture of the sacred and profane proved just as perfectly compatible in my own mind.

Although the events that brought an end to the First Empire have passed into the realm of history and have been described by fair-minded men, I cannot pass over this period entirely in silence, for, I repeat, it is of my moral being that I am writing. Though I was then a young girl, such shocks leave behind a lasting impression in one's mind and necessarily change one's thinking.

As this change of dynasty neared, agitation overcame all ranks and all ages. As my father's official reader, I would recite aloud the reports from Napoléon's army. Like him, I was deeply affected by our triumphs and our reverses. Because of my shyness, this further initiation as reader did not make me a grandiloquent orator, but from that time on, I knew in my heart what patriotism meant!

I lived among the people and I shared their feelings. Like them, all the love that I felt for France led me to detest all those who took any part in her humiliation. Thus, in 1815, when the time came for everyone to fight for her independence, it was with pride in accomplishing a sacred and indispensable duty that I embraced my father and older brother, who were both going off to the gates of Paris. My father joined the ranks of the National Guard, and my brother was a member of the Patriotic Federation of the Suburbs. As for my brother Philippe, he had belonged for several months to the army of the Loire.

That cruel day that saw the misfortune of France fulfilled will never be erased from my memory. It seemed interminable to us. The enemy was there at our gates. Each blast of the cannon that he fired at our defenders might deprive us of a loved one. At last, toward evening, our two patriots returned, black with powder stains, weary, discouraged, and furious. My father cursed the faint-heartedness of the Regency Council and all those traitors who were responsible for defending us but had just handed over France by surrendering Paris to the foreigners. "Oh," he said, "if Napoléon had been there to lead us, no enemy soldier would ever have seen his savage native land again." His words echoed the sentiments of the immense majority. I was in a position to testify to that fact after my mother and I made our way through the populous quarters, for our mounting anxiety pushed us here and there in search of news. I assure you that in that supreme hour, no woman held back her husband or her son. Yes, the people of Paris, for their part, wished to defend their capital. [. . .]

The years following the Restoration were terribly distressing for workers to live through. Poverty, our longtime acquaintance, came once again to knock at our door. This woeful visitor weighed above all on my mother who, out of devotion for her family, shouldered the greater part of the burden. Moreover, her health changed from that moment on, and the terrible disease from which she would die three years later began its ravages, though not the slightest complaint on her part occurred to awaken our concern.

When, one day, education is offered on an equal basis to both sexes, and women with an aptitude for studies will compete, like men, to earn a doctor's diploma, how many female victims will be saved from a cruel and premature death! They will not wait, as my mother did, until the last stages of this terrible disease before entrusting themselves to science. During the long years that I practiced my profession, I was constantly in a position to observe that women hesitate to speak of certain symptoms.[17] Everything in them rebels at the thought of revealing to a doctor those details that offend their imagination and modesty. *All* conceal the seriousness of their symptoms or mention them too late. In Russia, where I practiced my profession for seven years, I observed how little well-to-do women would allow themselves to be questioned by their doctor. There, as in Egypt and America, he must guess everything, while the terrible cancer has already left its imprint on its victim's features, and inexorable death prepares to seize her.

To women, and *only* to women, belongs the right to assist the members of their sex, not only in the admirable work of maternity but also in all those illnesses from which chastity suffers so much when they must be divulged to a man.

But enough of that for the moment. This important matter of our rights and our responsibilities in society cannot be treated incidentally. Let us return to my mother who, for three years, concealed the first symptoms of her illness. During those years of remission, when the disease seemed to be arrested—for its advance is that insidious—my mother had the joy of seeing the marriages of her two sons, the elder's in 1818 and the younger's in the following year. The modest dowry of Philippe's wife permitted him to become his father's partner. Good cheer and liveliness reappeared along with work, but this period of serenity and hope did not last long. For my family it was a calm between two storms.

MY MOTHER'S ILLNESS AND DEATH

After thirteen months of marriage, Philippe lost his young bride in childbirth, and I lost a devoted friend and sister! I had no time to dwell on this sorrow, for my mother, already very ill at the time of this catastrophe, immediately had to take to her bed. I went to get Mr. Lacour, our venerable old doctor. My impatience made his visit with my poor mother seem very long. After this consultation, I ran toward him, uneasy, wishing to know if the patient's condition presented a serious danger. "Yes, my child, your mother has a fatal illness that she has kept hidden too long. She is dying of cancer that has reached an advanced stage," he told me brusquely. On

---

17. Voilquin was certified as a midwife in 1837.

hearing this diagnosis, I grew pale, fell ill, and did not hear the few words of consolation that he felt called upon to add. He was an educated and charitable man but he was a bachelor. If he had had children, he would not have added to my misfortune with this brutal way of speaking. He would have left me hope. As it was, for eight months his cruel words prevented the rebirth of the serenity of hopefulness in me. I did not leave my mother day or night. For that length of time, I wanted nothing—no entertainment, no outings—nothing but my beloved patient. I had, moreover, to take my mother's place in the family. At first, I was very awkward in these various tasks. But children of the people learn very fast. From childhood on, poverty makes them independent.

Though I was small and frail, I could manage anything. I was twenty years old, but my size and features gave me the appearance of a Parisian of fifteen or sixteen. My childhood had subjected me to too many privations, and it seemed that I had been stunted as a consequence. Up to that time, hygiene—that great medicine of the future—had been completely lacking for us. My life had been spent in a dark and unhealthy house located in one of the smallest streets in the center of Paris. If, during those eight months, I was able to endure the unparalleled strain that I imposed on my sickly body, I owe it as much to my filial affection as to the strength of will that I get from my father.

The evening hours usually brought a slight lull in the sufferings of my beloved patient. At such times, we were alone, and I was all hers. Those hours seemed sweeter for her. She would consecrate them by pouring her heart out in a way that it is impossible for me to forget. We were two friends, the older of whom had at last found the opportunity to pass on an account of her life and her past sorrows to a sympathetic heart that was quite happy to accept her melancholy confidences.

One evening I made her smile by asking about the early days of her marriage!

"Our honeymoon, my dear curious one! I don't even know what the word means. The revolution stole it from me. The sudden commotion of that whirlwind carried off everything in its path. The intimate joys of the family were replaced by meetings on the public square, religion was replaced by clubs in which people spoke of the Supreme Being but forgot the God of charity. Alas, as you well know, I have often been disheartened in my innermost beliefs but, being weak and timid, I had to bend before the hand of a master whom I loved and feared too much, while constantly offering my submission to the gentle Savior of mankind. I was never able to find in maternal love the only compensation that I desired. To be sure, you children might have been my consolation and reward if I had not seen your childhood wilt in poverty—and I mean not just relative poverty but genuine destitution, what you, Suzanne, used to call the blackest poverty, as if to avenge yourself for all the privations it made you endure.

"God forbid that I should rail against His will, but as you see from the grief that burns my bowels, it is too heavy a cross for a mother's heart to bear. May you, my child, never know such sorrows!

"Several times, dear daughter, I've seen your innocent heart make you guess at the many mysteries that exist between your father and me. I preferred not to speak of them with you, so as not to weaken the respect that is due to him. Until life and its lessons bring you the kind of tolerance that understands and pardons, let me tell you of his paternal tenderness, of his invincible courage, so that these memories may balance in your heart the rigor of your judgment.

"My beloved Raymond has always been a gentle, steady worker who thought only of the happiness of his children. His sole ambition was to rise above the precariousness of his status as a worker, but he was much too trusting and perhaps not educated enough to succeed.

"At the time when the great abundance of paper money managed to revive business, it was easy for him to carry out his plan.[18] He started a hat shop, hired a few journeymen, and set to work. If he had enough stock on hand, he would journey on foot to the fairs. He would do a day's march of fifteen leagues and never traveled any other way. His handsome face, his great integrity, his open demeanor caused him to be noticed at the fairs of Guibray, Caen, and Beaucaire. What he didn't sell at these markets, he would leave on consignment with provincial retailers. You remember how we welcomed and celebrated his return each time. He was happiness and abundance personified. These profitable trips only redoubled his courage! For several years, this impoverished worker must have congratulated himself on his vigor and believed that his family was saved from calamity. [. . .]

"As business prospered, your father was obliged, in order not to crowd his shop too much, to place more goods on consignment in the provinces, since production and sales didn't always proceed apace. Alas, that's where my dear husband lacked common prudence, for he would accept risky notes with long maturities. How often I saw those notes come back unpaid! When this happened, he had to resort to borrowing to cover his obligations, for the credit of a small-time manufacturer is quickly exhausted. By resorting to such burdensome means, he was able to deal with the initial

18. Paper money was issued by the revolutionary government in the 1790s in the form of *assignats*—warrants or promissory notes. Before that, coins containing precious metal were the accepted medium of exchange.

difficulties and redeem his signature. I approved of this, because it was important above all to maintain his self-confidence. But it meant mortgaging our future.

"I don't know what occurred in the political realm, but at a certain moment, business ground to a halt for many months. We needed to survive. My husband was obliged to sell, little by little and at very low prices, all the merchandise we had on hand. Then, when the notes that had been renewed fell due, he had to resign himself to selling his tools and the hat works. Everything was paid off, thank God! But for all his effort and toil over several years, what did this industrious worker—the head of a household with four children to feed—have to show for it all? Nothing! Nothing! Absolutely nothing!

"This trial was too much for him; his courage was vanquished. He fell so dangerously ill that for six weeks he was too delirious to recognize us. At the beginning of this illness, his closest friend, Mr. Morales, advised me to have him taken to the Hôtel-Dieu hospital where he would not lack for doctors and medicine, as he would at home. My extreme poverty forced me to consent.[19] I can still see him, lying in bed number forty of the Saint Charles ward, unable to recognize anyone in his raging delirium. Forced to abandon him in this state to the care of strangers, my tears, even more than my entreaties, called him to the attention of the woman who was the head of that ward. In those days, one could visit patients every day. So I'd spend all the time with him that was allowed, before returning home to you children a little more heartbroken than the day before.

"Listen and be amazed at how *chance*—oh, no, dear Lord, I'm wrong! It was Your holy providence that used me, Your unworthy instrument, to bring this poor breadwinner back to life. I had barely arrived one morning when good Sister Elisabeth, without letting me approach my husband, took me by the hand and led me before a statue of Christ. She said, 'Take courage, you poor mother! Commend yourself to the Savior of mankind so that He may come to your aid, for your husband is very sick today. The doctor has just prescribed a powerful medicine that should either save him or else. . . . He must be given *six drops* every quarter-hour in a spoonful of

19. The Hôtel-Dieu was the oldest hospital in Paris, then located on the Ile de la Cité to the south of the open space before the Cathedral of Notre Dame. Hospitals were public institutions, usually operated by the Catholic Church, to serve those too poor to pay for their care. Voilquin's mother communicates the strong sense of pride and self-sufficiency felt by members of the working class and the shame they experienced when they were unable to provide for their own needs. She also expresses the reluctance that workers often felt when forced to contemplate the admission of a loved one to a public hospital from which, experience showed, the patient might never return.

herb tea. I am entrusting this vial to you. Don't forget: every quarter-hour, just six drops,' she repeated as she withdrew.

"I cried so much on seeing your father's dull eyes and his livid face that no longer seemed to belong to this world, that I forgot the good Sister's instructions. The patient's hand stirred and appeared to be searching for something. I thought he was thirsty. I poured a bit of tea into his glass and then a half-teaspoonful of the fatal potion and made him drink it all. Sister Elisabeth, returning from her rounds, came up to us at just that moment. Judging how much he had drunk from what was missing in the phial, she said just these words to me: 'Unfortunate mother, what have you done?' This sentence, which brought the prescription back to my mind, fell like a weight upon my heart. I became ill and was carried home to you, my poor children, half mad with sorrow, blaming myself for your father's death. I spent the night in prayer. At dawn the next day I ran to the Hôtel-Dieu. It was not nearly time for the gates to open, but the charitable Sister, who had felt a presentiment of my arrival, sent word by the ward attendant that toward morning an appreciable improvement had occurred in the patient's condition.

"A deadly weight was lifted from my spirit. I went to Notre Dame to pray. I lit a candle before the altar of the Holy Virgin Mary, to whose intercession I believed and still believe I owed this miracle, for I'd prayed to her so hard all night!

"I'd hardly entered the ward when the Sister came to me, saying, 'Rejoice, my child, God has chosen not to abandon you to despair. Your unintentional error has had a happy outcome. Yesterday, after you left, for some hours we thought your husband was dead. But then a profuse sweat broke out, giving rise to a crisis that has turned out to be so beneficial that the doctor has now judged him to be out of danger.'

"Can you comprehend my joy on hearing these words? All I could do was cry and kiss the hands of this gentle creature. I will not speak of my happiness on seeing my husband's gaunt hand reach out to me: he recognized me! He wasn't able to speak yet, but his gaze was already so alive. Oh no, that's something that cannot be expressed!

"Reassured that our breadwinner would live, I turned my attention to you, poor children, whom six weeks of anguish had made me neglect. Alas, how did we live during that period of time, you and I? I don't know. Your godfather, the pawnshop, and some charitable neighbors helped us get through somehow or other.

"After a few weeks, your father—still thin, weak, and famished—returned home. He would eat anything to satisfy the insatiable appetite that tormented him. You'll shudder, my child, to learn the degree of poverty your parents were reduced to. Instead of giving my dear convalescent a bit of wine or the sort of tonics that his condition called for, I was forced to meet his imperious need to live by going to the barracks to collect the scraps of ration bread, which I was never refused. When I'd gathered what I could, I would bring it home, boil it with a bit of salt, and serve it to him several times a day in enormous quantities. It was on this same diet, insubstantial as it was, that your father had to return to work. All our resources had been exhausted. Everything we could carry had been taken off to the pawnshop. Only your father's labor could save us. His strength failed him more than once, but the shining courage he'd had before came back with his health.

"Soon after this he had need of that courage, for I could no longer hide my suffering. Though I was only eight months pregnant, I was forced to leave you in your father's care so I could go in turn and occupy a pauper's bed in the maternity hospital. The great weariness I'd experienced at the time of our financial losses, and above all my recent afflictions, all pushed forward the time of my confinement, but the child I brought into the world was so sickly that he couldn't live for even one whole day. Despite our poverty and our responsibilities, a mother, you can believe me, never loses a child that she's felt moving in her womb without experiencing heartbreak. This new grief complicated my state of health. I fell seriously ill. For a month your father would bring you children every Sunday. You barely knew how to walk. Not wanting to deprive me of your presence, he was forced to carry you the whole long way. The sight of all that I loved in the world would bring me happiness for the entire week. With what noble pride your father would tell me how his work was going! 'My strength has come back too,' he would say. 'I knocked off thirty francs' worth of work this week. You see, woman, how the kids are coming along? Here, they've brought you some biscuits and sugar. I want you to deny yourself nothing, and come back to us quickly.'

"Twice a day he would take you to a little workers' restaurant where they made food that, although it wasn't very elegant, was healthy and abundant. These meals, enlivened by your babbling and by your hearty children's appetites, were a source of joy for him. In the evening, after a hearty supper, he'd take you back to the house and put you to bed with the patient tenderness of a mother, just as I might have done myself.

"Oh my daughter! Love and respect your father in memory of that time, for in his courage and his devotion to his young family he proved his nobility."

My dear patient's confidences also taught me about her husband's continual efforts to climb to a higher station and also of his incurable trust in those who took the trouble to ingratiate themselves with him. This led inevitably to the same result, just as negative, though not as disastrous as it had been the first time.

She also told me of the grief she had suffered as a mother at the loss of three other children who died as infants, before the birth of my Adrienne.

Alas! her death approached without her seeming to fear it or even to be aware of it. She maintained a perfect calm that was never breached up to the final moment. When, after intolerable crises, peace would finally return, she would hold me in her arms and say, "When I'm well again, how I'll have to love you, my good and courageous child, to make up for all your present sorrows!" As for the hope that she would make gleam in my eye, did she believe in it? I don't know. Perhaps she only wanted me to believe it, but at that time those gentle words were my consolation. They still make my weary heart quiver as if they were a noble reward for a duty well done.

When my mother died, I took refuge in a dark room where I could cry to my heart's content over my dear departed, for the reluctance to show genuine sentiment is so strong in me that ordinary consolations are mere words whose meaning escapes me.

But my Adrienne constantly came to wipe away my tears with her hugs and kisses. "You are my only mother now," she would say to me. "Why do you want to abandon me too?"

My father came to find me. He was kind and gentle. He managed to calm the fears that I had not even expressed by swearing to us on the memory of my mother that he would not take another wife before we both were married.

In the end, *duty*—our mother's watchword—reasserted its control over my awareness and helped me to shake off the gloomy apathy I had fallen into. It made me return to active family life, at least insofar as a languishing illness of several months' duration permitted.

Reading became the only distraction I wished to pursue. It was the end of 1821. [. . .]

The works of Voltaire, Rousseau, de Volney, and others were rather heavy for so untutored a mind as my own. Of Voltaire, the only works that I read with interest were his plays. I preferred Rousseau. I read with pleasure his *Emile* and especially his *Julie*. Despite the shivers of terror that its terrible preface caused me, and although I convinced myself that I would remain strong against its influence, it worked its charm over me. I did not feel that I was the same person after reading this book. I still sought out my same old reliable authors, but I was forced to admit to myself my preference for works of romance because they spoke to the imagination. Madame

Cottin and Madame de Genlis, the charming storytellers of that period, were my favorites. As for the learned Madame de Staël, I took pleasure in reading her books—*Delphine*, and especially *Corinne*, that latter-day Sappho, in whom, they say, she wished to portray her own triumphs and sorrows.

These various works, all celebrating love, colluded with nature itself in sharply stirring my imagination and filling my heart with unknown desires.

[Not included in these excerpts is a chapter in which Voilquin recounts her first love. Her courtship with Stanislaus, a medical student, lasted some ten months before he brought it to an end, leaving Voilquin broken-hearted and disillusioned.]

THE LIVES OF WORKING WOMEN IN PARIS

The two years from 1823 to 1825, the period of my marriage, will teach you something about the lives of working women as well as their tribulations when, left to face the demands of day-to-day life on their own, they have only their labor to provide for their needs. Cherish them too, my child, and protect all those whom you may find along your path, for they are not without merit, these daughters of the people who, in their pride and dignity, know how to resist temptations of all kinds, relying for their daily bread on work alone.

The partnership between my two widowers proved unable to save our household.[20] Their business affairs were in a bad way and threatened us with ruin for the fourth time. Everything in our domestic life took on a sad and gloomy hue. Just then, my father, anxious about my state of health, decided to take me on a trip that combined business and pleasure. He had some important business to take care of in Saint-Omer. He said I could help him look over the muddled accounts of an agent who was running a business in that town on our behalf.

Naturally, Adrienne was taken along as well. We left her in Amiens with a family of friends until we returned. Then my father and I continued on to Saint-Omer, where we completely surprised our agent. Alas! It did not require a very long or very thorough inspection of his books to see the deplorable result produced by the inexperience of my brother in combination with the incorrigible confidence of my father. The agent, who was managing a substantial warehouse of goods in Saint-Omer that was constantly replenished with new shipments, was a man more unlucky than culpable. He possessed no business skills and was, moreover, burdened

20. Voilquin refers to the business partnership between her father and her brother.

with a large family. He managed to support them from the sales proceeds of our store, constantly hoping to make up the deficit by his own hard work. In response to all the letters asking for a summary of the accounts, he would send us back small payments on account, along with evasive replies. This was the state of affairs that had made necessary a visit from the boss. In short, by the time we arrived, all we could do was to confirm the disaster. The sale of the entire remaining stock did not even cover what was owed. This unhappy outcome prodded our poor household a bit more rapidly toward its ruin.

I remembered my mother, who had always been so forgiving in such circumstances, and I took pity on this poor family. I begged my father not to press charges against his unfaithful agent, whose labor, if accepted by another employer, might continue to put bread on the table of his young family.

We left Saint-Omer too preoccupied with our losses to think of seeing anything more than its massive fortifications and its beautiful Gothic cathedral. But before returning to Paris, my father wanted to keep the promise he had made me earlier that he would show me the sea. He took me to Dunkerque, that beautiful port on the North Sea. We stayed only forty-eight hours in the native city of Jean Bart.[21] This short time was enough for us to wander through the magnificent anchorage, the commercial port, and the shipyards. But the place to which I inevitably returned was the jetty which ran out from the port far into the sea.

What intense emotion I felt as I contemplated that vast ocean, me, a poor Parisian who had never seen anything but the bends of the Seine! With a mysterious inner joy, I looked out over that grandiose spectacle, a vision of the infinite. On that jetty, I experienced at last a calming of my sorrow and shed the first tears that were sweetened with hope.

In the presence of that vast element, I was surprised to find myself envying the fate of sailors destined to live between the sky and these majestic waves. I little suspected at that time that these great oceans would later become the customary byways for my peregrinations.

After this too brief interlude, we had to return to Amiens, spend a few days with our friends, then return to Paris with my sister after an absence of a few weeks. This trip was very healthy for both my body and my spirits. Upon our return, I regained my past energy and the force of will that has never since failed me in any circumstance of my life.

Given the state of our financial affairs, I foresaw that our labor would

---

21. Jean Bart (1650–1702) was a celebrated privateer whose seamanship and daring brought him lavish rewards from Louis XIV.

soon become our sole resource. I urged Adrienne to join me in resolutely pursuing this set purpose. We had, from time to time, embroidered on a loom at the home of our sister-in-law, whose specialty this was. It was this gracious occupation that we chose. Necessity, that great tutor of the children of the common people, made us achieve successful results right away and helped get us through the practical difficulties almost as if they were trifles.

That inauspicious year had not run out before the two partners, my father and Philippe, were forced out of business. Everything was sold, but everything was paid up. They at least had the right to withdraw with their integrity unblemished.

My father's indomitable courage had not been able to ward off his bad luck. At the age of sixty, all hope had expired in him. He had to turn over to some luckier man his shop, his honest and carefree workers, and his numerous trips across France. A case of pneumonia, caused by this change in his life and by sadness, nearly took him from us in the space of a few days. At the end of a month, he was on his feet again and ready to start over, he told us. We left our old and hideous house—so dear, all the same, for all the memories with which it was filled—and went to find refuge, all three of us, high in the Faubourg du Temple.

From then on, our life as working women began in earnest. For the first time, we had to leave our father's house and go ask strangers for our daily bread. The first embroidery shop where we were taken on as workers was located in the Rue Saint-Martin, in the house of a woman who was very religious, but not in the manner of the three Sisters from Normandy, whose religious feelings were so genuine and so untainted by any worldly interest.[22] In the case of my new employer, on the contrary, it was a matter of outward form and self-interested hypocrisy. Miss Marie was a previously unmarried woman about thirty-five years old who had just recently joined her shop, her savings, and herself to Mr. Martin, a long-time clerk, crippled with rheumatism, whose wages were as slight as his person. Bored with an unmarried state that had gone on infinitely too long, these two had joined forces and complemented one another perfectly. I soon came to understand the mirth of the six young girls who constituted the work force in Mrs. Martin's shop. Her devoutness, ridiculous in its attention to details, in combination with the affectations of a new bride, more than justified the jokes of which our overly strict employer was the object.

22. Voilquin refers to the Sisters with whom she spent three years in her childhood. This period is described in a portion of her autobiography not included in these excerpts.

On account of Adrienne, I was pleased to have fallen into the midst of this swarm of mad young women, for indeed, my sister came to life again in their company. Until then, she had suffered more than I from the changes in our lives and from our lowly station. Then too, her passionate and moody character did not incline her toward happiness. This was true to such an extent that the healthy crisis that makes a child into a young woman had a very hard time taking hold and often caused me intense anxiety. That is why I was so happy to see her vital force achieve a better equilibrium and her youth at last blossom out, once the gaiety of that shop's young energy had won her over bit by bit.

Our task was arduous, however. We had to be at our looms at seven o'clock sharp and, even before setting out on the long race to get there on time, we had to carry out all our little household duties as quickly as we could. If certain details made us late, Mrs. Martin would accept no excuses and offer no reprieve. We had to pay in kind, that is to say, make good those few minutes at the end of the day's work. When our days were prolonged in this way, I had a horrible fear of meeting on my return one of those contemptible men who make a game of accosting young working women and frightening them with disgraceful remarks. When this happened, my nerves were always on edge and I lacked all physical courage. It was quite otherwise with my proud and pretty Adrienne. She would say to me, laughing at my timidity, "Dear sister, aren't I here?" (She was barely fifteen.) "If the occasion arises, why then you'll see that *a person's worth is not measured in years!*" And indeed, one evening, she gave me positive proof. Around nine o'clock, we were in the Rue du Temple near Saint Elisabeth's Church. We were stopped by the vulgar words and filthy gestures of some poor wretch. As always, I stood there trembling and unable to speak before this reviler. Adrienne, on the contrary, experienced a moment of sublime energy. She managed to find such a tone of resolve, while brandishing an enormous key before his eyes, that he backed away, and, when we reached the corner of the main street, we were delivered from his insolent remarks.

Mrs. Martin seemed satisfied with our work, and we were accepted as regular employees. And so, at the end of the first week, we were very proud to deposit on our father's mantelpiece the eighteen francs we earned as wages. It was the same each week, for he had made himself the provisioner for our little group.

That cruel year was brought to an end by an accident that nearly caused my sister the loss of her right hand. My father's wail when he thought his child had been maimed for life was heart-rending. He cried! Twenty-two years later, in America, I saw this poor old man cry a second time when, bareheaded, he followed the remains of our dear, departed Adrienne.

Around this time, my father wanted to marry us off. The esteemed Mallard, who has since earned the respect of all Saint-Simonians, was courting my younger sister. Everything about this marriage seemed right and promised happiness for the young couple.

It was not the same for me. The widower whom my father begged me to marry was fairly well established but neither handsome nor pleasant nor witty. Moreover, he came with a son twelve or thirteen years old, a charming Parisian street urchin who had been very badly raised. As a result, my heart, my mind, my senses, my whole being rebelled against the thought of such a match.

My father ardently desired this marriage and never ceased portraying this suitor as the paragon of husbands. "And that way," my father would add, revealing his more self-interested motives, "I won't have to go work for strangers any more. After your marriage, Mr. Bitard will have to put me in charge of his workers. You see, my child, we won't ever have to leave one another." In short, I saw this marriage as an act of filial devotion. I told myself that God would perhaps grant me a child, and I would be saved in my turn! But this sacrifice never actually came to pass. The first banns had already been read at the church when a business discussion between my father and his future son-in-law made me decide that my devotion was pointless and without consequence for my father's happiness. I immediately said *no*, and everything was called off.

I am telling you about this prospective marriage, which very fortunately was never consummated, in order to help you understand the strange resolve that my father adopted as a result of this great disappointment. Cheated in his desire to marry us both off (which would have restored his freedom of action) and above all impelled by his attraction to women (a weakness of character that had troubled both our mother and ourselves), my father, despite his tenderness for us, got the idea of leaving Paris—but not *alone*—to go try his luck once more in the city of Amiens, where he still had a few friends. Before leaving, he set us up in a small room in the Rue Michel-le-Comte and furnished it with our old household belongings, the sorry remnants of the shipwreck of our family. He then set off, leaving me a power of attorney to marry off my sister when I thought best.

This abandonment, which, alas, had the consequence of greatly increasing our poverty and isolation, did not, however, cause me inordinate grief. Hardship had already taught me to count on no one but myself. My sole preoccupation was to protect my sister, that frail and charming creature, from any overly harsh contact with fate.

The quarters we then occupied were located right near our work. That was their only advantage. The house was ugly and had no concierge.[23]

Our only room, on the third story, had a single window that looked out on a narrow and somber courtyard. Just the sight of this house wrung our hearts. When we returned from work in the evening and had to cross that dark alley and, holding hands, climb that foul-smelling stairway to reach our room, we would experience insane terrors. We would feel that there was no protection nearby to guarantee our safety. [. . .]

In this period, we also made the acquaintance of what is most painful in the life of a worker: *unemployment.* It was the end of the reign of Louis the Desired.[24] Everywhere the luxury trades had ground to a halt, for the decorum of the court demanded dreariness. Balls and celebrations were proscribed. No more of those gold- and silver-spangled dresses, nor those delicious whims of fancy which, even as they adorned the privileged beauties, at least provided a livelihood for the working woman. Mrs. Martin's workshop was reduced by three-fourths. Since we were the last hired, we were the first to be let go. That was fair. But the resulting uneasiness that Adrienne experienced again compromised her health. I had to look elsewhere, all over the place, for work. All I was able to find at the exporters' were job lots of embroidery that were very badly paid, but we had to accept them or die of starvation. We rented looms and worked in our room. During those two months, the most we earned in a day was *one* franc for each of us, and that required beginning at six in the morning and keeping at it, often until midnight.

This miserable existence could not have lasted long without exposing us to risk. This forced labor, along with rather insubstantial food, were already exhausting my poor sister, both in her body and her spirit. On this austere regimen, her beauty, so delicate and so pure, began to change. This

23. A concierge was the person, male or female, who lived permanently in most urban residences and apartment buildings, serving as caretaker and supervisor. The concierge might perform a variety of tasks connected to the cleaning, maintenance, or administration of the premises, such as putting out the garbage, doing minor repairs, collecting the rent, and sorting the mail. Perhaps the primary function of this position, however, was to oversee the comings and goings of visitors. For this purpose, the concierge's apartment was typically located in a corridor or courtyard through which everyone who entered had to pass.

24. Voilquin uses one of the popular epithets for Louis XVIII (1755–1824), who became king with the restoration of the Bourbon monarchy in 1814. Because he reigned at a time of considerable austerity for France and was, moreover, a widower, the life of his court was rather subdued, and the trades which catered to the demand for luxury goods suffered accordingly.

dear child had an aversion for real life. Her emotional nature, always elevated to the heights of the ideal, could not accommodate itself to the shabby and prosaic life that we were leading. This instinctive revolt of all her feelings made her reject this daily struggle, honorable beyond all doubt, but full of pain. She was wasting away and yet could not decide to say *yes* to the entreaties of her fiancé. [. . .]

If, by my endearments and by the arguments that my affection inspired me to expound, I managed to tip the balance in favor of this marriage, it was only her happiness and self-respect that I had in mind. If their relationship later ceased to be calm and steady and—at the end of 1832, when Saint-Simonianism was making such a furor—a certain anguish and discord took hold between them, I could only pity them both, for I loved one as much as the other. But that was no reason to regret the past, for I was convinced in my heart of hearts that I could not have done anything better or anything different.

Voilquin goes on to describe her own unhappy marriage and her gradual involvement, beginning in 1830, in a circle of disciples of the visionary socialist theoretician Saint-Simon. Later sections of her autobiography chronicle her travels, first through France and then in Egypt, where she joined the community of Saint-Simonians that had been established there. The text concludes with an account of her return to France and preparations for her 1838 departure on a second great voyage, this time to Russia.

3   Agricol Perdiguier
Memoirs of a Compagnon

Born in 1805, Perdiguier was the first of these authors whose life was situated entirely in the nineteenth century. He was a true child of the Midi, or southern region of France, who, like so many workers of the period, grew up in the countryside. Though his first work experiences consisted of chores on the family farm, his father was also a joiner whose mind was set on having one of his sons follow in his footsteps. If Perdiguier first inherited his trade with some reluctance, he would come in time to be its most eloquent and effective spokesman. His memoirs are above all the story of his Tour of France, the four-year journey he undertook to hone his skills before returning home to his native village.

In the process, Perdiguier also broadened his personal horizons. As a child, he had spoken not French but the distinctive dialect of his region and had received no more than the primary education typical of his circumstances. He possessed, however, a reflective nature as well as a gift for observation. The account he wrote of his travels as a young journeyman, completing his circuit of French towns, remains the most complete and precious contemporary description of workers' brotherhoods as they existed in the first half of the nineteenth century.

This memoir was drafted in 1852, in Perdiguier's middle age, while he was in exile in Antwerp as a result of the coup with which Louis-Napoléon brought to an end the French Second Republic. The story was initially serialized in a Swiss periodical and first published as a book in 1854, a year before the author was able to return to his own country and resettle in Paris. The book was an immediate success and with time became the best known and most widely read example of the genre of workers' autobiography in French literature. Though Perdiguier published other volumes before and after, Memoirs of a Compagnon stands apart for having been reprinted many times since his death in 1875.

MY CHILDHOOD

Morières; My Family

Morières is a small town of 2,000 souls, situated one and a half leagues from Avignon, of which it is a dependency. It has no officials of its own: the mayor of Avignon is its mayor, and the municipal council of that city is its municipal council. This makes for an extremely subordinate and rather odd situation, which can only stand in the way of its intellectual and material progress. This tiny district lies along the road between Avignon and Apt, at the foot of a hill covered with vines and olive trees. This hill is always green and always alive, offering the most beautiful of panoramas. Travelers visiting the Fontaine de Vaucluse pass through this district, but the map-makers seem not to know its name.[1]

That is where I was born on 3 December 1805, the son of Pierre Perdiguier, a joiner, and of Catherine Gounin, a seamstress.[2] I was their seventh child, and two more would follow me, but there were never more than seven of us living at one time—Simon, Madeleine, Elisabeth, François, Agricol, Marie, and Marguerite—three boys and four girls.

Though my family was large, it was not badly off, for my father owned an ample number of fields and vineyards in addition to the saws and planes he used as a joiner. Moreover, he made good use of his children's labor. He wanted to make us hard workers rather than gentlemen and ladies, and in this he did right.

When the Revolution of 1789 broke out, Pierre Perdiguier was in his prime and full of enthusiasm. When the time came, even though he was

1. The Fontaine de Vaucluse, a large natural spring, is the source of the Sorgue River.
2. Perdiguier observes the customary practice of including his mother's maiden name so as to identify both families from which he was descended. He uses the French term *menuisier* to designate the trade that he, like his father before him, practiced. The word is sometimes translated "carpenter." As the description of his training makes clear, however, he is referring to a highly skilled branch of the woodworking trades that encompassed a good deal more than the rough framing and construction of buildings. Joiners did not erect entire wood-framed structures, which were in any event quite rare in France, where stone constitutes the preferred building material. Joiners were instead responsible for much of the detailed finished work—doors and windows, paneling, staircases, cabinetry, and other built-in furniture—that was a common element of nineteenth-century construction, both residential and commercial. The height of the joiner's art was often seen in the pulpits and altars of European churches or the sumptuous woodwork of public buildings. As a seamstress or dressmaker (*couturière*) in so small a town, Perdiguier's mother would likely have undertaken a variety of jobs involving both the making and the mending of clothes.

married and the father of a child, he enlisted in the Avignon volunteers and left to join the army being sent to Italy. He held the rank of captain, which his comrades-in-arms had conferred upon him by election. He defended his country. He would later be reproached for this act of civic duty, so praiseworthy in itself, as if it were a crime: 1815 would see him treated as a thief and outlawed.[3]

My older brother Simon was the godson of my mother's father, Gaspard Gounin, who had special affection for him and wanted him to have a bit of education. This brother therefore learned French and even Latin from the village priest, Mr. Bonnet, a hard, harsh, brutal man who nonetheless succeeded in educating a certain number of students.[4]

The time for Simon's draft lottery came in 1809.[5] He drew a bad number. A dockhand from Avignon who had been luckier offered to trade places with him in exchange for three thousand francs. The offer was accepted and the money changed hands. The dockhand left for the army. But soon afterward it turned out that the supposedly saving number was not good enough, and Simon was obliged to replace his replacement. He went to Spain and then to Portugal, where two years later he was captured and sent to the English prison ships.

Aside from Simon, for whom grandfather had a special attachment, our schooling was completely neglected. My father thought that girls could get along very well without knowing how to read or write; as for the boys, he was hardly any more enlightened. His ideas were no doubt the product of a certain selfishness, but let us just say that the joiner had a big family and

3. After Napoléon's final defeat and exile in 1815, the Bourbon monarchy was restored in the person of Louis XVIII, brother of Louis XVI, who had been executed in 1793. Under the Restoration, those most closely associated with the Bonapartist regime found themselves in disfavor and, in many cases, the object of prosecution and punishment.

4. The reader may be surprised that Perdiguier's brother went to school to learn French, but at the turn of the nineteenth century, many people in rural villages spoke only local dialects (see introduction, page 23). These dialects were sometimes specific to a village community, and its members might experience considerable difficulty in understanding the speech of those who lived even relatively nearby. Particularly in the south of France, French tended to be a language reserved for use in relations with outsiders and especially with the official representatives of the state. Many peasants' command of the language remained imperfect their whole lives long.

5. The draft lottery (*tirage au sort*) was a system of military conscription still in use during much of the nineteenth century. Young men of draft age were obliged to draw a number that determined the order of their induction into the army. If one drew a good number, one was effectively exempt from the draft. If one drew a bad number, all was not necessarily lost. One could sometimes arrange to trade numbers with someone in a more favorable position by paying an agreed-upon sum of money. This person then became one's "replacement" in the army.

was not able to make us all literates and scholars. He had need of our labor and, happily, he knew how to put it to good use.

School; Mr. Madon

Every one of us nonetheless set foot in the village school for a time. The girls were sent by mother, the boys by father. The monthly rate was one franc for children who were learning to read, and one and a half francs for those who were studying both reading and writing! My mother, that good and courageous woman, paid the fees for her daughters with the money she earned (all the while she was managing her considerable household) by making little children's bonnets, a task at which she excelled. My father paid only for his sons.

François, nearly three years older than I, had been going to school for fifteen months when I was sent to sit on those same benches, veritable benches of woe. I experienced genuine anguish. Just the word "school" made me shudder; its sound was ear-splitting and heart-rending.

But my father had spoken: the next day I was to make my entrance at Mr. Madon's. Gripped by fear, I hid as best I could. For several days in succession, at the same early hour, I repeated the same trick. But one morning my father took me by the hand and said, "Come along."

I offered not the least resistance and uttered not a single word, but streams of tears ran from my eyes, pouring down my cheeks. I was devastated. Had I been led to the site of my final agony, my terror could not have been greater. But Mr. Madon made me welcome, patting me on the head and calling me his friend. My tears ceased, and calm and hope filled my heart. I was no longer upset at having been forced against my will to go to school. The next day, I returned all on my own. In fact, I was never absent, and there was no schoolboy more punctual or more hardworking than I. [. . .]

The Two Schoolteachers

Mr. Madon would hit us, and our families were not very happy about it, but there was no choice; he was the only teacher in the village. We either had to take our beatings or remain completely ignorant, and the latter was the greater evil. Fortunately, at about that time Mr. Pinolle, a native of Fontenay-Tressigny near Meaux, moved to our area. He passed for a Parisian, even though he was a true Briard and even though, with time, he ended up mixing more than one Provençal expression into his French.[6] The

---

6. A Briard is a native of Brie, a region just east of Paris, best known abroad for the cheese that is produced there. Provençal is a language spoken in Provence, the

new schoolmaster was a fine man and was very well received. Soon he had many students, my brother and I among them.

Except for beatings, with which Mr. Pinolle was sparing, the two instructors had the same style of teaching. They charged the same fees and assigned the same books. What were those books? First, *The Alphabet*, next the *Spelling Book*, and then the *Roman Book of Hours*, all in Latin. Was the idea to instruct us in the language of Cicero and Virgil? Not at all. But it was thought that only through Latin could we learn French. This rough and zigzag path appeared to our teachers, quite incorrectly no doubt, the most direct, kindest, and surest route.

Next we read *The Duty of a Christian, The Holy Week,* and *The Imitation of Christ,* splendid books, to be sure, that were written in French, and in proper French at that. But we were small children, and all this was far above our heads at that age. One might almost say that after Latin we were given, so to speak, Greek.

If my reflections hold true for those who come from the North, think how much more true they are for those of us who lived in the Midi, for we spoke the local dialect or *patois* not only in the streets and in our houses, but also at school. That was all we knew, all we dared utter, and our schoolmasters did not require anything more. When we read aloud, we could say "sapeau" for *chapeau* [hat], "ceval" for *cheval* [horse], and "zé" for *je* [I]. Our teachers did not correct us for such minor faults. [. . .]

When I had been to school for barely two or three years, I knew how to read, write, and count, though not very well. It was time, however, to start working. [. . .]

My First Jobs as a Country Boy

To make our land productive required manure. This filth, this muck, so despised in cities, is highly prized in the countryside. It is a treasure to which we owe the most precious and beneficial things and those most pleasant to the senses of smell and taste. This I knew, for I had been taught as much from a very early age.

I would wander the streets, the main roads, the places most heavily used by horses, mules, and other animals, carrying a large basket made of unfinished willow under my arm. That which gentlemen and well-dressed ladies fled in disgust, holding their noses, pleasantly caressed my nostrils, attracting me and arousing my cupidity. I would gather it up with a passion. When my basket was full, I would return to the house to drop off my treasure and go off in search of more.

---

southeastern region of France which includes Perdiguier's native department of Vaucluse.

I did not stop at picking up dung in the streets. I would also carry straw to a muddy ditch and let it rot for several days. Then, with my little wheelbarrow, I would cart it to our farmyard. Sometimes, if there were two of us, I would use a sort of handbarrow, called a stretcher. When this was done, I would mix the straw and dung, make it into piles, wet it down, and turn it from time to time. In this way I managed to make excellent manure. When I had a good pile of it, my father would buy it from me and, it should be noted, he paid me a premium price.

Pierre Perdiguier also put his daughters to work, especially the two oldest, Madeleine and Babet [Elisabeth]. François and I, meanwhile, had grown up and were becoming young men. Our father had little pitchforks made for each of us. He told us, "If you work three days a week, on Sunday you will have three sous.[7] If you work six days, you will have six sous. As many days as you work, that's how many sous you will have on the day of rest."

That was a long time ago, and we were very young. I couldn't have been more than seven or eight. We would go tend the vines and till the soil, working incredibly hard to put in a full week. We would brave the rain, the cold, the raging winds. We wanted to earn our six sous for Sunday. When bad weather overwhelmed even our most determined efforts, we would shed tears of despair. In those days, we would spend our money frivolously, but it was ours to spend, for we had fully earned it. How I thank my father for having taught us from an early age the meaning of work, weariness, and the inclemency of the seasons!

After the pitchfork came the spade and another tool that we called the *içade*, and later other agricultural implements. We would till the soil and tend the vines. We would hoe, harvest grapes, reap, disbud, and pick olives. We would climb into the mulberry trees and pick leaves for the silkworms. In short, we did all kinds of farm work. Madeleine and Babet worked alongside us, just like men.

Details Concerning My Family

Soon after his arrival in Spain, my brother Simon, the oldest child in the family, deserted and managed to return to the village. My father refused to take him in or even allow him to visit. My mother and my aunts hid him for a time. But they were assailed by fears, for military law was terrifying. In the end, however, father softened and got involved, and Simon went back to Spain to rejoin his regiment without being subject to punishment. From Spain he went to Portugal, where he was taken prisoner and sent off to an English prison ship. From England he went to North America.

7. A sou was 5 centimes (see chapter 1, n. 10).

He was alive, but soldiers returning from Spain brought back all kinds of news. They told us that they had seen him die, had closed his eyes, had buried him. We therefore thought he was dead.

My last two sisters, Marie and Marguerite, were too young to help us with the work in the fields, and even when they were older, they never got much involved. They learned to weave, to make taffeta, and never worked except on their own account. They lived at home without ever paying a cent. Everything they earned went toward filling out their wardrobes. Fathers often have a real weakness for their youngest children!

You have seen me as a dung gatherer, a digger, a carter, and a plowman, but that's not all. When the weather was good, François and I would work outdoors. This suited us just fine, and we were happy to do it. But when it rained or there was too much frost, and even the hardest-working peasants were forced to stay home and rest, Pierre Perdiguier, that clever man, would have his sons gather in his woodworking shop and set them to work planing planks, hammering nails into the corners of the panels of pine doors and shutters, assembling tongue-and-groove joints and rabbet joints, and fashioning mortises. In short, he made the best use of us he could, and he was right to do so.

As for school, we had long since been able to go only in the evenings, and only winter evenings at that. We could read fairly well, write rather poorly, and do just a little arithmetic. Our sisters were about at our level at best. Simon was the only one who could speak properly—even Latin. He was the scholar in the family, but he took no special pride in the fact. We had about the same level of education as all the other young country boys, neither more nor less.

Before leaving for the army, Simon had worked in joinery. When he returned from America after an eleven-year absence, my father wanted him to take up the trade again. He refused, claiming he would never be more than a very mediocre workman and saying he preferred working in the fields. After failing with Simon, my father next asked François, who also preferred the farm to the workshop. He worked his way down to me, saying, "You have to become a joiner."

"I'd rather be a farmer."

"Simon doesn't want to be a joiner. François doesn't want to be a joiner. I need a joiner, and that's what you're going to be."

"Not me."

"Yes, you."

He was the master, and so I gave in. I was then thirteen or fourteen. My father did not want to see his workshop close. One of his three sons had to carry on and make it shine in the eyes of posterity. That was his way of thinking, his ambition, his unshakable will. Would he get his way? The rest of this story will tell.

So there I was in the shop, working as best I was able. But my master was demanding, hard to please, and not much inclined to helping an apprentice make progress. That was the real reason Simon and François preferred the farm to any trade, though they never said so, and for good reason. My timid refusals had been similarly motivated. [. . .]

1815

We were then approaching a terrible period. Foreign armies had invaded France. Napoléon had been overthrown and Louis XVIII reascended the throne of his ancestors. Tired of the Empire's pointless wars and outraged at the loss of public freedoms, many republicans greeted this first restoration with resignation but not all that much discontent, for it was not in the least bloodthirsty or savage, though it was mean spirited and petty minded. The royalists raised their heads high and taunted the patriots.[8] The latter, even though they had reason to complain about Napoléon, began to wish for his return. They did not have long to wait.

The prisoner from the isle of Elba returned to take power once again.[9] Once again the tricolor flag flew from bell towers and public monuments. My father was overjoyed. With his own hand he attached the glorious standard to the clock tower in our village and joined in the dancing and collective merrymaking and general celebration. [. . .]

Second Restoration; Fall of the Tricolor Flag

My father had rejoiced at the return of Napoléon. As for me, during this brief reign, I had played soldier with a passion, embellishing my shoulders with the golden epaulets of a captain in the imperial army. I sang the glory of heroes and would gladly have gone off to fight for France, though I was not yet ten years old. Did that make me too a criminal and a brigand?

Woe to those who had acclaimed the second reign of Napoléon. We had

8. In the period in question, the term "patriot" referred to partisans of the Empire and therefore opponents of the Bourbon Restoration.
9. After his abdication in April 1814, Napoléon was permitted to retain his title of Emperor and to rule the sovereign principality of Elba, a small island off the coast of Italy. In reality, he lived under a glorified form of house arrest. In February 1815 Napoléon escaped from Elba, landed on the southern coast of France near Cannes, and marched to Paris, gathering a small army as he advanced. His attempt to restore the military hegemony of France during the period known as the "Hundred Days" ended with his defeat at the battle of Waterloo on 22 June 1815, and his second abdication four days later. This time he was banished as a prisoner of war to the island of Saint Helena, where he died in 1821.

hardly learned of the return of the Bourbons before my father made haste to run off and hide. When the royalists came to our house to force him to take down the tricolor flag, which he had placed on the clock tower with his own hands, and replace it with a white one, he was nowhere to be found. God granted us that favor. In his absence, they went to find his brother-in-law, the mason Demorte, who had married his sister Marguerite.

Because our house was next to the clock tower, I could see everything through one of our casement windows. A cord was cut, the flag tumbled down, slicing through the air, and fell heavily to the pavement. The street was thronged with royalists, milling and swarming about. Some men took hold of the tricolor, making a noise, yelling, throwing it on the ground, tearing it in shreds. Raising their heads, they shouted to their confederates to throw down the mason as well. I trembled in fear for my uncle, one of the most peaceful of men and one with no strong political opinions. Had my father been in his place, he would have been sacrificed. [. . .]

MY STAY IN AVIGNON

I Go to Work for Mr. D——

Let us return to the subject of work. I said earlier that I had yielded to my father's will by entering his workshop and training to become a joiner. Let me repeat: my father lacked patience and was too severe. As for me, I was rather sensitive. I did not want to displease him and would rather have plunged a tool into my flesh and given myself a deep gash than spoil the smallest piece of wood. In the end, I succeeded in making proper mortise-and-tenon joints and in using saws, chisels, and both block planes and smooth planes with reasonable skill. I could make casement windows all by myself, and that was no mean feat.

One of my father's friends, Mr. D——, a master joiner in Avignon, came to visit us in Morières on Easter Sunday. This was in 1822, and I was sixteen years and three months old. He took me aside and urged me to come work in his shop. I answered that I was willing if my father would agree. They had a conversation, and my father gave his consent. I was free to do as I pleased. The next day I left Morières for Avignon.

Mr. D—— gave me room and board, nothing more. Certainly not the least word of encouragement. He had me get up every morning, winter and summer alike, before five o'clock and work until eight or nine in the evening. We ate our meals in a few minutes. In the course of the day, whether he was there or not, I used my time as best I was able. On Sunday, I would tidy up the workshop and the attic where scrap wood was kept, and I was rarely free before ten o'clock or noon. I was shy and oversensitive. If I had ever been scolded, it would have brought me to the verge of despair.

I slept on the fourth floor. Mr. D——'s bedroom was on the floor below. He would wake me in the morning by thumping on his ceiling with a sort of pole. He did not even have to get out of bed. One night, he thumped. I got up but I was still tired and sleepy. I looked out the window and saw that they were just closing the pharmacy of M——, our neighbor. I could make no sense of that, but I got dressed and went to work. It was eleven o'clock at night. I therefore had to remain on my feet all night and all the next day. My master was not afraid of making use of my energy, or even of using it up.

Mr. D—— would give me wood to rip and rough-plane. Then he would trace a pattern. I would make mortise-and-tenon joints, and cut grooves, rabbets, and ornamental mouldings. His part was to take the trouble, or rather the pleasure, of assembling. Then I was left with pegging everything together, planing things down, making everything flush, cleaning up the joints, and doing all the finish work. With this division of labor, we made casement windows, doors, the window displays for the front of shops, and other pieces. He often had me make packing crates for Mr. Poncet's silk. This was rough, crude work that was not very pleasant for the worker but highly profitable for the master.

I had been with Mr. D—— for six months and he had never given me a cent to spend on Sunday despite the fact that I was sixteen. I deserved better. I told my father that it was impossible for me to remain under these circumstances, that his friend had never let me trace or assemble anything, that I still did not know the color of his money, and that, in short, I wanted to leave his shop. My father advised me to stay, adding that he would give me ten sous every Sunday. This was not much, but it was enough for me, and I tried to be patient.

Mr. D—— continued not letting me trace or assemble and still gave me nothing on Sunday, so I decided that I would stay with him no longer. I asked my father to please inform my master. He did so and, what's more, even though he and Mr. D—— had no such verbal or written agreement, he told him that if I had not earned my keep, he was ready to make up the difference. Mr. D—— replied that I had earned my keep. I should think so! He might have added that I had made him a certain amount of profit. I left that workshop on Easter Sunday, having worked there one year to the day.

As for the color of Mr. D——'s money, I finally got to see it. I am happy to say that on the first day of 1823, he gave me one and a half francs as a New Year's gift. But that was the extent of all his presents and all his encouragement during twelve very full months, even though, when business was brisk, he would make me work all through the night. That was real stinginess.

Mr. D—— had not treated me like a friend but rather like a selfish master who engages in speculation and who purposely keeps a young man ignorant of his trade in order to be able to exploit him longer. When I entered his shop, I already knew how to handle tools and produce. He had me work at things I already knew how to do and nothing more. If I made any progress in his workshop, it was without his knowledge or instruction and entirely as a natural consequence of constantly practicing the trade. I nonetheless took every conceivable precaution not to anger him in leaving, and my father did the same on his side. All our efforts were in vain. Mr. D—— sulked anyway.

Mr. Poussin's Shop

After leaving Mr. D——, I went to work for Mr. Poussin, another friend of my father's. [. . .]

Mr. Poussin hired me for a daily wage. He fed me, housed me, and paid me ten sous a day besides. That made three francs every Sunday! An enormous sum! What riches, all of a sudden! I was charmed, delighted! This was a fellow without peer! Later I was placed on a piece rate and went to eat at the inn like the workers on the tour.[10]

At Mr. Poussin's, I made casement windows, shutters, doors, and fanlight windows.[11] Two of the latter were placed in a building situated opposite the arcades in the Place Pie, where the shop of Mr. Crémieux, the clothier, is located.

Mr. D—— had never taught me how to trace or assemble, nor given me any training whatsoever, either theoretical or practical. Yet I executed all the jobs I was assigned without experiencing difficulty. I understood with no great effort the designs the master gave me, drawn on ruled paper. I did my work without anyone's help or intervention.

The Compagnonnage System and the Various Brotherhoods

While I was working for Mr. D——, I had been in daily contact with *devoirants,* or Compagnons du Devoir. If I had begun my Tour of France

10. The Tour of France—the main subject of Perdiguier's autobiography—was the journey made by aspiring artisans around a circuit of French towns. According to his estimate of his own travels, the entire tour amounted to some 660 leagues, or 1,600 miles. Its ostensible purpose was to expose the novice craftsman to regional variations in technique and to perfect his skills under the supervision of a variety of mentors. In addition, it served to integrate the new initiate into the community of workers practicing the same trade. Much the same custom existed elsewhere in Europe; in England it was known as tramping, and in Germany as the *Wanderjahre.* At the time of which Perdiguier writes, only a minority of French workers undertook a tour, but the tradition continued to be widely observed in a number of highly skilled trades. By the 1840s, however, the practice had entered a period of decline, and during the second half of the century it became more exceptional.

11. A fanlight (*éventail*) is a window in the form of a half circle, often with sash bars arranged like the ribs of a fan, whence its name.

immediately upon leaving that workshop, I would have become a zealous member of that brotherhood. But Mr. Poussin employed *gavots,* or Compagnons du Devoir de Liberté, and in their company my ideas underwent a change.[12] But, in those first few days, the members and adherents of their brotherhood, with which I was not yet acquainted, were far from friendly toward me.

After all, I had come from a workshop of *devoirants,* so I had to be a candidate or at the very least an *esponton,* or "hopeful," and therefore a rascal whose only desire was for absolute independence and who scorned any form of association. Furthermore, I was young, and could therefore only be a shoddy workman. It was this kind of thinking that led a few of my coworkers to tease me. This was especially true of the three apprentices, two of whom, Louiset and Pinçu, were a few years older than I, and the other of whom was my age. The day I entered the workshop, I made a mallet that I needed and split a few pieces of wood. They praised me sarcastically for my skill. I caught their drift and said not a word. But when I had finished the first four windows that the boss had assigned me, they mellowed and became polite. By the time I had assembled my first four shutters, and they saw how the cross-pieces and slats fitted perfectly against the vertical members even before they had been pegged together, I received unanimous and sincere congratulations. The two who had completed their apprenticeships and who had thought themselves my betters, understood that they had made a mistake and changed their attitude

12. Perdiguier is referring to rival branches of the compagnonnage system. These workers' societies recruited unmarried journeymen and apprentices, most of whom intended to set out on a Tour of France. Each brotherhood operated a number of chapters in major French cities. The inn where the chapter was located was typically run by a couple, referred to as the "father" and "mother." By extension, the chapter itself was called the "Mother" (*mère;* or sometimes *cayenne*). Each brotherhood incorporated a number of trades, but the members of any single trade might be divided among two or more brotherhoods. The rivalries among these brotherhoods gave rise to the bitter and occasionally violent clashes which Perdiguier deplored and struggled actively to overcome. On the history and organization of the French compagnonnage system of the nineteenth century, see Perdiguier's *Livre du Compagnonnage* (Marseille, 1878) as well as Ernest Coornaert, *Les Compagnonnages en France, du moyen âge à nos jours* (Paris, 1966). The best general bibliographic source on the subject of the compagnonnage system is Roger Lecotté, *Essai bibliographique sur les compagnonnages* (Marseille, 1980).

In general, I have left untranslated the term *compagnonnage,* which may refer either to a brotherhood or to the system of brotherhoods. I have done the same with *compagnon* or sometimes rendered it as "fellow," rather than the frequently used "journeyman." Workers who were members of a formally constituted association of artisans-in-training, of the sort that Perdiguier describes, were compagnons; those who were not members of such an association might be journeymen but not compagnons.

toward me completely. They became my friends. I remember with pleasure Louiset d'Orgon, Pinçu de Carpentras, and Ravoust de Barbentane and would be happy to see them all again.

I quickly earned the affection of the entire workshop. All the journeymen were friendly, gentle, kind, and willing to give me help. These *gavots*, whom their adversaries had portrayed in such dark and hideous terms and whose very name was enough to make me shiver, seemed to me to be charming and delightful. They took me walking with them on Sunday and on several occasions invited me to their Mother, where I was always well received. I was pleased to see young men from every part of France living as brothers, helping one another, and offering mutual support. The serenity, honesty, and respect that reigned in that house made a strong impression on me.

At the Mother of the other brotherhood, I had observed more merriment and heard more noise and licentious talk. They were all on familiar terms and kidded one another.[13] But the character of the new community that I now had before my eyes was completely different. They did not use the familiar form of address or make outlandish remarks, and in all their relations there was something wonderful, sublime, and fraternal that I found attractive. I was won over, already halfway toward being a *gavot*.

I Am Hired at Mr. Ponson's

Carcassonne-the-Kindhearted and Provençal-the-Just, both excellent workers and men of honor, advised me, upon leaving Mr. Poussin's, to get myself hired and become a member of the Compagnons du Devoir de Liberté.[14] I was happy to go along with this idea, though I did request that

13. The French text reads, *tout le monde se tutoyait*, meaning "everyone used the familiar form of address." In the period in question, the pronoun *tu* ("you") was a sign of intimacy generally reserved for members of one's family and close personal friends; for everyone else, the more formal *vous* (also "you") was used. In the various workers' brotherhoods, this distinction took on special meaning. As noted in this passage, among the Compagnons du Devoir, all members were addressed as *tu*. Among the Compagnons du Devoir de Liberté, on the contrary, use of this familiar form was banned as a sign of mutual respect, and any member who employed it in the Mother was subject to a small fine.

14. Perdiguier refers to his fellow workers by their *noms de compagnon*, the names they were given within the compagnonnage. The custom of taking such nicknames originated in the days when workers' brotherhoods were clandestine associations which protected trade secrets and the society's rituals from being divulged to nonmembers and tried to control entry to the trade. Among compagnons, most workers went by names that combined a reference to the town or region where they were born with an epithet that evoked some personal trait or quality which their fellow workers associated with their character. Thus, Perdiguier's *nom de compagnon* was *Avignonnais-la-Vertu*, or "Avignonnais-the-Virtuous."

they find me a job in the shop of Mr. Ponson, an old friend of my father's whom I had often heard mentioned and whom I had seen just once in our house in Morières. They spoke on my behalf to Languedoc-the-Gentle, who was then *First Fellow* of the local chapter, who said he could satisfy my request.[15]

When the "roller" or "compagnon on call" received from the head of the brotherhood the order to find me a job, he took me to meet the *bourgeois* in his shop in the Rue d'Amphoux.[16] All three of us gathered, our hats in our hands. Mr. Ponson took five francs from his pocket and placed them in the roller's palm. The roller gave them to me, saying "Here are five francs that the *bourgeois* is giving you as an advance. I hope you will earn them." I replied that I would surely earn that and more, for such is the hiring ceremony. It is identical for full-fledged compagnons and for new initiates, at least in our brotherhood. Once I had been hired, Mr. Ponson, who I thought did not know who I was, addressed me in familiar terms. "Listen, son, you mustn't follow your father's example. Back in those days, he was supposed to accompany me on the Tour of France. He made me wait a week, then ten days, then two weeks, and kept putting if off. Finally, I went off without him, and your father never left the area. You, however, must travel." I told Mr. Ponson that that was precisely my intention. "So much the better," he replied.

At Mr. Ponson's, I made walnut armoires with curved, oblique, raised panels on the doors and hand-carved mouldings. I also made stars, hearts, and other sculpted ornaments on the main cross-pieces, top and bottom. I was being paid a piece rate, so my earnings for this work were modest. Still, I got along. I ate at the Mother and slept there too.

---

15. The First Fellow (*premier compagnon*) was responsible for guiding the internal affairs of the Mother and seeing that all workers were fairly treated. As the title implies, the *premier compagnon* was merely first among equals. The office was elective and turned over once or twice each year.

16. The roller (*le rouleur*) or registrar was charged with many practical responsibilities in the daily operation of the brotherhood. The job was circulated on a frequent, often weekly, basis. The most important of the roller's duties was to arrange for the employment of newly arrived journeymen. This assistance was indispensable to itinerant workers who possessed no knowledge of the local job market. The roller's presence also served as an assurance to the employer that the new recruit would perform with competence and conscientiousness or risk losing face among his peers or even be subject to fines imposed by the brotherhood.

Perdiguier refers to his new master as *le bourgeois*. The term conveyed a respectful acknowledgment of the owner's status and had little if any of the pejorative class connotation it would acquire toward the end of the nineteenth century (see chapter 5, n. 10). It was used in much the same way as a contemporary worker might use the word 'boss' for his or her employer.

My Admission to the Compagnonnage

[. . .] Every brotherhood would hold a general assembly on the first Sunday of every month to assess each member his share of the costs common to all. I had been hired through the brotherhood and now had to be introduced to the company of my assembled colleagues.

The roller had made the rounds of the workshops on Saturday and notified each member of the brotherhood to be present at the Mother the next day. At the agreed time on Sunday, he first had all the compagnons, then the affiliates, go upstairs to the meeting chamber. I was left all alone in the room below. Then the roller came down, took my hand, and led me upstairs, giving a special knock at the door, which immediately opened. He took me into the meeting room, where I was surrounded by a circle of men, standing calm, silent, and neatly dressed, their outfits decorated with blue and white ribbons. I was dazzled, astonished, and perplexed. He had me cross the length of the room to meet the First Fellow, who was presiding, telling him, "Here is a young man who asks to become part of the brotherhood." The First Fellow asked me, "Do you wish to become a member of the brotherhood?"

"Yes."

"Do you know which brotherhood this is?"

"It's the Society of Compagnons."

"That's true, but there are several brotherhoods: there's the Compagnons du Devoir, or *devoirants;* then there's the Compagnons du Devoir de Liberté, or *gavots.* Which of the two do you wish to affiliate with?"

"The Compagnons du Devoir de Liberté."

"They're both good, and if you've come to the wrong place, you're free to withdraw."

"It's definitely this one I want to join."

When he had finished reading me the regulations, the First Fellow asked me, "Can you abide by these rules?"

"Yes," I answered. He added that if I did not feel capable of observing them, I was free to leave.

I approved of what I had just heard and I promised to comply. The First Fellow proclaimed me an *affiliate.*[17] The roller led me to the place reserved for me. Since I was the newest member of the brotherhood, I was lowest in rank.

17. The rank of affiliate (*affilié*) was a preliminary or probationary status within the brotherhood, bestowed upon candidates for full membership. Perdiguier later describes how he became first a "recognized fellow" (*compagnon reçu*), then a "finished fellow" (*compagnon fini*), before himself being elected to a position of responsibility by his fellow members and being accepted into the third order in the hierarchy as an "initiated fellow" (*compagnon initié*).

Next we took care of association business. Everyone paid his dues. The common expenses were shared equally. [. . .]

Preliminaries to the Tour of France

I was now an affiliate. I attended all meetings and paid my dues promptly. Everything I had seen, except for the hatred and violence, pleased me. After a while, I was ready to undertake my Tour of France. My father was not opposed to the idea, but he had agreed to make a portable walnut baldachin for the church in Morières and wanted to put me in charge of its execution.[18] My trip would have to wait until it was finished.

I made this baldachin all by myself. It had four fluted columns and four ornamental brackets sculpted with acanthus leaves, and the whole thing was crowned with the figure of an egret that had been textured with an engraver's tool. It also had a small cornice and a very simple pedestal. I served as both joiner and sculptor on this project, and in the village I was thought to have created a masterpiece. That baldachin is not terribly valuable. It can claim distinction neither as an object of art nor as a demonstration of skill, but I was only eighteen when I created it. It was not bad for that age. It still exists, for I saw it in 1850. It is in perfect condition, and the inhabitants of Morières value it highly. They never look at it without thinking of young Agricol, who is not so young now and who lives in exile.[19]

MY TOUR OF FRANCE

Journey from Avignon to Marseille

The moment of my departure was approaching. In those days, compagnons often fought among themselves, and leaving to do one's Tour of France was almost like leaving for war. For that reason, my mother experienced a certain anxiety and advised me to make my confession before beginning so perilous an expedition.

Until then, all I had ever worn was a plain jacket. My father had a coat made for me, and a few shirts and some other clothes, and he bought me a trunk to hold them all. He gave me thirty francs, in six five-franc pieces, the largest sum that I had ever possessed. On the third day of Easter, [Tuesday,] 20 April 1824, having sent my trunk ahead by carriage and carrying a small bundle hung from a stick on my shoulder, I left Avignon on foot with a friend named Jargea. He was nicknamed Vivarais-the-Palm-

18. A baldachin is a solid canopy of the sort that might be built over an altar or throne or, as in this case, cover a statue or relic to be carried in a church procession.
19. Perdiguier's autobiography was written while he was living in exile after Louis-Napoléon's coup d'état of 1851.

of-Glory and, like me, was going to Marseille. The other compagnons saw us on our way with songs, as was the custom.[20] Then, fraternal embraces were exchanged, and they left us to continue our journey alone. As we made our way forward, I looked behind me for one more glimpse of the town I had just left. [. . .]

At Saint-Andiol we entered an inn to drink a glass of wine and have a bite to eat. A gendarme followed us in and asked for our passports.[21] When he saw that we were joiners, he sat down beside us and offered to serve as roller by finding us jobs, for there was a shortage of workers in that region. We could not accept his offer, as we were in a hurry to reach Marseille, but the gendarme had been kind to us, and we returned the favor by offering him a drink. We clinked glasses, and then went on our way, as delighted with him as he with us.

We made our way under a brilliant sky. Soon we ran across four compagnon coopers carrying the sort of large axe that is called an adze. We were somewhat afraid of being "hailed."[22] Fortunately, these men were extremely tired and contented themselves with passing alongside us and giving us dirty looks. This was a mild display of ill will, and worse things could happen. More than once, coopers have been known to use their adzes in fights to lop off their adversaries' arms and shoulders. We knew this, and it would not have been very pleasant to find ourselves disabled at so young an age and at the start of our first campaign.

As we passed through the town of Orgon, we came to an inn whose sign read "Mother of the Compagnons du Devoir." We belonged to the Compagnons du Devoir de Liberté, so we quickly walked on by.

As we arrived in Sénas, the good weather turned stormy, and huge drops of rain began to fall. We entered an inn to have supper and spend the night. The rain lasted five or six hours, so the road was sure to be in poor condition. We decided to take the coach when it passed through rather than continue on foot. We were up at midnight, listening for the arrival of the

20. Perdiguier uses the expression *faire la conduite*. This refers to the ceremony of departure or escort, which he describes in more detail later (see also chapter 1, n. 12).
21. A gendarme—literally, a "man of arms"—was technically not a civilian policeman but a member of the armed forces with responsibility for keeping the peace in the countryside. Throughout most of the nineteenth century, passports were required for travel within France (see chapter 1, n. 3).
22. There is no precise English equivalent for the French verb *toper*. It refers to the practice, among traveling compagnons of certain brotherhoods, of sounding a signal (occasionally a whistle or a noise, but generally the single word, "Tope!") whenever other journeymen were encountered. The hail might lead to fraternal embraces if the signal was returned in kind, or to a violent brawl if not. Perdiguier's brotherhood did not practice this custom, and its members were forbidden to respond to the hails of others.

coach from Avignon. When it stopped, we learned there was room for us. We climbed aboard and made good time. [. . .]

My Employers in Marseille

My friend Vivarais-the-Palm-of-Glory found himself a regular job, and I was placed temporarily in the shop of a master joiner barely twenty-two years old who was called by his first name, Michael. Mr. Michael's work-shop, opposite the port, had no wood, no tools, and none of the essentials that a journeyman requires to work.[23] If Mr. Michael was lacking in materials, he was even worse off when it came to skill. He paid me by the day. The two of us made a very long bread-kneading trough in the shape of a hopper. We had to cut some planks lengthwise, using a two-man hand-saw. This saw had an extremely thick lead blade. It would not cut. It refused to bite, to penetrate the wood, and no amount of effort could make it sharp. Mr. Michael and I would stand facing one another, holding the four ends of the saw's two arms in our hands. We would make strenuous efforts, but try as we might to draw that saw back and forth and get into a rhythm, it simply refused to budge. Mr. Michael would grip it con-vulsively in his sinewy hands, would lie on it, hit it, twist it, dripping with sweat all the while (and me sweating just as heavily). It was all a waste of time and effort, and our work was of poor quality. I would say to my employer, "*Bourgeois,* instead of mistreating your saw and making it suffer, you have to take care of it, sharpen it, and make it cut. Then it'll work without effort." Mr. Michael would not hear of it. He claimed that time spent putting a tool in condition, making it cut, was really time wasted. He was, like other workers I have known, very miserly with that kind of time. A curious theory! On the basis of that glorious principle, so injurious to his own self-interest, he condemned me to spend the most awful day.

The next day, I did not have the heart to go back to Mr. Michael's, though he was in other ways a worthy man. Later, he did not refuse to pay me, as soon as I asked, my one and only day's wages. Mr. Michael was young. He may since have become a skillful worker, a knowledgeable joiner. The years bring many changes and sometimes much progress.

My next job was also strictly temporary, and so I did not have to pay the expenses associated with a regular hiring. It was in the shop of another

23. The expectation in most joiners' shops was that the master would supply at least the larger, more expensive tools that itinerant workers would have found difficult to carry with them. This arrangement was common in trades where many different implements might be required for the wide range of jobs undertaken; however, as Perdiguier's mention of the coopers' adzes makes clear, there was considerable variation among occupations.

owner, whose name escapes me. My coworker was a compagnon from the town of La Voulte, whose name was Maurice Abraham and who was called Vivarais-the-Triumph-of-Love. We worked on setting up a cobbler's shop. The counters and cupboards were already in place. Our job was to cap the rest with an ornamental cornice. The owner, who had not provided designs—and you'll see why—came to me and said, "Do you know how to draft?"

"Yes, boss, a little."

"Are you familiar with any of the fashionable styles of cornices?"

"What kind of fashion do you mean?"

"Design me some kind of a fashionable cornice."

I did so, and right away the owner said, "That's it. That's it exactly. Now make it." So I made the cornice just as I had designed it.

After this experience, I did not think it necessary to ask how the capitals and the bases of pilasters should be executed. I drew two small cross-sections on a plank, took some wood, and worked it. All that remained was to carve the moulding. Then the owner arrived and saw what I was doing. So what did he do? He took the piece I had prepared as a base, picked up a pencil, and began copying, though not very well, the cross-section I had just completed onto one of its ends. He had my drawing lying right in front of him, but he only glanced at it on the sly, so that I would not think he was copying me. Then he showed me the product of his genius, saying "Here. That's about what I want for the base."

"Very well, *bourgeois*!" I replied. He did the same thing with the capital. You can see that this gentleman was extremely inventive. On other occasions, to give us even clearer proofs of his abilities, he would use the tip of his finger to show us an imperceptible hollow in something we were working on, saying, "There's a chip there." Or else he would take a door or some other piece of assembled work and look it over, winking as he told us, "It's at least two hairsbreadths out of line." He would rack his brains to find some trifle that any other master would have paid no attention to, yet he would not notice genuine defects. The more he sought to hide his stupidity, the more he made it stand out. Such men can never learn or acquire genuine skill. They refuse to lower themselves to the role of student, pupil, or disciple, for it makes them blush. They like to give the semblance of knowledge but can never succeed. They remain ignorant for fear of appearing so. To make you think that they know everything, they never learn anything. Their conduct is silly, stupid, and fools no one. Woe to anyone who would follow this ridiculous example! As soon as my coworker and I had finished the cobbler's shop, we left this *bourgeois*, who combined conceit with ignorance.

I was hired by Mr. Riboulet, who lived in the Allée de Meilhan, on the right side opposite the fountain. Instead of the two francs fifty centimes a day that I had been earning from my previous employers, I was paid two francs seventy-five centimes and improved my skills in the bargain. I was delighted with such a handsome salary and did not fail to mention it in my letters to my father and tell him how happy it made me.

Mr. Riboulet did not resemble my first employers in Marseille in any way. He was proficient in both architecture and drafting, knew how to cut wood to perfection, and was a real joiner. When I entered his workshop, he was making a church pulpit and he had me work on it with him. This man combined talent with simplicity. To obtain the most perfect shapes possible, he would often produce several different designs for the same object and then show them to his workers, asking their opinions. Though I was the youngest, he would not fail to consult me and he placed a certain value on my judgment. He clarified his thoughts through our remarks, then reflected on his own, and arrived at his choice.

Still, this honest man and excellent joiner was not always in his right mind. He was a bit dotty. He would sometimes tell us the most extraordinary things. One day, after a flood of other remarks, he said: "Oh, but I have so many jealous and envious souls who are my enemies."

To this I answered, "Then you will be victor over them all."

And he responded with great energy, "My name is Victor: Victor Victorious!" After that, he began telling me stories of all the victories he had won, among them the following: "One day," he said, "I had walked and walked aimlessly, without any destination in mind. All of a sudden, I looked around. Without suspecting or realizing it, I'd reached the summit of a high mountain. Now that was a victory. And how many such victories I have won!"

When Mr. Riboulet spoke, we had to listen attentively, not make a sound, not move. But after a long narration, he would notice that the time had flown and that no work was getting done. Then he would change his mind, look at his two apprentices, and cry out, almost in despair, "Oh, my Lord! Marius! Joseph! We have got nothing done all this week! Let's hurry, let's hurry." And then he would work with all his strength, his apprentices trying to imitate him, and the workers, understanding that if he had not uttered their names it was only out of politeness, would follow suit. There was complete silence. No one would open his mouth for the rest of the day, especially if the owner stayed around. [. . .]

Mr. Portalès and My Classes in Geometrical Drafting

Mr. Portalès, my landlord in Marseille, was a joiner who had done the Tour of France as well as the Tour of Italy, had lived in Rome, and was very learned in architecture. Nothing could match the perfection of his tinted drawings, his shading, his Corinthian and composite capitals. That is why the compagnons had nicknamed him Languedoc-the-Capital. He had written a song about the five orders of architecture that was mediocre as a piece of poetry but fascinating for its technical details.

Those who shared a bed in a dormitory-style room paid Mr. Portalès five francs per month if they did not take his drafting classes, and six francs if they did. A month of drafting lessons therefore cost just one franc, next to nothing. But it has to be mentioned that Mr. Portalès was getting old, and his enthusiasm for teaching was disappearing. Despite his skill and the beautiful shapes he could create, he did not have a room in which to assemble his pupils, so the students did not get demonstrations. The teacher merely loaned out his drawings, which were supposed to serve as models, and everyone learned from them what he could. Like the other youths, I would do my drafting in the darkened room where the four of us slept, two to a bed, using the bed as my drafting table. [. . .]

In Avignon, the worker's day lasted from five in the morning to eight at night. We went off to eat as soon as it was over. We were in class before nine o'clock and drew until eleven. In Marseille, the Compagnons du Devoir worked until eight o'clock, but the Compagnons du Devoir de Liberté only until seven. I do not know if this difference between the two brotherhoods still exists, but because of it we had a little more time to draw than in Avignon.

In Avignon, after leaving Mr. D——, I had worked for nine months for Mr. Poussin, then three months for Mr. Ponson. During this period, I had lived the life of a compagnon, eating at the Mother, at that time located in the Rue Bonneterie. In Marseille I continued the same lifestyle. I ate three meals a day—breakfast, lunch, and supper—at nine in the morning, at two in the afternoon, and in the evening at the end of my day's work. The other towns were no different in this regard. In Marseille, because fish was inexpensive, we could feast on it. I saw mackerel sold in the streets at six sous a pound, and then go as low as two sous, and then lower still. The catch had been so abundant that it was spoiling, and they were forced to throw out large quantities. In the fish store, you saw a lot of large fish, especially tuna. The riches of the sea had overflowed onto the land. [. . .]

I Decide to Leave Marseille

[. . .] In order to judge things in perspective, we need to have seen a great deal. We need some terms of comparison, and at that time I had none. Thus, I more than once permitted myself to say that Marseille was just a hick town. I thought better of it later.

But there was a good reason why an inner voice stirred within me, telling me, "Move on." For someone from Avignon, Marseille was a sort of dead end. In order to continue my Tour of France, I would have to retrace my steps to a point very close to Avignon. "If I stay here much longer," I told myself, "will I then be able to pass so close to my native district without being tempted to go and pay it my respects? And if I go back there, will I have the courage to tell it good-bye a second time? Now, that's a very complicated and involved question. Come, come! Rather than trust my own willpower and abandon myself to temptation, let me be on my way." And that is how I decided to depart.

I went to notify Mr. Riboulet of my decision. He was very distressed because he wanted to keep me, but I explained my reasons and he understood. [. . .]

My Stay in Nîmes

We arrived in Nîmes and went straight to the Mother. The First Fellow and the roller welcomed us. We handed them the letters of recommendation that we were carrying from the First Fellow of Marseille. They brought out the bottles of wine that the brotherhood owed us as new arrivals, and we clinked glasses. They found us jobs, and we went to work.

Mr. Journet

The name of my *bourgeois* was Mr. Journet. He had me make some walnut chests of drawers with columns, stained the color of logwood and polished with wax. I was being paid a piece rate.

Like the other workers, I was fed at the master's table. We paid him a fixed sum for our daily subsistence that he deducted from our wages. Mr. Journet acted the role of family patriarch. He would serve us all the food, except that we could help ourselves to bread. By by some curious coincidence, our host almost always sat with his elbow on the bread. And even though we might still be hungry, we would not dare say, "Boss, move your arm." So our stomachs were the dupes and victims of our timidity. Why was that elbow positioned in that way? Was it a conscious calculation on the part of our employer? I don't know. I'll leave it up to you. [. . .]

Saint Anne's Feast Day; Compagnonnage and Combat

In Nîmes I took part in the feast day of Saint Anne. In the morning, we went to mass. We then held an election for the new head of the chapter, an office that rotated every six months. In the evening the banquet took place. There is nothing as beautiful, as sweet, as fraternal as these compagnons' celebrations! We would sing in chorus and join together in friendship and enthusiasm. We developed the capacity for mutual sacrifice, to the point of being ready to die for each other. But unfortunately, certain ominous shadows darkened this picture. Groundless, pointless struggles continued between one brotherhood and another. The regions of the Midi have witnessed veritable wars among workers. [. . .]

In each brotherhood, members learned how to handle a walking staff and quarterstaff, and how to subdue a man quickly. The strongest, the most terrifying, the most daring were also the most famous and beloved of compagnons. To kill your peer, as long as he was not a member of your own little brotherhood, was not a crime but an act of courage. The Tour of France was completely belligerent. Compagnons were warriors, and their brotherhoods were enemy armies, rival nations that dreamed only of crushing one another.

Despite the efforts of policemen, gendarmes, soldiers, judges, prisons, and the most rigorous penalties, the warlike spirit did not weaken in the least. Each brotherhood revered its heroes and martyrs and cursed those of their opponents. That frame of mind stood in the way of the training and education of the young and of the entire working class. Moreover, it embraced no political or philosophical ideas, no historical, literary, or moral learning. Unless he commanded great respect by force of character, the worker who read books was an object of derision. Our song writers sang of war, inflamed our pride, our sense of superiority, our prejudices and our biases. According to them, we were gods, while our adversaries were thieves and idiots, stupid and wicked animals, so unworthy of living that we had to exterminate them. [. . .]

Journey from Nîmes to Montpellier

I had stayed in Marseille less than two months. After barely six weeks in Nîmes, I wanted to move on. I still felt that I was too close to Avignon and was afraid of being tempted to return there before it was time. Marius, one of my friends from Marseille, insisted he would not part company with me. [. . .]

So on the night of 30 July 1824, we found ourselves on the top deck of a coach, a seating arrangement that corresponded to the lightness of our purses, leaving what is perhaps the most remarkable city in all of France, with its ancient ruins and its old monuments. [. . .]

My Stay in Montpellier

[. . .] We had arrived in Montpellier without a cent, but thanks to the brotherhood, to the compagnonnage, we found work as well as credit at the Mother for both our room and our board.

My friend Marseillais and I kept one account for the two of us. Our expenses were mixed and mingled, for we were like two brothers. At the end of the first two weeks, our *bourgeois* paid us in full. We each went to see Mrs. Palas with our money. "How much do we owe you, mother?" She added it up and told us to the penny. "Fine!" we said, and we paid up.

Ah! We no longer owed a cent. We were square with everyone and still had . . . what? . . . how much? Can you guess? Twenty francs in four large coins. What riches, what good fortune! How happy we were!

I took this quantity of coins in my hands and flung them against the wall. They clanged, fell, and rolled across the flagstone floor. Marseillais picked them up and took his turn flinging them with all his strength. We were playing ball with our little shiny coins, acting crazy, laughing, rejoicing in our riches, which were no mere trifle! Four five-franc coins for the two of us! Our game amused the other compagnons, and the mother, who was not much given to laughter, burst forth heartily.

The Dialect of the Midi

While I am speaking of the mother, that good woman Mrs. Palas, I should point out that she always spoke to us in the dialect of Montpellier, which gave us cause for much laughter. Why? I'll tell you. My friend was from Marseille and I was from Avignon, while the mother was from Montpellier. Her accent was not the same as my friend's or my own. What is more, she used words that were not part of the dialects of Bouches-du-Rhône or Vaucluse. That's why we were always breaking up with laughter. "She certainly speaks badly," we would tell each other. And Marseillais would think to himself that there was nothing to rival the dialect of Marseille, while I would whisper to myself that the Avignon dialect was the king of all *patois*.

That is how we reasoned, all the rest of us dialect speakers, especially when we had just left our village and were still quite green. At that stage, we are merciless: we mock and jeer any aspect of language that is different from our own. The dialect of our own locality is presumed to be the standard by which to judge every dialect in creation, and any that are different must obviously be terribly provincial.

This prejudice, of which Marseillais and I had such a healthy dose, is common to Gascony, Languedoc, Provence, Béarn, Périgord, and Limousin. The cities, towns, villages, and hamlets in the same canton all say the same things about each other. Two villages will ridicule and banter with one another on account of their accents, or a few words, or nothing at all. When I had traveled more, I corrected my error, my injustice. I understood that I was just a fool, and that the dialect of Montpellier, which I had been stupid enough to laugh at, is one of the prettiest in France.

Mr. Pradoura; Drafting; I Become a Recognized Fellow

After finishing the library that Dauphiné-the-Rampant had assigned me to do, I was hired by his compatriot and friend, Mr. Pradoura, with whom he would go each morning to drink a glass of white wine.[24] We called him Weak Chin. He was a kind old man, for whom I had genuine affection. Mr. Pradoura fed me, housed me in a garret built at the rear of the workshop, and gave me eighteen sous a day. The lovely Ursula was a servant in the household. Is she still alive? Is she happy? Does she know what became of Avignonnais-the-Virtuous? I loved her like a sister, but that was twenty-seven years ago. [. . .]

The good Mr. Pradoura introduced me to the completely novel idea of becoming a recognized fellow. It seemed to me that I was still too unskilled in my trade to receive so high an honor. One evening at the Mother, Clermont-the-Resolute, who was First Fellow or dignitary, also whispered a few words in my ear.[25] He led me to understand that it was entirely up to me if I wanted, like him, to carry a ceremonial walking staff, wear the colors, and bear a new name.[26] I was shy and did not expect enough of myself, and so some kind of initiative had to be taken to get me to pluck up my courage and rise within the hierarchy of the compagnonnage.

Joseph Buyé, one of the friends I had worked with in Mr. Ponson's, where he had been an apprentice, had soon afterward followed me to Marseille and then to Nîmes. At length, he came and joined me in Montpellier, where we became inseparable. Marius was our mutual friend, and we had a number of other good friends, among them Ferdinand Eméric from Cucuron.

All Saints' Day, which the Montpellier brotherhood still celebrated at that time, was approaching. Urged on by predictions delivered with such assurance, we dared to speak up and were made recognized fellows. Buyé took the name Avignonnais-the-Prudent, Marius was Marseillais-the-Well-behaved, Eméric became Provençal-the-Faithful-hearted, and Per-

---

24. Perdiguier actually refers to a *chopinette* or quarter liter of white wine. Had their rendezvous not taken place in the morning, they would probably have ordered the more common portion, *la chopine* or half-liter of wine, served in a tall mug or carafe.

25. "Dignitary" is the additional title that was bestowed upon a First Fellow who had also achieved the status of initiated fellow (see n. 15 above). Perdiguier employs these terms (along with "president" and "captain") somewhat interchangeably.

26. Perdiguier refers to three of the outward signs of full membership in a workers' brotherhood: the hefty walking stick that had both practical and symbolic value for the itinerant worker; the colored scarves that signified the precise branch of one's trade as well as one's specific brotherhood; and a *nom de compagnon* for use among one's fellow members.

diguier was renamed Avignonnais-the-Virtuous. So there we were, the proud owners of walking sticks, blue and white ribbons that we were to attach to our buttonholes at general assemblies and on important ceremonial occasions, and new names that were quite pleasant and very flattering, though difficult to live up to. But my friends, with whom I have not lost touch, have always proved themselves worthy of them. [. . .]

Misadventure

One Saturday evening, there were twelve of us at the Mother. It was hot, but according to the rules of the brotherhood, we had to remain dressed in our ties and jackets. Beauceron-the-Virtuous, the most senior of us compagnons, said, "Shall we take off our jackets and get comfortable? If someone comes along and we have to pay a fine, then we'll pay it, but we'll surely drink our share."[27] His proposition was greeted with cheers, and we removed our jackets and ties.

The First Fellow entered, counted us up without saying a word, and then shouted out, "Mother! Bring twelve bottles of wine!" The bottles came. It was decided that we would drink them strictly according to the rules, observing all the formalities, with each person reciting certain words that must be pronounced without stammering or getting so much as one syllable wrong. Just then Mr. Bedos, Mr. Ducros, and others of Montpellier's most lively and high-spirited residents arrived. They had completed their Tour of France not long before and from time to time honored us with their visits. They also profited from this unexpected windfall. So we drank according to regulation, toasting the fine and all those who had to pay it. The dignitary was the very first to make a mistake by getting the toast wrong. That meant he was at fault and had to pay a fine himself! "Mother," a voice cried out, "bring two bottles of wine to be charged to the First Fellow." Two bottles were served, for when the First Fellow violates the regulations, he always pays double; that is the law. We all had a wonderful time. [. . .]

The Use of the Term Pays in the Brotherhood

Among themselves, compagnons do not call each other "mister" but "brother."[28] Whether you are a German, Spaniard, Turk, Italian, Russian,

27. Minor infractions of the brotherhood's regulations—such as using foul language, being tardy, or violating the dress code in the Mother—were subject to a fine. One form a fine might take was being required to buy a bottle or a round of drinks for those present.
28. The French term is *pays*, signifying someone who comes from the same region, much in the sense that we might say "fellow countryman."

Englishman, Kalmuck, American, Asian, African, or Frenchman, it's all the same. You are all *brothers*. The compagnon is a cosmopolitan. For him there is but one sky, one earth, one world, and just one native land. That is why, wherever he goes, he always remains in his native land and why all other compagnons are his *brothers* or *fellow countrymen*. Wherever you were born; whether your face is white, black, yellow, red, or brown; whether your prophet or god is Moses, Manu, Mohammed, or Jesus— none of this matters. You are a compatriot, a fellow countryman, a brother. I have seen Spaniards, Germans, Americans, Belgians, Swiss, Italians, Savoyards, and Moroccans win elections over Frenchmen and become First Fellows, captains, or dignitaries in our brotherhood. Now there is something beautiful, something that always delighted my soul!

But the battles between one brotherhood and another corrupted this beautiful harmony, mingling something base and hideous with that which was noble and grand. It cast a somber, dark, appalling shadow over this picture that no one seemed to be aware of at that time, except perhaps myself.

My First Act of Resistance; A Compagnon Who Became a Doctor

My opposition to what I saw as injustice began to manifest itself in Montpellier. When one of our brothers is in the hospital, a list is drawn up on which the names of all the members of the brotherhood are written down in order of their rank and seniority. Each must go and pay a visit in turn, taking whatever object or comfort the patient needs, reporting on his condition to the First Fellow, and finally passing the list to the next person after stating what new requests he might have made.

I was given such a list. I looked it over and said to myself, "Mine is the twentieth name on this list. The patient has been in the hospital for just twelve days. It can't be my turn yet. Eight compagnons have neglected to do their duty, and I disapprove of that. I'll explain to the First Fellow why I refuse to accept the list today and don't expect to get it back for eight days." I, a mere recognized fellow, thus presumed to oppose the finished fellows. This was serious.

The head of the brotherhood replied that another compagnon had previously fallen ill, and that eight of the more senior compagnons had visited him. This other patient was due to leave the hospital the next day, so rather than start over, the list was being taken up at the point where we had left off. This explanation seemed quite fair.

The first names on the list are generally those of finished fellows, who, it is true, often end up doing double duty. But in this case we were speaking of a matter that was six months old. Since that time, a lot of turnover had occurred within the brotherhood, with some compagnons leaving and others arriving, for that is the life of a journeyman. The first eight names on the new list were for the most part quite new in town. For that reason, they could not have visited the previous patient and therefore had a duty to fulfill. Once again I refused the list and waited for the general assembly to give my explanation. My reasoning was the following: "Let the leaders set a good example, and I'll be happy to follow in their footsteps."

They sensed that I was in the right and everyone did his duty. I visited the patient in my turn, just as the regulations require. I also visited him out of turn, of my own free will. My opposition did not make me any enemies.

I remember a recognized fellow from Rouergue whose nickname was "the Wise" and who had long been working in the Montpellier hospital making coffins, doors, and windows, and doing repairs. In his free time, he would study anatomy, medications, the nature of illness and of the ill. He ended up getting a diploma as a health officer: the joiner had transformed himself into a doctor.

For a compagnon to become a doctor and thus cross the barrier that separates joinery from medicine—now that was something novel! It was Rouergue's destiny to realize such an achievement and prove once again that nothing is as strong as the human will, and that, more often than not, where there's a will, there's a way. [. . .]

Journey from Montpellier to Béziers

I had been in Montpellier for nearly seven months. I was still working for good old Mr. Pradoura. I resolved to be on my way, and I set a date for my departure. A young man from the village of Lansargue came to tell me he wanted to leave with me, and on Shrove Sunday, 13 February 1825, we set out. The compagnons saw us on our way and we bid them farewell. [. . .]

My Stay in Béziers

We arrived at Béziers just as night fell. The welcome we received from the local father, mother, and sisters could not have been better. Some of my close friends had preceded me; others were soon to follow.

I was hired at Mr. Garadot's, where I was paid a piece rate. Like all the other compagnons, I was fed and housed at the Mother for twenty-two sous a day. We would all eat together. Mr. Durand, seated at the head of the table, served us each in turn. This father of compagnons behaved just like the father of a real family, and we were all his children. Everyone helped himself to bread and wine.

Wine and Drinkers; Our Entertainment and Songs

I have noticed something. I have seen workers who often got drunk and others who never did. It all depended on the region where they were born and on habits they had acquired at a very early age. Which ones got drunk most often? Was it the men from Provence or Languedoc? No, it was those from Brittany and Belgium. And why? Here is the reason: if there is a lot of wine in a region and if it is very cheap, then people consume it, but that is all they do. But if it is rare and dear, the opposite happens. They go back and forth from privation to abuse, from abuse to privation, in a never-ending cycle and end up doing themselves harm. I will return to this question later.

On Sundays, we would go out to play a game of *boules* or *roulette*.[29] We would sometimes go drink white wine in the Bagatelle district or some such place. On these occasions, we would join in songs of the compagnonnage or sometimes songs of war. The emperor was in the back of our minds. For my part, I was a Bonapartist. [. . .]

I was a Bonapartist and at the same time I was a republican. To me there was no difference between Napoléon and liberty, and all my friends reasoned in the same way. We were familiar with the glory of the great man and had no idea how he had perverted liberty and the principles of justice and humanity. We were unaware of how he had slighted the dignity, the fortunes, and the very lives of the men whom he proscribed, whom he crushed, whom he pulverized as if they were no more than vile insects. Our compagnonnage songs were also songs of war. We celebrated might, always might. Might had taken the place of right and virtue. Might was the god that we had learned to revere, in which we believed, and this lay at the origin of the struggles and bloody battles among workers. [. . .]

Mr. Garadot and the Bit of Candle; the Squaring of Accounts

I mentioned that when I arrived in Béziers, I was hired at Mr. Garadot's. He was a tall, thin man who was extremely miserly. [. . .]

Our working day—as in Avignon, Nîmes, Montpellier, and nearly everywhere else—began at five in the morning and ended at eight at night. At nine o'clock, we took one hour for breakfast; at two, one hour for lunch; and we ate supper at the end of our day. Thus, we had to put in a full thirteen hours of work each day and consequently had precious little free time. It was a hard life!

Mr. Garadot had me making wide, deep windows out of hawthorn, a wood that is fibrous, tough, and difficult to cut. This was unpleasant work. As a result, despite all my efforts, I was earning very little money. It was

29. Both these games are played with heavy balls about four inches in diameter and rules not unlike those of the game of horseshoes: each team tries to place its throws closest to a small target ball.

the end of February. One morning at five o'clock, I was making tenons.[30] But my wood was of poor quality, stubborn, obstinate, contrary, hopeless. Once my saw had penetrated a few inches into this wood, it would bind in such a way that I could not get it to move any further. But I did not have the least scrap of pork rind or fat with which to grease it, and the boss was still in bed! What was I to do? Leave? Waste my time? No. I cut a tiny end off the tallow candle that was providing me with light. The saw accepted this bit of nourishment and showed its gratitude. My work progressed.

Soon it was nine o'clock, and we went to breakfast. While we were gone, Mr. Garadot visited his shop and inspected our work. And what did he see? What he saw, dear Lord, was hardly to be believed! He saw the end of a candlestick on my workbench. Was he ever furious! He shouted, he raged, he threatened. Ruining his candle! Wasting his tallow! That was unpardonable! He would fire the rascal who was trying to bankrupt him in this way. Lansargue was present and saw and heard everything. He hurried off to let me know.

When my breakfast was finished, I returned to the workshop. I resumed my work, waiting for the storm to break. Mr. Garadot approached stealthily, all gloomy and intent, holding in his fingers the incriminating bit of candle. Glancing around, he asked, "Who cut this off?"

"I did, *bourgeois*."

"Why did you cut it off?"

"To grease my saw because I couldn't get it to work."

"Why didn't you ask me for a piece of pork rind?"

"Because you were in bed."

"Why didn't you ask me for it yesterday evening?"

"Because I didn't think of it and had no idea I would encounter this morning's difficulty. The wood you've given me is atrocious."

"The point is, this is my shop, and I don't want you ruining what belongs to me."

"Mr. Garadot, there's no need to get angry over something so unimportant. Your candle was worth three sous. I cut off about an inch, less than a tenth of it. Here's a sou, and stop crying." Mr. Garadot made a terrible face and withdrew grumbling.

This row made me think about leaving Béziers. As soon as I finished

30. A tenon is the projecting, blade-shaped end of a wooden part that has been made to fit precisely into the slot or mortise of the adjoining piece. The skilled joiner relied on his skill in making a perfect fit, rather than on metal fasteners or glue, to give strength to the joint once the mortise and the tenon were pegged together. Inferior raw materials could make it difficult or impossible to achieve a proper fit.

what I was working on, I settled up with the boss. He paid me, and we parted company. But there was one formality yet to complete, to which all members of the compagnonnage are subject when they leave a workshop: this was the squaring of accounts. The roller took me back to see the boss. The three of us formed a triangle, our hats off, just as in the hiring ceremony. He asked the boss if I had done my duty, if our accounts were square, and if I was free to go as far as he was concerned. The boss replied in the affirmative. The same questions were addressed to me. I gave the same response, but I could not help adding, "Give the gentleman a good worker to replace me but tell him, above all, not to touch the candle." Mr. Garadot smiled, but it was a smile without mirth.

A bit of candle was the reason for my leaving that workshop. But two friends, stung by the behavior of the *bourgeois*, also quit. The man's miserliness had served him badly. [. . .]

The Journey from Béziers to Bordeaux

[. . .] That evening, we arrived in Valence, which is located in the Quercy region. We entered an inn and ate supper. They served us some delicious small birds for one sou apiece. Good food at a good price is always an excellent stroke of good fortune! And yet we were not happy. There were some workers, about our age, who were staying there and, like us, were making their Tour of France. They were so drunk that they frightened us. Why, you ask? Because they were blacksmiths and therefore our enemies. We were at their Mother, in their lair.

We were taken to our sleeping quarters in a large, crowded room. *Gavots* were mixed in amongst *devoirants*, which did not seem healthy to us, for something awful might happen. We got up early the next morning and set off at a rapid pace. We were worried that we might be pursued by the enemies in whose home we had stayed the night, and even though our feet had blisters, this fear gave us the speed of stags. But the smiths were well behaved. They let us continue our journey in peace, which says a lot in their favor. Oh, the times! Oh, the mores!

It is, they say, three leagues from Valence to Agen and three leagues from Agen to Aiguillon. That makes six leagues in all, if I am adding correctly. That was the distance we were to cover that day. You may think it was not much, but it was a lot.

We had passed through La Magistère, a little village consisting of a single, very long street. The sun beamed down its most direct and hottest rays. We could see Agen in the distance. A young man came walking along in our direction. He could not have been more than four feet seven inches tall. On his back he was carrying an enormous goat-hair sack. In his hand he carried a walking stick that he no doubt thought insufficient. He set his sack down at the side of the road, placed his stick next to it, jumped over a stream, went to cut a tree branch, returned to take up his position on the road, and waited for us. When we were twenty paces away, he cried out to us, "*Tope!*" We continued forward without answering. He repeated the word, "*Tope!*" We kept going. He said to us, "Does that mean you're not workers?" I replied, "We're workers, like you, but we're not members of the same brotherhood. Our brotherhood forbids us to hail others or to respond to those who hail us." "Then you're *gavots.*" "Yes, *gavots*, joiners, Compagnons du Devoir de Liberté. And you can see that if we were ill-natured, it is not you who would be the strongest. Pass on by, and let us pass in turn. That's more reasonable and the best for all concerned." And we all continued on our way.

We were soon passing through Agen, following a street populated mainly by coppersmiths.[31] What a racket, what a din, what music they made by beating their hammers on copper! These men watched us pass by. Nothing strange in that. But we were concerned that they might come out in the street and attack us as we passed. [. . .]

We also passed through Port-Sainte-Marie, where the sign on the Mother of the Compagnons du Devoir caught our eyes without delighting our hearts. No oasis in this desert for us! The sun began to set, and little by little, night spread its black veil over the countryside and all of nature. We further punished our weary legs in our efforts to arrive at our resting place. We climbed a hill, and as we reached the summit, at a turn in the road, six very tall compagnons suddenly appeared. We could not believe our eyes: these were six colossi! They wore velvet jackets and had gourds strung over their shoulders and across their chests on red twists of cord.[32] They carried enormous walking staffs five feet or more in length, and they had hairy, surly-looking faces. These six men together would have struck fear into the heart of the devil himself. My companion Provençal was horror-stricken. As for me, I recognized the danger the situation presented. I told him, "This is a terrible fix. These are enemies and they appear determined. We run the risk of being maimed or killed. If they hail us, let me answer." Then we heard that formidable cry: "*Tope!*" We

31. Coppersmiths (*chaudronniers*) primarily made watertight metal containers. Their traditional medium had been copper and its related compounds, bronze and tin, but in the course of the nineteenth century, the use of sheet iron became far more widespread. Coppersmiths were increasingly in demand in industrial applications as boilermakers, but they were better known to the general public as the makers of pots and pans and kitchen utensils of all kinds.
32. Dried, hollow gourds, sometimes ornamented with symbols specific to the owner's brotherhood, were often used for carrying water.

continued forward. A second shout of *"Tope!"* We still advanced. A third shout: *"Tope!"* We came face to face with the six giants, who blocked our path and bluntly asked us, "Why don't you answer? What are you, then?" I answered, "Conscripts. We're on our way to Bordeaux to join up with our regiment." The giants were not convinced but they let us pass, however reluctantly. A lie had saved us.

A lie is distasteful, but it is sometimes dangerous not to use one. Yes, I was due to take part in the draft lottery the following year and I might even be drafted, but that is not my excuse. Were we obliged to reveal our identities to these strangers, these fanatics, these terrible adventurers who might turn murderous? Not to my way of thinking. And yet we were careful not to brag to our colleagues about this act of prudence, which would have been deemed a sign of cowardice. [. . .]

That was an eventful journey! Ten times we nearly drowned or perished. And yet, in spite of all that, it is still one of my fondest memories! It pleased me then and it pleases me still. Traveling on foot, then by boat and mingling with all kinds of folks. Experiencing annoyances and miseries but also pleasant surprises and moments of joy. What could be sweeter or more delightful? To have traveled twenty-four leagues in this way: now that means something, that counts in life. Crossing a thousand leagues in a stagecoach or on a railroad—enclosed in a sort of prison cell that you cannot escape and from which you cannot see anything—that means nothing, absolutely nothing. That leaves no imprint. That is why I say, long live travel by foot and in total freedom!

My Stay in Bordeaux

We arrived at the Mother and were well received. We gave fraternal embraces to a crowd of compagnons who had preceded us as well as to father and mother Bertrand, for you do not have to have already met *fathers* and *mothers* to greet them in this way. There was a little celebration in our honor.

Mr. Moulonguet and Local Workers

Young Portalès, who was called Marseillais-the-Corinthian, was dignitary. He found us jobs that very day at Mr. Moulonguet's. I remember that when the roller said, "I've brought you two workers, as you requested," the *bourgeois* looked at us and answered, "They're very young." Then he turned to us and asked, "Where are you from?" One of us replied, "From Avignon," the other, "From Provence." "Oh, good!" said Mr. Moulonguet, who was always sparing with words. He feared, no doubt, that we might be from Bordeaux. Why? Is it because men from Bordeaux are not the equal of those from elsewhere? I didn't say that. Here is what I maintain. As a general rule, masters from Avignon don't like workers from Avignon just as masters from Marseille, Nîmes, or Bordeaux don't like workers from those cities. The reason? It is because young men native to those regions receive considerable support from their parents and have not experienced the difficulties, hardships, and bad luck with which life is strewn. They often drift into laziness, listlessness, or idleness. They sometimes occupy a workbench in the shop without producing all that it is possible to get from it, for each workbench must generate a return. That is why, as a general rule and with certain exceptions, masters prefer compagnons and journeymen who are engaged on their Tour of France or who have already completed it to youths from the local area who have stayed in their nests. It is not a matter of prejudice. Their preference is based on experience, which cannot deceive them. [. . .]

Devigne; My Readings; the Compagnonnage

In Bordeaux, after spending my day working in the shop, I continued going to drafting classes until eleven at night. It was also in that city that I acquired a taste for reading. I will tell you how.

I was sleeping in the same room and the same bed as Provençal-the-Kindhearted, and Poitevin-the-Pure-hearted had the bed next to ours. In the room next to ours were Vivarais-the-Rose, Narbonne-the-Hopeful, and Provençal-the-Faithful-hearted, all recognized fellows like ourselves, along with Devigne, an affiliate from Switzerland who had formerly been an apprentice at Mr. Portalès's shop in Marseille.

We would sometimes gather in the evening in the room where Devigne slept with Narbonne and the others, and he would pick up *Othello*, or *Hamlet*, or the tragedies of Ducis, or Racine's *Phaedra* and read them aloud. I was enthralled, and suddenly my fondest wish was to own a few tragedies myself.

The very next day, I made the rounds of the bookstores. I bought *Gustave Wasa* by Piron and a few comedies by Poisson that we read among ourselves. We were especially fond of gloomy, terrifying plays and, I have to admit, the more deaths there were at the end of a tragedy, the more we found it sublime, magnificent, perfect.

One day, I was taking a walk in an arcade near the stock exchange. I stopped in front of a bookseller's window. I saw four small volumes bound in red on whose backs was written, *Dramatic Masterpieces of Voltaire*. What could that title mean? I went in to take a look. I opened a volume and leafed through the pages. But these are tragedies!

"How much for these four volumes?"

"Four francs."

"Here you are." I was now the proud owner of Voltaire's dramatic masterpieces. I owned tragedies! I went as quickly as I was able to sit on the grass in a public garden, and there, all alone, I perused my volumes. I read verse; I read prose, beautiful prose, even though, like the *bourgeois gentilhomme* and most of my fellow workers, I did not then know the word for it.[33] My friends also read my tragedies and, like me, they were enchanted with them.

The four volumes by Voltaire, which I read and reread, taught me about classical theater, modern theater, dramatic action, and the unities of time and place, and about poetry. They gave me an appreciation for all this. They acquainted me, at least by name, with Sophocles, Euripides, Aristophanes, La Fontaine, Boileau, Regnard, Molière, Racine, Corneille, as well as English, Italian, and Spanish authors. A whole new world opened before me. My mind was enlarged. The wars among brotherhoods of compagnons, which already seemed stupid to me, became still more horrible and abominable in my eyes.

About this time, we received a letter from Nantes. A battle had just taken place in that city. While our compagnons were conducting an orderly ceremony of departure, the blacksmiths organized a mock ceremony. The two brotherhoods met, and soon blood flowed. One smith lost his life. Many of our men were sent to jail, where they received assistance from those of us on the Tour of France who sent them money. [. . .]

A Thief and His Punishment

I have mentioned Lansargue. He had departed Montpellier with me, and I had left him behind in Béziers. When he arrived in Bordeaux, I welcomed him, even though I did not like his character. One Sunday, he went out with us and spent rather extravagantly. When we got back to the Mother, he ate six portions of roast at thirty centimes each, and talked about eating as many again. In the end, I went to bed and left the glutton at the table.

The next morning, I got up and dressed for work. Provençal-the-Kindhearted and Poitevin-the-Pure-hearted were still in bed. Poitevin said to me, "Avignonnais, what time is it?" I went to look at his watch, which at night was hung from a nail driven into the wall above the chest of drawers. Not seeing it, I told him, "Your watch isn't there."

"What do you mean my watch isn't there?"

33. Perdiguier refers to Monsieur Jourdain, the title character in Molière's comedy *Le Bourgeois Gentilhomme*. When introduced to the distinction between poetry and prose, Monsieur Jourdain is astonished to learn that he has been speaking prose all along without even knowing it.

"I see the key and the piece of cord, which has been cut, but nothing else." Poitevin leapt out of bed and Provençal did the same. We started searching, but our efforts were in vain. The watch had disappeared. There were only three of us in that room, and if Poitevin was apprehensive, his two roommates were even more so, even if they did not show it to the same degree. I told him, "Hurry and tell the First Fellow what's happened." He followed my advice.

The First Fellow, once notified, ordered an assembly and gathered information. Everyone joined in the search and investigation. We shared what we knew or thought we knew. Everyone wanted to uncover the truth, and all efforts were directed to that end.

Lansargue, the one who had been so extravagant the previous evening, had not gone straight to bed after leaving the table. He had passed through several rooms in his bare feet and had been noticed. Suspicion hung over him.

It was not just the roller who made the rounds of the workshops inviting all members of the brotherhood to make their way to the Mother, as would have been customary. Instead, all those who were willing—and there were many—set forth, and the task went extremely quickly. By ten o'clock, all compagnons and affiliates were gathered in the common room.

The dignitary or First Fellow, who presided over all assemblies, removed his hat, saying, "This meeting is now in session." As always, everyone took his hat or cap in his hand, for in all our gatherings, even the most informal, nothing happens until all heads are bare.

"Brothers," he said, "a theft has been committed; a silver watch was stolen last night from a room here in the Mother. The guilty party must be found and punished. No one may leave. Roller, and you, Poitevin, go through all the rooms, inspect all the trunks beginning with my own. Here are the keys. Do all you can to discover the thief."

The First Fellow and then each member of the brotherhood in turn, without exception, had to answer the roller's call and open their trunks, allowing their belongings to be searched. Nothing was discovered. Once this first operation was complete, everyone's pockets were searched right there in the midst of the assembly, beginning with those of the highest ranking member.

Everyone had their eye on Lansargue. Two five-franc coins were found in his purse. "Where did this money come from?" the First Fellow asked him.

"I earned it," replied Lansargue.

"When you arrived in town, the father gave you credit. You said you didn't have any money."

"I just said that."

"We went to see your *bourgeois* and we know how much you've earned. We've seen your account at the Mother and we know what you've spent. You can't have a cent of savings left. Where do these ten francs come from?"

"I had them when I arrived." [. . .]

I intervened in the dispute. "Lansargue," I said to him, "a theft has been committed in the room where I sleep. Everyone wants to discover the person responsible, and I perhaps more than anyone. Last night you went into rooms where you had no business."

"I deny it. That's a lie."

Several men spoke up at once: "I saw you." [. . .]

Everyone told what he knew about Lansargue. They came at him from all directions. He was bold in his denials. When everyone was quite worn out, the matter had to be left there. The First Fellow then said: "We are going to separate for a while. Everyone should continue the investigations and inquiry. At two o'clock, we will assemble again. No one will be absent. As for Lansargue, until further notice, he will remain here, in this room, guarded by four compagnons." [. . .]

Outside, a search was being conducted. We retraced the route the suspect had followed that morning. He had crossed the bridge and gone to the other side of the Gironde River. He had met with a candidate member of the Compagnons du Devoir, whom we found and who told us the truth. We gave him back his ten francs and returned with the watch. At two o'clock a second assembly took place with everyone present.

Lansargue was brought into the middle of the room. His cause was lost. The universal censure overwhelmed him. He was shown the recovered watch, and stern words were spoken. We made him get down on his knees and beg forgiveness of God and men. We made him swear that he would never boast of having belonged in any capacity whatever to the Compagnons du Devoir de Liberté. Then wine was brought. The compagnons and affiliates clinked glasses together, about ten at a time, and drank to the execration of rogues, swindlers, and thieves. Each time that a group of ten men clinked glasses and drank their wine, the convicted man had to swallow a glass of water. And when his stomach could hold no more, it was thrown in his face. Each member of the brotherhood drank a glass of wine, or two at the most, but as we were numerous and there were not enough glasses for all, there were several clinkings and several toasts of a rather unusual sort, and Lansargue had to swallow more water than he might have wished. Then the glass from which he had drunk was broken.

If he had been a full-fledged compagnon, we would have broken his cane and burned his colors. The roller made him rise, took him by the hand, and led him around the room, making him pass before each of us. Each gave the thief a light slap. He had to make a second round. A cane was passed from hand to hand as quickly as he advanced, and each man had to touch him lightly on the back. Finally, the door was opened and Lansargue was allowed to leave. At that moment, the roller gave him a kick in the behind with the end of his foot. Justice had been done.

Lansargue had not been physically harmed, and besides he was free. Yet I must say that I have never seen a harsher punishment. Those who have participated in a *conduite de Grenoble* are not tempted to do anything that would earn one for themselves. Because of Lansargue's unparalleled effrontery, this one was executed in all its rigor. More often—in fact, almost always—they are cut short. The guilty party is merely made to kneel and swear never to boast of having been a member of the brotherhood; then he is put out the door with a kick in the behind. The *conduite de Grenoble* that I have just described is the only complete one that I saw in my entire life.

After expelling a guilty party in this way, the compagnons send his description to all points on the Tour of France. In each town, it is recorded in the register of thieves, and the malefactor can no longer show his face anywhere, for he would be driven away.

Those who leave a town without settling their accounts or without letting anyone know, thus doing wrong to the *master* who employed them, or to the *Mother* that fed them, or to the *brotherhood* that protected them, are labeled "burners." Word is passed just as for thieves, and their names and descriptions are similarly recorded in a special book. Still, if they eventually repay what they owe and make amends, the bosom of the brotherhood is opened to them once more and they can continue their Tour of France and even hold positions of responsibility. As for thieves, it is the end: the brotherhood of compagnons ceases to exist for them. In extreme circumstances, however, if a man who has suffered this degradation were to find himself without a job and in cruel straits, he would not be refused information about where to find one. But no one from the brotherhood would accompany him, because we would not wish to vouch for him. Even if he were offered assistance, we would avoid him like the plague.

I do not know what became of Lansargue after being stigmatized and banished by the compagnons. I never heard of him again. [. . .]

My Opposition within the Compagnonnage

[. . .] The feast day of Saint Anne, our patron saint, had arrived. We gathered in a general assembly to elect a First Fellow, choosing among three candidates. To count the votes, one affiliate, one recognized fellow, and one finished fellow are asked to step forward. The ballots are opened by the first of them and read aloud. They next pass into the hands of the second, then the third, who repeat the names written on them. These ballots, tossed into three hats, are immediately counted, and the candidate who gets the most votes is proclaimed First Fellow. [. . .]

Around that time, I received a letter from Avignonnais-the-Prudent, with whom I had been made a recognized fellow. He had become a finished fellow and held the office of secretary of the chapter at Béziers. He told me, "I'm advancing in the ranks, and you should too." I answered him, "You're advancing in the ranks while I'm advancing on the Tour of France. You'll turn back on your own footsteps, but I'll continue my journey and finish it as planned. We'll see, when all's said and done, who has progressed further according to my way of thinking and according to yours." [. . .]

Journey from Bordeaux to Nantes

On 3 July 1826, I left Bordeaux. Several friends saw me off. I did not take a steamboat, since they were still rare and their departures infrequent, but rather a small sailing ship headed for Royan. In silence I said my farewell to that city I had liked so much.

We arrived in Royan without mishap. Its port consists, or consisted then, of nothing but the shore, rocky beaches, and reefs—in short, it was rather primitive, as if unworked by human hands. We disembarked. The customs officials made me open my trunk right there on the rocks that the salt water would come up and wet, and inspected it carefully. A helpful sailor, with whom I had made friends on board ship, gave me a hand with my trunk, and I dropped it off at the first inn I came to. We made inquiries about coaches. At that time, there were none in Royan that made the connection with Rochefort, where we wanted to stay the night. I therefore had to leave my trunk, which could not be sent to me that day or the next.

We set off on foot but had hardly gone a few leagues before the sailor, a poor walker like almost all men of the sea, was exhausted. We arrived at a village and entered an inn. We ate dinner and rested for a moment. The sailor was on his way home from Pondichéry and was returning to Nantes, his native region, where he had left his wife, fifteen days after their marriage, for a three-year voyage.[34] The innkeeper was an old soldier of the Empire. Napoléon was his hero, his god. The sailor who, on his way

34. Pondichéry (Pondicherry) is a port city on the southeastern coast of the Indian peninsula. For most of the time between 1683 and 1954, it was the principal settlement and administrative capital of French India, a colonial possession of some 193 square miles.

back from India, had made a landfall at Saint Helena, began speaking of the great man's tomb, over which he had said a prayer.[35] He took a billfold from his pocket, opened it, and carefully took out a tiny twig of willow. This twig had come from below the equator, from Saint Helena, from the weeping willow that shades the tomb of Napoléon. He had picked it with his own hand and carried it across the depths of the ocean so it could shine there before our eyes. He gave us each a leaf. The innkeeper was in heaven! He kissed that holy leaf, that peerless relic, a hundred times. He cried with tenderness and joy. He could not control himself. I shared his emotion, for, as I have said, not knowing of the arbitrary and unjust deeds of Bonaparte, I was a Bonapartist. I kept that leaf, given to me as a present, for years. I was truly sad when I lost it. [. . .]

Beyond Marans, I entered the Vendée region. I saw Luçon, Mareuil, and the town of Bourbon-Vendée, perched high up on a hillside. Each change of government has brought a change of name for this small hamlet. First it was called Bourbon, then it was Napoléon. It has been baptized and rebaptized twenty times, and its tribulations are not over. No, nothing is less stable than a royal or imperial name in the times in which we live. [. . .]

Nail Makers and Blacksmiths

The compagnonnage had many members and was very active in Nantes. Battles among compagnons were also frequent. Since the terrible combat between *gavots* and blacksmiths, which cost the life of one smith, other disorders have taken place.

Nantes is the headquarters city for compagnon nail makers. Members of this occupation stand out because of their number, their dress, and the nature of their ceremonies. They preside over their assemblies, or did so then, in high hats and knee breeches. They wear ponytails and pigtails on the back of their heads. When one of their brothers is buried, they untie their hair and let it hang, wave, fly about their necks and in front of their faces, however the breeze blows it. In this state—hatless, grave, and silent—they accompany the deceased to the cemetery where a singular and curious ceremony takes place.

Compagnon nail makers are very charitable. They provide fraternal support to one another. If a compagnon is on the road and finds himself without work, what does he do? He goes to the first nail maker's shop that he finds along his path and explains his difficulties. One of the workers will surrender his hammer and his place at the anvil, and go off to travel in turn,

35. Saint Helena is a small, remote island in the South Atlantic Ocean, where Napoléon died in exile in 1821.

or else the new arrival is given assistance, which is not charity but a loan. After reviving a bit and shaking the hands of his friends, he will then continue on his Tour of France. Compagnon weavers employ the same procedures. The traveler finds brothers everywhere. These practices are very ancient.

Blacksmiths have one of the strongest associations. They are widely distributed in both cities and villages. But are they ever rough and tough! They will not tolerate any teasing about their brotherhood. They have wrists that can twist iron and they know it, and so all too often they get in fights. They also have customs all their own. Here is one I have witnessed:

A group of blacksmiths were gathered in a field alongside the road, doing what they called their "duty." This was a ceremony in the open air, a formal departure ritual for a member who was leaving. Their walking sticks were stuck into the ground. Red, white, and green ribbons hung from their buttonholes. Standing side by side, they formed an immense circle, with all of them facing the center. One of them, holding in his right hand a glass full of deeply colored wine, started to run completely around the outside of the circle, crying out, howling, until he was back at his place, where another fellow—the one leaving, no doubt—was waiting for him, holding a glass in his hand as well. They stood facing one another, staring at each other intently. They made certain signs, stepped forward, and each leaned to one side, passing his own right arm around the other's and bringing his glass to his lips so that they both drank at the same time. The one who ran and shouted returned to his place. His neighbor stepped out and imitated him, until they had all, one after another down to the very last, repeated the same set of actions. There were also a few collective shouts.

The departing compagnon moved off, his goatskin sack on his back, his long walking stick in his hand, his gourd hanging from his side. Two handsome golden earrings, embellished with a horseshoe, shone in his ears. The others all called out to him and called again, but temptation had no hold on his soul. He marched off without a backward glance, without showing any weakness. The others redoubled their provocations and enticements, but to no avail. He proudly walked straight ahead. Suddenly he grabbed his hat in his hands and threw it back over his head, far behind him, and started to run away. The other compagnons ran to pick it up, pursued the runaway, finally reached him, and shoved it down on his head. The departing compagnon remained indifferent, as if he did not know and did not want to know who had replaced his hat. He walked on with a firm step, looking neither right nor left. He was like a statue; nothing surprised him, nothing moved him, nothing could deflect him in his course. The other compagnons retraced their footsteps. The departure ceremony was over, the departing fellow had given proof of the firmness of his resolve. [. . .]

I Fall Sick; the Hospital; Mother and Compagnons

I had arrived in Nantes in a sorry state. I got a job anyway and started working, but all the while I worked, I was suffering. After nine days of persistent effort, I had to set my tools aside and shut myself up in my room. I had passed through Rochefort during July, in the dog days, the period of fevers and sickness in that region. Still, the origin of my illness came from still further away. I had brought it from Bordeaux.

Until then, in every town I had passed through, I had found compagnons' Mothers that were truly worthy of so fine a title. I had been properly cared for and offered every consideration. For their part, the compagnons, despite differences which I have mentioned, had shown themselves to be noble spirited and brotherly. This was not the case in Nantes, and if I am still alive, it is no thanks to the people with whom I was in contact there. Why this change? Had I been done a bad turn by an unfavorable letter from Bordeaux? Had I been denounced as dangerous because of my momentary disobedience, which I thought legitimate, just, and necessary? I do not know. [. . .]

During the ten days I remained in this weakened condition—delirious, getting up and walking around without knowing what I was doing—I received visits from a few friends, but the brotherhood and the Mother completely forgot me. My bill for those ten days—counting herb tea, hot broth, food; in short, my total expenses—came to just three and a half francs. My strength abandoned me. Even on days when my fever did not return in intensified form, I was unable to sit up.

I asked to see the First Fellow. Unfortunately, it was no longer Bugiste-the-Esteem-of-Virtues but the locksmith Clermont-the-Royal-hearted. I begged him to have me admitted to the hospital as soon as possible. [. . .]

On hearing my request, Clermont had taken certain steps and obtained a document, signed by I don't know who, without which it was impossible to gain admission to the hospital. I do not know if one still has to go through the same formalities. He gave orders to the roller, Rochelais-the-Rose-of-Love, who accompanied me, his arm passed through mine to support me, cursing and swearing under his breath. We arrived at the hospital, a magnificent establishment that was truly vast and yet crowded with sick people. Every bed was occupied and there was not a single place for me. We were obliged to return to the Mother and postpone my admission until the following day.

I was waiting for the roller bright and early the next morning. When he arrived, I said, "Let's go."

"I went with you yesterday," he replied. "You know the way. Why don't you go on your own."

"But if I go by myself, which would be very hard for me to do anyway, the brotherhood will not know in which room or which bed they've put me, and the compagnons won't be able to take turns making the customary visits." Rochelais-the-Rose-of-Love, a very handsome man, an excellent dancer, an accomplished quarterstaff fighter, and a skillful worker, showed his resentment. He answered me curtly, "That's none of my affair." If he is still living and happens to read this account, and if he agrees that he was wrong and reproaches himself for it, then I forgive him for having failed me.

Poitevin-the-Agreeable, one of the oldest compagnons, was present. He offered to accompany me in place of Rose-of-Love. Along the way, he criticized the conduct of the roller, who had thus been shown wanting in both his duty and his sense of humanity.

I was admitted to the hospital and placed in a bed just as an attack of fever overcame me for the sixth time. The head doctor, while making his rounds, accompanied by a number of students, looked me over, gave me an examination, and then moved on without saying anything, leaving me in a state of drowsiness. I lost consciousness again. The next day was my good day. I was bled and then bled some more.[36] I followed the prescribed treatment exactly. They took wonderful care of me, and I had no recurrence of those terrible attacks. Fortunately, the illness promptly diminished.

When one of us takes to a hospital bed, he is supposed to receive every day, as long as nothing interferes with this ancient rule of our brotherhood, the visit of a fellow worker. The dignitary, for his part, must verify firsthand if anyone is failing in his duty by going to see the sick person once or twice a week. Our rules were not being observed, for I saw very few people from outside.

I slowly recovered my health and climbed my way back up from death to life while so many others around me followed the opposite path. I saw many die. *Gavots* and *devoirants* are two inflexibly divided camps even among the dying. My neighbor in the hospital was a worker perhaps

36. Bleeding was the practice of drawing small amounts of blood from the veins of a sick person in the belief that this would purge the body of the substance responsible for the illness.

twenty years old, and therefore the same age as myself. One day he asked, "What is your occupation?"

I told him, "Joiner."

"What brotherhood do you belong to?" he asked.

"To the Compagnons du Devoir de Liberté," I replied.

He made a grimace, became angry, and worked himself into a fury. He told me he belonged to the Compagnons du Devoir, that it was the good brotherhood, that mine was bad and could only bring dishonor, that *gavots* were not men but vile and evil creatures who were ignorant and incompetent, and had to be stamped out. But aside from this mad patient, I also met some pleasant fellow workers, made good friends, and even earned a certain respect among them. I became especially close with an Englishman and a Parisian, who represented two extremes as far as personality was concerned, though both were very decent sorts.

I wrote my father about my situation and asked him for money so I could leave for Chartres as soon as my strength permitted. When the fever broke, I shed the gray hospital gown and prepared to leave. I had been a patient for twenty-four days, and my stay had done my health a great deal of good. As I was getting ready, a hospital attendant told me, "That's a very handsome pair of pants you have."

"Why do you say that?"

"I had claimed them for myself and never expected that I would be returning them to you."

"I must have been very sick, then?"

"Three-fourths dead, or more. But you're a good sort, so I'm just as happy to see you walk away. Good luck."

I left and went to the Mother. "Good morning, mother." She barely responded and asked no questions about my health. "Mother, have you received a letter for me?"

"No."

"I'm expecting one."

"Well, if it arrives, you'll get it."

I needed to eat, but I didn't dare say so, because I still owed the three and a half francs I have mentioned, as well as two-thirds of a month's lodging.

Just then, the mailman entered, holding a letter in his hand: "For Agricol Perdiguier."

"That's me! Hand it over." I took the letter, opened it, and shouted, "Seventy francs! I'm so happy. I'm rich. I'm off to find the First Fellow to tell him that I want to leave."

"Don't leave," the mother said in a sweeter tone. "I'll speak to him, put in a good word for you, and he'll place you in a good workshop as soon as you are completely recovered. Until then, I'll see to your convalescence."

"Thank you, mother, thank you, but your kindness comes too late. It's not me you want but my money, and you shall not have it."

I went to find the First Fellow in the shop, where he was working some wrought iron. I informed him of my decision to leaves Nantes immediately. He convened a two-hour meeting of the elders. They gathered, deliberated, and arrived at the following conclusion: "The town lacks workers. The brotherhood enjoins Avignonnais-the-Virtuous to stay and help us in our work. We accept his declaration of today as notice. He shall leave in two weeks if he wishes, but not before." They had me enter the room and conveyed to me the decision they had just made.

"But," I told them, "you can't hold me to the usual regulations in these circumstances. I've just gotten out of the hospital, I'm weak and unable to work. If I stay two weeks doing nothing, I'll have been of no use to the brotherhood, but my money will have disappeared and it'll no longer be possible for me to go where I wish. The rules that compel healthy compagnons can't apply to those who are sick, for you can't require them to do things that are beyond their strength. I can sense that the city air is bad for me. I have to get away. My plan was to go on to Chartres, but if you prefer, I'll only go as far as Tours. Once that city has received me as a compagnon, it'll be able to send you another in exchange, one who will doubtless be worth more than I am at the moment."

The compagnons who were members of this assembly paid no attention to my arguments and insisted on imposing two weeks of work on me, even though I was unable to work. They told me, "If you leave, the brotherhood will no longer count on you."

"What you're doing," I told them, "is totally unfair. When I was sick and still living in the Mother, I was left without care. While I was in the hospital, very few of my colleagues came to see me. The First Fellow came to visit me just twice in twenty-four days, and if I'd left one day earlier, I would have seen him only once. You haven't done for me what you do or are supposed to do for all compagnons and all affiliates. I've been treated without consideration or humanity. And now you say the compagnons of Nantes will no longer count on me. Well, I no longer count on you. I am going at once to have my passport stamped, not for Tours, since it makes no difference to you, but for Chartres, as I had originally intended."

I left and slammed the door behind me. I went to the town hall and had my passport stamped for La Beauce. Then I went to reserve a seat on the next day's coach. I had to hurry, for I only had a little money and wanted to make the best possible use of it.

That same evening, I was at the Mother and saw a lot of people arrive. That meant there was to be a general assembly, an assembly for a departing compagnon. Was it for me? Maybe it was, and maybe not. They had told me, "If you leave, we will no longer count on you." And this threat had not intimidated me. I therefore needed to be on my guard.

The compagnons and affiliates were sent up into the assembly room while I remained alone below. They called for me. I obeyed and took my usual place. The First Fellow told me, "Come forward and stand next to me in the place reserved for the departing compagnon. Cover your head." I covered my head. It is only when a compagnon is about to depart and the meeting has begun that he keeps his hat on his head. The First Fellow asked me, as custom demands, if I had any complaints to make about the brotherhood or any of its members. I answered that I did not. He asked all those present if they had anything to complain to me about and received the same response. I went with the roller to see the mother. We returned, and he declared that I did not owe anything, that my bill was paid. The First Fellow affirmed in a loud voice that my accounts were settled with the mother, the brotherhood, the compagnons, and the affiliates and that, since all the formalities had been observed, there was nothing more standing in the way of my departure. The affiliates and then the recognized fellows withdrew. Only the finished fellows remained. Clermont-the-Royalhearted said to me, "You complained that we neglected to go see you in the hospital. When I asked if you had complaints to make, you should have spoken up, and all those who you said failed to visit you would have been forced to pay you what they owed you." I answered, "When I was sick in the hospital, I looked forward to visits from all my brothers. At that time, I would have accepted the least assistance with thanks. Their presence alone could have done me the greatest good. But now I'm free. What's more, I've received some money, so I'm able to get on my own whatever comforts I might need. I ask nothing from anyone and I have no complaint to make of anyone, except perhaps yourself."

"Me?"

"Yes, you."

"Would you please explain?"

"The flock travels where the shepherd leads them." That produced a great uproar, a din, as well as exclamations. I did not waver. The more my physical strength had diminished, the more my moral force had grown. Injustice had aroused my indignation.

The First Fellow had the nerve to argue, in our discussion, that I had brought my illness with me from Bordeaux and that, strictly speaking, the Nantes chapter owed me nothing. This was a ridiculous sophism, to which

I responded victoriously because for us there is no Bordeaux chapter separate from the Nantes chapter, but just one unified brotherhood, the Compagnons du Devoir de Liberté. It cannot be divided up but remains one throughout France. We therefore owe each other care and assistance wherever we may be and never cease to be colleagues and brothers.

With this first part of the debate out of the way, the First Fellow said to me, "Where are you going?"

My response was, "To Chartres."

"You had promised to go to Tours."

"Yes, if you had wished it. But you said, 'If you leave, we no longer count on you.' I took you at your word and acted without constraint."

"If you don't go to Tours, we can't consider you to be in order."

"As you wish. My papers are stamped for Chartres, and that's where I am going. And the compagnons of that city will make good the difficulties I've endured in this one. They'll see my pale, emaciated face, my sunken eyes, the wrinkles on my brow, my nearly hairless head. They won't be able to imagine how you could have required two weeks of work from me when I'm barely convalescent and completely without strength. I go to them with complete assurance. It's not me they'll blame, but you."

Journey from Nantes to Chartres

The next evening, 31 August 1826, a few affiliates and a few recognized fellows, among them Gandiole, called Vivarais-the-Frank, accompanied me to the coach. I gave them fraternal embraces and climbed up to the top deck, a seat that suited my purse if not my state of health.

The horses were harnessed, the driver had taken his seat, and the postilion had mounted his horse.[37] The driver was just grasping the whip in his hand and raising it; we were ready to leave. At that moment, Goutille, called Châlonnais-the-Key-to-Hearts, the First Fellow's secretary, came running up. He said to me, "The brotherhood didn't want to let you leave without being in order, and they've asked me to give you this." He handed me a document. I said, "You needn't have bothered, but since you're here, I accept it." This man, whom I then hardly knew, has since become one of my best friends.

The whip cracked and the horses pawed the ground with their feet. The coach got under way, began to roll faster and faster, and moved off from a city that I was departing with my eyes dry and my heart at peace. That is what I was thinking as I left Nantes. [. . .]

---

37. The postilion rode the left-hand lead horse in a harnessed team of four in order to assist the driver in guiding and controlling the coach.

Mr. Luton's Shop in Chartres

I had been at Nogent-le-Roi two months when the compagnons of Chartres wrote to tell me that I should return because they needed my services. I answered their call. They got me a job at Mr. Luton's shop in the lower end of town near the Porte Guillaume. Across from us was the Mother of the compagnon tanners, where we went every morning to eat bread rolls the size of walnuts and a little drop of brandy. These enemies of ours were not mischievous, and we never were greeted with insults. Not long afterward, it is true, there were a few incidents between joiners and tanners, but fortunately they were short-lived. Mr. Luton gave us room and board, as was the custom in that region. We were quite content in his shop.

Life in the Workshop

Employers and compagnons sometimes exchanged teasing, antagonistic words, and jokes of questionable taste. When it snowed, an employer might say to his workers, "Do you see those white flies swarming in the air?" What this meant was, "It's your slow season. Be careful what you say, act a bit more humble, and watch your step, because I'm in a position of strength." During the winter, the boss was the one who did the teasing. But compagnons knew how to get their revenge, and they had three favorable seasons for every unfavorable one. Their advantage was the subject of a bizarre song of which I remember just this verse:

> When the season of icicles arrives,
> We compagnons wish we'd never been born;
> When the season of icicles arrives,
> Those rascal *bourgeois* heap us with scorn.
> But when the thaw comes after all,
> We have all spring, summer, and fall
> To pay them back.

I may not have reproduced it exactly, but I am certain that I am not very far off.

There are all kinds of jokes that make the rounds of the workshops, concerning both masters and workers: A certain master, who is referred to by name and who has therefore become famous, has a peculiar way of telling his workers the height and width of a window or a door he wants them to make. After getting their attention, he throws his cap up in the air, saying, "That's how tall it must be." Then he spreads his arms horizontally and tells them, "That's the width. Now get moving, and hurry up." And they all laugh at the employer's strangeness and eccentricity, which they much exaggerate, you may be sure. A certain Mr. Lemoine of Marseille must often have felt his ears burning.

If the master comes in for a lot of ribbing, so does the shoddy workman, the one who doesn't manage to keep busy. A master was absent from his workshop. One of his workers stood between two workbenches and placed one hand on each. He then straightened his arms, lifting himself off the ground, and swung back and forth like a church bell, singing:

> The master pays me by the day,
> Tirra-lirra-lirra, tirra-lirra-lirra.
> The master pays me by the day,
> Tirra-lirra-lirra-lay.

The master returned without a sound, crept back in on tiptoe, and swung into action by singing his refrain to the worker while keeping time with the kicks he delivered to his backside:

> I'll pay you for the work you do,
> Tirra-lirra-lirra, tirra-lirra-lirra.
> I'll pay you for the work you do,
> Tirra-lirra-lirra-loo.

And everyone laughs at these jokes and applauds the master who paid the worker what he deserved.

Then too, when a master does a worker some injustice, we have all seen how the worker will exact his revenge by damaging his last piece of work. If he was making a chest of drawers or a writing desk, he might, unbeknown to anyone, glue the drawers shut and then take his leave. The piece of furniture might look perfectly fine, but it would later be discovered to be worthless. By then, however, the worker was far away. Such things happen rarely. The compagnonnage would punish one of its members who was guilty of such an act, because it is supposed to intervene in disputes and it insists on maintaining good relations with masters. There were, in short, wrangles and conflicts between masters and workers, and it could not have been otherwise, for men are not angels. But there were also cordial relations.

On Saint Anne's feast day, the compagnons held a ball to which they invited their employers and their spouses. The following day, it was the masters' turn to hold a ball and return the favor. These entrepreneurs would also feed their workers. They all sat at the same table, ate the same bread, and drank the same wine. And on certain days, there would be a banquet. They were all part of the same family.

I recall that in Montpellier, when the days grew short and we had to lengthen them morning and evening by burning candles, Mr. Pradoura would inaugurate the new season by buying us what was called the "late-hours pie."[38] This was a fancy dinner that culminated with a pie and was enlivened by singing.

In Mr. Moulonguet's shop in Bordeaux, where we were paid a piece rate and no meals were supplied, even though we were not invited to sit at his table at that time of year, he gave three francs to each of his workers, telling them, "Go have dinner together to usher in the late-night hours."

In Chartres, the custom of the late-hours pie was still in general usage and became the occasion for fraternization between masters and workers. Some of the old ways were truly good ones.

Since those times, I have never seen the late-hours pie being observed. What is more, the masters, at least in big cities, have all stopped feeding and lodging their workers. Relations between the two groups have suffered a great deal as a consequence. Nonetheless, good feelings persist and the brotherhood does what it can to maintain and encourage them.

I Become a Finished Fellow; Entertainment

Until then, I had remained a recognized fellow, but a few of my friends strongly urged me to advance in the ranks. Among them was Languedoc-the-Kindhearted (Moynier), a native of Mauguio near Montpellier, where I first met him. He was a charming young man, as likable as his nickname implies. And so I joined the ranks of finished fellows. From then on, I took an active part in the administrative affairs of the brotherhood.

At that time, there was no drafting instructor in Chartres. Compagnons were not in a position to extend their working day by spending a few hours learning architecture and design. Like everyone else, I was forced to neglect my studies. But you will never guess what I found to occupy my free time in the evenings. I learned to dance. I was, after all, not some gloomy philosopher. What I really wanted was for thought and action, the serious and the cheerful, to be combined and to work in concert.

On Sundays, we would go as a group to rural fairs. We would find some young women and leap about like madmen. The band was usually composed of two musicians majestically seated on stout chairs that were like raised thrones, their four feet resting on two large pedestals (more commonly referred to as kegs or casks or barrels). The sound they made was not that of the fife and the long narrow drum as in Avignon or Marseille, nor the sound of the oboe and the rolling drum as in the region of Montpellier, nor the sound of the musette or southern bagpipes as in

---

38. The expression *pâté de veille* may well refer to a meat or poultry stew, cooked inside a pastry crust.

Auvergne, nor that of the Breton bagpipes as in Limousin and Brittany, nor even that of the hurdy-gurdy as in the mountains of the Alps. Theirs was the sound of a hoarse, shrill, discordant violin and of a bass drum, which makes up in volume what it lacks in harmony. This music was not intoxicating, nor did it give wings to the dancers' feet. It was not capable of resurrecting the dead, nor of charming a crown prince, nor of building a new Thebes as in the times of Linus and Amphion.[39] But we were young and needed to move about, and nothing could wear us out or get us to stop.

The Compagnons' Songs

[. . .] I got the notion to write a poem or perhaps a song. But I needed some kind of spur to set me to work with courage and perseverance. Let me tell you how this came about.

One Sunday, several of us were gathered around a table. We had downed a few glasses of wine and were singing. "What!" you may ask, "Is it possible? You would go to a *cabaret* and sing?"[40] Why not? Put yourself in our place. In the morning, we were at our workbenches at five o'clock sharp. In the evening, we got off work at the stroke of eight—six days a week, winter, summer, forever! The seventh was our day of rest and recreation. But since we were strangers to that city and had no money, no place of our own, no family, no relatives, no circle of acquaintances like those that fashionable people can always find, no drawing-rooms, no gardens, no parks, no horses, no pack of fox-hounds, no hunting, no fishing, no plays, no games, and neither hearth nor home, what were we to do? What was to become of us? Where were we to go? How were we to spend our time, where were we to sit around and relax? How were we to entertain ourselves, find distractions even for a time?

I have said that we were not rich, and I will add that we were not very well educated either. Because we lacked sufficient instruction or experience, we could not join in religious, political, philosophical, historical, literary, scientific, or artistic discussions—in short, we could not participate in any of those noble, high-minded, varied, or interesting pursuits that might have kept us occupied for an entire day. So, what would we do? We would sing, for that was the easiest thing within our reach. So we sang.

39. In Greek mythology, Amphion, a son of Zeus, built a wall around Thebes by charming the stones into place with a lyre. Linus was a master musician whose prowess was celebrated in various myths.
40. The French *cabaret* of that period combined elements of what today would be called a bar, a café, and a tavern. The *cabaret* served meals as well as alcoholic beverages and might offer overnight accommodations. It was a multifaceted institution where workers could assemble for entertainment and companionship.

After a few mediocre songs, someone would hold forth with one of the rougher, more barbarous sort, like the one whose last verse goes like this:

> The man who wrote this song
> Was known as Sincerity-of-Mâcon.
> He wrote it while feasting on the liver of four devouring dogs,[41]
> And cutting off the head of one of their candidates.
> And on the heads of these cowards,
> He wrote his worthy *nom de compagnon*.

This curious composition was sung with enthusiasm, even with passion. I was distressed, shocked, and could not hide my feelings.

"What's the matter?" one of my table companions asked me, "don't you find our song pretty?"

"I find it detestable."

"Could you write one like it?"

"I'm not bragging that I could."

"You're right not to."

That was the provocation I spoke of. It was because of that incident, trivial in itself, that I resolved to create, not songs of progress, but at least something that would not embitter people's minds and lead to brawls.

Like all brotherhoods of compagnons, we had our poets and our song-writers. But most of their compositions were bellicose, violent, and insulting toward the rival Compagnons du Devoir. On this crucial point, I wanted to depart from the example of my predecessors.

In the evening, after my day's work, I returned to the room that I shared with Vivarais-the-Well-behaved at Mr. Luton's, and made my first attempt. Its title was "Hymn to Solomon." Was it good? Was I satisfied? Of course not.

I owned the major tragedies of Voltaire and all of Racine's. As I read these plays, I would get a feeling for the cadence and the harmony, and this brought me pleasure. Yet I had no understanding of structure and strict meter, the secret of verse. In this respect, I was like any other reader who lacks formal training. What's more, my verses merely rhymed without having meter. It was really prose with rhyming lines, and even at that, the rhymes were not always well interwoven. Try as I might to sing those miserable couplets as I wrote them, I could sense their defects but did not understand them or know how to fix them.

There was another compagnon who was considered well educated be-

---

41. The song puns on *dévorants*, "devouring," which was also a common nickname for *devoirants*, the members of the rival brotherhood, the Compagnons du Devoir.

cause he had written ballads. I entrusted my song to him and asked him to teach me. He took it away with him and returned it after several days, telling me, "It's good." I was more demanding. I was not happy with my piece of work. But in the end, by continuing to read my cherished authors, I managed to discover the mechanics of verse. And then I would rewrite and touch things up.

Not long after that, I wrote a second song, which I entitled "The Embattled Spirit." It was about a compagnon in love whom the brotherhood orders to leave the city where he is staying and to travel. It was about love in conflict with duty. Duty ends up winning out. My compositions, which contained no provocations against *devoirants*, were not badly received, and people sang them. [. . .]

Distractions; Love; Attachment to My Native Region

Particularly in the wintertime, the sole refuge and place of entertainment for the worker in Chartres was the *cabaret*. There was a theater but no resident company. Actors on tour offered occasional performances. I saw presentations of Scribe's *Le Mariage de raison* and Favart's *Oreste, ou Les Rêveries renouvelées des Grecs*. The first of these, a light comedy, made me think without ever winning over my heart, even though I think the author is right. The second, a parody, made me laugh a lot.

In the summertime, we were happier. When nature is renewed and the countryside grows green again, when flowers dot the fields, hillsides, and valleys and the birds fly from branch to branch, singing their gentle harmonies, that is when gatherings and village festivals start up again and the countryside becomes infinitely preferable to the cities. We would attend these festivals and have ourselves a wonderful time. For my part, I got a taste of happiness there, enormous happiness, a happiness that was intense even if it was incomplete. My heart wanted something more. But on the one hand, I could not take pleasure in fallen women who I was not in love with, and I did not want to deceive young Sophie, so sweet and tender. I did not want to drive her into misery or offer her only dishonor in exchange for her love.

To seduce a young girl with noble promises or with solemn declarations of undying affection, to make her pregnant and then abandon her, to disturb her mind, bring her despair, break her heart, kill her spirit, these were not consistent with my principles or part of my character.

I loved, I burned, I suffered, I was buffeted, shaken, pushed in opposite directions by my emotions and my conscience. If my emotions wanted one thing, my conscience would say, "Stop, that's bad." Ah, what it costs a sensitive, loving man with a passionate heart to make himself the slave of his reason and his honesty and not weaken. What a difficult task!

I did not want to form attachments and settle outside the region of my birth, for it meant everything to me. My family was there, my relatives. I wanted to return home and settle near them. Those were my feelings concerning my family and my native region.

When I would see a compagnon interrupt his Tour of France, get married, and settle down far from his father and mother, his relatives, his place of birth, it was beyond my comprehension. How far I was from thinking that it would be my destiny to do just that! But all that happened only after long disappointments and genuine misfortunes, as we shall see. [. . .]

My Stay in Paris

At last I reached Paris, that great and beautiful city, which all by itself has a population as large as several of our departments. It is the residence of kings and princes, of the powerful, of intellectuals. It is the seat of government, the nerve center of France, the theater of revolutions and political and social change. Paris is where talent, bursts of genius, science, the arts, and all manner of astonishing things are on display and have a chance to shine. Paris is a district made beautiful by its quays, its boulevards, its Champs-Elysées, its public squares, its vast gardens, its innumerable monuments, its rich countryside! It most assuredly is worthy of our admiration.

Yet I was struck by a painful contrast. This magnificent region was, for young travelers like myself, less hospitable than many others. In provincial cities, as soon as we arrived, the First Fellow would greet us, the roller would take us to see an employer and get us hired. At the Mother, we would find food, a bed, and credit. There can be nothing as delightful as that! In Paris, it was completely different. We would indeed meet many comrades who, as individuals, treated us well and took an interest in our affairs, but we would not find a brotherhood organized as it was elsewhere and presenting the new arrival with a veritable family.

At the time we arrived, jobs were scarce. What added to our difficulties was that Parisian masters required workers to supply their own tools.[42] We had neither the tools nor the money to buy them. If we had wanted to make furniture, we could easily have found work in the Faubourg Saint-Antoine, but joinery was more our line. We made the rounds of the city and its suburbs, presenting ourselves at many workshops, asking in a loud voice, "Are you hiring here?" This was rather unpleasant for us, since,

42. This is consistent with Bédé's observation that Parisian masters in the woodworking trades had succeeded in shifting to the workers the responsibility for this expense, a change that appears to have taken place early in the nineteenth century (see chapter 1).

until then, the First Fellow and the roller had spared us this kind of drudgery, and work had come to us without our having to worry about it. We got many rejections and a few positive responses. But we still needed tools that we did not own—block planes, smooth planes, saws, and so on. Still, Caderousse and Bagnol managed to get themselves hired, and some fellow workers loaned them tools. As for me, I still had not found the local chapter of the compagnonnage, and my thoughts were turning to the countryside.

I wrote my father, who was already urging me to hurry my journey along, asking him to send me money that would get me as far as Lyon all in one burst. [. . .]

Journey from Paris to Chalon-sur-Saône

I received an answer from my father, who sent me one hundred francs. I could pay my little debts and get myself to Lyon.

Vivarais-the-Happy-hearted and I, having sent our trunks on ahead by coach, each slung a small bundle over our shoulders and left Paris on foot. Some compagnons provided us with an escort, and after giving us friendly embraces, sent us on our way. [. . .]

But the roads were bad, and we were walking in water and mud. My shoes suffered, came unsewn, and gave out on me. I was forced to walk barefoot. At the first opportunity, a cobbler put my shoes back in a state that I thought acceptable, but not much further on, I had to pay four francs for another pair that was hardly any better.

We passed through Villeneuve-le-Roi on market day. Two ancient gates and some beautiful alleys skirting the town attracted our attention. After we had gone a bit further, we decided it was best, in light of the condition of the roads, to climb aboard a rattletrap coach and ride along in that ghastly—and I do mean ghastly—vehicle.[43] The coach drivers were even more ghastly. They would stop at every inn, tavern, and watering hole they encountered, and have a few drinks. Once drunk, they would ridicule the poor passengers who complained about the lack of speed. I had never in my life seen anything so gross, so blunt, so crude, or so insolent as those rattletrap drivers from Burgundy. They were truly the scourge of the region. [. . .]

I said earlier that the inhabitants of regions rich in wine do not get drunk, but I was not speaking about the drivers of rattletrap coaches. I

---

43. A rattletrap (*patache*) was the sort of primitive coach likely to be in service in rural areas. As it had no suspension, it gave its passengers an extremely uncomfortable ride.

make an exception of them, for they make a mockery—to the point of outrage—of the general rule.

Stagecoaches, railways, and other forms of transportation set up to serve small localities have done away with the old rattletraps, those proletarian vehicles which, because they were the property of their drivers and operated without rules or regulations, were so free and independent. The rattletrap drivers cried, "Robbery!" and complained bitterly, but their complaints did not move me in the least, because they had no redeeming virtues, no dignity, no consideration, no pity for the poor passengers. They deserved their downfall.

"What?" you may say, "The rich organize corporations and vast workshops! They develop all sorts of businesses, take over the highways, the streams, the rivers, the canals, the earth and the sea! They make workers their underlings, their instruments. Either by themselves or through their associates, they provide the impetus for everything! Under their supervision everything must run with precision, order, reliability, and speed, but in the process they do away with independent work and crush private enterprise with their competition! They turn a profit on everything! They are rich and constantly getting richer! They lure all the silver, all the gold, all the capital of France into their hands! Should we see this as progress? Where can we find independent workers? What will become of the people? What, then, will be its fate in the future?"

Yes, that is one outcome, one fundamental consequence that is slowly coming about. Workers do not stand up for each other. Because they lack mutual respect, because they fight among themselves, because they struggle to see who can devour the other, they have lost their status, their independence, and their well-being. That is a great misfortune. But a new day is dawning. Workers will gain in understanding, in intelligence, in virtue, in wisdom, in industriousness, and in justice. And a society that has undergone renewal will pay them back with interest for what they have lost. They must develop their minds, constantly consult the voice of their conscience, become the champions of fraternity, love their neighbors, and above all hope. Justice will one day be done. But they must not forget that in this world (not to mention the other), they will earn their reward, whether it is heaven or hell, according to their merits. [. . .]

The Tour of France; Capturing Towns

For members of the Compagnons du Devoir de Liberté, the recognized stops on the Tour of France at the time I did it were: Avignon, Marseille, Nîmes, Montpellier, Béziers, Bordeaux, Rochefort, Nantes, Tours,

Chartres, Chalon, Lyon, and Valence.[44] While I was working in Bordeaux, we had added Toulouse. While I was staying in Chartres, we took possession of Blois. Auxerre and Sens, through which I had just passed without stopping—and for good reason—were to be captured later and become towns on our Tour of France. Rochefort, where too many people came down with fever, had to be abandoned for La Rochelle.

Aside from these cities, called "brotherhood towns," where there is an actual chapter that welcomes compagnons, there are others such as Toulon, Cette, Saumur, Alais, Uzès, Annonay, Vienne, and Paris where members of our brotherhood are living but where no accommodations are available and the brotherhood has not formally been established. For this reason, these are called "bastard towns." A given city may be a bastard town for one society and a brotherhood town for another. Angoulême is the charter city for the shoemakers' brotherhood and the primary town of their tour. Orléans, Dijon, Agen, Angers, Vendôme, and Paris are of central importance for other trades.

I have said that during my stay in Bordeaux we recaptured Toulouse and that while I was in Chartres we took or "captured" Blois. To capture a town meant to send compagnons, found a Mother, and establish our brotherhood in force, making it a stop on the Tour of France. The capture of towns sometimes had to be paid in blood.

The Compagnons du Devoir were well established in Blois and exercised control over it. We, the Compagnons du Devoir de Liberté, also wanted a foothold, a right to stop and stay over in that city. A prefecture was being built in Blois, and we had been promised work. The masters were waiting for our arrival.

All chapters of the Tour of France were consulted in this matter. The brotherhood as a whole decided to make Blois a "brotherhood town." This resulted in certain measures being taken. It was agreed that a certain number of men would be sent from each point on the vast circumference of the circuit: so many from Chartres, so many from Tours, so many from Nantes, Bordeaux, Lyon, and elsewhere. Paris sometimes furnished its contingent. All the men selected would set forth at a prearranged moment and travel toward a common destination. Once arrived, they would join forces, make their entry into the new city, and go to a house prepared in advance, where they would name a mother and get the brotherhood established.

44. See the map on page 3. The names of these towns are given in the order in which Perdiguier, departing from his native Provence, visited them (he did not visit Rochefort, Tours, or Valence), but they formed a circuit that could be begun at any point.

It sometimes happens that the rival brotherhood tries to repel the new arrivals. Terrible fights then take place. The compagnons who open up a new city generally come from the brotherhood cities that are closest by. However, because these towns deplete themselves and thin their ranks of men, they are often unable to meet employers' needs, and the whole Tour of France is shaken up, thrown into an uproar, and forced to react. Even the most distant towns make some effort. Compagnons who are on the road are ordered to head in the direction where men are lacking in order to reestablish a more uniform ratio between the amount of work and the complement of journeymen available to execute it.

The capture of Blois led to conflicts and horrible battles. Men were injured and killed. All other towns on the Tour of France were obliged to send money to help our brothers in their immediate need and in the process of adjustment that they would soon have to undergo. Chalon did its part.

The compagnons who take part in the entry or capture of a city earn a certain seniority, a right of precedence over other compagnons. It is, in effect, a military campaign and it confers advancement.

Compagnons' Strikes

In that same year of 1827, a strike took place in Nîmes. Several of our compagnons were put in jail. We had to come to their aid, just as we had done for our brothers in Blois, by collecting money in each city.

Competition is something that comes naturally. Every master wants to get work and, in order to attract business, will offer to produce and deliver at a lower price than his colleagues. Cheap goods create pressure for more cheap goods. But when masters set up businesses that are marginally profitable (or not profitable at all), when they fear losses (or actually suffer them), what do they do? They lower the cost of labor, the wages of the worker. These wages sag and fall from one year to the next, as a natural consequence of our very human tendencies, for there's a little bit of the peddler in us all.

When the worker labors for a very low wage and is unable to make ends meet; when he finds that he is unable to shift onto anyone else a portion of his overwhelming burden or to effect a proportional reduction in the price of meat, bread, or rent; and when he nonetheless wishes to live as a man of honor and meet his obligations, what does he do? He goes on strike.

No other avenue is open to him in his effort to obtain justice, raise his lowered wages, and balance his income with essential expenses. The most intelligent workers, the most active, the most devoted, the most courageous, and those who are often the leaders of the different brotherhoods in the trade—for in these matters, *gavots* and *devoirants* act as one—draw up a wage schedule, pegging the value of each type of work in the trade. They then parley with the masters.

If the masters choose to listen to their complaints and demands, the opposing parties negotiate, arguing for their respective interests, and together set either the price of a day's work or a piece rate, so that everything is settled amicably and, as it were, all in the family. But if the masters refuse to listen or are too demanding, the compagnons pass the word and *gavots* and *devoirants* alike stop working all at once, the shops empty, the employers have no more workers, and production is suspended.

It sometimes happens that the masters, finally exhausted, make concessions to the workers' demands and sign a new wage schedule, in which case order is immediately restored. But in other cases, they call on the courts to help them, set traps for the leaders of the strike, and subject them to legal action, conviction, and even imprisonment as leaders of a conspiracy.

In Nîmes, three Compagnons du Devoir and an equal number of Compagnons du Devoir de Liberté were thrown in prison as their reward for their devotion to their brothers. This resulted in a collection being taken up in Chalon as elsewhere, and in the cooperation of compagnons from all points on the Tour of France.

I would like to ask the rulers and judges of France why they imprison men who are asking only to live by their own labor. When wages are too low, when these men can no longer support themselves, are they supposed to wrong their innkeeper, their landlord, or any other kindhearted man to whom they may be indebted, by being dishonest? Or are they supposed to remain honest by not eating when they are hungry, by destroying their health and their physical constitution, and becoming an impoverished, stunted race incapable of serving France or defending her if needed? Those are two extremes that you cannot allow, and I feel certain that you will reject them both.

So workers must be honest and yet they must not perish. Well then, let them go on strike. Let them arrive at an understanding that will help prop up slumping wages. Let them be permitted to withhold the products of their hands and minds from sale at too cheap a price, for those are their only wares and their sole resource. Take heed of these men, who are your brothers and who do useful labor, for their wretched existence forms the base, the true foundation of more fortunate states of existence. Compare their lives to the lives of others! And yet without workers, what would become of society? There would be no rich, powerful, and influential people, no princes or kings. Would there even be a hint of civilization, prosperity, or comfort anywhere to be found?

If, however, their strikes prove violent, if they mistreat some employer or some worker who refuses to stop working and join them, bring them to judgment and punish them for their acts of violence. But allow them the freedom to struggle over the price of their sweat and blood, of their lives. Let them live by their labor.

[In sections that have not been included here, Perdiguier recounts his journey to Lyon, where he was immediately hired in the workshop of Mr. Audry and where he became deeply involved in the affairs of the Compagnons du Devoir de Liberté. The chapter in Lyon, the nation's second most populous city at that time, was perhaps the most active on the entire Tour of France. At a general assembly in December 1827, Perdiguier was elected First Fellow and subsequently inducted into the third order as an initiated fellow, giving him the right to the title of Dignitary. His administration was devoted to setting the chapter's house in order, from both a fiscal and an organizational point of view, and proved somewhat controversial. By the end of his six-month term, however, the affairs of the Lyon brotherhood had been placed on a sound footing.]

An Induction into the Brotherhood; a General Assembly

Let us now take up detailed consideration of specific facts relating to the affairs of the compagnonnage which portray not only the practices and customs of workers but also the spirit and deportment of their professional associations.

One day when I was at the Mother, I witnessed the arrival of a charming young man who had curly blond hair, blue eyes, the sweetest of faces, and a good bearing. He told me, "I am an aspirant, a candidate for membership in the Compagnons du Devoir. I have come with the intention of changing brotherhoods." I had him sit and asked him, "Do you have cause for complaint against your own?" He told me of the injustices that its members had done him. I answered, "That is evidence against certain men, but not against your brotherhood. You would perhaps do well to remain a member and not to change. I cannot promise you that you will never have cause for complaint if you join us. Our rules are good, but those who are responsible for applying them may understand them incorrectly, interpret them badly, or do the opposite of what they command."

"Yes, but in your brotherhood there is friendship and equality between affiliates and compagnons. In ours, it's just the opposite. That's something I can't stand. If you'll accept me, I want to belong to yours."

"You're quite sure, then?"

"Yes, very sure."

"Were you of steady conduct as a member of the Compagnons du

Devoir, both in the Mother and in your employer's workshop? We'd have to settle your accounts so that there are no black marks against you."

"I have nothing to fear; I did my duty."

"If you persist in your resolve, come back tomorrow. The roller will accompany you."

The next day, this young man, who came from Saint-Symphorien near Lyon and whose name was Chavana, indeed came back. The roller went to settle his accounts with the Compagnons du Devoir and with his employer. His conduct had been good, and they had nothing to reproach him for. I got him hired immediately.

On the first Sunday of the month, we held a general assembly. I stood in the most visible spot in the room, opposite the door by which we had entered. On my immediate right and left, I had my secretary and my four elders. The others took up positions according to their rank or seniority in the brotherhood, with the finished fellows nearest, then the recognized fellows, and then the affiliates. All were clean and well dressed. I was dressed in my gold-fringed scarf. In the buttonholes of their jackets or frock coats, all the compagnons wore the blue and white ribbons that were the colors of the Compagnons du Devoir de Liberté. The meeting opened with everyone standing, hat in hand. The preliminary business was soon completed.

There had been several recent arrivals, new men who wanted to join us. They were downstairs in the Mother, waiting for us to have them come up.

I told the roller, "First bring in the man from Lyon." He came back, leading a young worker by the hand. He introduced him to me, saying, "This is a young man who asks to join our brotherhood." I questioned the new arrival in these terms: "Do you wish to belong to our brotherhood?"

"Yes, sir."

"That word is not appropriate here. You must say, 'Yes, brother,' for, wherever we may have been born, we are all countrymen, all brothers, all part of the same family."

"Yes, brother."

"I must tell you that there are several brotherhoods. There are the Compagnons du Devoir and the Compagnons du Devoir de Liberté."

"I know."

"And which do you think you are addressing at this moment?"

"The Compagnons du Devoir de Liberté."

"You're correct. But if you had been mistaken, you would have been free to withdraw. All brotherhoods are good. You must choose freely."

"I'm not mistaken. This is indeed the one I prefer."

"In a little while, we'll acquaint you with the regulations."

I then addressed the person who had brought him to me and who had remained at his side: "Roller, take the brother from Lyon to his place. Because he is the last to arrive, he must be the last in rank. Then bring the man from the Vivarais region."

The roller brought in the worker from the Vivarais and then each of the other new members in turn, and I asked them all the customary questions before having them placed according to rank, one behind the other. When they had all been through this process, I told them, "Come closer. We're going to acquaint you with the regulations which we all must submit to. Pay close attention."

I gave a sign to the secretary, who read the regulations. In abbreviated form, their principal articles are the following:

> Whenever you arrive in a town, make your way to the Mother and ask for the roller. He will have a bottle served at the brotherhood's expense so that you can clink glasses. After he is given the order by the First Fellow, he will then get you hired.
>
> While in the Mother, it is forbidden to take the holy name of God in vain, to use the familiar form of address, or to quarrel. We must treat each other with mutual respect, behave with decency, and show respect for the father, the mother, and all those who serve them.
>
> You may not enter the Mother on Sundays or holidays without stockings or gaiters. During the week you may not wear shirt sleeves or your work apron or come without a tie.
>
> In your place of work, be respectful to your *bourgeois* without being servile or groveling or being a bootlicker.[45]
>
> If any of our members are in the hospital, everyone will visit them in turn. But if someone is there because of his debauchery, the brotherhood owes him nothing.
>
> If any of us were to go to prison for upholding the honor and interests of our brotherhood, he would be entitled to our every consideration. But if he is there because he started a fight, the brotherhood owes him only its scorn for having brought it dishonor and will expel him immediately.
>
> Any member who misses three assemblies in a row, after being ordered by the roller to attend, will be expelled from the brotherhood.
>
> Everyone must pay his monthly dues to defray the expenses of the brotherhood. Anyone who gets more than three

45. Perdiguier employs the expression *pousser la doucine*, a joiner's metaphor which literally means "pushing the molding plane." This tool was used to make fancy moldings with both a convex and a concave surface and had to be manipulated with great delicacy.

months behind without a legitimate reason will be expelled
from the brotherhood.

Each time you leave a city, you must be certified by the
brotherhood as being in order if you expect to be welcomed in
the new city to which you are going.

Each time you leave a workshop, you must settle your accounts. You cannot be hired elsewhere until this formality has
been completed.

The brotherhood is accountable for a certain sum of money
for each of its members in the Mother. Anyone who leaves
without settling accounts and paying up is considered a
"burner" and is reported as such throughout France. He is excluded.

"And those, my dear brothers, are our regulations. Wherever our
brotherhood exists, they are the same. If they suit you, you may remain
with us. If not, you are free to withdraw."

Once the rules had been read, I said to the new inductees, "Do you feel
able to comply with these regulations? If they're not to your liking, if you
can't observe them, you've been told and I tell you again, you are free to
withdraw."

"We can observe them and they do suit us," they would say, each in his
own way.

"Then you are now members of the brotherhood," I added. "Return to
your places."

Secret ceremonies, the admission rites for compagnons, and the great
code of regulations, all this is for the best, but I cannot and must not say
anything more on these subjects. [. . .]

The First Fellow

A First Fellow is a president, a captain, an arbiter, a judge, a brother, and a
father. He summons and presides over all assemblies, accompanies those
who are leaving, welcomes those who are arriving and gets them hired. He
watches over the operation of the brotherhood, over the affairs of each and
all. He reprimands or encourages, approves or disapproves. He is in daily
touch with workers and with masters, and intervenes in their disputes.
Sometimes it is the master who is unfair and wants everything his own
way. Sometimes it is the worker who, though he has not produced work of
acceptable quality, makes unreasonable demands and wants to receive an
elevated price. I remember one affiliate from the Vivarais region who had
made some windows for Mr. Martelin. The latter wanted to pay four sous
per running foot below the going rate. The worker from the Vivarais called

on me to appraise his work and speak in his favor. The *bourgeois*, on his side, accepted me as arbiter. When I had finished my examination, I took Vivarais aside and told him, "Your work isn't up to standard, and I can do nothing to plead your cause. Take what you're being offered. You could do worse." He took my advice and everything was settled.

The First Fellow is often called upon as an unofficial judge. I intervened in many disputes, in many conflicts. I patched up many such affairs and restored good relations among lots of people who were falling out. And I made one hundred friends for every enemy. [. . .]

My Certificate

I was by then about to end my Tour of France. I was, I repeat, all square with the brotherhood. It was grateful to me for my zeal, for my administrative work, for the enormous results I had achieved. It had grown in size and was sound, even flourishing, and in complete peace.

The moment of my departure was approaching. An assembly of departure was called in my honor. My accounts had just been settled with the Mother and with the brotherhood, and we were all square with one another. In addition to the document that each compagnon must carry on the road, I also held a certificate stamped with the seal of the brotherhood. It read as follows:

> We, the compagnon joiners of the Devoir de Liberté of the City of Lyon, certify that brother Avignonnais-the-Virtuous (Agricol Perdiguier) served his time as Dignitary from Christmas to the feast day of Saint Anne and that he performed his duty with honor and integrity. The brotherhood declares him to be in good standing and is grateful for his services.
>
> We have therefore issued the present certificate to serve him in case of need.
>
> Executed in session before us, the compagnon joiners of the Devoir de Liberté of the City of Lyon, this eighteenth day of August, 1828,
>
> > Limousin-the-Pure-hearted, D. G. T.
> > Vivarais-the-Calm, Initiated Fellow

[. . .] My Arrival in Avignon and Morières

Even though I had friends and relatives in Avignon, I preferred to go to the Mother of the compagnon joiners of the Devoir de Liberté who, four and a half years earlier, had provided my escort as I set out on the road to Marseille. They had been the last to bid me farewell at the time of my departure from the region, and they would be the first to welcome me back, take me in, and help me celebrate my return.

I ate supper with these friends and slept in one of their dormitories. The next morning, I set off on foot for Morières, the place where I was born. A few compagnons accompanied me.

The road from Avignon to Morières is gently sloped, smooth surfaced, and bordered by two streams that are always cool. Its banks are planted with poplars and willows whose enormous boughs meet, overlap, and interlace, forming an immense vaulted avenue under which the traveler always walks in shade. The countryside is flat, full of madder vines, cereals, and good grazing land. We arrived at the little canal, then at the larger Canal de Crillon, whose salutary waters have transformed stony fields and red, rocky, arid, and infertile lands into an earthly paradise.

Near the Pont de la Fuste, I entered our garden and stopped for a moment. I picked a flower and a piece of fruit. What fragrance! What flavor!

Here and there along my route, I had met a few of my fellow villagers, both men and women, who were going off to the city in carts or on foot or mounted on donkeys. They had all given me proof of their firm friendship.

I arrived at the village. Everyone looked at me, called out to me, came up to me, rejoiced over me. My aunt and my uncle, the Turins, heaped affection on me.

At last I arrived at the threshold of our dwelling. I entered. I hugged my father, my brothers, my sisters, and my mother, who started crying. I could not contain my emotion and my chest swelled. Words failed me, and tears ran from my eyes.

Only our mother can move us, can play upon our heartstrings in this way. I made an effort to hide my emotions and my weakness, to display courage, firmness, and a manly spirit.

The news of my arrival spread. My aunts, my uncles, my cousins, my godmother and godfather, my friends, our neighbors, a swarm of kindly people came to the house. One gang followed another. My, but that was a beautiful day! Many tears of joy were shed.

At so sweet a memory, I can feel those tears reborn, flowing from my eyes and dampening the paper on which I write these words. Great sorrow and the most profound joy are expressed in the same way, in the same language: tears!

The whole village demonstrated its genuine affection for me. If my relatives, my friends, my fellow citizens have stood by me, I can do myself this justice: that I have not repaid them with ingratitude and have always stood by them as well.

I have said it once and I'll say it again: if, far from my village, I had been offered the most beautiful, the richest, the most perfect woman in the world and been told, "Take her and remain here," I would not have been tempted. It would not have made me renounce my family and my native region. That is why I never could understand the compagnons who got married on the Tour of France and, in so doing, said farewell forever to all that was associated with their place of birth. I would think to myself, "I could never do that."

On 24 August 1828, after four and a half years of traveling, I returned to the place from which I had started out. I was twenty-two years and nine months old. From time to time I had received a little money from home, but I had used it well. I had tried to learn, to increase my understanding, for that is the sole purpose of the Tour of France. My responsibilities as First Fellow of Lyon had cost us money, but it was not a total loss. It had prepared me to direct and govern men, to study and understand them in depth, to gain experience, and all of this was worthwhile.

I returned to the village thinking I would never leave it again, that I'd stop traveling, settle down, get married, live and die right there. Soon after, I formally "thanked" the compagnon joiners of the Devoir de Liberté, which meant I was resigning. There is a ceremony, a very sweet celebration, that takes place on such occasions. I was issued a certificate on parchment, covered with secret symbols and the seal of the brotherhood, that had been sent from Marseille at the request of Avignon because Avignon did not have the right draftsman or a certain stamp.

It seemed that my life as a compagnon was over. My relations with the compagnonnage would thenceforth be those of one of its former and faithful adepts, and later those of a master and employer, and that was all. I would lead the life of a villager: isolated, obscure, peaceful, and happy. My ambition was fulfilled and I wished for nothing better.

In point of fact, Perdiguier's life followed a subsequent course entirely different from the one he anticipated in the closing lines of his memoirs. Though he resumed work in his father's shop after returning to Morières, he grew bored and restless after just nine months. He soon headed for Paris, despite the unfavorable first impression it had made on him, arriving in time to witness the Revolution of 1830. In addition to earning his livelihood in his trade and pursuing his studies as a form of self-improvement, he managed to publish a volume of compagnons' songs in

1834 and the first edition of Le Livre du compagnonnage *in 1839. Now married, he started a drafting school to supplement his income, as he was increasingly afflicted with a series of debilitating, work-related illnesses. His writing projects embroiled him in controversy with other compagnons, who felt that he had been too revealing of the societies' secret inner workings or had sought personal recognition at their expense. But his status as a worker-author also brought him into contact with a new world populated by such luminaries as George Sand, whose patronage made it possible for him to undertake a second tour of France in 1840 to promote his writings.*

His visibility also won him election as a workers' representative to the National Assembly under the Second Republic, where he was associated with the moderate republican faction. Perhaps because of his support for Ledru-Rollin in the presidential election of 1848, his name was placed on a list of eighty-four individuals proscribed after Louis-Napoléon's coup of December 1851. Arrested and placed briefly in Sainte-Pélagie prison (the same one in which Bédé had served his term some thirty years earlier), he was soon expelled from French territory and forced into exile in Belgium. There he briefly shared a one-room apartment with Martin Nadaud. In 1855 he was allowed to move back to Paris, where he opened a small workers' bookstore in the front of the building in which he also rented rooms, sold wine, and offered drafting lessons as his health permitted. Despite his many difficulties, he persevered in his writing projects and even made a triumphal third tour of France in 1863, greeting old friends and new, and trying to breathe new life into a compagnonnage system that had experienced a serious decline in the interim. With the liberalization of the mid-1860s, Perdiguier was able to resume his public advocacy of republican politics. He played a minor role during the siege of Paris in 1870 and spoke out in opposition to the Paris Commune, a position which led to attacks in the working-class press. He died in Paris in 1875.

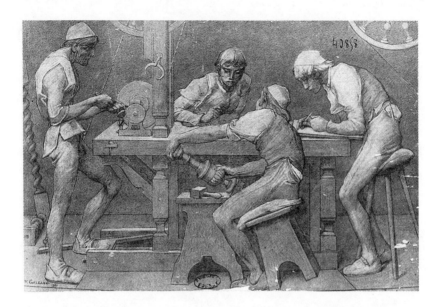

A wood turners' shop. This drawing dates from the late eighteenth century, toward the time when Bédé was born. Note the treadle-powered lathe at left. Bibliothèque Forney, Paris.

A wood turners' shop. Rough planks are being split; and recently arrived, unfinished wood is being handed up for storage in a loft. Bibliothèque Forney, Paris.

A working-class *cabaret*, the California, in 1856. The activities portrayed, as well as the mix of men and women, children and adults, suggest a midday meal. Engraving by Flameng. Bibliothèque Nationale, Paris.

The Departure. Engraving by Bauce. A young woman is leaving her native village for the city. Her search for wage employment would likely lead to a job in domestic service or in industry. Bibliothèque Nationale, Paris.

A joiners' workshop. Strewn about this exceptionally spacious and airy shop are the tools and raw materials typical of the joiner's trade. Among the items being made are a door, a casement window, and a curved wooden panel. In the court-yard, two long-sawyers are ripping the wood to size. Behind them, lengths of unseasoned wood have been stacked in piles to dry. Bibliothèque des Arts et Traditions Populaires, Paris.

Compagnonnage: Arrival at the Mother. The itinerant worker, still carrying his possessions on his back, enters the local chapter of his brotherhood to be greeted by the "mother" and the "roller." *Journées illustrées de la Révolution de 1848* (Paris, 1848–49), p. 95.

Compagnonnage: The roller and the new hire. The roller would introduce the newly arrived worker to the employer and oversee the ritual exchange that bound the two parties in an unwritten contract of employment. *Journées illustrées*, p. 94.

Compagnonnage: The new hire pays for a round of drinks. His fellow workers offer a toast to the recently arrived journeyman in return for this gesture of good colleagueship. *Journées illustrées*, p. 94.

Compagnonnage: The departure. A worker, bound for the next stop on the Tour of France, sets off on foot with his staff and bundle of belongings. He is followed as far as the edge of town by a retinue of fellow workers who pretend to try to restrain him before bidding him farewell with wishes for a safe journey. *L'Illustration*, 22 November 1845, p. 185.

Seasonal migrants head for Paris. A small convoy of workers takes to the road in search of temporary employment in the urban cash economy. *L'Illustration*, 31 May 1862.

Construction site. Workers unload materials, mix and carry mortar, and, in the distance, erect the building, while the contractor and owner consult in the foreground. Bibliothèque Forney, Paris.

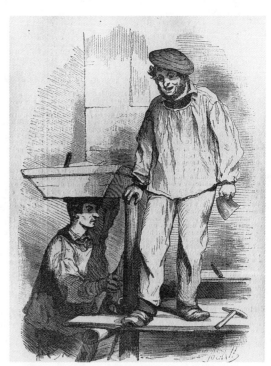

A mason and his assistant. The laborer carries a hod full of fresh mortar up a ladder. The mason waits, trowel in hand, impatient to resume his work. *L'Illustration*, 9 October 1847, p. 92.

Open market, itinerant peddlers. This scene from the Boulevard du Temple, a working-class neighborhood of Paris, is typical of the lively, crowded, sometimes squalid environment of the great cities to which so many rural residents were attracted in the course of the nineteenth century. *L'Illustration*, 10 February 1844, p. 376.

Navvies at work. Brick makers, ditch diggers, and earth workers were among the least skilled and worst paid male members of the working class. Bibliothèque des Arts et Traditions Populaires, Paris.

A weaver at his loom. Although the apparatus pictured here is relatively elaborate, it was quite common for silk workers like Truquin to set themselves up in their homes and make use of the labor of their wives and children. Bibliothèque Forney, Paris.

Le Creusot in the nineteenth century. The town where Dumay was born and lived most of his life was unusual for its time in that a high proportion of its economic activity depended on large-scale factory production. Bibliothèque Forney, Paris.

Smelting in an iron foundry. Among the characteristic new forms of heavy industry in the nineteenth century were ironworks like this one in Saint-Gervais. *L'Illustration,* 17 February 1849, p. 393.

Embroiderers working at home. Women workers tended to be concentrated in a few sectors of the wage-earning economy, especially those involved in the production of textiles and clothing. Much of this work was done at home, where it could be accomplished along with domestic tasks. Bibliothèque Forney, Paris.

Le blanchissage

A laundress at work. Young women employed as maids worked extremely long hours for very little pay. Their duties would typically include the full range of household chores as well as child care. Bibliothèque Forney, Paris.

4 Martin Nadaud

*Memoirs of Léonard, a Former
Mason's Assistant*

*The title of Nadaud's book is curious but significant. He calls himself
Léonard, which was, in fact, his father's first name. Given the warmth and
intimacy of their relationship, as revealed in these pages, Nadaud's choice
is most readily seen as an expression of his filial respect and affection.
Maurice Agulhon has suggested that Martin Nadaud may have preferred
to use a first name more typical of the Limousin region than his own.*[1]
*Certainly his intention was to tell a story of more than personal scope, to
communicate not only his own and his forebears' experiences, but to introduce the reader to a distinctive way of life.*

*Born in 1815 to a family of poor country people, at age fifteen Nadaud
joined the bands of seasonal migrants who sought to supplement their
meager incomes by making their way to the great cities of France to work
as masons during the yearly peak in construction activity. The terminal
points of this journey — his native department of Creuse and his adopted
city of Paris—remained the dual poles around which the events of
Nadaud's life revolved. Though he rose to prominence in both local and
national politics, his identification with the working class was unwavering.*

*His memoirs, begun in 1891 after he had retired from public affairs, re-
viewed a lifetime that very nearly spanned the nineteenth century. Published when he was eighty, just three years before his death in 1898, they
remain profoundly optimistic about the progress achieved by France and
by its workers in both political and material terms. Several editions of this
work have appeared in French in the course of the twentieth century.*

1. See Martin Nadaud, *Mémoires de Léonard, ancien garçon maçon* (Paris, 1976),
p. 179 n. 1.

MY BIRTH; VILLAGE CUSTOMS

I was born on 17 November 1815 in a small village called La Martinèche, located in the commune of Soubrebost and the ward of Bourganeuf. [. . .]

In our village, evening "vigils" would always take place in the same house and under the supervision of one particular old woman to whom we would listen attentively and with the greatest respect.[2]

Old Fouéssoune, considered to be the voice of authority, was the village midwife. She had assisted our mothers when each of us was born. She also knew the medicinal properties of every plant. She was the only doctor who had ever practiced in our village. Accustomed to never being contradicted, she would affirm with imperturbable self-assurance that Tom, Dick, or Harry, who had been dead for several years, had come to visit his former neighbors and told them the names of others from the village who had gone either to heaven or to hell. She would also tell us the names of those known to be werewolves as well as those who had exerted themselves to vanquish them. At that point, the eyes of everyone present would shine with joy, for we all would have liked to be one of those resourceful men who had brought down a werewolf. [. . .]

Eugène Sue tells us, in his *Histoire des prolétaires à travers les âges*, that in the fifteenth century few peasants had family names.[3] They were given made-up names, usually nicknames relating to the occupation of the head of the household.

Our home was called Rag Paper. This nickname came from the fact that one of my ancestors had been a ragpicker.[4] It is well known that after the

---

2. The *veillée* or evening vigil was a common practice in rural villages between the months of November and March. As the weather grew colder and darkness fell earlier, most of the tasks that could be usefully accomplished took place indoors. From suppertime to bedtime, neighbors and relatives would gather in a barn to take advantage of the warmth of the animals and to conserve both light and heat. These intimate assemblies provided the occasion for storytelling and socializing as well as the accomplishment of domestic tasks.

3. Eugène Sue (1804–57) was the author of several popular novels that were widely read in the mid–nineteenth century. He was also a Socialist who, like Nadaud, served as a representative in the Legislative Assembly in 1850 and 1851.

4. The term "ragpicker" (*chiffonnier*) might designate someone who sorted rags in a paper mill; more frequently it referred to a person who collected discarded bits of fabric or worn-out clothing that were resold for making writing paper. Because the search for such materials often involved rummaging through refuse, it often developed into the trade in scrap materials of all kinds. Men and women who earned their livelihood in this way typically existed on the margins of society. The practice of naming houses and of calling inhabitants by the names of their houses was common in small villages, where most people were closely related and there might be several households with the same last name.

invention of printing, this occupation became rather lucrative. Since there was not enough parchment to meet the needs of commerce, people had to resort to the rag basket. From those beginnings, a new industry was created in France. Through their involvement in this trade over several generations, my ancestors managed to become the owners of several plots of land and, toward the middle of the fifteenth century, to build themselves a little house. I cannot say whether my family encountered misfortunes in an age when, from one day to the next, peasants could be despoiled by the lords of the manor or by bishops. All I know is that, though my ancestors managed to hold onto what they had acquired at the beginning of the sixteenth century, their level of prosperity made no further progress through all the centuries that followed.

It was not until 1808 that the ragpickers' hut was transformed by my grandfather and father. My father's oft-told description so effectively conveys the condition in which peasants lived that it is worth a few lines. The front door still stands in its original condition. People and animals alike would come in through this entrance. The animals would turn left, where a simple partition separated them from the room that served as both bedroom and kitchen to the family that slept pell-mell on wretched litters of straw.

But that was not its greatest drawback. The animals' fodder was brought into the loft above and spread out to dry on a floor of unjoined planks that separated it from the room in which we lived. As a result, hay seeds and bits of straw were constantly falling onto the table where we ate our meals. The conditions which my family confronted indicate, beyond all possibility of doubt, the general state of the population a little more than a hundred years ago.

Peasants may have lived in a state of poverty and degradation when it came to their dwellings and health, but from the point of view of the products of their labor, they were still slaves and serfs. If a peasant was known to have set some savings aside, the lords were not satisfied with their right to a tithe but would lay hold of the animals or claim the right to unlimited credit, perhaps bringing complete ruin to the unfortunate peasant.

A MASONS' CELEBRATION; WILL LÉONARD GO TO
SCHOOL OR WON'T HE?

One of the mason's greatest pleasures, upon returning to his village, was to take his wife to the nearest town on the very next Sunday. There friends would meet and, after an exchange of friendly handshakes between those who had migrated and those who had not, they would go to the *cabaret* to have a drink.[5]

The good cheer that reigned at every table could not have been more complete, nor could the conversations taking place have been more friendly. Everyone would welcome the return of the recent arrival and insist on knowing if he had had a hard time finding work, if he had been lucky enough to find a job with a good master, and whether the wages had been decent or the price of bread had been high. The air of contentment, as well as the smiling and gracious faces of women overjoyed at their husbands' return, gave these little pleasure outings a feeling of incomparable satisfaction.

On one such Sunday, we accompanied my mother and father to Rouchon's in Pontarion. Before long my grandfather came along to join us. Soon I was treated to ear-splitting noise. People were calling each other by name from one table to the next, but always with a smile on their lips. I was pleased to see how well my father was liked and respected by the young migrants. That was because he had led most of them on their first trip to Paris and had made sure they got started off on the right foot. Everyone knew, moreover, that he was one of the best workers from our area and that with his numerous contacts he was often in a position to get them work.

Old Faucher, the churchwarden of Pontarion, was sitting opposite our table, also having a drink. The old man was universally respected by the people of the region. My father knew that from time to time he took children into his home to teach them the alphabet and a smattering of writing.

My father placed his hand on my head and told him, "Here's a young lad who I'd gladly send you if you'd agree to take him." The answer was affirmative. I will never forget the emotional reaction that these words elicited from my grandfather and mother. The conversation immediately turned to the usefulness or uselessness of sending country children to school. My mother protested in the most vigorous possible terms, saying that she needed me to work in the fields. My grandfather agreed with her, as did the other peasants who were quick to join in the conversation. They

5. Nadaud's native region was the department of Creuse, located roughly in the center of France, some three hundred fifty miles south of Paris (see the map on p. 3). This region produced a large proportion of the masons employed in the construction industry of northern France. They would spend several months of the year in a center of construction activity like Paris, working feverishly to accumulate money which they could then bring home to their village to supplement the meager livelihood which rural families managed to scratch from the soil in this region.

For *cabaret* see chapter 3, n. 40.

all claimed that for country children, what they could learn in school would not be of much use, except for writing occasional letters and carrying a missal to mass.

"Since your return from Paris," my grandfather said to his son, "not a day has gone by without you telling us what you're going to make of your boy. You'd have done better to stay in Paris than to come back and talk about your plans for schooling. Not a one of us—not my brothers, not me, not yourself—ever learned to read, and yet we've never starved, all the same.

"I always said that all those old documents from the war (the Bulletins of the Grand Army) that you used to buy in the Saint-Jean market would end up scrambling your brain.[6] That's what happened to my tenant in the Rue de la Mortellerie. He had a son and he wanted to send him to school. And what did he become? A little troublemaker who would only talk to us when he wanted to make fun of us. Later on, he brought shame to his family by becoming a real scoundrel."

Nonetheless, my father's firmness of character and the unshakable will he exhibited in all things overcame the resistance of his father and my mother. One morning, after eating breakfast earlier than usual, he placed in my hand a pretty little basket that he had woven himself, and sent me off to Old Faucher's in Pontarion. A few days later, my father set out once again on the road to Paris. I was not to see him again for nine months.

Every morning, after I had taken the sheep back to their shed, I would go to Pontarion. I would spend barely two hours at the old churchwarden's before returning to the fields in the afternoon. During the harvest season, I stayed home altogether. I spent the year learning the alphabet and how to spell syllables.

When he returned from Paris, my father was not very satisfied. He was told that I was slow-witted and that I refused to listen to the venerable old Faucher. There was some truth in this reproach, for, like all strong and vigorous children, I loved to play and, what is more, I was boisterous and quarrelsome.

The following year, a professional teacher by the name of Rioublanc was supposed to come to Pontarion. Would I be sent to him, or wouldn't I? This became the subject of a new quarrel in my family. The principal argument advanced by my mother and grandfather was that the family had already

6. The Grand Army was the popular name for the vast military apparatus organized by Napoléon. As he gradually extended French imperial control over most of continental Europe during the first decade of the nineteenth century, the Bulletins of the Grand Army were enthusiastically read by the patriotic supporters of the Empire.

squandered twelve francs on my education and that our sheep and cows were poorly tended.

These words sent my father, who had just returned from Paris, into a towering rage, and woe to anyone who pushed him too far. He silenced his wife by threatening to slap her and he reproached his father for preferring to spend money at the *cabaret* rather than think about his grandson's education.

So I was to be sent to the new teacher. He was ordered to keep me for as long as classes lasted, afternoons as well as mornings. What tempered my mother's and grandfather's bad humor was that Mrs. Rouchon, who was always so kind and affectionate to me, offered to feed me lunch along with her children.

Rioublanc was a man who had a passion for his profession. He was harsh and perhaps a bit too moody. He soon introduced a severe discipline in his school. Woe to anyone who dared laugh or play in class or come to school without having studied his lessons, for he was sure to be sent to the cellar or the attic as punishment. [. . .]

On the day when prizes were to be given out, our teacher, Rioublanc, took us to the old feudal manor, and awards were conferred upon those students who had most distinguished themselves. When it was my turn to come before the baroness, she placed a crown of oak on my head and gave me two small religious books that must have cost all of four or five sous apiece. My parents were so overjoyed they neither tried to hold back their tears nor to skimp on their hugs and compliments.

When we got back home, my father said to my mother, "Do you still regret the money we're spending on our son? Poor child! I certainly hope he'll be able to do what I couldn't do myself. If I'd known how to read and write, you wouldn't be as badly off as you are. I've had plenty of chances to make money but, because I was ignorant, I had to remain a simple worker whose nose was always buried in the hod."[7]

The next day, I went to watch some workers who were putting up a wall that was to separate our barn from the animal shed. I fell from a height of four or five feet and landed on my back. I was in bed or in convalescence for about three months. By the time I got better, my excellent teacher was no longer in Pontarion. He had gone to die, I believe, near Chénérailles. [. . .]

My father, whose burning desire was to see me get an education, took me one day to Saint-Hilaire. A man named Dypres [a retired army officer who had set up a school there], immediately arranged an interview with

7. A hod is a wooden trough, borne on the shoulder or head, in which masons carry mortar or bricks.

me. He was soon able to inform my father that I knew almost nothing but that I seemed to him to be alert and intelligent.

The thing that bothered my family was that Saint-Hilaire was too far from our village, La Martinèche. I would have to board in town, and that involved expenses beyond our means. "Money is no object," my father said. "The most important thing is to educate our son."

An agreement was struck, stipulating the following conditions: we would pay the teacher five francs a month, and three francs would go to Jeannette Bussière for my bed and board. My mother ended up with a difficult and exhausting task: each week, for eighteen months, she had to bring me a loaf of bread and a wheel of cheese. And so every Sunday I would go out to meet her, carrying her burden over her shoulder on the end of a stick. Jeannette would have her rest a moment, then my mother would hug me, give me lots of advice, and return home, happy to see me thriving and to hear Jeannette, and sometimes my teacher, singing my praises.

One day, my father sent the teacher a beautiful pipe all the way from Paris. It was made of meerschaum, embellished with silver. The teacher was extremely pleased with it and redoubled his efforts on my behalf. In the letter of thanks that he sent my father he told him, "If your son continues to apply himself with the earnestness that he displays at present, you will make of him something other than a mason." If I had not come in contact with this man, whose voice and imperious authority profoundly stirred my soul, I would never have learned arithmetic or the difference between a noun and an adjective. [. . .]

I PREPARE TO DEPART FOR PARIS

I got up long before daybreak and put on the outfit that my mother, according to regional custom, had made me for this purpose. What kind of material had she chosen? It was, naturally, drugget, made from the wool of our sheep.[8] Jacket, vest, and pants were all of the same material. The outfit was as stiff as cardboard and nearly paralyzed all bodily movements. With it went some huge shoes that were soon scraping the skin from my feet, and a high hat in the style of the day, which we had gone to buy in Saint-Georges. It was with this armor on my body that I had to set out on foot to make the journey from the department of Creuse to Paris.

On 26 March 1830, decked out in this way, I joined my father in saying farewell to my family. We actually had to escape the embraces of my mother, my grandmother, and my sisters. That was a painful and difficult

8. Drugget is a coarsely woven woolen fabric, often used as a lining or floor covering. Because of its durability, it was sometimes used to make the practical but unstylish garments worn by people on low incomes.

moment. I do not believe that the cries of these women would have been any more heartrending had they been seeing us to our graves.

My grandmother was so fond of me that I had to be torn from her arms. Though I was young, the care and consideration that this worthy woman had for me are engraved in my mind even today, and I can affirm that I have since known the grandeur of spirit as well as the treasures of goodness and devotion that are locked in the hearts of most women.

Françoise Tixier, my grandmother, had been born in Le Theil in the commune of Saint-Hilaire. When she was orphaned, however, she was brought to Saint-Armand, at the southern end of our department, to live with some distant cousins who were very poor sharecroppers. As soon as she was strong enough, she was sent from village to village in search of her daily bread. That is how she grew up, without knowing her last name or her place of birth.

One day she was told that she had a cousin who sold chestnuts at the market in Bourganeuf. This relative was Anne Nadaud, my godmother. Anne liked the young girl and introduced her to her brother, Jean Nadaud, who married her soon after. My father was born of their marriage in 1786. Hardworking and thrifty, Françoise Tixier proved to be the guiding spirit of our family.

This fine woman would overwhelm me with her attentions. To get her to laugh, all I had to do was ask if she had known how to dance when she was young. "Oh yes, my lad," she would answer, "when I was at a barn dance, I wasn't the last one to be asked." She must not have been lying, for she was pretty and full of grace. She died of chills, as they say, in 1832.

My grandfather had preceded her to the grave by a few years. He was also a handsome and hearty fellow, built like Hercules but kind to the point of simplemindedness. All he had to do was go into a *cabaret* and down a couple of half-liters and he was well on his way to getting drunk. That is, in fact, what caused his death at the age of sixty-three. One evening he was returning rather late from Pontarion. He sat or fell down next to a little stream that emptied into the Thaurion River above Machecou. He fell asleep with his feet in the water and got a chill which resulted in pneumonia, soon leading him to his grave.

After these initial scenes of tenderness, themselves sufficient to break the hearts of the members of such a genuinely close-knit family, I went on to experience new emotions almost as moving as these. My young childhood friends, Martin and Michel Vergnaud, as well as the two Tabourys, François and Jean, were waiting for me in front of our door. We went off to the barn to say our farewells and share our feelings of true youthful friendship.

My dear friends were leaving for Lyon, and I for Paris. Alas, we were never to see each other again. Three of us, Martin Vergnaud and the two Tabourys, were never to return to the village. They died, prematurely and most sadly, on the construction sites of Lyon, something that is too often the fate of the unfortunate pariahs of Creuse.

At length, we had to part, even before we were able to dry our tears. A moment later, I arrived in Pontarion at Old Duphot's inn, where we were expected by friends who were heading to Paris with us and by those, even more numerous, who had come to see us off. People started emptying bottles of white wine, while the old men who were staying behind directed encouraging words our way, telling us above all to behave ourselves and always retain a fond memory of our native region.

When we arrived at Le Marivet, a tiny village not far from Pontarion, more traveling companions were waiting for us. Above Sardent, we began taking back roads, for in those days the road from Sardent to Guéret did not yet exist. The footpaths that we had to follow were barely passable because so much rain had fallen the previous evening.

Beyond Saint-Christophe, we entered the forest of Guéret, where the roads, which the water had made muddy and had channeled with gullies, were even worse. In certain places, tree branches nearly blocked our way. Whenever we touched them, a fine, cold rain would fall on our shoulders, which was, as you might guess, not very pleasant. The water had already seeped into my shoes, and I confess that if I had only dared, I would have asked to turn back.

Around eleven o'clock we arrived in Guéret. We were a bit tired and footsore, but our goal was in sight, and we went to eat at Old Gerbeau's, where my father and several of our traveling companions were highly thought of.

Migrant workers, who passed through twice a year, had inns at which they regularly stopped and which they very rarely changed. Gerbeau was as well known by these masons as Napoléon was by his soldiers. Not one of them would pass through without stopping by his place, because he never tried to fleece us and served decent food at a good price. What's more, he was never too cheap to buy us a drop to drink after our meal.

As my father introduced me to this innkeeper, he said, "Gerbeau, here's a new customer." Gerbeau immediately had his wife come give me a hug and fill my pockets with all kinds of treats. From that moment, I formed a permanent bond with that establishment and never passed through Guéret without paying a visit to their inn. We maintained contact so well that later, when I placed my daughter in Mrs. Bailet's boarding house, which was just opposite their inn, Miss Gerbeau, who had become Mrs. Audoine, never missed a day of lavishing a mother's kind and affectionate attention on her. In 1870, I became Prefect of the Department of Creuse. Mrs. Audoine had all my meals brought to me at the prefecture for the modest price of 1.75 francs. When she died, I felt as much grief as if she had been one of my family.

On that first trip in 1830, before we left Gerbeau's inn, our traveling companions each placed ten francs in my father's hands. He became treasurer of our little group as far as Paris. His honorary duties consisted of going on ahead along our route to arrange to have our meals prepared, choosing the menu, figuring how many bottles of wine to order, and negotiating the cost of the meal. His election imposed on him an even greater responsibility. Since this route was used by many migrants, each group chose a strong walker whose job it was to be the first to arrive at the inn each evening in order to reserve the beds. My father, who was of average size and very solidly built, liked to boast that he had never met his equal at walking fast and for a long time. That must have been true, for our friends never dreamed of withdrawing their confidence in him.

As we left Guéret, we headed towards Genouillat, stopping only at various inns to have a drink. Up to that point, there had been no laggards and, in an effort to buck up those youngsters who were beginning to tire, the veterans would hum in their ears a few of the old songs of our native region. This would make us laugh and forget the exhaustion that was beginning to overcome us.

At nightfall we arrived at Genouillat, where my father had arranged for supper at the baker Meillant's inn. But in walking ahead with a few other friends, they had noticed that a considerable number of migrants who, like us, were on their way to Paris, had come on the road from Jarnages. While we were eating, my father pointed out that it was in our interest to eat a quick meal and continue two leagues further to Bordessoule, so that by the following day we would be well ahead of most of the crowd.

Everyone understood, and as soon as dinner was over, we got underway in the light of a superb moon. A good number of us continued to strike up cheerful songs, but in spite of this, our legs lost strength and a few stragglers lagged behind. I was among them. One of our traveling companions, Chabannat, a strong and vigorous fellow, came up to me, gave me encouragement, and offered to carry my pack. I would have experienced enormous relief if he could have rid me of my bulky, brand-new shoes, which were rubbing the skin right off my heels.

At last we arrived. I found that by the end of that day I had completed a first lap of fifteen leagues. Overcome with fatigue, I was more in need of restorative sleep than the dinner that they were going to serve us.

Our inn was known as a gathering place for carters and mule drivers. The rooms of this establishment were spacious and contained everything necessary for those sorts of people. Two mule teams arrived at the same time we did. One team was wearing enormous bells that made an indescribable chiming. It is well known that at that time France was lacking in means of transport, and these animals were being used to carry double goatskins of wine along the roadways. The other team, consisting of young mules, had been assigned to supply the nearby markets, even those of Paris. To those of us who had just left our village, the looks of the mule drivers were astonishing. Their raucous voices were frightening to hear, and their puffed, reddish, impudent faces made them appear to be what they were not: veritable highwaymen, always ready to rob travelers. The cracking of whips, the tinkling of bells, and the barking of dogs made an enormous impression on me.

We entered the inn and found ourselves in a vast kitchen, where you could hear a buzzing like the sound of a menagerie. In a disproportionately large fireplace were roasting enormous quarters of meat that we all looked at greedily. I, like my young companions, was remarkably disoriented. It felt as though we had lost our bearings.

We went to sit down at the end of a very long table that had been placed alongside two others, around which a fair number of travelers were gathered. Since we had eaten at Genouillat, we were more thirsty than hungry. My father had me drink a few swallows of mulled wine that I had difficulty getting down, so overwhelmed was I from the fatigue of that first day.

We needed rest. We were taken up a small stairway, where we saw the straw pallets that had been set aside for us. My father helped me take off my shoes and stockings and was quite surprised to see that my feet were torn and bloody. He put grease on them and wrapped them in a few small pieces of cloth. Then we lay down not on beds but on grain husks and straw that had been broken up by previous use and that was naturally full of vermin.

When you opened the sheets, you saw that they were black as soot and bore, in addition, various signs of uncleanliness. This gives some indication of the indifference of the innkeepers along our entire route at that time. Around the middle of November, when it was time for the migrants to pass through, they would set out clean sheets that had to last until the middle of March, unless they really got too dirty or were torn. That is how the health laws were observed as far as the masons' migration was concerned.

Such laws existed at the time, but only for the benefit of the rich, who were developing ostentation and extravagance in their houses and castles. Since the Catholic Church and the royalty have never considered the people to be more than a herd of slaves, there was nothing surprising in our being penned up haphazardly in such a pigsty. We were, moreover, careful not to undress. We would wrap our heads up so that our faces would not touch the bolster and we would cross our arms on our chests because we did not know where else to put them. Hard as it may be to believe, as we crammed ourselves into these filthy litters, we were laughing rather than grumbling. The old carters were not the least bit surprised. They would tell us, "Lads, you'll see many more of them. You'll even find that exhaustion makes your sleep pleasant and deep even when you're being rousted by fleas and bedbugs."

They had spoken the truth, for the night went nicely and sleep seemed to lighten all the weariness I had experienced the previous evening. It was hardly light the next day before some of us were already animated by insane mirth. We got ready, laughing and singing all the while. When some said they wanted water to shave, others replied, "Don't hold your breath." Those were circumstances in which one had to make do. We were forced to use our shirt tails and a little spit to wash our eyes lightly until we could find clear water along the road.

Just as we were leaving, we drank some white wine. Everyone was ready, his pack on his back. For the first few hours, there were no stragglers, the road was in good condition, and the general cheerfulness persisted. Having arrived at Nohant, where the beautiful house of George Sand was located, we set off into the Saint-Chartier plains.[9] We had to take some very bad roads that had been torn up by wagons and were full of little puddles or big stones. This stretch of our walk was all the more difficult because from time to time we would sink up to our ankles in water and mud. The water would slosh inside our shoes, which contributed in no small degree to making this stint very disagreeable for us.

The most annoying thing for us youngsters was seeing our elders marching along and not being able to keep up. To subject thirteen- or fourteen-year-old children to such harsh trials would strike me today as an extreme form of cruelty.

When we reached Issoudun that evening, a quarter of us were completely worn out. I was convinced that I would be unable to undertake a similar march the next day. In consolation, my father told me, "I made the journey from the Vendée when I was even younger than you are, and I didn't whine like you seem to be doing."

I told him that if my shoes had not caused me so much suffering, I would have been less tired. He cut them for me again and asked me—begged

9. George Sand: see chapter 2, n. 12.

me—not to sulk over my dinner. Wanting to please him, I did justice to the meal. We had arrived at the Moreau Inn. Although dinner was cosy, the sleeping accommodations were not. That night, there were no fewer than one hundred men of Creuse, who had come from every corner of our department. To lodge all those people, about thirty of us had been crammed into a room in which half the floor tiles had been torn up and where our beds were right up against each other. As at Bordessoule, we were careful not to undress, for it was just as filthy.

Nonetheless, the cosy meal that we had been served at the Moreau Inn, along with a little too much wine that I had forced myself to drink, contributed to loosening my tongue for the first time. My father, who loved me very much and who was proud of the bit of education he had obtained for me as well as of my physical strength, received compliments from some of our traveling companions, who told him, "Oh, that little imp sure can talk a blue streak. Once he's done a few campaigns, it won't be easy to keep him in check."

I was, in fact, a bit sharper and less awkward than the other youths who, like me, were making the trip for the first time. [. . .]

After this little escapade, we made our way toward Salbris, where we were supposed to spend the night. [. . .] There as elsewhere, we knew our inn and went straight to Labonne's (if my memory is to be trusted, for I am writing these lines sixty years after the fact). There we ate a hearty meal, and those kind folks offered my father the bed that belonged to one of their children, which meant that we had that rarest of luxuries—clean sheets— and that our sleep was as sound as possible.

Nor did our companions have any complaints about that inn. In the morning, as we were about to leave, we were informed that that day was to be our last lap on foot. Naturally, we were overjoyed. We threw our hats in the air to show how happy we were. In fact, that very evening we arrived in Orléans, and from there we knew we were to take rattletrap coaches.[10] [. . .]

The basket that was suspended from the vehicle's axle held four of us. Its motion was rather like the rolling of a boat. And so, tossed about in this manner, I arrived in Paris.

My father was to take me to Mrs. Champesme's boarding house at 62 Rue de la Tisseranderie.[11] But before going there, he took me to the Quai

10. Rattletrap coaches: see chapter 3, n. 43.
11. The Rue de la Tisseranderie no longer exists. It was a westward extension of the Rue Saint-Antoine in the cramped, populous working-class quarter located immediately northeast of the Paris city hall. On boarding houses, see the introduction, page 17.

de la Grève, on the banks of the Seine, so I could wash my face and hands. I needed that wash, as my hands were black as coal. By rubbing them with sand, I managed to whiten them a bit. I had taken off my jacket and vest to hunt the vermin that were devouring me.

When we arrived at the boarding house, all we found were the two Champesme girls, Caroline and Eléonore, both dressed in mourning clothes. They had just lost their mother. The older daughter immediately came to give me a hug. I lowered my eyes and did not dare look at her. She said to my father, "Why, Father Nadaud, you told us your son was so forward, but he seems very shy to me."

My father answered, "Wait a few days and then tell me what you think." Five minutes later, we had left to go see François Thaury, who was a foreman near the Place Saint-Sulpice. We found him in front of the entryway to his work site, supervising the unloading of cartloads of sand and wagonloads of quarry stones. It was the first time I had seen a mason in work clothes, and it struck me as rather strange. As we were headed for a wine merchant's to have a drink, Thaury called out to his assistant by his nickname: "Hey, Joy-of-My-Life, come over here." Finding that his laborer was not obeying quickly enough, he shouted at him in an angry tone, "Are you coming, good-for-nothing?"[12] Then he said to him, "If the boss shows up, come find me in the corner wine merchant's."[13] And off we went. Not ten minutes had passed before Joy-of-My-Life came to tell him that the architect and the boss had arrived. Thaury left us.

I was not done walking, for we still had to get from the Place Saint-Sulpice to the Place de la Bastille. There we climbed aboard the coach from Raincy that took us as far as Villemomble, where we had jobs with one of my uncles.

Thus, in four days' time, we had marched sixty leagues from Creuse to Orléans, without counting the time spent in those accursed rattletraps to get to Paris. It was, I believe, a rather difficult trial for a child of fourteen.

I have insisted on going into such detail concerning this journey because the men of my generation were the last to undergo such harsh tests of endurance. In fact, with the advent of the railways, a golden age was about to begin.

---

12. The French word *garçon* (literally, "boy") designated any apprentice, assistant, or common laborer employed in a subordinate status in a skilled trade. Among masons, *garçons* might range in age from adolescents to adults in middle age, and included those who still aspired to become independent craftsmen in their own right as well as those who would never progress beyond the level of unskilled laborers.
13. Thaury uses the slang term for boss, *le singe*, literally, "the monkey."

LÉONARD ASSISTS THE MASONS

The day after my arrival, I might have thought that I was still in La Martinèche. There I was, at my uncle's home and in the company of his children, two of whom had been born in my father's house, so there was no question of being bored. My uncle was especially pleased to see me there beside him because, up until then, he had been obliged to rely on strangers to keep his records, for like my father, he had never learned to read or write.

At that time, he was contractor for three houses underway in the Rue des Trois-Frères in Villemomble as well as other substantial projects in the castle and park of the owner, Mr. Leval. He had me brought up to date with his bookkeeping by the village sexton, who was a sort of giant but with a pleasant and simple personality. The latter did not hesitate to point out to my father that my education left much to be desired. "I always had my doubts that he was really expert in the subject." So it was then agreed that the sexton would give me lessons in the evenings. He soon tired of that. When he found someone to buy him a glass of wine, he did not hesitate to abandon his pupil.

I got room and board at my uncle's. He did not assign me to assist a journeyman right away.[14] I was put to work on projects in the castle and the park, rolling wheelbarrows full of sand, pebbles, and quarry stones back and forth. In the evenings, I would mark down the workers' daily wages and enter notations in a book for all the merchandise we had received. For this purpose, my master's lessons proved rather useful to me.

One day, as I was hanging around a group of workers who were digging an artesian well, three or four of them who were bolder than the others began to tease me. "Hey, you little skunk! So you didn't have any more chestnuts to chew on back home and came to eat our bread?"[15] Others added, "Give us the address of your tailor; your outfit suits you to a tee." Another came up and knocked my cap askew on my head. I got red in the face and I gave him a kick in the shin with the toe of my shoe. He gave me a gentle slap. By then I was crying tears of anger and rage, and others came to console and coddle me. A version of this little adventure got back to my uncle, who did not get upset at all and assigned me to assist a man named

14. Nadaud uses the term *compagnon*. Whereas for Perdiguier it meant a formally initiated member of a workers' brotherhood (see chapter 4, n. 10), for Nadaud it simply signified a journeyman who was recognized as an independent practitioner of a trade and who worked for a daily wage.
15. In the central regions of France, chestnuts were gathered from trees that grew wild in the forests and stored in stone sheds for consumption during the winter. It was this custom that gave rise to the pejorative nickname "chestnut eaters."

Henri Raymond from Gagny, a village not far from Villemomble. This journeyman was very good to me. He had himself once been my father's assistant. We were working on some outer garden walls. I did my job as best I could while we worked on the part below ground level and until we reached a height that required scaffolding.

But when it came to lifting those enormous quarry stones up onto that scaffolding, I lacked the strength. I would roll them onto my stomach as best I could, and my journeyman would take them from me in his hands. He would take pity on me from time to time and often come down off his scaffolding to get the stones himself. But while he was doing so, the mason who was working next to him would have built his section up, so that my journeyman's lagged behind. A proud and skillful worker, he would fume at seeing himself "buried" or "eaten up," as they say on the construction site, by fellow workers who were not his equals. But my uncle never wavered in his confidence in him all the same.

I have never seen Henri Raymond since, but the memory of how he took care of me when I was just a weak child has always remained imprinted in my mind. Later, when he learned that I had been named a representative of the people, he would send residents of Gagny to me so I could get them a pass to the Chamber of Deputies, and in this way I would hear news of my first journeyman.

THE REVOLUTION OF 1830

Around that time, the Revolution of 1830 arrived. The population rose in rebellion and raced toward Paris. My father was not among the last to set out, and I followed him at a healthy pace. We reentered Paris by the Montreuil gate. It was July 31. Need I add that I was full of emotion upon seeing barricade after barricade as far as the Place de la Bastille? But we could go no further.

What a picture! For a child who had just left his village, it was a grandiose spectacle, beyond all words, to see an entire nation in the streets, proud of its victory over a king and his perverse ministers who had sought to steal those few shreds of freedom that the Charter of 1815 had granted.[16] It was enough to send us into ecstasies and to strike us mute with astonishment.

The last shots had been fired the evening before, but the entire population, combatants and noncombatants alike, was outdoors, the people

---

16. The Charter of 1815, promulgated at the time of the restoration of the Bourbon monarchy, placed limitations on the power of the king and provided guarantees of certain limited individual rights.

shouting for all they were worth, "Long live the Charter! Down with the Bourbons!" [. . .]

The same difficulties that we had encountered that morning in making our way down through the Faubourg Saint-Antoine also hindered our return. We tried our best to make our way through side streets, but the congestion was everywhere the same. Nonetheless, by dint of giving and receiving elbows, we managed to reach the undeveloped area of Charonne and then rejoined our route above Montreuil. Two hours later, we arrived at Villemomble. Everyone wanted to hear the story of what we had been able to observe on our trip.

We went into the shop of a wine merchant by the name of Guérin and spent the night talking, drinking, and singing. [. . .]

Mr. Leval, the owner of the park and castle, who for years had employed large numbers of workers by opening limestone quarries in that region and who had had so many houses built, suddenly found himself bankrupted by the events of July.

All of a sudden, all work stopped. The residents experienced such genuine sorrow that when people came to carry out a writ of arrest against Mr. Leval, the local National Guardsmen took up arms and for several days guarded all the castle's entrances.

But that could only continue for a time, and Mr. Leval took refuge in Switzerland, never to reappear in Villemomble again. The departure of this truly good man caused the ruin of my father and uncle as well as many other men in construction and small business. We shall see subsequently that it also swallowed up all the savings that I was to make between 1830 and 1848.

Linked by a verbal partnership, the two brothers lost about twelve thousand francs, half of which remained my father's responsibility. Everything in life is relative. This sum was obviously beyond his means, as a simple worker, to repay. Honest to the point of simplemindedness, my father had never taken an advance on his salary beyond what was necessary for him to live and buy clothing.

Unfortunately, he had emptied the purses of several of his friends because he did not dare ask money from Mr. Leval, who was presumed to be a millionaire several times over. What is more, he had no right to make the slightest demand on him, since everything was in his brother's name only, and the latter always advised him to wait.

I witnessed quarrels between the two brothers that were certainly violent and might easily have become still more regrettable had not several friends intervened. But the misfortune was total, and there was nothing to do but resign oneself. The crowning anxiety and regret was that my father had just bought his brother's share of our little property in La Martinèche for fifteen hundred francs.

The result, when all was said and done, was that, at the time of our departure from Villemomble on 27 September 1830, my father owed a little more than eleven thousand francs. I have never in my life met a more sincerely scrupulous and honest man than my father. One day he told me, the witness to his troubles, "If it weren't for your mother and you three children, I would throw myself off the Notre-Dame bridge. How will I hide my shame when the bailiffs come to seize everything we own in La Martinèche? If I were still a young man (he was then forty-six), it would be easier to find a way out, but in three or four years they won't want me on the construction sites any more." His laments would then redouble.

"Come, come, father," I would tell him, "in a few years, I'll be a mason and I'll help you. Between now and then, we'd have to be very unlucky not to earn enough to pay the interest." We left Villemomble to come work in Paris.

When we arrived in Paris, we went to the boarding house where my father had spent his youth and where he had taken me the first day of my arrival. This was Mrs. Champesme's boarding house at 62 Rue de la Tisseranderie, which, since her death, had been run by her older daughter, Miss Rose. She took me to the fifth floor of that house, showed me my bed, and set my little pack on a shelf. Then she introduced me to the men who shared the room, being careful to tell me that they were all well behaved, which was true, and that they would take care of me, which was also true, and that in addition they were all from my commune or from Pontarion.

There were six beds and twelve tenants in that room. We were so crowded in on top of one another that there was just barely a space of fifty centimeters to serve as a passageway through this room. It did not take long, in fact, to get to know my roommates. Morning and evening, I would hear random bits of conversation, one more amusing than the next, always trivial when they were not outright irritating or degrading to a child's ears.

There were two streams of conversation in our dormitory room: the skinflints' on the one hand, and the spendthrifts' on the other. From the former, you learned to count your pennies. In general, skinflints are backbiters, always ready to make unfavorable judgments about anyone whose character traits are different from their own. [. . .]

The kind of skinflint I am speaking of did not lack either integrity or honesty. On the contrary, he loved his family and perhaps his friends, but he was his own body's tormentor. He could not spend more than fourteen or fifteen francs a month. This did not include his expenses at the boarding house, where he got bed and broth for six francs a month, or his bread, which he bought "on the cuff" and also paid for each month.[17] Each morning he would leave one piece on a shelf that was rarely dusted.

The landlady would come along and gather up all these pieces of bread in her apron and, without knowing which piece belonged to which tenant, she would pour some sixty to eighty bowlfuls of soup over the bread as soon as the water in the large pot was hot.

Our man would place the second piece of bread under his arm, gnaw on it all the way to work, and deposit the remainder, as necessary, in a convenient hole in the wall or wherever. He would fetch it at nine o'clock and go spend five to seven sous on his breakfast, depending on whether or not he had a bowl of hot stock. If there was plenty for breakfast, he would save the little piece of meat that he was served in the morning for his two-o'clock meal, which he would eat sitting right there where he was working or in some corner of the construction site. That's what they call "crushing the screenings."[18]

In the evening, the soup was sometimes poured over the bread an hour or two before our arrival, depending on the distance we had to travel from the construction site to the house. If it was too cold or if the bread had drunk up all the broth, the late arrival would ask for more, but there was not always more to be had, and he might then let out a mild curse. The landlady would not get mad. Ours, who had the wit to say the right thing, always found some friendly words to make us laugh. And soon some other conversation would get started, for we loved our good-natured Rose and would not have caused her trouble for anything in the world.

You're never bored in a boarding house, unless you are a melancholy soul or some kind of lout. Some start talking about home. Those who are not married tease those who are, about the wives they have left all alone. And then they praise or criticize the boss. "He's a miser," someone will say, "who won't pay a decent day's wages. He expects you to knock yourself out on his behalf, and then see if he'll come through for you." Another employer is said to be generous, and they pay him all sorts of compliments.

17. Nadaud uses the expression *prendre le pain à la taille*, literally, "to take bread by the cut." This refers to the custom of using a *taille* or small piece of wood which the baker would set aside for each customer buying on credit. Each time he served the customer, the baker would cut a small notch in the piece of wood. The account was settled at the end of each month by counting up the number of notches.
18. The lime that masons used for mixing mortar had to be sifted through a sieve or screen to remove the lumps or "screenings." These lumps could be reused only after they had been crushed into a fine powder. The self-deprecatory humor of masons, obliged to take their midday meal at the job site, rendered this practice as "crushing the screenings," which also suggests the frugal worker's desire to use every last bit.

At that time, neither books nor newspapers made their way into our boarding houses. You might say that we ate and slept without ever thinking about cultivating our minds. Then we would go back up to our rooms to breathe fetid and stale air, and, to top it all off, the only lavatory in the house, for use by more than sixty people, was located on our landing. I confess that it was not easy to enter. [. . .][19] And when the men from our room removed their shoes to go to bed, taking their sweating feet out of filthy socks they did not always change from week to week, you had to be very used to that kind of life in order not to hold your nose.

I have said that alongside the conversation of skinflints, there was that of spendthrifts or squanderers. Money melts in their hands. They spend it either bit by bit, drinking little nips or glasses all day long with whoever happens along; or all at once on payday or the day after. Then, for the rest of the week, they eat dry bread or try to borrow money that they never pay back.

The spendthrifts' conversations provided us with a great deal of entertainment, because the skinflints had a special knack for getting them to chat. Skinflints would take momentary pleasure in spendthrifts' stories about women or their other adventures. One would almost have said that they regretted not having taken part.

Among the spendthrifts, there were some who came home at all hours of the night and would sometimes wake us up by making a racket. But if you did not answer them, they soon fell asleep. Fundamentally, these folks were not hooligans. They maintained steady work habits. If you were nice to them the next day, they were happy, for the truth is that a man needs the respect of his peers to be able to bear life's burdens.

There was one in particular who was a real drunkard, but of a rather particular variety. When he opened the door, he would close it gently. He did not always have the strength to undress, but no matter; he would just lie there, dumb as a fish, either on his bed or on the floor.

Besides, the men I am speaking of were far from having fallen into the final stages of drunkenness and degradation. Their capacity for always maintaining the taste for work had ended up making several of them serious men who were worthy of respect.

One of my roommates, a good worker and a good friend, was named Big Dizier. He had an assistant whom he called Nine O'Clock. Two days after I arrived, the latter took me to the Quai de la Grève, where he bought me a

---

19. Nadaud presumably refers to the overpowering smell, but he then adds an obscure phrase, "even though there were stones piled upon stones on either side of the toilet" (*bien qu'il y eût de chaque côté de la lunette pierres sur pierres*). I have been unable to decipher his precise meaning.

hod, a shovel, a skullcap well stuffed with rags so that the mortar trough would not hurt my head, and a work shirt and work pants.[20] And off I went, with my new friend, to what used to be 29 Rue de la Chaussée-d'Antin. Once there, he took me to the spot where they mixed the mortar, where we were surrounded by fifteen to twenty masons' assistants. The first words that I made out were these: "He's a colt, he's a colt!" That is the term they used for someone who had just come from the provinces and did not know the trade. Then they added, as they crowded around me, "It's your treat, buddy." I had been warned, and so I replied that I hadn't a cent. When they learned that I was supposed to assist the master mason, they left me alone.

I was very surprised at the noise that all the assistants constantly made in answering their journeymen. At a certain point, everyone got ready to mix mortar. If there was not enough water in their own pail, they would grab one out of someone else's hands, resulting in frequent arguments and sometimes in violent shoving matches that would end in threats or even blows. One of them told me, "Instead of looking at us like a little canary, why don't you go to the well?" I went, but imagine my surprise to find that the rope to the well, which was made of braided willow branches, was full of knots. To get them to run over the pulley required pulling with more strength than I possessed, and I had to let the pail fall back to the bottom of the well. Nine O'Clock, who had brought me to the construction site, spoke to his journeyman about this, and he spoke, in turn, to the foreman, François Thaury, whom I was supposed to assist. Thaury told me, "Unless I call for you to mix mortar for me, you don't have to listen to that rabble of assistants, half of whom are just good-for-nothings." That meant one less problem for me. So then my comrades told me, "Since you won't go fetch water, here's a mallet. You can help beat the lumps out of the lime."

At that time, the lime came from the quarry without having been sifted. It had to be reworked with a shovel and passed through screens. The bits that remained were spread out on the ground, and when there were enough, the assistants took up heavy mallets and crushed them. This job,

20. The job of the mason's assistant was to maintain a steady supply of materials, especially fresh mortar, so that his journeyman's time could be used most efficiently and so that he could sustain a pace coordinated with the other masons working alongside him. This required that the assistant mix mortar on demand, working on the ground floor of the construction site where the sand and unslaked lime (*plâtre*) were stored in piles, then carry it in a trough, balanced on the shoulder or head, up the scaffolding, to where the mason was at work. In between deliveries of mortar, the assistant would ferry bricks or quarry stones up to the work area or carry out other preparatory tasks like sifting sand or beating the lumps out of the quicklime.

which made us swallow lungfuls of dust, was unpleasant for another reason: using the mallet tore up my hands. Mine were soon covered with blisters to the point where I suffered a great deal. But there was nothing to be done about it, for it was part of the trade.

One day, my journeyman began plastering the peaks of the building's chimneys, a job that involved applying by hand long tongues of plaster to the walls. A mason who was skilled at this task was as much in demand in those days as one who is skilled in ornamental mouldings today.

I had to start carrying the mortar trough up to the sixth floor, and this was no laughing matter for me. My journeyman would only ask me to bring a few trowelfuls at a time, but all the same I had to leg it up those six stories about twenty-five to thirty times a day. My neck was being shoved down into my shoulders. Often, halfway up the ladder, I seemed to be out of breath. But I could not even think of resting, for if I took too long to climb up to the sixth floor, the plaster would be half set and my journeyman would be unable to stir it in the mortar trough.

When this happened, he would take an enormous wad of tobacco out of his mouth and become furious, without, for all that, ever addressing any recriminations my way. He stuck by me because I was the son of his friend and roommate. Sometimes he would tell me, "Don't mix your batches quite so close together and try to get them up here faster. You seem to have good legs." And, in fact, I was stronger than most kids my age. But I was not used to this difficult and exhausting work. In the evening, when I returned to the boarding house, my father, who was never heartless where I was concerned, would take me out to drink a half-bottle at the wine merchant's. He would order bread and cheese and encourage me with all sorts of kind words. What bothered him was that he knew I did not like meat and when I went to the greasy spoon with Nine O'Clock I would trade my bit of meat for some vegetables. "You won't hold up," he would tell me, "if you go on like that." It was all because, in raising us at home, my mother had fed us nothing but soup, bread, oilcakes, potatoes, and good dairy products.[21] For more than a year, instead of beef I started eating Italian cheese that I would find at the pork butcher's. I gorged myself with it to such an extent that I have never eaten it since.

Once these chimneys were up, topped off, and stripped of their scaffoldings, my journeyman had enough to do just supervising the workers and, although he kept me busy, my work was less exhausting.

Before me, my journeyman had had another assistant, whom he as-

---

21. Oilcakes are made from the residue left after the oil has been pressed from linseed, rapeseed, cottonseed, and so on. This waste material is also used as animal fodder and fertilizer.

signed to the stone setter in order to be able to take me under his own supervision. I was afraid that his former assistant would take a dislike to me, because he might think that as soon as I had learned the trade, he would be sacked. But our journeyman had reassured him on that point.

Among my new friends, there was one who would take pity on me when he saw that I was tired. He would carry friendship to the point of mixing the mortar himself and carrying my mortar trough as far as the third floor, where I would take it from him and put it on my head. This man was Laurent Luquet from the village of Planet in the commune of Saint-Alpinien, whom I will have occasion to speak of several times in this outline of my life as a worker.

Luquet was the first of all the construction workers from our region to defy the prejudices of the times. He never kept his opinions quiet, whether at the work site or at the boarding house or in the greasy spoons. I want to state that if I became what I believe I have always been—a defender of the people and a convinced republican—Luquet was not without a certain influence on my conduct and my thinking in my earlier years. As assistants to the foreman, we were the last two to leave the construction site. We had to sweep up the street, light the lanterns, and pick up crowbars, ropes, and other implements. If the other laborers got a notion to pick a fight with me, as they often did with youngsters who were not strong enough to defend themselves, Luquet, who knew well how to command respect, would take my side. [. . .]

A word about our wages: when I was working in the Rue Coq-Héron, we got thirty-six sous a day, and forty when we worked overtime.[22] Stonemasons earned from fifty-five sous to three francs; masons were paid from three and a quarter to three and a half francs.[23] These figures make it possible to follow the changes in wages from that period to the present day, demonstrating that our century is one of the most marvelous in our history from the point of view of the increase in well-being among the people.

But let us return to the month of April 1831 and to the construction site in the Rue de la Chaussée-d'Antin. We immediately set about rebuilding the gable that had been demolished. For a time, I was assigned as assistant to a journeyman named Dufour. He was surely the most violent-tempered,

22. There are twenty sous in a franc. See chapter 1, n. 10.
23. Stonemasons or *limousinants* (from the name of Nadaud's native province, Limousin) were masons who made rough-walls using unfinished quarry stones which they cemented together with mortar and often covered with a coat of plaster. Because these rough stones were large and somewhat irregular, the work was less skilled than work with finished stone or brick.

grumpy man you could hope to meet. He was constantly at war with his fellow workers, always wanting to be top dog but always running up against others much more skillful than himself. When that happened, he would flush with anger or froth with rage, and he would naturally try to vent his fury on his assistant. One day he needed a piece of wood to support his scaffolding, and I did not find one ready at hand. "Wait a minute," I told him, "and I'll go find one."

"What do you mean, you little good-for-nothing? There's one right there before your eyes. Can't you see it?" I could see it perfectly well; it was lying across the well-hole of the stairway. He threw a small wedging stone at me to make me hurry up. Ignoring everything but my sense of daring, and blinded by anger, I ran over and began pulling this piece of wood toward me, but unfortunately one end went between my legs and I was dragged over, falling from the fourth floor to the basement.

A shout rang out: an assistant had fallen. It was up to whoever was the first down the ladders to come and pick me up. A certain Michel Dizier jumped from the ground floor into the basement and tried to lift me. I was already covered with blood and both my arms were broken. In this state, they carried me to the mortar-mixing room and stretched me out on the plaster.

A doctor soon arrived. He bandaged my head, where I had extensive injuries, and at the same time confirmed that both my wrists were fractured. In the blink of an eye, all the workers had stopped work to come see me, and everyone found it miraculous that, having fallen from such a height, I had not been killed outright.

Once the doctor confirmed that I had no broken bones other than my arms, the question of how to carry me back to my boarding house arose. Instead of getting a stretcher, I was tucked into a hackney carriage with two of my friends sitting on either side to support me.

When we were somewhere near the Rue de la Ferronnerie, the horse, which had stopped to let other vehicles pass, stumbled, and I fainted. They thought I was dead and took me out of the carriage to lay me down in a pharmacist's shop. I soon regained consciousness. But the pharmacist explained to the friends who were accompanying me that they needed to get a stretcher, which took some time. It was in this condition that I arrived at my boarding house on 4 May 1831.

New and agonizing suffering awaited me, for the stairway that led to my room on the fifth floor was relatively narrow. I could barely stand on my feet. They had to help me lift one foot after the other to go up each step. The bandage which was wrapped around my head and covered my eyes further increased my suffering. Every jolt tore heartrending cries from my lips. At last they somehow managed to set me on my bed. The regular doctor of the house, Mr. Bénassy, arrived shortly thereafter, at the same time as my father, whom someone had gone to fetch in the Rue Choiseul where he was working.

The first question to be decided was this: Will he go to the hospital or not? "He won't go," my father answered, "even if I have to spend my last cent."

Then Dr. Bénassy confirmed the two fractures and examined my head wounds. He did not seem inordinately upset. He used scissors to remove the clothes that were in his way: my smock, shirt, and pants. Finding that my arms were too swollen, he put off the start of his treatment to the following day.

The strange thing was that rest brought an end to my suffering, and, as the night had gone rather well, Dr. Bénassy appeared satisfied. His examination showed that the fracture in my left arm was not very serious, though the same was not true of the right arm, which had more or less been crushed. He was so afraid that gangrene might set in that he would undo the dressings every day, but little by little he set his mind at rest and set ours at rest as well.

Once it was decided that I would not go to the hospital, my father wanted to get me a sick-nurse. But Miss Rose Champesme, my landlady, immediately spoke up, saying, "There's no point. I want to take care of him myself during the day and you, Father Nadaud, and your nephew Hippolyte Julien, will be in charge at night."

The worthy woman kept her word. Never has the most devoted nurse or sister of mercy shown greater devotion in the exercise of her praiseworthy functions than my landlady showed for me. You would have to have experienced the depths of dejection into which a young man can fall following such a catastrophe to know how much healing comfort a woman's friendly gaze or gentle word can bring a patient. When I needed to sit up, she always found someone in the house to assist her. Once the bandages had been removed, she would come sit at the foot of my bed and take up her needlework. I was never bored. Though I could not make use of my arms, I was not in pain once the bandages were done with.

At the time of this worthy woman's death, the voters of Creuse had elected me their representative. I approached her grave, thinking to say a few words of farewell, but tears stifled my voice and I could not speak a word. [. . .]

Three months later, I had to start working again. [. . .]

My journeyman, François Thaury, and I went to work for a small-time contractor named Thévenot, who was located in the Rue du Petit-Carreau.

A Parisian by birth, he was friendly and good-natured, and we were very happy working for him. He only did small projects in the old houses of his quarter. I rarely had to carry the mortar trough on my head, for we would carry our sacks of plaster up to the rooms where we were working. All we had to do was mix the mortar on the spot, so to speak. To make things even easier for me, my worthy employer would have me work in the shop, pouring plaster into sacks or doing other minor jobs that tired me very little. I would mix on the spot and my journeyman would help me carry my mortar trough by hand. I was regaining strength in my wrists by the day, and I did not lack spunk.

One day we were sent to the Rue de la Huchette to work in various rooms. To our great surprise, a virulent cholera epidemic was raging in that quarter. Soon that was all anyone talked about in Paris. In the building we were working in, there were three or four deaths, and panic took hold of the neighborhood.

Despite this, we kept on working in that building until we finished the jobs we had begun. One evening I got home to the boarding house and found a considerable number of our friends there, getting ready to flee to Creuse. Among them was my father, who wanted me to follow him. I insisted on staying. At one point, my journeyman told me, "Go pick up our tools and take them to the Rue Gaillon." The day after we arrived at that construction site, the man who had hired us was suddenly carried off by the horrible disease.

In the end, we too became concerned but, like sailors threatened by a storm, we would laugh and place ourselves in the hands of God. He protected us well, for we were not affected in any way at all.

Paris was a dismal sight. At one point, it was thought that the water supply was contaminated. Others maintained that the terrible disease was in the air. All one would see was people holding handkerchiefs to their lips and running through the streets in hope of escaping the scourge.

In that year, 1832, major work projects were undertaken in the Tuileries.[24] On either side of the Pavillon de l'Horloge, and especially on the left side opposite the garden, all the interior ceilings were torn down. My journeyman was hired on, and one morning I arrived carrying our tools on my hod.

---

24. Built on the site of a former tile works, beginning in 1564, the palace of the Tuileries was situated immediately to the east of the Louvre in central Paris. Since the time of the French Revolution, it had served as the seat of government in France. In the first half of the nineteenth century, the buildings were renovated and expanded. The Tuileries was partially destroyed by fire at the conclusion of the Paris Commune in 1871 and was completely demolished by order of the Chamber of Deputies in 1882. The name refers today to the vast, formal public garden that occupies the former site of the palace.

Given how weak my arms were, I could not have had a greater stroke of luck. Instead of having me assist my journeyman, they were going to use me as a spare laborer. This favor I also owed to François Thaury, who recommended me to the foreman, Lefaure. I did more or less what I pleased. About all they asked of me was to have a shovel in my hands, especially when the inspectors delegated by Old Fontaine, the architect, passed by, for our wages were stipulated in the contract. I held that job for four months. This wonderful piece of good luck allowed me to regain my strength completely.

I had already heard Louis-Philippe attacked in such violent terms that, often seeing him walking about with Old Fontaine or other members of his retinue, I mused that if it were true that this man dreamed of becoming a tyrant over our country, then getting rid of him would not be difficult. But that intention never crossed my mind.

I remember that one day the king had come to inspect the work being done on a bathroom. A plank had been placed on a double ladder that had been used for plastering over a lead pipe in the wall. The king waited until the plank had been removed and the plaster screenings cleaned up before entering. Then he put his hand to his hat and thanked us. He was a very good-looking man, tall and strong. Seeing him, what struck me was his simplicity and the heavy watch chain that he wore over a white vest.

LÉONARD SETS DOWN HIS HOD AND TAKES UP
THE TROWEL

One day my journeyman said to me, "You're now a big, strong lad. You can't go on forever serving as a mason's assistant, loafing around in the mortar-mixing room. I saw your uncle Martin yesterday. He's beginning a project in Bercy in the shop of a big wine merchant named Soulage. I told him he should have you start as a stonemason." I pranced with joy and, that very evening, ran to my uncle's.

As soon as he saw me, he said, "I sent one of my workers to go find you. You'll have to get tools, and then we'll see if you know how to use them."

I threw my hod and shovel to the devil and went the very next day to find myself an assistant at the Place de Grève.[25] And there I was, a journeyman. I was seventeen and had been a mason's assistant for nearly three years.

25. In the early nineteenth century, the Place de Grève, a public square located at the center of the capital's largest working-class district, served each morning as a sort of open-air hiring hall where workers in search of employment and employers with jobs to offer could meet. In those days, the expression *faire la grève* referred to the practice of making the rounds of the square looking for work and therefore, by extension, it meant "to be unemployed." In contemporary French, the same expression means "to go on strike."

Proud of this new status, I thought that the king was barely my equal. When I got back to the boarding house, I ran and hugged my landlady and received the congratulations of my friends with a satisfaction that is easy to understand. "Well now," they said. "For you to become a mason like your father is everything we might hope for you."

The assistant I hired at the Place de Grève followed me back to the boarding house, where he was supposed to pick up the tools I had just bought. What must have been going through his head? Did he guess that I was just a beginner by looking at my youth and at the two brand-new mortar troughs that he was about to shoulder? In any case, as soon as I had bought him a drink, he made his escape without saying a word.

Now I was really stuck. I returned on the double to the Place de Grève and found another assistant, whose appearance was neither very pleasant nor very prepossessing. But at least he came along, though it was nearly ten o'clock when we arrived at the construction site. Everyone was off eating breakfast and my lad did not have a cent, so I had to advance him ten sous for his first meal. He gave me no cause for complaint, however. He paid me back my money and proved to be hardworking and well behaved.

The foreman, a man named Lavergne, was my uncle's brother-in-law. He was a tippler who liked to have an occasional drop and who ended up acquiring the habits of a drunkard. Little by little, he became demoralized and besotted. He met a terrible end; I even think he went off to die in the hospital.

Lavergne set me to filling in the foundation of the wall of a shop. He never thought that I did enough. He went so far as to tell my uncle that I had no style and even that I was an idler. I think he had it in for me because I was a witness to his misconduct, and he feared that I would do him a bad turn with my uncle, who lived in Villemomble and rarely came to the project site.

Not daring to fire me as soon as the rough-stone work was finished, he set me to work "in plaster," that is to say, with masons who were doing ceilings and the finish coats on walls. Lavergne knew very well that I was just beginning and that everyone has to learn. He had the nerve to tell me I would never make a mason like my father. I got angry and told him to mind his own business.

The winter of 1832–33 had arrived, and I was overcome with homesickness. As it had been three years since I had last seen my mother and my sisters, I decided to leave. But I was lacking one essential: money. The three months of unemployment that had been forced on me after my accident in 1831 had eaten up all my little savings and even forced me into debt. I went to one of my good friends, Jean Roby from Saint-Hilaire, who knew my actual situation, and he loaned me two hundred francs. Overwhelmed with joy, we went together to the Temple district to buy clothes, old things that had been redone and appeared brand new.

As a result, I could proudly put in an appearance on Sundays and days when dances were held in Creuse, and I was happy to see my family again as well as those pretty and beloved girls of our native province.

In those days, it was a great honor for us to make a show of ourselves before our parents and neighbors, dressed to the nines, complete with necktie. The fashions inspired by the variety of cloth and materials that our burgeoning factories and mills had begun to produce and make available to the public were taking hold of the minds of workers. That was entirely natural. All we had ever known was drugget, which made us into heavy, ponderous beings who moved clumsily and turned with difficulty.

If we insisted on fancy clothes, it was, from another point of view, because when people saw us well dressed, they would take us for young people of taste and upright conduct. [. . .]

A TRIP BACK TO THE VILLAGE AFTER
THREE YEARS' ABSENCE

[. . .] When the migrant worker returns to his home region, everything changes, for the locals all recognize one of their own. Feelings of hostility and scorn are transformed into hugs, and sometimes the hugs develop into frenzies of joy, involving not just the family but the neighbors too.

They are right to welcome the migrant with such testimony of friendship, confidence, and respect. It is plain to any man of judgment and good sense that the migrant worker has been an agent of progress and civilization for our department.[26] Many of our simplest farm laborers' children have brought back to our villages, long dominated by an ignorant or miserly petty bourgeoisie, habits of honesty and openness that the intelligent worker acquires from contact with those who are his superiors and with whom he constantly rubs shoulders in a big city.

When this man returns home, he becomes the object of public curiosity. Everyone wants to know what he has done, what he has seen, what he thinks. Everyone listens to his least utterance with the greatest indulgence, as long as he is neither a braggart nor a troublemaker. [. . .]

[Migrant workers develop] peculiar ideas about their home region after hearing it slandered by people who are superficial and unreflective. We would get to the point where we no longer wanted to be identified as

26. On the role of seasonally migrant workers and their importance in integrating the provincial regions into the national economy and culture, see Alain Corbin, *Archaïsme et modernité en Limousin au XIXᵉ siècle, 1845–1880* (Paris, 1975).

coming from Limousin. We were so afraid of not being distinguished enough that we would try to change our pronunciation. To roll our *r*s and lose our natural accent seemed to us the height of distinction.

When we arrived at Pontarion, my traveling companion Desservière and I entered Old Duphot's inn. The latter's daughter Jeanne served us a bottle and brought a loaf of bread. She did not recognize either of us, so much had her godson grown in five years' absence, and I in three.

We began by making as much trouble as possible. We spoke to one another with exaggerated respect, calling each other Mr. Victor and Mr. Théophile. We asked if we were far from Bourganeuf.

The worthy woman, whose name is still held in such reverence in the region, answered all our questions, but there was something she did not like in the least about the clever game we were trying to play. When she needed to leave the room, she began by removing the keys from all the chests of drawers and cupboards, thinking that we might well be a couple of rogues who, in her absence, might taste her liqueurs or slip a few bottles under our smocks. Just then, we burst out laughing and said to her, in the local dialect, "So you don't recognize your own godson and Martin, the son of la Mignon?"[27]

Suddenly she cried out, "Oh! So it's you, you two miserable wretches!" Then we followed her into the kitchen, where we met some people from Pontarion who had known us when we were growing up. We all hugged one another, laughed, and soon after I slipped off to La Martinèche.

Upon entering our house, I found my mother and sisters at the table, eating soup and a plate of turnips. My father, who had gone to Bourganeuf, came in a moment later. "How tall you've grown, my poor little one," my mother said. "I was afraid I would never see you again after you fell from such a height in Paris."

At last I left everyone in a state of joy and went to bed. It was barely light the next day when my mother came to ask if my exhaustion had kept me from sleeping. "Oh no," I told her, "but my bed isn't very soft. It feels like my ribs are broken and my body is in pieces." [. . .]

My mother told me, "Here's the jacket, pants, and vest that I had made for you. I hope that all these clothes fit you properly. The tailor took the measurements from Michel Vergnaud, who's a year older than you, but it's better for them to be too big than too small."

Then the peasant woman in her suddenly changed the topic of conversation, and she said to me, "You don't want to keep your purse on you. Give it to me for safekeeping."

27. Here, for the first time, Nadaud refers to himself by his own first name, Martin. He also refers to his mother as "Mignon," a corruption of "Miyon" (for "Marie").

"Mother, dear mother, you're going to be very unhappy with me, and father will be too. You may think I've behaved like a wayward and ungrateful child who's forgotten all that you've done for him, but I don't have any money. Look in my pockets and you'll find less than a hundred francs. Don't forget that I had to pay my doctor, my baker, and my landlady, and that I spent three months not working after my fall."

She then started shedding a flood of tears. Through her sobs, she told me the story of the difficulty in which we found ourselves. She did not fail to remind me that for three years my father had earned nothing, and that the savings he had set aside over four years had disappeared in the unfortunate Villemomble business. On top of that, the harvest had been bad, we did not have enough wheat to last until the following summer, our cows were not producing a drop of milk, and she did not know where to begin when it came time to prepare our meals. Then she added, "I have another worry: your sister Magdeleine is twenty years old. Someone's asked her to marry him, and we have to scrape together a little dowry." I listened without saying a word, but my heart was torn.

As soon as she had left my room, she went to bring my father up to date on our long conversation. On the matter of money, my father told her, "I expected as much. Above all, don't reproach him for it. He's a good boy, he has heart; but he's sensitive and at the same time quick-tempered and hotheaded. If we can reach him at an emotional level, reestablish his sense of connection with his native region, then I don't think he'll abandon us."

Then, during a dinner consisting of whey, oilcakes, and potatoes, my father told me, "Well now, you dandy, I hope that you're going to come help us thresh in the barn." I nodded my agreement, and that afternoon the three of us went to thresh the sheaves. This is exhausting work, because it lasts fifteen days straight. But I held up well all the same.

In the evening, just before nightfall, I would take the axe and cut either branches or big logs to feed the fire that would burn in a fireplace more than two meters wide during our evening vigils.

At these vigils, which the neighbors attend, the mason always gets to speak. People like to hear his stories about Paris, and if he has the least gift of gab or imagination, his narrative is always enjoyable rather than boring, especially when the young women take part and begin to sing, or when the subject of prospective marriages is raised. [. . .]

But where the migrant's influence really holds sway is with the women, and especially the young marriageable women. The mother of such a young woman will sing the praises of a returning migrant at the evening vigil. The reasons she gives will exert their influence on the father, and if the suitor is well decked out and suitably attired, the young girl easily falls in love.

In our villages, dances are always held in barns, where people pile in. This sort of entertainment nearly always begins with that ancient Gallic dance called the *bourrée*, which has been kept alive in our region from generation to generation, as proof of the attention and respect that our youths used to profess for their elders. In fact, custom demands that for this first dance the young folks ask the oldest persons present to dance. The radiant faces of those women, who are getting along in years yet who effortlessly display their grace and comeliness, are a sight to be seen. This is what gives this dance greater appeal than is often assumed.

I never attended one of these gatherings without being amazed at the enormous number of pretty women there are in Creuse. On this subject, I will always remember hearing a great artist who was a maker of chignons say that nowhere except perhaps in Italy did women have such beautiful hair as in Creuse.[28] Observe our local women with their long, thick heads of black hair. There are some who are radiant with beauty, especially when they have taken the trouble to interweave their curls on each side of their foreheads, giving such charm to their faces and bringing out the brilliance of their large black eyes.

It is quite rare that such an occasion takes place without there being some talk of marriage. Four or five weeks after these preliminaries, the marriage is generally an accomplished fact. It is practically an absolute necessity that these marriages be rapidly concluded. The month of March chases us from our villages. Paris or other cities call us back for the construction of their houses. That is why any marriage that is not consummated during the months of January or February is necessarily put off until the following year.

It was in that same year of 1833 that my sister's hand in marriage was requested by a very honest man, Louis Soumis, who was to make her so happy for more than fifty years. There was some difficulty in reaching an agreement about the dowry. The Soumis family was asking fifteen hundred francs, but my father only wanted to give twelve hundred and to make that payable in installments of three hundred francs every other year.

Finally, for the sake of peace, the Soumis family accepted these terms.

Unfortunately, we had no money, not even to meet the initial expenses necessitated by the marriage. That is what tormented my father, a man who was shy and sensitive beyond all telling. To make his agony worse, a

28. A chignon is a knot or detachable coil of hair worn at the back of a woman's neck. During the period in question, commercial chignons were made from human hair, typically purchased from peasant women who thus were able to earn a bit of cash. Nadaud's comment not only compliments the women of his native region but indirectly indicates the relative poverty of the rural population of Creuse.

rumor had just gone around that François Thaury had foreclosed on a mortgage in the amount of four thousand five hundred francs that he had loaned my father so he could buy out his brother's share of our little property.

We were known to have other debts, the total exceeding ten thousand francs without counting my sister's dowry. This was just about what the property in La Martinèche was worth. Who could we approach for a new loan when everyone in the area knew about the wretched state of our affairs?

My father said to me, "Let's go see a man I know quite well, who lives in Soubrebost and has a very obliging nature." We found him in a *cabaret*. As we were drinking and chatting, my father told him the purpose of our visit. He immediately replied, "I have four hundred francs in my cupboard, but I need it to pay for a cow at the next fair in Bourganeuf, and I can't really touch it." In the end, he decided to loan us this money for four months. I signed the note, even though I was only seventeen; but to our great surprise, instead of handing over four hundred francs, our man gave us just three hundred sixty. He thus began by retaining the interest on his money at a rather high rate.

On our way back home, my father and I were outraged, each as much as the other. But when I saw him choked with tears, I tried to console him. As we were passing before the gate of our cemetery, he entered without saying a word to me. He made his way to the graves of his father and mother and knelt. I had difficulty getting him to stand up. I was as moved as he. Having those forty francs withheld on a four-hundred-franc loan for four months had deeply distressed him. In a voice interrupted by bitter sobs, he shouted, "To be reduced to borrowing at thirty percent interest! Ah, if that got out, my friends would no longer have the least confidence in me, and it would just be a question of which of my creditors would be the first to send the bailiffs after me."

He added, "To find myself in such distress, I who work so hard, I who was always frugal! Death is a hundred times preferable to living like this."

This scene, which took place in the middle of a brilliantly moonlit night in the cemetery where for several generations our ancestors have been laid to rest, was to leave indelible memories in my mind and in my heart. I know of nothing that did more to elevate my thoughts and make me understand the duty that a son owes to his parents.

My mother, who was anxiously awaiting us, immediately asked to know the result of our efforts. We told her that a friend had helped us out of our difficulty and naturally we told her nothing of his predatory conditions.

Three days later, we went to buy the bride's clothes. In those days, the taste for fancy dress was not widespread in our rural areas. A solid black dress of ordinary material, a kerchief instead of a shawl on the shoulders, a coif or cap, either with or without lace, wooden shoes with pretty straps, one or two silver rings which acquired significance in the eyes of our young newlyweds when the priest had blessed them—this constituted the wedding attire of our pretty country girls.

At last, my sister married Louis Soumis. My sister, who today carries her seventy-nine years rather well, could not have done better and never had reason to complain of her husband, who was as good for her as he was for our entire family.

Three or four days after this marriage, I went to borrow sixty francs from Chopinaud, one of my uncles from Masbarreau. I gave twenty francs to my father and with the rest I set off for Paris to begin a new campaign.

MY RETURN TO PARIS;
THE CONSTRUCTION CRISIS

No sooner had I arrived in Paris than some friends from the boarding house informed me that construction was going very badly. Some of them assured me that they had not worked a single day during the entire winter. The next day, at the crack of dawn, I went to the Place de Grève, where I soon found that the information I had been given the previous evening was in no way exaggerated. This square, the last vestige of the old slave markets of antiquity, was chock-full of men who, though haggard and emaciated, were adapting, without too much melancholy, to their situation as starvelings. You could see them shivering with cold in their sorry smocks or in jackets worn to the seams, stamping their feet on the paving stones to warm themselves up a bit.

When, toward nine o'clock, they left this place of desolation and misery, some would head for the gates of the army barracks to snare a few spoonfuls of soup, thanks to the generosity of our gallant soldiers. Others would stop along the quays where one of the numerous itinerant women peddlers would sell them a cup of bad coffee, a bit of bread, or some fairly good potatoes for one or two sous. But most of them would go home to their boarding houses. These were not the ones to be pitied most, and I was fortunate enough to find myself among them. Generally, the baker let us buy on the cuff, and we had credit with the landlady. As for the rest, we got hold of a little meat from the pork butcher and lived as best we could, awaiting better days.

During the sixty years that I have lived in Paris or London, I have seen construction workers endure some very painful crises, but with the exception of 1848, none could be compared with that of 1833 to 1834, of which I am speaking. The people were all the more saddened and angered due to the great hopes that had seized their spirits following the promises that had been lavished upon them by the government of Louis-Philippe. [. . .]

No, there is no torment quite the same, no worry quite so overwhelming for the worker as what he experiences in these great and poignant crises. Each morning he goes off in search of work. Each evening, as he makes his way back to his boarding house after having tramped the streets of the city in all directions, seeing foremen and buying drinks for Tom, Dick, and Harry, he returns with empty pockets, overwhelmed with exhaustion. And he senses that he will find himself in exactly the same situation the next day. His anxiety, far from diminishing, is increased by the fact that he cannot foresee whether the calamity that pursues him will be of long or short duration.

This had been my situation for three weeks when my father returned to find me sad and profoundly demoralized. He began by telling me, "You have to go back to working as a mason's assistant. Then, before long, I'll get you hired as a stonemason."

In fact, that same day, my father found work with a man named Laville who lived in the Rue de Vaugirard. He asked me, "Do you want to be my assistant?" I accepted and there I was, a mason's assistant once again, earning forty-two sous a day while stonemasons earned fifty-five sous and masons three and a half francs.

This was a boon and a great stroke of luck for me. As soon as I had carried the mortar trough to my journeyman, he would have me stir the plaster up a bit and even have me try my hand at plastering ceilings. I did not fail to improve my technique under the watchful eye of my father, an elite worker who had such a favorable reputation in the construction sites of Paris for doing difficult work.

His great renown was also based on his muscular strength. He liked to flatter himself that he had never found his equal at handing quarry stones up the ladder, nor in the one-to-one competitions that took place for a bet, nor in the games journeymen play among themselves. Today, it is almost impossible to imagine how highly strength was prized in that era.

The reason was that masons from Creuse were just then beginning to develop that sense of pride and independence which kept them from thinking themselves inferior to the workers of any other trade. This idea of placing might in the service of right, as the diplomats say, made many youths decide to win themselves respect by going to the savate and quarterstaff academies that were very numerous in our quarter.[29] But we will return to this subject later.

Toward the end of April, I stopped being my father's assistant, for he got me a job as a stonemason working for a certain Fanton, who was beginning a building in the Rue Blanche. There too, as in the Rue de la Chaussée-d'Antin, I was to have a painful and terribly unfortunate accident. I had been assigned to build cellar walls out of dressed quarry stones. I had an assistant named Barbat from Vallière. After choosing where I was going to start work and showing him my pile of quarry stones, I went back down into the cellar. But just as I was bending down to pick one up off the ground, he tossed another one down onto my left arm.

Fortunately, my arm was hanging free. The blow flung it backwards. It was just a bruise and not a break. It swelled up on the spot, and I fainted. The barracks in the Rue Blanche were just opposite our work site. I was taken to a surgeon-major, who gave me first aid. One of my young fellow workers then took me to the boarding house in a very sad and downcast state.

When kind Miss Rose Champesme saw me come in, she was stricken. She still had a vivid picture in her mind of the condition in which she had seen me three years earlier. She cried out, "Poor young man! How you're to be pitied! What will become of you, at your age, if you're crippled? What will your poor father say when he comes home this evening?"

In fact, my father had hardly entered the kitchen before he noticed that everyone around him had a mysterious look. At last, Miss Rose came up to him and said, "Eat your soup, Father Nadaud." There was no way to persuade him, and they had to tell him the painful news.

What went through his mind? He was overcome with anger. He threw down his soup bowl and broke it at his feet, shouting "For God's sake! If I go up to see him in his room, I'm going to strangle him." His nephew Hippolyte Julien, instead of calming him down, stirred him up further: "Let him kill himself once and for all and good riddance. He's careless and completely scatterbrained!"

When he came to my room, he was choking with anger. He looked at me without saying a word, and the look he gave me was ferocious. I was overcome with remorse and got the idea of going to the hospital the next

29. Savate is a French form of boxing in which blows from the feet as well as the hands are permissible. A quarterstaff was a stout length of wood, six to eight feet long, used as a weapon in hand-to-hand fighting. The popularity of such forms of combat among the youths of mid–nineteenth century Paris had given rise to the proliferation of "academies" where training could be obtained, much like the martial-arts schools in contemporary American cities.

day. Sure enough, as soon as my roommates had left for work, I told Miss Rose, "Take me to the hospital." She resisted this idea, and I could not persuade her. So I suddenly jumped out of bed, saying: "Why then, you'll see," and at the same time I ran toward the window to throw myself into the street.

She let out a loud shout, as did two other masons who were not working. I repeated my words with such insistence that she grew afraid and had to take me to the Hôtel-Dieu. Two hours later, I was crossing the square in front of Notre Dame and finally reached the hospital. I was immediately given a bed. One of the Sisters, seeing that I was very disheartened, welcomed me with gentle and kind words. I was undressed and I went to bed.

The next day, when the famous Dr. Dupuytren made his rounds, he examined me for a minute or two and then said a few words to one of the interns who was accompanying him: "There's no fracture; we have to concentrate on making the swelling go away." I was given every possible attention and I slept all night without waking up.

When my father returned from work that evening and was informed of my departure for the hospital, he was silent for a time and then went up to his room without saying a word to anyone. Miss Rose did not hide from him that all our friends in the boarding house condemned his conduct and some had even made very offensive remarks about him.

I was perhaps the only one who understood that his anger resulted more from his excess of tenderness than from anything else. He came to see me and found me seated near a window with other patients. I got up to go meet him, he gave me a hug and quickly saw that I had no feeling of resentment toward him. We immediately made our peace.

The third time that the doctor bandaged my arm, I moved my fingers without pain. From that point on, I had no further worry, counting on a prompt and complete recovery. [. . .]

After taking two weeks' rest, I went back to the same construction site in the Rue Blanche. The building was covered over, and the foreman, Fanton, put me in the cellar making the joints in the walls and the vaults, work that was not very difficult. Every time this worthy man came to see us, it was to tell me not to tire myself out.

As soon as Fanton found it necessary to lay me off, I went to work up in the Faubourg Saint-Denis, but as I did not know anyone at that work site, they did not keep me on very long. The construction crisis was still raging, and I prowled about from one project site to the next without finding work. In the end, a certain Mr. Gasne, a foreman for a man named Dayras, had me bring my tools and accompany him to the Rue des Bons-Enfants.

Unfortunately, the carpenters' strike of 1833 broke out around that time. It lasted several months and work had to come to a halt. I went five weeks without a job.

This was one of the hardest times of my life. Just out of the hospital and burdened with all my preexisting debts, too young to inspire much confidence, and out of work, I became very poor. I have since understood the words that Beaumarchais put in the mouth of Figaro: "I've experienced more difficulty earning a living than Charles V had governing Spain."

Fortunately, my baker, who had long been my father's baker too, did not refuse me bread any more than my landlady refused to serve me soup. I learned the meaning of the words "to scrape the bottom of the barrel."[30] A worker is said to scrape the bottom of the barrel when he does not have a cent either to go to a greasy spoon or to drink a glass at the wine merchant's at dinnertime. The barrel scraper lays himself down on the plaster at mealtimes and takes a bite of his piece of bread or munches on an apple, if he still has a sou to his name, and drinks water if he is thirsty.

Today's worker is very rarely reduced to this extreme. If he wishes, he can ask to pay in installments. He is rarely refused, even if he asks at each meal. Sixty years ago this practice did not exist and one had to wait for payday to get money or borrow a few sous from whomever one could. But those who had too frequent recourse to daily loans were not respected and were looked at askance by their fellow workers, who considered them to be people of questionable conduct, incapable of obtaining the slightest credit either among their friends or in their boarding houses.

Those of us who were young, however, would promptly leave behind the lamentable state of boredom, sadness, and misery that resulted from our lack of work by practicing the sports toward which we were impelled by the ardor of youth. In the morning, after making the rounds at the Place de Grève, we would return to the boarding house. We would then begin by piling our beds one on top of the other and converting our rooms into boxing or savate halls. These hand-to-hand combats would bring us moments of pure joy. From time to time, we would spend our evenings in the academies of Gadoux or Le Mule, who were considered the two most skillful masters of savate of that era. For my part, I grew to like these exercises and became fairly good at them.

Early one morning, Giraudon, who was from Lyon, came to tell me that he was going to be starting a building in the Rue Saint-Ambroise as foreman for the contractor Gémon. He hired me along with one of his

30. Nadaud's phrase is *battre les gravats,* the same mason's metaphor noted earlier in a different context. It means "to crush the screenings" (see n. 18).

cousins. His cousin told him, "We'd gladly buy you a drink, but we don't have a cent between us." Giraudon let out a raucous laugh and added, "They're never happy. I give them jobs and still have to loan them money." And indeed, he gave us ten francs each.

The truth is that our families were linked by close ties of friendship. The four Giraudon brothers were natives of a small village called Le Masdarier. As each of them turned fourteen or fifteen, the age at which masons left for Paris, their father, a very honorable peasant, entrusted them to my father, who did his best to find them work and never stinted his advice. As these young men were all well behaved and good workers, relations between us became extremely friendly.

Giraudon was just their cousin, yet I had found in him a friend who was to have a very great influence on my life as a young man. He was better educated than the workers of that period and a man of fine and noble character as well as gentle and kindly manners. We had enormous respect for him. Giraudon had been trained in first-rate schools in Lyon, where his father was a contractor, but when the latter was killed on one of his construction sites, his son came to Paris to join his cousins.

While he was working at the construction site in the Rue Saint-Ambroise, this worthy comrade, who knew that I already had the beginnings of an education, persuaded me to spend my evenings going to the school of a surveyor that he himself attended regularly. Our idea was to perfect ourselves in our trade. Unfortunately, I soon found myself obliged to abandon this school. As soon as the job in the Rue Saint-Ambroise was over, I experienced new difficulties and went two weeks without finding work. I had to start wandering the streets all over again, prowling from one construction site to another, without managing to get myself hired.

I watched that year of 1834 slip by without earning any money. "How," I asked myself, "can I keep my word with my creditors and with my poor father if misfortune continues to pursue me with such pitiless severity?"

The scarcity of good job opportunities forced me to go to work at the Barrière du Combat for a man named Mérigot who had contracted to build lime kilns and supporting walls to prevent cave-ins in the quarries.[31]

I was worn out by this exhausting work and by the hour-and-a-half journey that I was forced to make morning and night, and lack of time and fatigue prevented me from going to school. It is true that this difficulty lasted barely two months.

31. The Barrière du Combat had once been used as a tollgate, to levy taxes on goods being brought to the capital for sale. In the time of which Nadaud is speaking, it marked the boundary between the city of Paris proper and the commune of La Villette to the north.

Many workers from a variety of trades were to be found in those parts, and at mealtimes we would crowd into the same wine merchant's. You would be making a great error if you imagined today that in those days people were indifferent to politics. Though we were a little unsystematic in our reasoning, we had the right idea all the same. The spirit of France, a spirit of common sense, was not deceived by the deadly blows that Louis-Philippe and his ministers dealt to the Revolution of 1830. People figured out that the only purpose of their middle-of-the-road politics was to lull the nation to sleep so as to consolidate the dynasty more quickly. Newspapers were sold in the streets just as they are today.[32] Every morning in the wine merchant's shop, I would be asked to read aloud Cabet's *Le Populaire*.[33]

One morning I was approached by a young medical student named Macré, the son or nephew of the foreman at the quarry. He complimented me on the tone and energetic manner in which I read certain passages. He came back several times after that to hear me. That was the first time that someone from the middle class had come up and shaken my hand, and I confess that I was very flattered by it. He asked me if I wanted to join the Society of the Rights of Man,[34] to which he belonged. He saw immediately from my response that I was already a republican.

What is more, on the construction site in the Rue de la Chaussée-d'Antin, Luquet, my foreman, never stopped telling me about the Republic or about this important society, so dreaded by the government, which I was determined to join. We arranged a rendezvous, and our young student introduced me and my two comrades, Luquet and Durand, into his chapter, which was located in the Rue des Boucheries-Saint-Germain.

We were received with the warmest enthusiasm. From the moment of this baptism, I felt that I could never be bold or daring enough to earn the confidence of this group of young republicans, so openly devoted to the

32. Nadaud implicitly contrasts the situation under the politically repressive Second Empire (1852–70) with the generally more liberal regimes that existed under both the Orleanist Monarchy (1830–48) and the Third Republic (instituted in the 1870s and still in force at the time he was writing this account of his life).
33. Etienne Cabet (1788–1856) was among the best-known Socialist theorists of his day. The son of a cooper, Cabet practiced law in Dijon and had been elected to the Chamber of Deputies as representative of that city, before he was forced into exile in 1834 for his criticism of the government of Louis-Philippe. *Le Populaire* was the republican newspaper through which Cabet tried to propagate his early ideas to the working class.
34. The Society of the Rights of Man was a republican club whose members were recruited mainly among Parisian students and workers. In its manifesto, written in 1833, it called for the extension of political rights, including universal suffrage, and aimed at a social revolution that would improve the plight of the working class.

interests of France and of the people. But in order to make my narrative as clear as possible, I have devoted a special chapter to my political activities between 1830 and 1848 and I now return to the subject of work.

After finishing these projects at the Carrières de l'Amérique, highly disagreeable projects for a young man hoping to improve his skills in the trade, I went to work on another construction site that was no less unpleasant than the one I had just left. My friend Roby was beginning an important project at the Barrière de la Courtille on behalf of the big wine merchant Dénoyer, so well known at that time by all fanciers of light bluish claret and by women of loose morals, who were drawn to his place from every quarter of Paris. [. . .]

What did they have me do for a start? I was working as a carter. I used the owners' carts to drive the debris resulting from the demolition and the earth resulting from the excavations to a dumping place located at the top of the Rue Saint-Laurent.

When this operation was completed, the excavations, which were very deep in some places, had to be filled in. This required working in amongst timber props, creating enormous difficulties and continual dangers for us. For nearly five months, I continued working on this project, receiving a miserable wage of fifty-five sous a day at first, and three francs later.

There was no way to learn anything useful on such a terrible job, and this caused me a great deal of annoyance. But you cannot always find the job you hope for in such times of crisis. You take what you can get and are happy with that.

REGRETTABLE ABSENCE OF RELATIONS AMONG WORKERS

[. . .] Among those of us who were from Creuse, there were little clans, petty rivalries between cantons or even communes. Workers who came from the regions of La Souterraine, Le Grand-Bourg, and Dun were christened *brulas*, while those who came from the neighborhood of Vallière, Saint-Sulpice-les-Champs, Saint-Georges, and Pontarion were called *bigaros*.

When members of these groups found themselves on the same construction site, they would start to stare at each other menacingly. Moreover, a foreman or a worksite supervisor who was a *bigaro* would be careful not to hire *brulas*. If, by chance, they happened to be on the same construction site, the question was who would "eat up" the other and "dismantle" him.[35] This would produce one of those struggles in which the em-

35. Nadaud employs the expression *déchaffauder*—to take down someone's scaffolding.

ployer was the only one to profit. The two adversaries would work to the point of "twisting the shirt off their backs," or in other words, to the point of complete exhaustion. Once the battle was over, if the two rivals had been equally bold, they would go have a drink together. When they left the wine merchant's, they were no longer *bigaro* and *brula;* they were friends, and peace had been made.

The crazy jealousies and rivalries that existed among workers in a single trade or from a single department were even more intense among those of us who were young. When we would go on walks to the city gates or when we wanted to go to a dance, we would everywhere meet with such disdain that the need to win respect made us into fighters. It was this frame of mind that accounted for the proliferation of savate academies in our neighborhood.

The first savate master to become a celebrity in our circles was a man named Toulouse. He had a student named Gadoux who came from my village and who succeeded in earning a reputation as a grand master. I asked to enter his academy, but my father had made him promise never to accept me, and he kept his word.

Since my father had gone to spend the winter of 1834 back in our native region, I lost no time in going to Le Mule's academy in the Rue de la Vannerie. Because I was adroit and highly agile, Le Mule soon decided that I could become one of his most capable students and he was careful not to neglect me. On the contrary, he would teach me different attacks and, after close observation, would lay bare my weak points and take great pains to perfect my technique.

In our neighborhood, there was a great outbreak of shameless behavior that lasted two or three years. The freedom to which we aspired and which the newspapers were promising us daily, exacerbated what were already our natural inclinations. As we had little training or education, at the least insult we would kick like feisty mules being whipped in the fields. We would tell each other that we had to learn how to use our fists to punish those who had such a poor opinion of the "chestnut eaters" from Limoges and from Creuse. The little dance-hall girls would refuse even to dance with us when other, more elegant young men were in attendance.

There came a time, however, when it was our turn to be feared by the troublemakers and false swaggerers. We would follow each other around in gangs. At the least gesture, at the slightest word, it would come to blows. The police rarely intervened, though twice within a fairly brief span of time I happened to get picked up and had to spend the night in jail. I confess that I then experienced very great remorse.

What a scene it was to spend the night in the midst of that rabble, as they shouted, raged, and covered the floor with thick gobs of spit or their vomit! Anyone who did not consider himself depraved would be led to despair. The thought that would lodge in his mind was to promise never again to get involved. My father wore himself out giving me advice. He set François Thaury, Roby, and Giraudon on my trail, three of the worthiest of men, for whom I had the greatest respect. The truth is that one should never give up hope of leading a young man back onto the path of upright conduct as long as he seeks men of integrity as friends. This is a quality which I have always possessed.

These worthy men, who were very fond of me because I sought out their company, summoned me to Bertuzi's, the wine merchant's shop near our rooming house, where we went to have a glass or a bottle to drink. The conversation, though rather animated, especially on the part of François Thaury, always retained a certain goodwill toward me. I listened to these kind and loyal friends with all my nerves trembling and I told myself in my heart of hearts that I was better than they thought. They accused me of hanging out in savate academies and fighting over trifles. But the most serious of their reproaches was that I got mixed up in street brawls, so frequent in that period, and that I spoke too much of the Republic.

Giraudon, the one from Lyon, was a sober man with much common sense. He advised me to leave the boarding house and change neighborhoods so as to escape the bad influences that were tugging me this way and that. This thought appealed to me quite a bit. For some time already, I had been considering it, for the desire to educate myself had never left me, any more than my attachment to my family.

The new acquaintances that I intended to maintain were a few good masons and a few young people I met with once a week at the Society of the Rights of Man; but I could not admit this to my worthy and honest friends, who never adopted any political position.

Roby, in turn, said: "I'm living alone in my room with Jacques Lafaye. If you want to join us, I have the sheets you will need, and we'll set up a bed." I accepted his proposition on the spot, and five or six days later, I was living at 7 Rue des Barres.

It was a peculiar dwelling that I was going to inhabit. It was located on a sort of mezzanine between the ground floor and the first floor and had such a low ceiling that you could hardly stand up straight. On these premises, which were rather a mess, there were mortar troughs, masons' rules, planks, and scrap metal of every variety. I should add that it was barely ventilated at all and that half the floor tiles were missing. Now that there are laws about unsanitary dwellings, the police would not fail to prohibit this sort of slum. But in those days, our room was hardly different from those that workers lived in everywhere else.

"Let's not stay here," I began saying to Roby after a few days. "We'll soon be devoured by fleas and bedbugs. I'm already all marked up from the bites of those relentless parasites." We gave notice to our landlord in the Rue des Barres and went off to rent a rather spacious room at 23 Rue Saint-Louis-en-l'Ile. It was on the fourth floor, at the back of a courtyard.

I had thus accomplished what my friends had advised and what I myself so much desired, namely getting away from the neighborhood of the Place de Grève. All I had to do was redeem my conduct in the eyes of those honest men who found that my youthful indiscretions had gone a bit too far. But they were forgetting that the reasons for my behavior had been, as in the case of duelists, matters of honor. Neither my friends nor I had ever been able to resign ourselves to hearing masons from Creuse being called insulting names. [. . .]

THE CONSTRUCTION INDUSTRY IN 1835 AND 1836

[. . .] It became easier to find work and we earned a few sous more per day: three francs for stonemasons instead of fifty-five sous and still three and a half or three and three-quarters francs per day for masons. The thirty million francs in advances made by the Bank of France to Parisian businesses, like those made by the discount bank, produced a marvelous effect at the time. The construction of monuments, which had remained in abeyance for many years, revived. This included the Arc de Triomphe, the Church of the Madeleine, the lawcourts and judicial headquarters at the Quai d'Orsay, the Ministry of Foreign Affairs, and the Church of Saint Vincent de Paul.[36] For its part, the private sector undertook several substantial enterprises, as indicated in a previous chapter.

Shopkeepers and workers everywhere displayed their satisfaction. By common accord, people started calling Louis-Philippe the king of the masons. This improvement in the business climate produced a renewal of his popularity that would have lasted longer if the clear-sighted men of the progressive liberal party had not found it necessary to issue a denunciation to all of France concerning the harmful policies of the king, who was destroying our liberties and electoral rights one after another.

As I was unemployed in February 1835 and knew that the month of March would witness a swarm of workers returning to Paris, I was very much afraid of finding myself without a job and of being forced to go shiver each morning in the Place de Grève.

I was, therefore, extremely happy when, arriving one morning at that

36. The Church of the Madeleine in central Paris had been begun in 1764 but was not completed until 1842. (Nadaud misspells it "Magdeleine," perhaps because he had an older sister of that name.)

site of desolation, Barozier, who was quite well known as a city employee hired to inspect for saltpeter rot,[37] got me and one of my friends, Pierre Dizier, hired by a man named Dutour, foreman for Mr. Bayle, a very worthy contractor.

The construction site was located in the Rue du Helder at the rear of a large courtyard. We didn't know a soul there, but when he hired me, Dutour had seemed to be a kind and decent man. I had not been mistaken. He had a great refinement of feelings and a way of commanding that was just as praiseworthy. He put us to work on a long facade, putting up five or six piers of identical dimensions.[38]

Because this building was located in a courtyard, once we had all gone in, they would close the door behind us and reopen it only at mealtimes. As a result, we had not treated our fellow workers or "paid for our welcome," and thus they gave us the cold shoulder. The regular members of the work crew were interested in finding out just how skilled the two new hires might be. So all the workers set about preparing their first course.[39] Suddenly, a short fat one with a pockmarked, spiteful face gave the order to have mortar mixed. With his first troughful, he laid three or four quarry stones into the second course of the pier. Without warning his fellow workers, he called up his assistant with another trough of mortar.[40] Dizier and I did not have long to wait before being left behind, or "eaten up" in the language of the construction site. But all of a sudden, someone cried out, "On the ladder!" for there were no more quarry stones on the planking.[41] It happened that two of our friends were located right above me on that ladder. They immediately noticed that I was passing the largest of the

37. Saltpeter rot is the white crystalline deposit that forms on damp stone walls, caused by nitrifying bacteria or by minerals working through to the surface. In the period of which Nadaud writes, the inspector's job was to see that saltpeter rot did not weaken the mortar used to join the stone blocks, thus creating unsafe conditions.
38. A pier (*trumeau*), as the term is used here, is a span of wall between windows.
39. A course (*rang*) is a horizontal row of bricks or stones that must be completed before the next higher row is begun.
40. The normal practice would have been for all masons to work on the same course at roughly the same pace until all were through, and then for their assistants to mix and bring up fresh mortar to all at the same time. By calling for new mortar without waiting for the others to complete their course, Nadaud's fellow worker announces his intention to humiliate the new arrivals by outperforming them.
41. A supply of stones was carried up and stored on the scaffold planks close to the mason, who would draw upon them as necessary. Once these were exhausted, the workers above would call for a new supply, requiring those below to interrupt their work and pass the stones up the ladders. Caught in this situation, Nadaud has the bravado to accomplish this task in a way which displays his exceptional physical strength.

quarry stones without resting them on my stomach, something they could not do. That was when I told myself, "If you don't behave, I'm going to have to bring you to your senses." The shame of seeing myself "buried" had made me turn red as a beet. In such moments, the journeyman mason becomes ill-tempered and upset. He gets angry at himself, his assistant, his fellow workers. He loses his head and often picks up a quarry stone that he should not, while the man who is keeping up maintains his composure, laughs up his sleeve, and works more efficiently than the poor idiot who is being mocked by those who see him in this state of confusion, turmoil, and anger.

When these piers had all been built up to the proper level, we were put to work on the gable-end wall. But I was doing better the second day than the first, and by then I had paid for my welcome, so we had all become good friends.

The foreman, after seeing me pass the quarry stones up the ladder, began to look favorably upon me. Then, over the next few days, he clearly saw that I was managing to work so as not to let myself "get eaten out of house and home" any more. As soon as the others saw that we could stand toe to toe with the rest of them, we made peace and only called to have mortar mixed when the whole row was ready.

What showed me, after two weeks, that I was on the foreman's good side was that he laid off first one and then another group of workers and I was not among those let go. My friend Dizier and I were kept on to rough-wall the timber framing and floor surfaces and even to do some plaster ceilings.

Meanwhile, the owner started another very big building in the Rue Saint-Fiacre, and we were sent there. Did Bayle wish to encourage us by keeping us on the payroll? He began by telling us, "Boys, you should be happy. Here you are with good jobs that will round out your campaigns." And as he was saying this, he gave us each a ten-franc tip.

We were overjoyed to know that we would have work for some time. It was an enormous satisfaction, especially for someone who had been tossed about from one construction site to another over the course of several years, to be delivered from those harrowing anxieties that gnaw at the heart of the journeyman who wants to work and cannot find employment.

I told myself that my family was counting on the money that I might manage to save. Nonetheless, there are pressing debts which weigh even more heavily on one's conscience, and one has to start with those. Every month I would make partial payments to my baker and I would pay back little debts of honor. For more than a year, I never left Mr. Bayle's employment and I saved thirty to forty francs each month.

The first thing we had to do in the Rue Saint-Fiacre was to demolish the vast workshops which had served as a repair shop for a shipping company. This quarter is known as the center of Paris's great export trade. Dizier, the foreman's two nephews, and I spared no effort. We very often arrived at four o'clock in the morning and quite often stayed until eight at night. We maintained these long hours until the building had risen above the basement level because we were working amidst props which supported the gable ends of the neighboring buildings and which the architect as well as the owner and ourselves were all in a hurry to remove.[42]

We were full of pluck at the age of nineteen or twenty. I have always remembered that the more overtime we did, the happier we were. It was not unusual for our friends, who did not have our luck, to show a certain jealousy, for the time had not yet come to talk of regulating work hours.

And so we enjoyed, for the first time in several years, a peace of mind that in a certain sense resulted from being constantly busy. Because we had fewer worries, we experienced less physical exhaustion even though we were working like slaves. [. . .]

Up to that point, I was just a stonemason, which is the first stage in achieving the rank of mason. When I announced to our honest and upright foreman Dutour that I was leaving to become a mason at the Marché Saint-Laurent in the Faubourg Saint-Martin, he expressed his warmest regards for me and shook my hand with affection. Then I invited my fellow workers to drink a glass of white wine. Once we were standing in front of the counter, everyone wanted to buy a round, but when we had emptied our glasses three or four times, we decided that was enough and we had to say our good-byes.

My new boss was named Claude Lefaure. We had known one another in the savate academies and had the reputation among devotees of that sport for being equally stubborn and obstinate. Before long we became inseparable friends, and not for just a day. Our friendship grew stronger until death separated us. [. . .]

At the Marché Saint-Laurent, Lefaure had only hired fellow workers who were energetic, cheerful, and good-natured with one another. So the only question was who might show me up as a worker; but since the job only called for ordinary plastering, I held my own fairly well. One day Lefaure told me, "If you take my advice, you'll quit this job. You can't really perfect your skills here, because we're not doing any moldings. I

---

42. It is customary in Paris to erect buildings that directly abut against the walls of their neighbors. When such a building is demolished in preparation for new construction, the adjoining buildings must be supported with massive wooden props until the new project is completed and the integrity of the multibuilding unit is restored.

know a certain Pouthonet who is foreman for Moreau from Saint-Georges, and who has some very elaborate projects to do. You should go there and really learn how to offset."[43] When Pouthonet hired me, he promised to give me a very good mason to work alongside of. He kept his word, and I made fair progress.

But one day, while I was busy rejointing a stairwell, I encountered a new source of annoyance. The joiners bringing up wood paneling obliged us to stop work from time to time and remove the planks we were standing on for scaffolding. These joiners simply refused to understand that once plaster is mixed, it has to be used. One of them felt that we were making them wait too long and, all of a sudden, he called me a clod. No sooner had he pronounced this insulting and vulgar word than I threw a handful of plaster right in his face. Naturally we had to grapple with one another, so we went down to the courtyard and started exchanging punches and kicks. The two of us fell down next to the rim of a well that was nearly flush with the ground. Everyone cried out in fear that we would disappear down this well. The owner and Moreau, the contractor, were there in the courtyard. The latter, who had been involved in many such fights in his youth, came over to separate us and whispered to me in dialect, "Dunk him!"[44] The owner was not in a joking mood and fired us both on the spot. But a moment later, the foreman passed along a message from the contractor that I should bring my tools to the Rue des Noyers. That is what I did. [. . .]

At that time, my father was working at the Marché de la Madeleine, in a building that fronted on the square, for a man named Sucherat who had as his foreman Georges Vidaillat. My father asked Vidaillat to take me on as his scaffold-mate, and his request was granted. We got along marvelously with Old Léonard.[45] He did not, however, find me a careful enough worker. He would have liked to see me plaster walls and especially ceilings with the uniformity and high finish that had earned him a reputation that followed him through all the construction sites in which he had worked. But it was especially when it came to moldings, to cutting an angle or a return on a fireplace, that he found me mediocre. When Georges Vidaillat climbed up on our scaffold, he would tell me, "The young can't compare with their elders." He was right. As far as I was concerned, I never had as sure a hand or eye as my father.

43. In construction work, to offset (recouper) is to leave wide setbacks in successive courses of stones so as to buttress the walls of buildings.
44. The contractor's words, in Limousin dialect, are "bougno, bougno-lo," an exhortation to Nadaud to give his opponent a bath—either by drawing blood or by tossing him into the well.
45. Though Nadaud tries to create a certain sense of distance by using "we" instead of "I," and by referring to his father by his name, his affection as well as his respect for the master craftsman shows through.

Georges Vidaillat had heard that I was fairly well educated. Moreover, at that time there were so few workers who knew how to sign their names that in our circles it did not take long to train a scholar.[46] Compared to my fellow workers, I deserved that reputation. Such compliments, coming from a man as serious as Vidaillat, very much flattered my pride. [. . .]

I LEAVE FOR A MEDICAL EXAM BY THE DRAFT BOARD IN BOURGANEUF

I was working in the Place de la Madeleine when I received a letter from my mother that caused me considerable resentment, just as it did my father, who was my scaffold-mate. It informed me of the date when I had to be in Bourganeuf to be examined by the army medical board. "There's always something going wrong for us," I told myself. "It's such a pity to have to leave a good job in the middle of the year, especially now that I'm earning a mason's wage, to go off for a stroll in the country."

My father was no less annoyed than I, for in our calculations we would tell each other, "It's not impossible that between the two of us we could save seven or eight hundred francs this year." My poor old man knew that if the fractures in my arms did not get me an exemption, it would be impossible, given the amount of his debts, to extract himself from difficulty.

Because my mother had drawn the number six on my behalf, all our plans had fallen through.[47] We were too poor to consider putting up money to buy my way out, and in any event the fear of increasing our total indebtedness had frightened us, and this scheme was abandoned.[48] My father immediately went to one of his closest friends, Colas from Buze in

---

46. Nadaud's ironic comment applies only to a limited number of artisanal trades in the capital. Nadaud's acquaintances were mostly masons from rural Creuse, who had a lower rate of literacy than the Parisian labor force as a whole. According to the survey conducted by the Paris Chamber of Commerce in the spring of 1848, about one-third of all masons working in Paris were illiterate, whereas 82 percent of those employed in the construction sector and 87 percent of all males working in Paris could read and write. See Chambre de commerce de Paris, *Statistique de l'industrie à Paris, résultant de l'enquête faite par la chambre de commerce pour les années 1847–1848* (Paris, 1851), pp. 83, 68. See also introduction, n. 45.

47. Since Nadaud had a bad number (see chapter 3, n. 5), his only remaining hope was exemption on medical grounds.

48. In all likelihood, Nadaud is referring to a system of "insurance" against the risks of being drafted. As described in Emile Guillaumin, *The Life of a Simple Man* (Hanover, N.H., 1983), for a sum of approximately five hundred francs, an entrepreneur called a *marchand d'hommes* would undertake to provide a substitute to serve the term of military service if the insured individual was chosen in the draft lottery (see chapter 3, n. 5). If, however, one waited until after having been conscripted, the cost of securing a substitute was considerably higher.

the commune of Saint-Pardoux-Lavaud, who loaned him three hundred francs for my journey and for our household expenses.

Meanwhile, I was advised to go find the doctor who had set my broken wrists at the time of my fall in the Rue de la Chaussée-d'Antin. The latter gave me a hearty welcome and provided me with a certificate to present to the examining physician of the army medical board.

I left for Creuse. The day after I got there, my mother told me, "Tomorrow we'll go to Pontarion to see our cousin Lafeuillade."

"And what are you going to ask him?"

"Just come. He's expecting us."

For thirty years, Lafeuillade had been a wood splitter in the forests of Dr. Cressant, who was the physician chosen every year to conduct the business of the army medical board. As soon as my mother had explained the purpose of our visit to the old wood splitter, he answered, "I could no more refuse you than you ever refused to feed me when I was working in your village."

We all left the next day for Guéret and went straight to Dr. Cressant's house. We had hardly been announced before the servant brought us down to the kitchen and served us breakfast. Dr. Cressant himself soon came to join us.

Lafeuillade first made all sorts of excuses to his master for having disturbed him and then added, "For thirty years, I've worked for you or for your father and never asked for anything. But here I have one of my cousins who has come from Paris for a medical board examination. Would you be so kind as to glance at a certificate that he was given by a Parisian doctor?" Dr. Cressant had me take off my jacket then and there. He carefully examined the old fractures, especially the one in my right arm, without saying a word to me. He changed the topic of conversation and said he hoped we would have a nice breakfast. And so we started out on the road back to Pontarion quite pleased with the welcome we had received.

On the day of my medical examination, I could barely recognize the man, for he was decked out in a uniform covered with gold braid. I handed him my certificate, and he took my right arm. I barely heard him utter the word, "Unfit." I was so happy that I ran, half dressed, out to find my mother who was waiting for me in the stairwell. Naturally she was happy, for she knew that, as poor as we were, the salvation of our family rested on my shoulders! [. . .]

We were in a terrible hurry to inform my father of this outcome. We entered the house of Mr. Antoine Berger, our family's lawyer and a man who took a very active interest in our affairs, and there I began my letter with these words: "Father, you can sleep in peace, for your breadwinner has not been taken from you."

The other conscripts from our commune were waiting for me to go out to dinner, but I could not get my mother to go into the inn. It was hardly the custom in those days to see masons' wives enter an inn, even in the company of their husbands. My mother was, moreover, a rather unusual peasant woman. She never knew a word of French and she never wore shoes on her feet. In her mind, this luxury was reserved for women of the bourgeoisie. Neither did she have, her whole life long, any coat to place over her shoulders other than the one she was given at the time of her marriage. All I could get her to do was to go into a baker's and buy a loaf of bread, and we set out once more on the road to the village. When we reached the Dupont houses, we took a little shortcut where there was a spring. She stooped down and folded over her apron so we could use it as a receptacle and drink to our heart's content; all this in order to save a few pennies. [. . .]

Our joy was then complete, for I had just escaped seven years of military service. In the days that followed, my parents lost no time in speaking to me about marriage. On this subject, they confessed that a year earlier they had arrived at an agreement with a widow named Lefort from Theillaucher in the commune of Sardent.

Their arrangement was rather clever. If it had succeeded, our debts would have been paid off. My father had been close friends with Mr. Lefort, who had lived in our village and managed to save seven or eight thousand francs in Paris. But Lefort had fallen ill and, sensing he was going to die, advised his wife to do two things: to have their daughter marry me and then come live with us herself. In this way, we would have had the money and the two women. This arrangement had great appeal for my family, which had such a pressing need for money.

I went to visit this girl. She was not the least bit displeasing to me, for she was more pretty than ugly. But, whether because I did not suit her or because she had promised her hand to a boy from her village, she lowered her head when I spoke to her and remained as dumb as a fish. Her mother came to inform us of her refusal, and the proposed agreement had to be abandoned.

Following this first failure of marriage plans, I was soon to have a second. One of my close relatives from Pontarion, who was a widower, was trying to get married again, to a young widow named Nina from the village of Cherolles. Together they cooked up a scheme to introduce me to a girl from that village who was thought to have a dowry of four or five thousand francs.

With Nina's recommendation, I went to visit the girl's family. I have never been able to think back on that evening without bursting out laughing and making anyone to whom I recounted my adventure laugh as well.

Upon entering their house, I found it full of women, some knitting, others doing their spinning. Whether they were there because it was the custom to gather in that house for evening vigils or just to see Marie's beau, I never had the opportunity to find out. The mother had me sit near the fire, in the corner of a wide fireplace, and the eyes of all those present turned in my direction. As I was a little sharper and less awkward than most young people, who have not traveled, it seemed to me that I had made a favorable impression on all those kindly peasant women.

After the brief, customary preliminaries, conversation died out, and I was reduced to stirring the ashes with the end of my walking stick like a downright fool. Suddenly the grandfather, who was lying down sick in his bed, his head covered with an enormous cotton bonnet which left only the end of his nose visible, opened his mouth and said to me: "I knew your grandfather. The poor devil wasn't happy. He owed three hundred francs to Jean Graule from Theillaucher." Everyone was struck with consternation by this outburst, especially the mother and her daughter. All I could do was to answer him, "Oh, that debt is long since paid." But the old man was far from done. He continued his insinuations and impertinences, which may not have been intended to offend me, but as an old mason from Lyon, he detested "Parisians." That was the way things were in those days: jealousy and hatred were the rule among workers.

This venerable old man also told me, "Parisian masons earn money, but they spend it as fast as they make it. And they don't hesitate to abandon their women and live with tramps." He then went on to cite the example of a certain X—— from a village near his own.

As I was leaving, the mother and daughter accompanied me a short way beyond the door and begged me not to pay attention to the old man's words. But the old codger was so stubborn that he went to find Nina to tell her that I need not trouble myself to come calling again.

That made two refusals I had received, one right after the other, and I admit that it hurt. The hurt did not run very deep, however. I had several times told my father in confidence that in my mind these marriage plans had no other purpose than to help us find a way out of our difficulties by securing a few thousand francs. Then too, I was just twenty-one and liked to run around with folks my age, so my regrets did not last long. [. . .]

Soon the winter season, always so joyous for the migrant who has returned to see his family, was over. It was time to say our good-byes to the charming girls of Creuse and affectionately shake hands with those who would stay behind to work the fields. They would give us their best wishes that we might return full of health and with a few hundred francs in our pockets.

Such is the power of old habits that we were laughing and singing as we set out to walk the hundred leagues that separate Creuse from Paris. It was at the beginning of the year 1837 that I undertook this journey for the third time. [. . .]

Almost all [my coworkers at my new place of employment] were Parisians who were used to working for piece rates. These Parisians would make good-natured fun of those of us who thought about trying to save. In the morning, practically as soon as we had put on our work clothes, we all had to go have a drop to drink; often we would make it two or three.

Since we would go eat breakfast at the Barrière de l'Etoile, where wine was cheaper than in Paris, we would drink a liter instead of a half-liter. We had to have another liter at two o'clock as well. When we went back on the job, we would work like slaves. Then it was time to go drink our four o'clock wine. Strong and vigorous by nature, I took to this life, which I found pleasant. And since Parisians looked upon men from Limousin as contemptible fellows, pride entered into it, and I made a point of doing as everyone else did. My only regret was when I was alone or on those evenings when I would find myself face to face with my father, who was in the habit of indulging himself only to the strict minimum. The look he gave me would make me sad.

"If you can't muster more strength of character," he told me, "you'll have no lack of opportunities to spend your money." I reaffirmed my resolve to leave this construction site so as not to cause my father, who loved me so much, any further sorrow. [. . .]

I went to see Dupont in the Rue Neuve-du-Luxembourg, which is today the Rue Cambon, and he hired me. When I took that job with the Delavallade enterprise, I managed to find myself a pleasant little nest, for I was to work there at various times during the next three years. [. . .]

One day, as the rough plastering of the building in the Rue Neuve-du-Luxembourg was getting well along, Dupont called me and my scaffold-mate Lombard over. The owner was with him. It was to tell us to bring our tools to the Rue Louis-le-Grand, where a building was waiting for us. In a brief, friendly, pleasant conversation, Delavallade told us, "I hope that you're going to make a special effort and urge your fellow workers to do the same in this new building. I'll give you five sous more than the others, but on condition that you tell no one." By accepting this arrangement, we became "company men." We weren't betraying our fellow workers but we identified more with the interests of the owner.

I was so happy to find myself solidly employed with an owner like Delavallade that I went back to school with my old surveyor. I seemed to have more of a taste for it than in the past. Age had added to the vigor of my mind, and I applied myself with great intensity.

A double ambition had taken hold of my mind. "Why shouldn't I become a foreman or even a contractor?" I asked myself. Moreover, in our political gatherings, I would meet men who were well spoken. This stimulated my desire to educate myself. I say this without false pride. All it took to stir up my passions and get me carried away, was for someone to talk to me about the afflictions of the people and the desire to ease their lot and lighten their burden.

At the lower end of the Rue Saint-Antoine, there was a little house, a sort of cheap restaurant whose sign read, "The Café Momus." The head of this establishment was good old Bulot, a former soldier who had been in the Imperial Guard. He adored his commander, the lion of those great battles, who had so excited the men of his generation. This establishment had become a meeting place for true patriots, and Bonapartists and republicans would fraternize there together. If a police spy managed to insinuate himself among us, Bulot would let us know with just a glance. People have no idea today to what an extent the police used to be suspicious and active, especially after the Fieschi attack.[49]

At the Café Momus, as soon as we were sure we were not being observed, there were always a few honest and courageous citizens who would strike up daring and highly interesting political discussions. Even if the only purpose of these conversations was to combat the moral terror that had momentarily taken hold of public sentiment, for us workers that was crucial. The revolutionary breeze that we would breathe at the Café Momus kept us from losing hope that one day we would see the realization of our dream, the advent of the Republic. [. . .]

From the day that I had hired on with Delavallade to the end of that campaign of 1837, I had been steadily and constantly employed, for we had worked every day, holidays and Sundays included. At the first cold snap, my father and I left for Creuse. We were somewhat less worried than in the past, for between us we were bringing back a little more than seven hundred francs. For the first time, we were going to be making a dent in our massive debts.

THE YEAR 1838; MY RETURN TO DELAVALLADE'S

[. . .] For my father and me, that campaign of 1838 was rather productive. I worked nonstop, holidays and Sundays included, without any layoffs, and for a wage of four francs a day. And it was in that very year that I opened

49. Giuseppe Fieschi was a native of Corsica who had served in the Napoleonic army. In 1835 he attempted to assassinate Louis-Philippe by means of a bomb. Although eighteen persons were killed and many others, including Fieschi himself, were wounded, the king was unharmed. Fieschi was tried and executed in 1836.

the school that my readers already know about and that earned me more than three hundred francs.[50]

For a time I had thought that those long workdays, which began at five in the morning and did not end until eleven at night, would be beyond my strength. But as I got used to them, and thanks to a strong dose of willpower and the little snack that I would take after my students left, I managed to maintain my robust health perfectly well.

In the end, I turned over seven hundred francs to my father, who had saved four hundred. We made a payment of one thousand francs. Word spread quickly among our acquaintances. People began to believe that we might manage to solve our financial difficulties, especially when our neighbors saw that father and son were getting along.

RETURN TO THE COUNTRYSIDE; THE YEAR 1839; MY MARRIAGE

Things went much as they had in the preceding year. No sooner had I arrived in the village than my parents were speaking to me about marriage. I strongly opposed their desire, pointing out that now that our neighbors had begun talking about the amount of our debts, they would not fail to talk about them some more, which would end up becoming extremely disagreeable and even humiliating for me. Two of my uncles, who had more confidence in me than I perhaps had myself, agreed with me.

"Now that you're a good worker," they told me, "show what you're capable of on your own and you'll silence many gossips." My uncles were basically expressing my own thoughts.

In Paris, I worked on the same construction site as a man named Chaussat, who came from the town of Faye. We called each other "brother-in-law" because he needed to marry off a sister whom I had chanced to see several times. My friend had promised to speak of me to his sister, as well as to his father and mother, and he kept his word. So I changed my mind and went to see this girl, a pretty brunette whom I liked a lot. I was introduced as a friend of her brother and welcomed with all the courtesy that one could hope for under the circumstances. But Mr. Chaussat himself, before getting down to business, as they say in our region, went to the recorder's office in Bourganeuf to check whether the allegations that had been made to him were true or false. There he uncovered two outstanding mortgage obligations which together added up to a little more than six

---

50. Nadaud refers to classes in drawing and design that he offered to his fellow workers in the evenings.

thousand francs. Very politely I was made to understand that there could be no further question of marriage, and everything was broken off.

François Thaury, to whom I had been apprenticed and who had always known me to be a hard worker, was our biggest creditor. He wanted to marry me to one of his nieces, but the young woman had promised her hand to a young man from Soubrebost. Whether for this reason or for a different one, she turned me down cold.

These two successive failures, along with those of the preceding years, gave rise to all sorts of gossip and kidding on the part of jokesters and idlers. "I know one who'd be good for him," someone would say, and naturally it turned out to be one of those women who are not very strict in their morals or behavior. People made fun of me.

In the course of one's lifetime, alongside innumerable annoyances and terrible disappointments, the man who perseveres will always find those happy moments that last long enough to fill his spirit and his heart with hope. One day, as I was on my way to Vallières with a friend named Périchon whom I had met in Paris, we stopped for a drink in an inn at Le Monteil-au-Vicomte that was run by a woman called La Pouchonnelle. Over by the corner of a vast fireplace stood a tall and beautiful girl in the company of her mother. We found her so shy, so gracious, so radiant with youth and beauty that we began to devour her with our eyes. Both of us had the glibness that one possesses at that age, especially when one has lived for several years in Paris. When it was time to leave, we became even more courteous. It was only later that I learned—for this young woman would become my wife—that they had thought us very well-behaved. We continued on our way.

A few weeks later, I found myself in Soubrebost, the county seat of my commune. A man named Bouillot told me, "I want to marry you to one of my nieces." It just so happened that my friend was the brother-in-law of the mother of the young person whom we had met in La Pouchonnelle's inn. "Come on," Bouillot told me, "let's take a day off and go visit my relatives."

No sooner said than done. The moment I set foot in that house, Mrs. Aupetit recognized me and, as she spoke of our first meeting, laughed a lot. Her daughter entered a moment later and naturally she recognized me as well. They had soon prepared dinner for us, with the father and all the children in attendance.

When Bouillot and I were left alone with the two adults after dinner, we told them the reason for our visit. They told us that on several grounds they were not interested in marrying off their daughter that year. The mother then took me to a barn where her daughter was busy cutting the tops off beets to use as feed for the animals. On hearing the word marriage, she lowered her head and said nothing. I confess that I must have seemed a fool to her. I did not know how to strike up a conversation. The mother saved us both from this awkward situation by asking me a few questions. I answered as best I could, but the girl still remained silent, and I became anxious to leave, which is what soon happened. When I asked if I could give her a good-bye hug, however, the permission was granted.

In that village of Lachaux lived a Paris mason named Dubost. I went by his house as I was leaving. I told my friend's wife about my lack of success, and she made a point of telling the Aupetit family and the young girl in particular how well her husband thought of me. Dubost enjoyed a fine reputation, and for good reason, as he was a frugal man, a good breadwinner whose property grew year by year. To be spoken of so highly by such a man earned me the good graces of the mother and daughter. Soon there was no further question of putting off our marriage.

Once arrived at that stage, marriages in Creuse go forward quickly, for the migrants do not stay much longer than two months each winter in the region. Visiting the home of Jean Aupetit as often as possible and finding an excuse to spend a few moments with this young and pretty peasant girl became my constant preoccupation. From then on, I never missed a chance, even if it rained or snowed, to go three or four times a week to see my fiancée. [. . .]

We had reached the point where it was time to discuss the conditions of the marriage contract. One of their other daughters was already married, and they told me that the terms would be identical for this one as well.

Still, before drawing up an agreement, the Aupetit family wanted to take a day and come to our house to make an inspection; in other words, to look over our house, our meadows, and our fields.[51] We agreed on a day, and on the appointed morning received a visit from the father, mother, and other relatives of Miss Aupetit. The tour of the fields did not take place, as Mr. Aupetit declared that he could judge the value of a property within a few thousand francs just by seeing the animals and the size of the granaries. They found everything to their liking, even though our property was less substantial than theirs.

We discussed the amount of the dowry. My future father-in-law gave his daughter three thousand francs, to be paid at a rate of four hundred francs per year, as well as furniture, a wardrobe, linen, and six ewes and

51. Nadaud uses the dialect term *vudas*, meaning "viewing."

their lambs. Such were the meticulously detailed conditions of this country marriage.

One of the brothers, who did not like me very much, wanted to raise the question of our debts, but his mother rather vigorously asked him to be quiet, saying that if she did not have faith in my character, she would not have gone this far. The question was dropped.

A few days later, we went to have the contract reviewed by Master Laforest, the lawyer in Le Monteil-au-Vicomte. The next day, we traveled to Aubusson to buy the bride's wedding dress. The daughter proved to be the least demanding of all, for when it came time to buy jewelry, she had her mother tell us that she only wanted two or three rings. Anything more, she indicated, could wait. Finally, two days later, her older brother and I went to Felletin to buy an old cow for the wedding feast. On 23 February 1839 the wedding took place.

For a country wedding, the ceremony did not lack a certain glamour. I was accompanied by about thirty young men, chosen from among my Paris friends, all full of high spirits and good cheer and all stylishly dressed. On her side, my wife had managed to choose a number of pretty young women, some of whom created a very gracious effect on the arms of my fellow workers.

As we arrived at the bride's house, preceded by two fiddlers, young boys observed our ancient custom by firing a volley of pistol shots into the air. They did the same as we entered and as we left the church, and the same ceremony was repeated at each of the villages that we had to pass through on our way to La Martinèche. As word spread that I was accompanied by a large party of attractive young people, the residents of all the surrounding villages turned out, either to dance or to see the bride, who was said to be very beautiful. [. . .]

Women who married masons had a curious destiny. Today, many masons bring their young wives to Paris or elsewhere, but in those days this custom did not exist. Each of the spouses had to live on his or her own, often until the age of fifty, except for the period of the winter season.

Two days after my marriage, I received a letter from my friend Claude Lefaure, telling me that his boss, Mr. Leloir, had just been awarded the contract to build the new institution for blind children, located on the Boulevard des Invalides. Lefaure had proposed that I take his place at the construction site in the Rue de Seine, and I had to give my answer right away.

When I told my wife about this letter, she cried and cried. Though I was able to obtain a two-week delay, I then had to leave her. I was not to see her again until nine months later. [. . .]

THE YEAR 1839; AFTER MY MARRIAGE

It is a sad and painful moment when, after seventeen days of marriage, a man must leave the woman he loves, a woman endowed with such virtues. But the imperious duty of living and serving our parents overcomes our personal desires and obliges us to leave.

Such were, as I have already noted, the old traditional ways which remained more or less general among migrants from Creuse. We observed them without much complaint. We would simply say, in an effort to console ourselves, "What our parents have done, we children must do in turn."

When I arrived in Paris, I lost no time in going to see my friend Claude Lefaure at the construction site in the Rue de Seine that was to be mine two days later. His first words were, "You got here just in time to replace me. I have to go start the new institution for blind children, so let me introduce you to the boss, Mr. Leloir. I have to tell you that he absolutely insists on having the plaster work done by jobbers.[52] So as not to let in outsiders, I've taken this work on myself."

On this point, I knew what to expect. Work that is subcontracted out by the owner to one of his own workers almost always leads to legal actions between the parties to the contract. When the work is concluded, the owner goes over and over the worker's accounts, meaning that he trims and pares them down to suit his own interests, just as he pleases. If the jobber refuses to accept the predatory conditions he is offered, then a lawsuit between the two interested parties is the result. Because the jobber is almost always operating without money and is harassed by unpaid workers who torment him and shake their fists in his face, he is forced to make a bad bargain that deprives him of the profits from his operation.

That is what was then known—and is still known today—as the freedom of the labor market, a false and misleading doctrine which those who were my teachers in democracy and socialism advised me never to accept as the truth.[53]

My friend Lefaure first explained the conditions that he intended to offer me. "First, you'll be paid five francs a day, and if there are any profits to show when the work is finished, we'll split them."

52. Nadaud makes reference to work done *à la tâche* or "by the task." Contemporaries also used the term *marchandage* to designate the practice of subcontracting specific portions of the overall project to "jobbers" on the basis of bids submitted to the general contractor. The low bidder was awarded the subcontract and then had to hire and supervise workers on his own responsibility and complete the work on budget in order to turn a profit.
53. Nadaud's precise expression is *la liberté de travail*, "the freedom of work."

I found these conditions satisfactory and I set to work. At that time, in 1839, a mason's daily wage amounted to three and a half francs and for some it might go as high as three and three-quarters or even four francs; but it was customary for subcontractors to pay their employees ten sous more a day.[54] So I found myself in the company of the best-off workers, and I confess that this situation flattered my pride a great deal, and all the more so because it was the first time that I had held the position of foreman.

When I arrived at this construction site, I began by hiring two teams of good, solid fellow workers, and we set to work with great enthusiasm. This building, which fronted on three streets, was very large. My desire to start off on the right foot as a foreman was, naturally, very great. The desire also to give satisfaction to my friend Lefaure was no less strong or intense. So, through the entire phase of rough plastering, I worked as hard as my strength would permit. At that time we were getting plaster that had not been screened. As soon as I noticed that the assistants were failing to supply enough to their journeymen, I would rush down the ladders, grab a mallet, and help crush the bed of plaster. My assistant was a certain Bouny from Pontarion, nicknamed Curly. He was better at carrying things on his head than anyone else you were likely to run into on the construction sites of Paris.

Bouny would always bring me troughs brim-full of mortar and containing at least two buckets' worth. For more than three months, my job consisted of helping him unload, mixing the plaster that had often begun to set, spreading it over the shingle boards to form a proper surface, and rough-plastering over the timber framing. The more my Bouny saw me getting tired, the happier he was. He would let out his hearty, good-natured laugh and add, "I always said that Pontarion would get the better of La Martinèche, and I'm going to get the better of you." I got along wonderfully with this colossus of a man who was as good-natured as a child and yet the terror of the other assistants.

Once this rough work was completed, the joiners set the doorframes and the interior walls in place. I then assigned two journeymen to each room and we continued working at full steam. Then, when we had a free moment

54. The daily premium of ten sous (one-half franc) paid to the employees of subcontractors made it possible to attract the most skilled and energetic workers and was offered in part as compensation for the faster pace and increased effort they were expected to bring to their labors. Despite this opportunity to increase daily earnings, many workers opposed the institution of subcontracting because of the changes it imposed on the conditions of work.

at mealtimes or in the evening after the day's work, everyone would round off corners. You could not have asked more work of a team of yoked oxen.

There is one way to make men work strenuously without having to order them around and without ceasing to be their fellow worker either. You have to give them a chance to earn wages that are higher than what they could get on other job sites. They have to recognize that you are capable of holding your own without being either arrogant or prideful toward them. If they offer you a drink, you must not be too stingy to buy your round. Ingrates and spongers are despised.

Because I possessed most of the qualities that make up what we call a "regular guy," I came across workers who would knock themselves out just to please me. This held true for the six months that this group of projects lasted. Right from the very first time that I supervised my fellow workers, I saw just how much courage and devotion the worker possesses when he is trusted and treated with a certain respect. [. . .]

That is how I finished the campaign of 1839. I had been lucky as far as work was concerned. I had not lost a single day during my entire campaign. I had steadily earned five francs per day and not given in to any foolish spending. I had saved five hundred fifty francs from my daily wages, plus three hundred more in earnings from my school. My father, who had to spend the winter in Paris, handed me an additional five hundred. This made a total of one thousand three hundred fifty francs that I possessed when I left.

I was proud of this result and very happy to be going to see my wife, whom I had left behind at the start of the campaign. I was going to give proof to her and her mother alike that she had linked fortunes with a steady worker, not someone who would squander her dowry and allow his family to be chased from its home by the bill collectors, as she had so often been told. [. . .]

I have never seen my mother happier than the day the Gadoux debt was paid off. Gadoux had a mother who was such a scandalmonger that she had managed to sow discord among all our neighbors. A score of times, in fits of anger and violence, she would come stand in front of our house and shout that as soon as her son returned from Paris he would sell off what she called our last rags. In this way, my father and I, by pooling our savings, had easily managed to rid ourselves of this debt. [. . .]

That winter, I did not neglect any of our usual tasks, the most important of which was the barn threshing, and neither my wife nor I put down the flail from morning until night.

That's when I got the idea of teaching her to read as I had previously done for my older sister and for two other girls from my village, Thérèse Taboury and Rosalie Vergnaud.

At last the season arrived when I once again had to abandon my village and my family to return to Paris. Such was the fate reserved for my wife and myself for the first eight years of our marriage.

CAMPAIGN AND ECONOMIC CRISIS OF 1840

[. . .] In those days, our laws were harsh and cruel. Besides articles 414, 415, and 416 of the penal code, which authorized the government to impose two years of prison on any worker who went on strike, we also had the law of 1834 which prohibited all meetings of more than twenty-one persons. It was as if the people were clamped in a vise, as if the public were an honest man caught in a circle of assassins. The workers of Paris raised a cry of despair. Public sentiment boiled over as if it were compressed steam.

Unexpectedly, all the trades started talking about going on strike. All one heard was the cry, "Come what may, it's duty that commands us. Our dignity requires us not to bare our necks to our executioners any longer. Let's summon up our courage and break the law against conspiracies. Perhaps our forceful acts will open people's eyes to the traitors who made such pretty promises after the Revolution of 1830 and never kept a one."[55] Construction workers, who had always been among the most patient, found themselves tormented by poverty. They would roam the streets in search of work, gather before the gates of the rare work sites that were still in operation, or return to their rooming houses, where they would utter the most violent recriminations against those entrepreneurs known to be against increasing their workers' daily wages. [. . .]

Despite these appalling laws, the masons, stonecutters, painters, and earthworks laborers were determined to lead the entire corporation in a formidable general strike.[56] But how were we to arrive at an understanding, how were we to meet when we were dispersed across every quarter of Paris? Though quite certain we were throwing ourselves into the lion's den,

55. Participation in the Revolution of 1830 was widespread in the Parisian working class and particularly among workers of republican political sentiments. After the overthrow of the Bourbon dynasty, these insurgents were disagreeably surprised to see the Orleanist monarchy installed. Their surprise turned to disillusionment and a sense of betrayal as the new regime soon proved itself to be no more liberal on many social issues than the one it had replaced.
56. In the following discussion, Nadaud uses the French terms *corps de métier* and *corporation*, here translated as "trade" and "corporation." In nineteenth-century usage, a corporation was a workers' association that comprised all members of the same or closely related trades. The traditional function of the semipublic corporations and trade associations of nineteenth-century France was to regulate affairs among the members of a trade and between them and their employers.

we decided that our meeting would take place on a Sunday, payday, in the plain of Bondy.

The first step was to organize a large committee of twenty persons. Two or three times, the most active workers—the ringleaders, as the saying goes—came to sound me out and ask if I would consent to direct this great and immense movement. I started out by assuring them I was willing, but I made them understand that in the interest of all, they should look to better-known and more influential foremen in our corporation than myself.

To form this committee, we went off to hide in a wine merchant's shop in the Rue du Bac, where several editors of *La Phalange* or *La Démocratie pacifique* often ate their meals.[57] At our second meeting, we indeed arrived at agreement among ourselves. Claude Lefaure agreed to be chair, the elder Chansardon became vice-chair, and I was named secretary and treasurer.

After taking every imaginable and conceivable precaution to escape the notice of the police, we sent volunteers to all the major work sites of Paris and to the rooming houses. Up to that point, we had foiled all the government's tricks. On the appointed day, a great crowd of six to seven thousand men arrived by a roundabout route at the great plain of Bondy. [. . .]

A delegation of members of the committee had gone early that morning to see the mayor of the commune. After we had informed this official of the purpose of our meeting and assured him that our intentions were entirely peaceful, he made us fairly welcome. But hardly had we left his home before a police commissioner went in to see him. What had he come to tell him? Obviously we had no idea, and we hurried off to rejoin our fellow workers. Our discussion began immediately. Our program was simple: to increase daily wages, eliminate overtime, and abolish supplementary tasks.[58] On the first point, the discussion focused on the amount of the wage increase. The most outspoken declared themselves in favor of four and a half francs per day.

That is where things stood when a cry escaped from that great assembly

57. Victor Considérant (1808–93), a disciple of the socialist philosopher Charles Fourier (1772–1837), was the founder of both of these periodicals, although *La Démocratie pacifique* did not begin publication until after the time of which Nadaud is speaking. Considérant used them to propagate ideas based on his interpretation of Fourier's writings. Nadaud's testimony underscores the extent to which republican politics, utopian socialist philosophy, and workers' challenges to economic injustice were intermixed in this period.

58. Here "overtime" refers to hours worked in excess of the customary working day but without any compensation beyond the standard daily wage. The supplementary tasks were presumably miscellaneous duties, unrelated to the worker's principal skill or expertise, which the employer might assign at his convenience.

of workers, oppressed and martyred by our infernal legislation and by the bourgeois government of 1830. The army had arrived. A squadron of cavalry was advancing upon us at a fast trot, their sabers unsheathed. Panic took hold of our ranks, and the strikers fled in all directions.

To the commissioner's first summons, enjoining us to disperse, we opposed not the slightest resistance. Still, it was good to see that the committee remained at its post and protested with firmness against this dishonorable measure.

It must be admitted that in those days, striking workers faced the opposition not only of the government but of public opinion as well. People hurled insults, or rather taunts, at us. The ministers were reproached for not having given the order to shoot into the crowd. In showing themselves to be violent and cruel toward the people, that caste of moderates and conservatives which had allowed Louis-Philippe to violate the principles of the Revolution of 1830, those impudent and rapacious monarchists, were displaying their gratitude for his having brought the starvelings to heel so effectively.

The contractors appeared radiant. In their joyous effervescence, they would have kissed the ministers' feet. But in celebrating its easy victory, the government was blind to the radical change that was taking place in the sentiments of the masses. People were telling themselves, "At the first opportunity, this unworthy government must be overthrown." [. . .]

Such were the men who, in 1840, organized the first strike undertaken by construction workers. They failed, it is true, in the specific objective of the strike. But these same men immediately prepared to found the mutual aid society called the Society of Construction Workers. Was it mere caprice on their part, a passing fancy conjured in their minds or, on the contrary, the result of some well-thought-out and deliberate conception or judgment which led them to create this useful institution? On this subject, there can be no doubt, for the Mutual Society of Construction Workers has existed ever since and today, even as it pays out annual pensions to its elderly and faithful members, has nearly 500,000 francs in its coffers. [. . .]

In one of the previous chapters, I stated that in the preceding year I had been hired as foreman with a salary of one hundred sixty francs per month by one of my former employers, Mr. Bayle. It would have taken a splendid opportunity to get me to leave this worthy man whose way of doing things suited me just fine. I therefore remained with him all year and had no reason to regret it.

One day, Mr. Bayle proposed that he subcontract out to me the construction of a small building located in the Clos Saint-Lazare and a series of enclosure walls, reserving for himself the provision of plaster and all materials. I accepted. In less than six months, with the assistance of three journeymen, I made a clear profit of thirteen hundred francs, including my daily wages, which my employer paid me upon presentation of my bill. I was overjoyed, and it seemed that my fortune was made. I was then seized by a certain uneasiness. Where should I hide my bundle? I did not have the least idea of what a savings bank might be and I was rooming with my faithful friend Jean Roby and Jacques Lafaye from Saint-Hilaire, who were just as inexperienced as I.

In the mattress? That was unthinkable. The concierge made our beds, and we did not know her well. "Suppose we put it in one of those balls of twine hanging from the ceiling," Jacques Lafaye suggested.[59] This was the only hiding place I ever used at the Rue des Barres. No sooner said than done. We untangled that bundle of twine, which resembled a sort of old cordage, and reattached it to the ceiling, convinced that no one would ever guess that it held a small fortune.

My father, who would come visit me from time to time and who saw that I was happy, very much wanted to know what I was earning, but I kept it a secret from him in order to save him up an even more agreeable surprise at the end of the year.

My employer Mr. Bayle next sent me to work on a mansion that was located up in the Faubourg du Roule. After spending a month there, it was time for the masons' departure, and my father and I had to come to some agreement about whether we would return to the country together or if he would go alone.

The dear man was tired of Paris. His age—fifty-four years—made it barely possible for him to work at our harsh trade any more. I knew from the reports of various of our friends that he had been overcome by homesickness, but he was so sensitive that he did not dare confess that fact to me, for we were far from having paid off all our debts.

"Well then," I told him, "it's time for you to say good-bye to Paris, old Léonard. But first let's see which of us had a better campaign."

The next day he brought me five hundred francs, and I handed over thirteen hundred to him. He gave me a hug and began to cry tears of joy. [. . .]

RETURN TO THE COUNTRY

When the end of 1842 arrived, it had been three years since I had gone to see my wife. I naturally wanted to leave as soon as possible, especially as

59. Nadaud appears to be referring to balls of the twine that masons use in their work to ensure the perfect alignment of the bricks or quarry stones they are laying.

my purse was well lined. I was such a novice in money matters that I did not even dream of changing my five-franc pieces into either gold coins or bills. I crammed it all into four sacks that I placed at the bottom of my trunk and set off in the stagecoach as far as Châteauroux. A second coach took us to La Châtre and then to Guèret. In that town, we found one of those vehicles that are placed in service in the season of masons' migrations to make the trip to Pontarion. From there, one of my cousins helped me carry my trunk to the house.

As you might imagine, it is not mere joy that the family experiences when the migrant arrives, especially when he is considered to be the source of livelihood and virtually the breadwinner for them all; it's more like delirium. Instead of laughing, everyone cries. Then, as custom demands, the wives prepare a soup of bread and milk. While our traveler revels in his welcome or warms himself in the corner by the fireplace, the laughter begins and he is brought up to date on everything that has happened in the household and the neighborhood.

When this conversation is exhausted, the new arrival is in turn expected to speak about his finances. That is the moment when he graciously shows the result of his campaign—in other words his purse—and everyone promises not to say a word to anyone else.

So, once I had placed my trunk on the long, tall kitchen table, I began to undo it. First, I took out a beautiful dress for my wife, two others for my two sisters, a winter scarf for my mother, and a pound of snuff for my father.

Next I took out a sack containing a thousand francs, and then another. At that point, my father, my mother, my wife, and my sisters could no longer contain their joy. They began jumping for joy and hugging me.

A moment later, I said to my wife: "Why don't you look around in the other corners; perhaps there's something else." She took out a third sack and said at the same time, "I think there's yet another." She took them and placed them alongside the first two. Everyone looked at one another, but sobs choked our voices and we were weary from hugging one another. "You have outdone me, Martin," my father said. "I worked very hard, but I never had such good fortune." We set to emptying the sacks and placing their contents in piles of one hundred francs, until the table was half-covered with stacks of dazzlingly brilliant silver.

It was past two in the morning before we stopped gazing at what we called a ravishing picture. When we were exhausted from our mutual admiration, we talked about going to bed. That's when I said to my father, "Do you know what I'm thinking: that we should take these piles of coins to François Thaury tomorrow."

"We're in complete agreement," he replied.

The next day, I put my treasure in a basket and, as it was rather heavy, cut a branch of holly as we crossed our meadow so I could carry my burden on my shoulders.

My wife accompanied me as far as the foot of the great mountain of Beaumarty and then returned to our house. When she saw the basket going off in another direction, her expression grew gloomy. It was obvious that she would rather have kept the bundle than have seen it pass into someone else's hands.

François Thaury, who had taken a strong interest in my affairs from the time I had been his assistant, was no less happy than my father. He told me, "Ever since those first days when you were working under me, you always inspired me with confidence, and I often said that you would be a man. If I weren't so old, in a few years I'd see you become a masons' contractor."

My old journeyman would never see me become a contractor, but he had the satisfaction of seeing me elected a National Representative of the people.

Nadaud was indeed elected to the Legislative Assembly as representative of the department of Creuse in May 1849. There he allied himself with the Democratic Socialist movement and spoke out forcefully on behalf of the rights of workers. He was among those singled out for arrest at dawn on 2 December 1851, in anticipation of Louis-Napoléon's coup d'état. Soon afterward, he began an exile that would last eighteen years. Most of that time was spent in England, where for a while he continued to work as a mason. Over the next seven years, however, he mastered English, completed his education and, with the help of émigré friends, eventually earned a position teaching French language and history in an English private school.

With the declaration of the French Third Republic in 1870, Nadaud returned home for good. The republican leader Gambetta named him Prefect of Creuse for a few months before they both resigned in February 1871. Nadaud, who remained essentially neutral in the events of the Paris Commune, was elected to the Municipal Council of Paris in November 1871. Under France's new constitution, he was elected Deputy from Creuse and served in that capacity until his defeat in the campaign of 1889. It was at that time that he retired to his native province and began work on these memoirs. There he died in 1898, just as the nineteenth century, which he thought such a glorious time to live, was coming to a close.

5   Norbert Truquin

Memoirs and Adventures of a
Proletarian in Times of
Revolution

Truquin's autobiography is by all odds the most remarkable and unlikely
document of all those collected here. It is remarkable because, unlike the
authors of the other chapters, he lived most of his early years at the very
margins of the working class. Truquin was an unskilled laborer whose
childhood was spent in incipient vagabondage and who, as a young adult,
found himself trapped in a succession of poorly paid, menial, unhealthy,
short-term, and dead-end jobs.

This text is also unlikely, in that it represents the detailed written record
of the life of a worker who was illiterate during the entire period covered in
these excerpts. Truquin was an extreme version of the self-taught worker,
whose First Communion lessons appear to have been the only formal
schooling he ever received. His memoirs express the mix of shame, frustra-
tion, dependency, and anger he felt when forced to rely on others for assis-
tance or when deprived of access to the knowledge of history or of current
affairs for which he thirsted. It was only shortly before his first departure
for Argentina at the age of forty that he seems to have acquired even the
most basic ability to read; and only on his later trip, once settled in Para-
guay, that he learned to write.

Truquin's fate was the more harsh because his mother died when he
was five and his father's career as a small-time entrepreneur failed soon
thereafter. This account of his adventures teaches us about a variety of oc-
cupations that the author took up more or less by chance: wool comber, er-
rand boy to two prostitutes, machine tender in a spinning mill, ragman's
assistant, itinerant peddler, grape picker, well digger, and more. In reading
of his experiences, we also learn about the occupational instability and
marginality of those without skills, without knowledge, without tools,
without the support of a family or a circle of friends—in short, without re-
sources of virtually any kind to help them in their struggle to survive.

Truquin's is also the story of an individual frequently unemployed, whose sole advantage in the nearly constant search for work was his willingness to accept almost anything offered. Briefly, in his midthirties, he appeared to have achieved his dream of establishing himself independently, after marrying another silk weaver whose meager savings were used to pay part of the cost of setting up their own looms. Yet even this modest degree of occupational stability proved temporary, collapsing before a combination of personal difficulties stemming from the political upheaval of the Commune of Lyon in 1871 and the structural crisis in the silk industry of that region. The excerpts from his autobiography for this period are particularly bitter in tone, and his rage and class hatred never lie far below the surface.

Of the composition of these memoirs, we know relatively little. They were written in the author's midfifties, after he had left behind his native France for the third and final time. Truquin addressed his reflections to his fellow workers and considered his act of self-revelation to be a responsibility he owed to others who shared the desire to destroy society's inequities. His text was originally published in 1888 by the bookshop and press of F. Bouriand, which specialized in socialist writings and put out a journal of internationalist perspective entitled La Tribune des peuples. *These memoirs, long out of print, were reissued in French in 1977.[1]*

I. CHILDHOOD MEMORIES; MY FIRST TRIBULATIONS; THE MARTYRDOM OF A SEVEN-YEAR-OLD CHILD; HOW SMALL-TIME EMPLOYERS EXPLOIT THEIR WORKERS

I was born in Rozières in the department of Somme on 7 June 1833, the fourth child in my family. My birth was a major event for my father, who already had three daughters but had set his heart on having a boy who would take after him. My baptism was the occasion for a splendid feast.

Until the age of five, my upbringing was truly that of a spoiled child. My sisters and the servants had to endure my every whim. But in 1838, this period of prosperity came to an end. My father had gone bankrupt, and we sold everything in our home and in the workshop, including the grandfather clock. All that remained were the four walls of the house, which belonged to my mother.

My father then became manager of a factory in Amiens of which he was

---

1. The reader may also wish to consult the excellent essay by Michelle Perrot, which I have drawn upon for these introductory comments. It has been translated into English as "A Nineteenth-century Work Experience as Related in a Worker's Autobiography: Norbert Truquin," in Steven Kaplan and Cynthia Koepp, eds., *Work in France: Representations, Meaning, Organization, and Practice* (Ithaca, N.Y.: 1986).

part-owner.[2] He took me with him, for we were inseparable. I stayed there for a year, but his salary was not sufficient to maintain eight people, including five young children and their maid, as boarders in a private residence. That was when my mother fell ill, never again to leave her sickbed. My father returned to the village and sold a parcel of forested land that belonged to him, along with all the odds and ends that he could turn to account. He had not given up hope of striking it rich, claiming that he possessed a secret for the manufacture of the flexible steel needles used to knit machine-made sweaters and stockings.

We then left for Reims, where he became partners with a man named Triboulet. It was 1840, and we had already been boarding in a private residence for three months. I had just turned seven when I got it in my head to tell the woman who owned the place where we were staying that my father would not be paying her for our room and board. At first this woman seemed to be disconcerted by this curious revelation. But deciding, and not without cause, that where there's smoke, there's fire, she summoned my father to her room after dinner and, in my presence, repeated what I had said. My father feigned surprise, but I understood from the embarrassed look on his face that I had committed a blunder, though it was too late to take it back.

A week later, my father led me to the home of a wool comber. He turned me over to him with the following words: "I've brought you this rogue and I'm leaving him with you. He's yours. If he fails you, be sure to let him have it, for you'll be doing him a service. Don't forget to have him say his four prayers every day. He may be good for nothing else, but I insist that he at least become a good Christian."

This artisan, whose name was Auguste, was a sixty-five-year-old Belgian who was very neat in his personal appearance and had a big white beard. He had served as a quartermaster in the Indies for fifteen years under both the Republic and the Empire, but he had spent part of this time as a prisoner on the English prison ships.[3]

---

2. The French word *fabrique,* as used in the period about which Truquin is writing, might variously be translated in English as "manufactory," "mill," or "factory." In this context it typically designated a site of production larger than a workshop (*atelier*) but smaller than the vast, concentrated factories of the twentieth century. Its labor force might vary from ten to one hundred workers or more.

3. In this context, "the Indies" refers to southeast Asia, where France possessed colonial holdings or exerted political and economic influence in what are present-day Vietnam, Laos, Cambodia, and Thailand. It was not unusual for a "Belgian," who might or might not actually have been of French citizenship, to serve in the French army, particularly under the Empire created by the conquests of Napoléon, whose armies were recruited on an international scale. In that period, France and England were at war.

At first I thought that my father was joking. When he left me, I had a heavy heart. Very early the next day, the Belgian had me take a basket and led me to town, where he bought five sous' worth of scraps. That is what they call the little bits of meat that remain stuck to the meat-hanging hooks and that generally smell bad. Butchers sell these scraps for five sous a pound. They are only to be found in middle-class neighborhoods. Then my master went to the market to buy a cabbage and other vegetables for making soup. Next he said to me, "You see how you have to go about it. Do as I do and drive a hard bargain. If you forget this lesson, I have a strap that'll help you remember."

Sometimes he would have me go in search of a sheep's head, for which I would pay five or six sous. It would give us an excellent broth for dinner and supper. This was a hard job for me. As the cook, I was responsible for cleaning the sheep's head, not such an easy task for a child of seven. When I would sometimes encounter large white worms in these heads, I would tell my master of the disgust I felt. He simply replied in a rude tone that it was of no great concern, and that all I had to do was throw the worms out. He told me that I might one day be reduced to eating the leather soles of my shoes.

Because these purchases could only be found in the lower part of town, I had to travel more than three kilometers from Saint-Rémy Square where we lived. To do so, I would pass in front of the cathedral. Since my master was very religious, he had gotten me in the habit of entering the church to take holy water, make the sign of the cross, and recite the Credo. As I could not enter with my basket, I would leave it by the door. One day it was taken by some kids, and I was forced to return without my basket and without having completed my errand. It was very awkward for me to explain this mishap. My master, after having me tell my story, had me kneel down and gave me thirty blows with a doubled-over strap, putting all his strength into it. I did not utter a single cry. "Ah, you rascal," he shouted, "I'll break you just as I've broken others." [. . .]

On the first night that I spent under this man's roof, he had set up a sort of bed for me on top of the table, and I had gone on sleeping there until that very day. But from the time of this incident, he sent me to sleep in the coal cellar that was located under the steps of a stone staircase. At first I thought it was to punish me for the loss of the basket, but I went on sleeping in this nook for three years, no matter what the weather, summer and winter alike. A sack was my only bedding.

My master would have me get up at three in the morning, as was his custom, to light the furnace so we could begin work at four o'clock, when the furnace was hot enough. His workshop measured three and a half meters long by three meters wide, not counting the coal cellar that was my bedroom. This room was lighted by a four-pane window which gave onto a corridor that was two meters wide and that led to an interior courtyard. Immediately opposite, a wall three meters high prevented the sun's rays from entering and warming up this hovel.

Let me provide a few details about the work we did. In large-scale manufacture, there is a furnace for every four combers, to warm their combs.[4] Since my master worked all on his own, he had made himself a furnace out of clay. When a comb gets hot, it is attached to a clamp. The comber takes a handful of wet wool in his right hand, and puts some oil, taken from a pot, on a finger of his left hand. He spreads this oil over the wool and greases the nearly red-hot comb. The result is a nauseating odor that hangs in the air from four in the morning until ten at night. Add to that the coal fumes that the furnace gives off throughout the day. Once this handful of wool is greased, the worker takes a second comb, which has been waiting in the furnace, and combs the wool until the fibers have become straight and silky. The comb is then put back in the furnace. Next, the worker takes the tapered end of the wool out of his comb and draws it out a centimeter at a time until it is three or four feet long. He then passes the drawn wool to his young assistant, who is generally situated to his left. Because impurities of various kinds have remained in this wool, the assistant takes it in his two hands, one on each end, and removes all these impurities with the tips of his teeth. He must not spit out these impurities. He has to make them run, like a string of rosary beads, out of the two sides of his mouth. It is not hard to imagine how unhealthy this work is for the child. *Nacteurs,* as these unfortunate children are called, have a wizened look and are for the most part rather brutish. They use their teeth to extract the impurities because the wool has to be held taut so as not to risk tearing the strands apart, and their two hands cannot be spared from this task.

I was therefore condemned to plying this trade from four in the morning until ten at night. For the first few days, I applied myself willingly and tried to do a good job, but soon I was so overcome by drowsiness that I was sleeping on my feet, despite all my efforts not to give in. To stay awake, I

4. Whereas wool of poor quality was merely carded, the higher grades of wool fibers were subjected to a process known as combing, prior to being spun into thread. Its purpose was to eliminate short, twisted, and knotted fibers and then to comb the remaining strands until they lay parallel, so that the thread, and ultimately the finished product, would be more regular and fine textured. By oiling or greasing the wool, these procedures could be carried out more easily and quickly. The oil or grease was later removed in a washing process. By heating the combs, the worker kept the wool fibers smoother and prevented them from tangling.

would go outdoors and take a breath of fresh air, but as soon as I came back in, I grew sleepy all over again. I would go back out to conquer my listlessness, but in vain. It was stronger than I, even though I was much in fear of my master. Every time I succumbed to fatigue, standing next to him, he would strike me a backhanded blow across the bridge of my nose and set off a nosebleed. This routine was repeated three or four times a day. The quantity of blood that this man made me spill was incredible. Though I would bite my hands or hit my head against the wall in an effort to resist the desire to sleep, nothing helped.

This barbarian, seeing that slaps were not enough, would have me completely undress and give out a shower of blows with the strap, accompanying them with his eternal refrain: "I'll break you yet. I've broken others cleverer than you."

One day, when I had gone into the rear courtyard, probably to play, the master came to find me, his broom in his hand. He hit me so many times on my head and back that the broom came off its handle. He continued to hit me with the handle and stopped only when he was overcome with fatigue. Fortunately for me, six months after I had started, an economic downturn occurred. It lasted two months and allowed me to sleep as much as I wanted.

This brute obliged me to get up at three in the morning all the same, to light the furnace as usual and then go get water. I was then free until eight o'clock, when it was time to go shopping. During those two months, we adhered to a strict regimen to save money. Previously, we had consumed each week five sous' worth of meat scraps, a sheep's head, potatoes cooked with their skins on, and rye bread that was horribly bad.

Let me give you a few details on what an ordinary worker earns. The wool that my master had been combing for the six months that I had been with him brought him two francs and forty centimes per kilo. An ordinary worker can prepare a kilo of it per day, thus earning two francs and forty centimes, from which seventy centimes have to be deducted for the cost of coal and oil. The wet wool is furnished to the worker in ten-pound bales. He must return his combed wool in the morning, but he goes to pick up his packet of unprocessed wool in the evening, causing him to lose a day of his time. This bundle yields about five pounds of combed wool. It is these five pounds that are paid at a rate of two francs forty centimes per kilo. Thus, the worker has to go take back the old and pick up the new wool twice a week, making for two lost days. Overall, deducting the cost of coal and oil, by working part of Sunday the worker and his assistant earn about eight francs a week, or from thirty-two to thirty-four francs a month.

When work picked up again, we were given inferior wool to comb. For this we were paid only one franc fifty centimes per kilo, even though our costs remained the same. We therefore had to redouble our thrift and privations. Two months later, we had fine merino wool from Spain, for which we were paid two francs sixty per kilo. My master had never earned as much, so he was happy. On Saturday evening he would go to the *cabaret* to drink a little rosé wine that sold for six sous a bottle. He would take me with him and make me drink a lot. Once he got started, he would make me dance, which annoyed me no end. Then he got me in the habit of fencing, which I liked better. However, every time that I failed to parry his thrusts according to the rules, my master, who had been a fencing instructor, would give me a slap on the head, causing me to stumble against the tables, and soon I wanted neither to dance nor to fence. But the lout would absolutely insist on making me start over just to amuse the crowd, and the customers encouraged me to drink with the same goal in mind. I would then take advantage of the noise of conversations to slip away and go to bed. As soon as the master noticed that I had fled, he would come badger me in my coal cellar, pulling me by the legs until he managed to drag me back, half asleep, to the *cabaret*. There I had to continue dancing and fencing, in between slaps, until the brute thought it was time to send me off to bed.

When he himself got home, he would tear me from my miserable bed and send me off to get fresh water from the fountain, which in winter was often iced over. I would go in my bare feet to avoid slipping and breaking the pitcher, an unpardonable crime for which I would have atoned with some extraordinary punishment.

During the fifteen months, more or less, that I had been living with my master, the clothes I had been wearing when I arrived had become completely worn out. He had given me one of his enormous cloth shirts, and it was, for an eight-year-old child, much too big. My pants were so full of holes that my shirt would stick out through the gaps and hang down to the bend of my knees. I also owed to his munificence a jacket of green broadcloth that came down to my knees. I had to do all my errands in this curious outfit. When I happened to be on the street at the time that school let out, the children would chase after me calling me names. They had baptized me with the nickname "the Marquis of Dire Poverty."

In the spring of the year 1841, my father came to see me. He brought me a package containing a pair of pants, a jacket, and a vest of checked wool. All this was accompanied by a velvet cap, also checked and topped with a golden pom-pom. There was also a little watch.

The following Sunday I put on my new clothes. You can imagine how proud I had suddenly become. I showed myself in this outfit on Saint-Rémy Square, where I met several boys my age who went into ecstasies over my beautiful clothes. "Oh, I have several others," I told them in a burst of false pride. I had hardly let the words out before I regretted having such a loose tongue.

When I got home, I informed my master that I was going to throw out my old rags. "I wouldn't do that," he told me. "Set them aside. You never know what might happen." In fact, my father returned very early on Monday morning, before I was awake. He took the package and the watch and pledged them at the pawnshop. Unable to find my clothes when I got up, I asked my master for them. He told me that my father, who had lost his money at cards the night before, had been forced to pawn my belongings for the week, but that he would bring them back on Saturday. I never saw them again, so I had to dress once more in the rags I had abandoned. I no longer dared to go out in such a state, but my master, who was very touchy on that subject, administered a volley of blows with the strap to get me back my taste for doing errands. "If your father comes back," he told me, "I'll throw him out. I hate gamblers who bring children into the world without worrying about how they are going to feed them."

As a crowning misfortune, my master was stricken with a white tumor on his knee which made it absolutely impossible for him to go out. I was therefore obliged to go return the work to the jobber. Since all those businesses were located at the lower end of town, I would pass by the cathedral and, as was my custom, instinctively begin to contemplate the paintings and other art objects that decorated the church. The light that filtered through the stained-glass windows produced a play of shadows and light that excited my admiration. Without paying attention, I would stay for hours in contemplation before this spectacle from which I could not tear myself away. The invalid would be waiting for me impatiently and would not fail to punish me with blows from the strap, but it did no good. I preferred to follow my fancy and receive the blows in exchange, knowing that his illness would prevent him from running after me. He worked with his leg stretched out on a footstool. We had, in consequence, become inseparable. I was his nurse. I dressed his wounds and washed his bandages.

This job disgusted me a lot, to be sure, the more so because I did not have any change of bandages. But whenever I would make a face, I received a fillip which bloodied my nose.[5] At length, the illness got worse, and my

5. A fillip is the small blow delivered by using one's thumb to hold one's finger down against the palm of one's hand, then suddenly releasing the finger to produce a rapid flick, in this case against Truquin's nose.

master was forced to abandon work altogether. He would send me to pawn his belongings: first a pair of pants, then a jacket or a coat, in exchange for which they would give me fifteen or twenty sous. With this money I would buy medicines, linseed meal, and so on. The only food we had to eat any more was boiled potatoes, with a salt herring from time to time.

Seeing that the illness was rapidly getting worse, I dared to advise my patient to go to the hospital, where he would be cared for better than at home. I had no sooner spoken these words than he gave me a slap. But this time there was no blood, for the patient had no more strength. That was the last time he hit me. "What would become of you if I went to the hospital?" he shouted. In reality, I had only made the suggestion in the hope of changing my circumstances, which could not have been worse.

He died on 19 December 1843. As soon as the body had been taken away, I was evicted and the door locked behind me. There I was, bareheaded and barefooted. I carried off with me one of the dead man's shirts as well as a pair of pants that I hid by fastening it under my armpits.

That residence had two wings. One of its facades looked out onto the square, the other onto the inner courtyard. A large stone staircase led to the second floor. Under this staircase, there was another that led down to the cellar. A dark recess, fouled with cat droppings, was located in the cellar, and that is the shelter I chose. [. . .]

I next made the acquaintance of a boy my age, the son of a paver, whose mother had died three months before.[6] He was just about as badly off as I, because pavers never have any work in winter. *We would make the rounds of the markets, picking up the carrots and other vegetables that had fallen on the ground. That was our food.*[7] [. . .]

The scheduled date of the local fair was approaching. For me this was a relief because it resulted in errands for me to do and helped me earn a few sous.

Around that time, I struck up an acquaintance with a half-dozen boys my age who would engage in petty theft. They would steal from the displays set out in front of grocery shops, carrying off whatever was within reach: figs, grapes, and so on. They would share with me and urge me to imitate them. I experienced an unconquerable loathing for this line of

6. A paver (*paveur*) was a semiskilled to skilled workman who surfaced public thoroughfares or private courtyards with cobblestones. In most French cities, cobblestone streets remained the norm well into the twentieth century.

7. Here and throughout this memoir, Truquin has made liberal use of italics, though his intention in doing so is sometimes obscure. In general, I have retained the italicization of the original.

work, but they gave me so many lessons and encouraged me with such enthusiasm that I decided to plunge my hand into a barrel of raisins and pulled out a handful. But I had hardly committed this theft before I began to think about the consequences and, then and there, I left the square where the great fair was taking place so that I would not yield to temptation any more.

II. HOW I WAS SAVED FROM POVERTY BY TWO
PROSTITUTES; FORGING PASSPORTS; THE PITIFUL
STORY OF A PATRIOT

One morning I was prowling around Saint-Rémy Square in our quarter when I was approached by a woman who lived in our building. She said to me, "Well, my little friend, so that's where you live?" I did not know how to reply, for I was offended by the trade which this woman practiced, that of prostitution. I remained silent, but she posed me questions, asking whether or not I had any relatives, how I came to find myself in this situation, and so on. I answered her rather curtly and expressed to her my amazement at the interest she seemed to take in me. But she responded as the woman of character that she was, and did not take offense at my brusqueness, knowing how much I had been mistreated and brutalized by my master. She went on to ask if I would agree to do an errand for her. When I said yes, she took me to her place and gave me two francs to buy a bottle of wine, a two-pound loaf of bread, and a one-sou loaf for myself.

This woman did not live alone but with another young woman who was from Mézières. She herself was *the daughter of an innkeeper from Nancy. After being carried off from home by a commander of dragoons, who later abandoned her, she was reduced to living by prostitution.* This did not prevent her from having a regular lover about twenty-five years old named Orblain. [. . .]

When it was time for dinner, they set me a place at their table. I was ashamed and did not dare to come near. But Orblain raised his voice to say to me, "Come over here! You have to eat to become a man." These words and the hunger I felt decided me.

After dinner, the women proposed that I stay with them and do their errands. Orblain had succeeded in putting me at ease with his jokes to such an extent that I accepted without further ado. The women heated water in a large kettle, cut my hair, undressed me, and gave me a bath. They scrubbed me until my skin turned red, for I was covered with vermin. Next, they set me up a bed on a couch and got busy outfitting me with a complete set of clothes with the help of one of Orblain's old garments. They made me shoes out of their ankle boots and covered my head with a tasseled cap. My joy knew no bounds.

My tasks consisted of sweeping the house, polishing the furniture, and shopping for supplies like bread, wine, and especially lots of water. But despite all the comforts that I encountered in this house, that kind of life, which required that I stay cooped up inside, did not suit my temperament.

These women took baths nearly every day. They would go out every evening between nine and ten o'clock and only come home at five in the morning. One night they returned on the arms of two young men from Strasbourg. These men had escaped from prison and were offering one hundred francs to anyone who could get them passports for Belgium. The women advised them to wait for Orblain, who was out. He returned almost immediately. They put their proposition to him and offered him an additional compensation for his trouble. To Orblain's questions about their doings, the travelers confessed that they had swindled a business firm in Strasbourg in which they were employed. Their declared intention was first to go to Belgium and then to Prussia, from where they could communicate with their families and return to live in safety.

Hearing this, Orblain promised the requested passports for that very evening. He went to fetch a man about sixty years old, tall and thin, who wore a top hat and a frock coat that came down below his knees. This individual produced the passports, and Orblain had their purchase price counted out.

Some time after that, the two women brought home a young woman from Alsace who might have been eighteen years old. She had come to take a job as a servant in Reims, but because she was an epileptic and her attacks occurred nearly every day, she could not hold a job anywhere.

These women offered her their hospitality for three or four days, gave her clothes to replace her old, worn-out things, and took her to the stagecoach, where they paid for her ticket and gave her all the money they had with them besides, so that she could return to her native region without mishap.

My hostesses were always gone at night. Orblain and the passport forger took advantage of this circumstance to come install themselves in the house with a group of card players. They played for high stakes, but without making any noise, as if they feared being surprised.

One night when Orblain and his companion were alone, the old man told him, "If you knew how to read, Orblain, I'd show you how to make a fortune with cards." Orblain replied, *"You mean you have to be educated to become a perfect rogue?"* The old man answered with an affirmative smile.

During the six months that I lived in this household, I never heard an off-color remark and never saw anything improper. One of the women called me her "little friend"; the other, her "little man."

One morning, Orblain returned home with the news that the two women were in jail, and then disappeared without giving me any further information. The police came to our place about eight or nine o'clock. They asked me my name and then, without any further ado, put me out and closed the door.

I found myself once again without shelter, but under better circumstances, all the same, than before. As I was fairly correctly dressed, I could make the rounds of the shops to look for work. They put me off until the following Monday. I was then asked questions about my address and my family. When I said I did not have any relatives, they would send me away with the excuse that they did not hire vagabonds. I got the same welcome everywhere. It was then the end of November, the streets were already covered with snow, and I was scantily dressed.

In the end, because no one wanted to give me work, I was forced *to start searching the gutters all over again to find a means of livelihood.* But with the snow, this was becoming almost impossible.

Under the second flight of stairs in my old building there lived a ragpicker named Drouet, who was said to be the brother of a general.[8] I decided to ask him if he would agree to give me lodging. [. . .]

He agreed to put me up and gave me a sack that would serve me, as he put it, both as a bed and as a means of livelihood. The only bed he had himself was a tarp of coarse canvas. I began roaming about the city picking up broken glass, bones, and even bits of wood for the kitchen stove. This occupation earned me about three sous a day. When my profit reached five sous, I would buy a sheep's head, out of which we would make a real feast. [. . .]

Mr. Drouet told me, "Next spring, I'll take you to Sompy in Champagne, to the house of one of my friends." At that time of year, he was in the habit of taking to the road to peddle combs, needles, pins, and various other haberdashery. After making his rounds, he would return to spend the winter in Reims.

On the first of March we set out on the road to Châlons. As we left the

8. On ragpickers (*chiffonniers*), see chapter 4, n. 4.

city, we were assailed by a freezing rain accompanied by a very strong north wind. The poor man, half crippled with rheumatism, could walk only with great difficulty by leaning on a cane. We took nearly six hours to do two leagues. I was cold, but it was more hunger that spurred me on. "You must be thinking," my old companion told me, "that I can't feed you."

"The thought never crossed my mind," I told him, but the truth is that I did not know how we were going to eat. The old campaigner pointed out a mill, advising me to go ask for bread there. I went, and, sure enough, they gave me a scrap of bread that I shared with the old man, who even gave me back a bit. As we were passing through a village, we bought two sous' worth of alcohol in a *cabaret*. I drank a drop, but as I was soaked and chilled right to the bone, that drop took away the last of my strength. For Old Drouet, on the contrary, it brought back his good humor.

Next he led me to a farm where he usually was offered hospitality. He suggested that I say I was his son. We were well received. They dried our worn clothes in front of the fire, cooked us eggs, and then took us to the barn, where we slept on straw.

The next day, Mr. Drouet went off to peddle his little stock of goods. We continued our rounds from village to village, traveling about a league a day. In the evening we would look for shelter. In the morning, he would go sell his odds and ends, pointing out a place for me to wait for him. When hunger became too urgent, I would decide to beg.

One day I noticed a sign on the door of a house. I made like the other beggars waiting at the doorway. Walking in as unpretentiously as possible, I asked for a scrap of bread. It turned out that I was in the house of the mayor, who asked me who I was. "I am the son of Mr. Drouet," I told him. He answered that begging was forbidden and that he was going to have me locked up in a house of correction. He had Mr. Drouet brought before him and asked if Drouet had a permit to peddle goods and if I was his son. Mr. Drouet answered in the affirmative, adding that he was authorized to peddle by virtue of being a military veteran. "You mean you're teaching your son an honest trade," the mayor went on, "the trade of begging?"

"Why don't you, who are rich," Mr. Drouet replied heatedly, "*teach him a better one? Here you sit in the comfort of your suite of rooms. Without your ever having done anything for anyone, you were made a judge. As for me, for twenty-five years I fought for France. My body is riddled with wounds. And after all that service, *your shameful masters didn't even give me any assistance!*"

The mayor interrupted him: "Don't shout so loud or I'll have you locked up!"

"Go ahead then, if you dare," Mr. Drouet retorted proudly.

The mayor chased us both out, and we went straight to a *cabaret* to buy two sous of alcohol.

A few days later, I showed the old soldier some little blisters that had appeared between my fingers. He looked at his own and observed the same thing.[9] "That's all we needed!" he cried. "We'll have to go straight to Châlons, where we'll spend a few days in the local hospital." Before entering that institution, he suggested once again that I say I was his son, because he feared that in my wanderings I would be seized and locked up in a house of correction. He explained to me that these houses were the anterooms to prisons; that the life that children led in them brutalized rather than improved them; that it was, moreover, a handicap in terms of getting work; that free proletarians already had quite enough difficulties to overcome if they were to manage to survive;[10] that those who got out of these institutions, having no experience of the social milieu and being badly thought of besides, were inevitably drawn into vice and ended up, for the most part, in prison or in forced labor camps.

We spent two weeks in the hospital. The food, which we thought very good, consisted of a big bowl of beans each morning and of peas and a big piece of bread each evening. In our room, there were a dozen people suffering from scabies, nearly all military veterans, who spent the day telling of their exploits, which had great appeal for me. We left this home for the destitute on the first of April and headed for Sompy, which it took us at least two weeks to reach. By then, the poor old man could walk only with great difficulty.

The countryside was beginning to deck itself out in greenery. Blossoming fruit trees gave off an intoxicating scent. When we were hungry, I would start to beg for bread, which my old friend and I would eat beside a stream. The freedom we had in setting our pace, that fresh air, and those flowers all brought me an inexpressible happiness which made me forget all the miseries of the past.

9. Truquin and Drouet appear to have been suffering from scabies, a contagious skin infection spread by microscopic mites that cause intense itching. Today this condition can be simply treated with sulfur-based ointments, but in the nineteenth century those too poor to pay for private medical assistance had to seek admission to a hospital.
10. Truquin's use of the terms *prolétaire* and *bourgeois*, signifying "wage worker" and "capitalist," reflects the influence of socialist theorists. He wrote his memoirs in the 1880s, long after the events described; in the early nineteenth century, French workers often employed the word *bourgeois* to mean simply "boss" (see chapter 3, n. 16).

III. OLD DUVAL; THE HUMANITY OF THE POOR;
THE INHUMANITY OF THE RICH; NEW
TRIBULATIONS; THE HOSPITAL IN REIMS;
BELGIAN NAVVIES; THE BOARDING SCHOOL;
RETURN TO MY FAMILY

At last we arrived in Sompy, at the home of Mr. Duval, another old soldier who had fought at Waterloo with my old friend. He had been fifteen at the time. Wounded at the same time as Mr. Drouet, he was treated in the same field hospital, where they had gotten to know one another. My companion introduced me to Duval. "I have brought you a fellow worker," he told him. "You're alone, and this might work out for you." Duval seemed satisfied. Drouet stayed with us three days and then left, and we never heard any news of him after that.

My new master ordered clothes and shoes for me, and then I started working with him. He was about forty-five years old and had a cheerful nature. All day long he would sing the praises of Napoléon's exploits. On Sundays, we would go out to look for nests or catch crayfish. I was happy. In the evening, he would take me to the *cabaret*, where he met old army buddies. They would sing patriotic songs and ballads.

Duval was in the habit of going each year to take part in the grape harvest around Epernay. That year he signed on to carry loads of grapes, while I became a picker, working for a big champagne company. Everyone received the same sum of ten sous a day along with a one-pound loaf of bread. There were seven or eight hundred harvesters working for that one firm. I stayed on twenty-two or twenty-three days and thought myself exceedingly rich, but I had the misfortune to contract jaundice. One morning, shivering with chills, I was unable to get up. This was at the beginning of November. A servant came to ask me to clear out of my spot, but I could not manage it. He went to notify the head of the firm. The boss's two daughters came to see me, saying that we had to find a way to have me taken to a hospital in Reims. Duval, who had been trying to find me for several days, arrived just then. The young ladies asked him to take me to Reims. "How am I supposed to take on such a responsibility?" he asked them. "It's seven or eight leagues away. You young ladies are rich and have horses and carriages. You could easily manage it." They answered that they already had much to do, taking care of the parish poor. At length, faced with the persistent ill will of these women, he told me, "Well then, let's go. I'll get you there as best I can." He led me to an inn, where he tried to get me to drink some hot mulled wine that I could not even sip. In the end, we left for Reims. Half the time I would walk, and half the time he would carry me. We slept that night in the forest of Monchenot. The second day we arrived at Reims toward seven or eight in the evening. There we spent the night at an inn. The next morning, Duval took me to the hospital. We separated, and from that moment I never saw him again.

They put me on a starvation diet for twenty days, with just two servings of broth per day. The medical officer who made the rounds was a man who had a fine presence, though his looks were quite ordinary. He was accompanied by a procession of seven or eight medical students. One of them always stayed behind to say a few words of encouragement to me. When I complained of not being given anything to eat, he would tell me, "Take heart, you'll be given something when you are better."

I had already been at the hospital for more than twenty days when a navvy who had a pain in his side was brought in.[11] He was placed in the bed on my left. A linseed poultice was placed on his side and kept there for four days. Every time he made his rounds, the medical officer said: "Starvation diet for Number 13." The fourth day, the navvy—now impatient—got red with anger. He ripped off his poultice and, in a rage, threw it into the group of medical students, demanding his certificate of release.

The medical officer was on the point of bursting out in turn, but he contained himself. The blame was placed on the sister on duty, and from then on the patient was a little better cared for. When the medical officer passed in front of my bed, I could not help looking him straight in the face, for I believed that he imposed the starvation diet on me out of pure caprice.

During my convalescence, I confided to my neighbor on the left that I did not know where to go when I left the hospital, that I had no home. In those days, a canal was being built from Strasbourg to Reims. He advised me to go to one of the villages along its route, where I would be able to find a job as a dishwasher in an inn. As soon as I felt strong enough, I asked for my release. The medical officer, who did not consider me to be fully cured, at first made trouble; but when I insisted, he decided to give in.

I headed in the direction indicated, but I was so weak that it took me nearly all day to go two leagues. When I arrived, I looked for a job, but my appearance hardly inspired confidence, and people were hesitant to respond. The owner told me, "We'll see tomorrow. You'll be hired if you can tamp soil." So the next day I was sent to the embankment and equipped

11. Navvies (*terrassiers*) are laborers who move quantities of soil, rock, and debris on large construction projects. It is rare to see such workers today, now that gasoline-powered machinery has taken over most such tasks, but navvies were ubiquitous in the nineteenth century, when this back-breaking work was carried out with little more than a shovel and a wheelbarrow. Because of the physical demands it placed upon workers and the fact that it was very poorly paid, this unskilled labor was considered fit only for workers who could find nothing better.

with a tamping tool. There I found three young girls, fourteen or fifteen years of age, who were tamping the soil. I, however, could not manage to lift the tool. Seeing this, the boss took the tamping tool in one hand and told me, "How come a man like you can't lift this tamping tool when these young girls manage to do this work perfectly well?" I was then forced to confess that I had just got out of the hospital. He had me go back to his home, where his wife used me for household tasks. She had me peel vegetables, make the workers' beds, carry water, and so on. There I was able to form a picture of the life that navvies led. It was December and therefore impossible to work the soil because of snow and frost. At that spot, they were cutting through a small mountain to allow the canal to pass. In certain places, the embankment was as much as twenty meters or more in height. The workers, most of them Belgians, would put crampons on their feet to be able to get their wheelbarrows up to the top. They would make this climb right into a wintry wind that whipped at their faces. The women, who were numerous among them, were subjected to the same conditions as the men.

Their food was inadequate. At noon, they had to pay forty centimes for a serving that consisted of soup in which there floated a tiny piece of meat. In the evening they were given a stew made from beans or potatoes with lamb. On average, they ate three pounds of bread a day and they were charged twenty centimes for a place to sleep. In the morning, they usually drank two sous' worth of spirits. Their daily expenses came to one franc seventy centimes without counting clothing. In the winter, they were not always able to earn their keep, because of the time lost on account of rain or frost. The workers' bedrooms consisted of large huts made of planks one inch thick. Their beds consisted of rye-straw pallets and cotton bedspreads. Truly, you had to be a Belgian navvy to stand these conditions in the cold weather we were having.

Their employers were jobbers who had subcontracted with the big entrepreneurs for one thousand to two thousand cubic meters of earth-works. Either because these small-time jobbers did not know how to manage their business or because they were scoundrels, they only rarely managed to pay their workers when the job was done. Some even disappeared with the money, so that the workers lost their wages and the innkeepers, in turn, lost the price of their room and board.

The workers who had thus been robbed first tried to sue those who owed them, but these poor devils knew nothing of the quirks of the law. Moreover, they lacked the necessary resources, and lawyers have a sovereign disdain for those whose pockets they sense to be poorly lined, even though the comforts they enjoy all come from the sweat of workers. Few among them live past fifty. Most die of pneumonia between the ages of thirty-five and forty-five. And to think that so many unfortunates, who have worked the earth for so many years, are reduced to utter poverty, even though they have earned the right to a retirement in their old age!

Soon it was March. I was sent on an errand to Reims. There I met someone who said he knew my father. My father had supposedly returned to Rozières and gotten remarried. I could not stand it any longer and decided to go see him. I returned to my employer's to inform him of the decision I had just made, but his wife took the news very badly, complaining that now that I had regained my strength and they needed me, I was taking ingratitude to the point of suddenly leaving at a busy time of year. I did not know how to respond, but I was determined to leave all the same. This employer did not pay me any wages. I still had twelve sous from the harvest, but as my shoes no longer had soles, I spent ten sous on a huge pair of red wooden clogs. With the two sous remaining, I bought rye bread and set out on the road to Soissons.

Because I was afraid of gendarmes and the house of correction, I took back roads instead of the main road to Soissons. The thaw was setting in and mud stuck to my clogs. I could walk only with the greatest difficulty. My clogs, which had no straps, cut into the tops of my feet. When I could stand it no longer, I took them off and walked barefoot in the fresh-worked earth. In the afternoon, I ran into an icy rain accompanied by a strong wind. I had to walk stooped over to stand up against the storm. At nightfall, I risked asking for hospitality at a farm. I was chilled and my teeth were chattering so badly that I could not speak. I was given some broth, which restored me a bit, and then I went to sleep on the straw.

The next morning, when I awoke, my joints hurt and my body was stiff, but I could not stay there. I had great difficulty getting down the ladder. Then I went to thank the farmer and his wife and was on my way. I had to give up wearing my wooden shoes, as the tops of my feet were all torn up. So that I could walk in greater comfort, I decided to get back on the main road, regardless of the consequences.

Two leagues outside Soissons, there is a little village whose name I cannot remember. It was noon. I had eaten nothing since the broth the evening before and I had a devil of an appetite. I went up to the first house that I encountered on the right-hand side. I immediately realized that I had come to a boarding school. I would gladly have retraced my footsteps, but the sight of all those young people intimidated me, and I thought it wiser to address the master. I took off my hat and greeted him. As he took his first steps toward me, I told him that I was a traveler and that, driven by hunger, I had come to ask him for hospitality.

He led me to the kitchen and had them serve me a pig's foot, as much bread as I wanted, and a glass of wine. Then they gave me a big piece of bread to take with me. He introduced me to his students, telling them, "Look carefully at this young man. He is poor, but he knew how to present himself properly." I thanked him, and he accompanied me to the door while lavishing his encouragement on me.

I arrived at Soissons at night, in a pouring rain. I wandered through town, barefoot in the mud. On a public square, I noticed several open wagons that had been unloaded. I settled myself into one of them to spend the night, but I took the precaution of leaving at the rooster's call to avoid meeting the driver. I next headed for Compiègne.

About three leagues from that town, I saw a castle set back quite some distance from the road. I went there to ask for bread. I entered a room furnished with a table that might have been five or six meters long. There was no one there! I was very perplexed. If I leave, I thought, they will take me for a thief. It is better to stay. I called out at the top of my voice. I banged my shoe on a bench. Absolute silence! At last, however, a man appeared, still putting on his clothes. He was bareheaded, his shirt was all frilly, and he wore red slippers. When he saw me, he angrily reproached me for making so much noise. When he had grown a little calmer, I asked him for some bread. He called me a vagabond, a thief, and threatened to have me arrested. But seeing that I did not lose my composure, he turned right around and went back up the stairway he had come down. I was still awaiting the outcome when, a quarter hour later, I saw him come back down all dressed up. He gave me twenty sous and sent me away. I left, thanking him politely.

Toward the end of the day, I caught sight of the forest of Compiègne. Before entering it, I bought a pound of bread in a village. Some carters whom I met informed me that I had four or five leagues of forest to traverse and advised me to turn back. But I continued my route without paying attention to their warning, and at three in the morning I reached the other side of the forest.

The crowing of a rooster told me that I was approaching a village. I was completely worn out and so sleepy I could hardly stand. Not far from the road there was a quarry surrounded with sheds. I went over and, not seeing anyone, sat back against a wall and fell into a deep sleep. When the workers arrived to begin work, they had some difficulty waking me up. Seeing that I was in such a pitiful state, my feet all bloody, they looked after me a bit. They put straw in my wooden shoes and one of them even sacrificed half his undershirt to wrap my feet. They wanted to have me eat, but I had no appetite. They informed me that travelers had the right to stay three days in the hospital and that it would do me no harm to go there in passing, but that I needed to obtain an authorization from the police commissioner.

The latter gave me a rather surly reception, calling me a vagabond, a do-nothing, and asking a slew of questions. Then, once he had calmed down a bit, he gave me thirty sous and a voucher for one night at the hospital. That's all I needed. With the forty-six sous that I owned, I no longer needed to beg.

I was not too badly received at the hospital, but it seemed rather strange that, after the Angelus, patients of both sexes should gather together to mumble their prayers for two or three hours.[12] This seemed to me to be rather stupid on the part of grown-up people. When I was still young, I had come to the conclusion that to ask something from God was to insult Him, to demand that He commit an injustice, for He could not help some without doing harm to others.

The next morning I was on my way again, and two days later I had reached my village. I went straight to my grandfather's house. My arrival was a major event for my family. First they heated water to clean me up. My clothing, which was infested with vermin, was thrown in the stove. The next day, which was a Sunday, most of the villagers came to visit me. They were amazed to hear me speaking proper French.[13] I stayed at my grandfather's. This worthy man had given his house to his daughter and, even though he was seventy years old, was working for his younger son in a town a league from Rozières.

I went to see my father, who was sick and poor. My stepmother, whom I called Madame, which very much displeased her, did not even offer me lunch. Then I visited with my uncles and aunts, for I had a large family. I had become the spoiled child once again. Everyone wanted me to stay with them.

I had been back one month when for the third time I was having dinner with an aunt who had taken on the task of raising my two older sisters. This good woman had the habit of reciting a prayer before and after each meal. In order not to seem foolish, I made as if I were reciting it too, even though I did not know a single word. My aunt noticed and wanted to know why. I was forced to confess my ignorance. She gave me a long sermon on

12. The Angelus is the church bell rung to announce the time for prayers. This custom dates from a time when individuals not only had a stricter sense of religious obligation but also lacked reliable means of knowing the time of day. It was not until the final decades of the nineteenth century that pocket watches came into widespread use among people of modest means.
13. His neighbors, of course, expected him to speak the local dialect. Compare the similar experience that Jeanne Bouvier reports in chapter 7.

this subject, telling me that it was a great sin not to know how to pray, not to thank God for the kindnesses that He heaped upon us, for the food that He gave us to eat, and so on. "Auntie," I answered, "God put man on earth, but if man doesn't work, he won't eat. So it's work and not God that gives us food." The poor woman was so upset by my remarks that she was nearly ill. My two sisters seemed very troubled. My aunt shouted, "The child is lost!" I left and never saw her again.

From that moment on, my other relatives grew cold toward me, though I could not figure out the reason for the change in their behavior. It was only later, when I reflected on the various circumstances of my life, that this answer, which I had totally forgotten, came back to mind.

IV. THE LIFE OF A BRICKMAKER; THE HORRORS
OF A SLAUGHTERHOUSE; THE BONE TRADE; THE
FACTORIES OF AMIENS; THE TRADE IN PLASTER
FIGURINES; ARRIVAL IN PARIS; THE ROOMING
HOUSE IN THE BOULEVARD DES AMANDIERS

I returned to the home of my father, who had me sleep in the attic. I then got hired in a brickyard where entire families were employed. To make bricks, you dig strips of earth three meters deep and one meter wide. This earth is heaved to the left, where it rises in a pile that can reach as much as four meters high. For this work, you would be paid seventy centimes per cubic meter. I could do three meters a day, but an able worker could do as much as eight. This rate of pay was never exceeded, for good-quality bricks sell for just eleven francs per thousand.

There was a Belgian family consisting of six persons who prepared the mortar and molded the bricks, for which they were paid three francs per thousand. These good people, who ate only bread and coffee without sugar, began their work at three-thirty in the morning and did not finish until ten o'clock at night. The son-in-law served as molder, two children carried the bricks, and the wife trimmed off the burrs with the help of her sister. In this way, they were able to make as many as three thousand bricks when the weather was good. When the children did not work the way the father wanted, he would fall upon them like a raging madman, beating them unmercifully. The other workers would watch him without flinching, as if it were the most natural thing in the world. I would say to no one but myself, "It appears that in Belgium it's the custom to treat children like beasts of burden." This reflection almost made me forget the grudge I held against my former master, Auguste.

Because this harsh labor had caused me to start coughing up blood after three weeks, I was forced to look for something less arduous. A half-hour from the village, there was a slaughterhouse where they made boneblack.[14] This firm's director happened to be one of my cousins. I was paid six sous a day, with a piece of bread into the bargain, because I was a relative.

This was in 1846. Bread cost six sous a pound.[15] My job was to use an axe to break bones that were then very carefully arranged in large pans so they could be cooked. I also cleaned up the slaughterhouse debris, which was extremely heavy and which I carried with extraordinary difficulty a distance of two hundred meters on a wheelbarrow that I then had even greater difficulty turning over. At the time, I was thirteen years old and not very strong.

This factory had two courtyards. In the first was located the director's residence, the storehouse for fodder, and the stables. The boilers for cooking the meat and making boot polish, the mill for grinding the boneblack, and the slaughterhouse itself were relegated to the second courtyard.

Nothing could be more sinister than the appearance of this second courtyard. There were always sixty to eighty horses of all kinds to be found there. Some had been used to pull the carriages of the high bourgeoisie, while others came from the carting trade or from the countryside. Those poor animals waited for up to two weeks before it was their turn to be slaughtered. I saw some that would search through the entrails of their

14. Boneblack is a very fine form of charcoal, made by burning the bones of animals in the absence of oxygen. It is used as a pigment and in a number of industrial applications.

15. Truquin is calling attention to the fact that the price of bread had begun to rise over the previous year and had reached a level that was driving workers to the brink of starvation. A major reason for the rise was the destruction of a large part of the potato crop in northern France by the same blight that was causing extreme hardship in Ireland and elsewhere. The shortage of potatoes greatly increased the French workers' dependence on bread, in a year when the wheat harvest was mediocre. The price of bread rose steadily to the level of six sous a pound that Truquin reports here. When the wheat harvest in the fall of 1846 proved to be truly disastrous, not only in France but all across the Continent, grain prices really shot upward. As Truquin notes later, it had climbed to seven sous by the fall, and it would continue to rise through the early months of the following year. It was only with the bountiful harvest of fall 1847 that grain became more plentiful and the price stabilized. For workers, whose diet consisted in large part of bread and whose wages left them very close to the margin of survival, any fluctuation in the price of this staple spelled potential ruin. This agricultural crisis had far-reaching political consequences, both because of its direct effect on the ability of the poor to feed themselves and because it prompted a crisis in the financial and industrial sectors as well. The downturn in the French economy, the widespread layoffs and unemployment that followed in its wake, and the movement for political reform begun in late 1847 all contributed to the outbreak in February 1848 of a revolution that toppled the monarchy of Louis-Philippe and led to the declaration of France's Second Republic.

dismembered fellow horses. Sometimes I would bring them a handful of hay on the sly. But what could this handful do to satisfy so many that were starving?

Some of them would whinny and still try to hold their heads high in spite of their exhaustion, stiffening their muscles and spreading their legs so as not to fall, then raising their heads as if they wanted to call God as witness to the hideous tortures they were made to suffer. [. . .]

I had noticed many poor people who came to sell bones, for which they were paid one sou a pound. I decided to roam the countryside, dealing in this same commodity. I took the thirty-six sous I was due from the slaughterhouse to my father, as I had done in previous weeks, and told him my idea. On Monday, he gave me back twelve sous and a sack, and I was on my way.

I made the rounds of the middle-class houses where they ate meat. I paid two liards a pound for bones.[16] With my twelve sous, I bought twenty-four pounds of bones that I carried to the factory. The proceeds from this sale allowed me to buy forty-eight pounds of bones, and in this way I carried on my little commerce. I only took on as many bones as I could carry, about twenty-five to thirty pounds. I made my rounds of six or seven villages to complete my load. Food cost me nothing. When I was hungry, I would ask for a piece of bread and I was rarely refused.

Soon I had enough money to buy the pelts of cats, hares, rabbits, sheep, and so on. I also sold knitting yarn and a few other articles that brought me a reasonable return. All this was a great help to my father, who was still sick. As my capital increased, I spent twenty francs on an old lame mule who had belonged to a miller. This acquisition was a great relief for me, for I had been obliged to walk all day long with a very heavy weight on my shoulders.

From then on, I was able to extend my commerce as far as Noyon. At a large farm, I bought an entire lot of pelts from sheep that had died of hoof-and-mouth disease. In this way I made a net profit of thirty-seven francs in one fell swoop. I used the money to benefit our household. My father, who was by then in somewhat better health and who saw that this trade was lucrative, decided to come in with me. Thereafter, we operated on a larger scale. We would buy sheepskins from butchers and use lime to remove the wool.

On September 15, we were passing through a village that was holding

16. The *liard* was a nineteenth-century monetary unit, no longer in use. One liard was equal to one-quarter of a sou or one and a quarter centimes. Truquin was therefore buying bones at one-half the price he was paid by the slaughterhouse.

its yearly festival. My father began playing cards in a *cabaret*. He lost everything we owned, capital and mule, and could not even pay his bill. I returned to our village in melancholy spirits, thinking about the approach of winter and realizing that it would be impossible for me to resume my little business.

A few days later, I went to my grandfather's. He worked, as I have mentioned, at his son's in Harbonnières. He already knew what had happened and was rather saddened by it. My clothes were in tatters and, even though the poor man had only his wages to live on, he bought me new ones all the same. He was in the habit of eating at the inn, so I was all alone while he was at work. I would go for walks in the woods, where I enjoyed myself a great deal. [. . .]

My grandfather was old and poor and could no longer take care of me. So that very night I decided to go work in the mills, since I still was not strong enough to look for jobs on the farms. When morning came, I told him of my plan. He gave me breakfast and handed me three francs and fifty centimes. From there I went to see my father and gave him this small sum, which he needed badly, for his wife had just given him a daughter.

Once I had obtained a piece of bread, I set out on my way. It was a Thursday in the month of September and already rather cold. At nine-thirty I arrived in Amiens, where I spent the night in an empty wagon, as I had done previously, because I did not have a cent to stay at the inn. I was lucky enough to get myself hired in a wool-spinning mill located on the road to Abbeville, a league and a half from Amiens. The only problem was that my job did not begin until Monday, and I had neither money nor a place to stay! They were loading apples in the port. I picked up those they had thrown away and that is what I ate until the next day.

On Monday, I was at the mill before six o'clock. When it came time for breakfast, a worker named Constant asked me why I wasn't eating. I simply answered that it was because I had nothing to eat. He then shared his meal with me. I told him that for lack of a place to stay, I was sleeping in freight wagons. He promised to take me to the home of an old woman who could probably give me shelter. Work at the mill ended at nine in the evening, but we didn't leave until a quarter of an hour later, when a bell rang. We had to travel a league and a half to get to the good woman's house, for she lived in the Saint-Leu quarter. We arrived at ten-thirty. Constant, who knew her, told her why we had come. "You make it impossible for me to refuse," she told him, after looking me over. "But you know very well that I only take in girls. I don't like to put up boys at all, but your protégé looks all right. I'll keep him." Constant left us, and this woman gave me the bed that belonged to her son, who was in the army.

Sixteen young working girls were lodgers in that house. Their wages varied from eighty centimes to one franc ten centimes a day. Those who earned over a franc, most of them warpers, thought themselves far above the others.[17] They wore bonnets that cost thirty sous and were decorated with red ribbons. Those who earned eighty centimes wrapped their heads in kerchiefs, walked in wooden shoes, and wore skirts that were half wool and half cotton. All these young women made do with two bowls of broth a day, eaten with bread. Each bowl cost them one sou. In the morning, they would munch walnuts or apples with their bread. On Sundays, the land-lady would cook a cow's head, serve meat broth at noon for two sous, and sell each portion of the head for three sous.

As for me, she loaned me a tin pot that I carried to the mill for dinner. She had another that she kept aside for my evening meal. I paid the same price for these portions of broth as the young women, but bread cost seven sous a pound. It was the end of the year 1846. I was eating a pound a day and could easily have eaten twice that amount, but that was impossible, for I was earning only twenty-two sous. With the long trip I had to make twice a day, I had only five hours left to sleep, which was not enough for me.

A few days after I started work at the mill, the director asked whether I had made my First Communion and had me enrolled in the catechism class given at the parish of Saint-Leu. He authorized me to be absent until eleven o'clock for this purpose. That made six leagues that I had to trudge twice a week. I was thinking not of my exhaustion but of the soles of my shoes, which were getting thinner every day. I was afraid that I would end up walking barefoot in town, which would have seemed the ultimate humiliation for me.

Since I did not know how to read, I experienced incredible difficulty in learning the catechism. I begged the workers to help me a little, but they were not always very willing. In Saint-Leu there was a Jesuit who taught catechism to the children from the mills. I would go there in the company of some of my young fellow workers. He was somewhere between forty-five and fifty years old. From the responses I gave to his questions, he recognized that I knew practically nothing. He seemed ill at ease in my presence, to the point where he could not perform his functions. I thought he was crazy. My fellow workers had never seen him in such a state. When I went back to his drawing-room the following Sunday, he made a grimace of disgust and abruptly sent me away. Several other children were no more

17. In a wool-spinning mill, a warper sets up the parallel strands of thread on the weaving frame across which the woolen cloth is to be woven. This may be done either by hand or on a warping machine.

able than I to get their lessons through their skulls, but the priest took the difficulty we were experiencing into account and did not make us repeat the following year, for fear that we would not come back.

The children from the mills were called into the sacristy. A tailor took our measurements and made us each a set of ceremonial garments out of cast-off army uniforms. But we were not given shoes. My outfit happened to be made of handsome black broadcloth. I had a white vest lined with cotton and a silk high hat. My landlady could not believe her eyes. She bought me white stockings and shoes with buckles that brought out the contrast with my fellow workers even more, for they were all shabbily dressed.

But before leaving Amiens behind, let me tell you a bit about the workers. Workers in Reims had to pay all their own costs of lighting and heating, as well as pay for the oil used to grease the wool. Workers in Amiens, on the contrary, were relieved of these expenses, even though they were paid the same wage. In consequence, the latter were less badly off and kept themselves cleaner. It is true that they had to get up very early in the morning so as to enter the factory on the stroke of quarter to five. The slightest tardiness meant a fine, and on the third offense, you were fired and given a bad reference that made it impossible for you to find another job in the region.

But despite all these disadvantages, the situation of mill workers was much more tolerable than that of home workers. Nothing is more brutalizing than work in confined quarters, even though it seems to be freer. All day long, the home worker breathes the unhealthy fumes given off by the coal and by the nauseating oil that it heats. In this manner, an entire family is half-suffocated in a space just a few meters square. To escape this isolation, which weighs heavily upon him, the worker goes looking for fellowship at the *cabaret*. There he finds out what price is being offered for labor and learns about working conditions. He drinks his bottle, sings a few verses, then goes home to his filthy hovel. In the mills, on the contrary, the workshops are heated, fairly well ventilated, and properly lit. Order and cleanliness prevail. There the worker finds fellowship. In those days, the foremen were less demanding about quantity than they were about quality. Your earnings could run as high as ten francs per week, and sometimes as high as twenty francs. They paid you the going rate without complaints. When the foreman was absent, workers would tell stories or recite plays. The jokers in the group would improvise a pulpit and amuse themselves by preaching. The time passed cheerfully.

To be more specific, one never heard any political or social opinions being expressed. If by chance it was learned that a worker had spread such ideas, *all the managers got together to refuse him work.* Constant, who had shared his meals with me, was an example. He was about forty years old and in the factory had been given the nickname "Cabet."[18] Constant had been in Paris in 1830. He had enlisted as a military settler in Algeria. He had continued to serve against the Arabs until obtaining his discharge at the end of eight years. Constant openly stated that the officers who commanded these battalions were all reactionaries. Officers despise "civvies," meaning civilians. *The military is incompatible with any form of civilization.* Then Constant would read to us from Cabet's *Voyage en Icarie.* I would ask him questions about the community described there. As for me, I was an anticommunist. It seemed to me that community required an iron discipline, before which all individual will would be erased. I was seized with the desire to roam the world, to visit Paris, the great cities, the seaports, to sail as far as the Indies. I feared seeing my freedom restricted. I believed there was no freedom if you had no money, and I was counting on the twists of fate to earn me some.

From another point of view, I would also reflect on the fact that we were living in conditions that were worse than those of community. If goods were held in common, we would not have to travel three leagues a day to get to work or to get back, we would not be reduced to eating nothing but broth, and children would not be forced to work so young.

The mill was really a special and rather different kind of community. The bourgeois monopolized all the profits for themselves alone and for their children. Since 1830, the bourgeoisie has not hesitated to use any means of exploiting the proletariat. On my way to work, I would pass in front of a mill run by Englishmen. More than four hundred young women would be waiting for the bell to ring so they could enter. Among them I noticed seven-year-old children who had to endure all the rigors of the cold weather.

To get back to Constant, the communist, the young folks would jeer at him by singing this constantly repeated refrain: "Let's divvy him up, let's split him among us!" One day, when he could stand it no longer, he told

18. Constant was nicknamed after the socialist Etienne Cabet (see chapter 4, n. 33). Cabet's most important writing was *Voyage en Icarie,* in which he outlined his plan for a utopian community organized around the principle of communal property. He described its central principle of operation in a maxim that would later be borrowed by Marx: "From each according to his ability, to each according to his needs." Cabet's followers, known as Icarians, founded a number of experimental communities in the New World. The first and best known of these was established on the Red River in Texas in 1848. Cabet went there in 1849 and lived in various communal settings in the New World until his death in St. Louis in 1856.

them, "You're a bunch of ignoramuses, and most of you will end your days in the poorhouse!"

What he said was only too true. I had already noticed that fifty-year-old men were refused work. Speculators naturally preferred to hire men at the peak of their strength. Those who were getting along in years were reduced to begging, soon condemned as vagabonds, and relegated to a poorhouse, which must be a hideous torment for these older workers, who are thus subjected to a fanatical oppression.

It was probably because of this outburst that Constant was let go the following Saturday. He could not find a job anywhere else. His wife was confined with his third child. The oldest was a girl five years old. Three months later, Constant died, and his wife soon followed him. *Such is the fate reserved for honest people!*

Soon the amount of work began to diminish. They first had us work five days a week, then four, then three. On days when I was not working, I took fencing lessons. I was afraid I would have to consume the capital of nine francs that I had amassed with great difficulty.

That is when I learned that my father was in Paris, where he was running a warehouse for wine. And even though no one could tell me his address, I decided I would go join him anyway. I was, however, at a loss to know how I was going to undertake this journey with just nine francs. I anticipated that I would be forced to spend them on the way and that if upon my arrival I did not find my father right away, I would have to look for work. What was more, the soles of the shoes that my grandfather had bought me were all worn out. I still had the ones from my First Communion, but I cherished those like the apple of my eye. I foresaw that in Paris a barefoot boy might not have an easy time finding a job.

While these thoughts were running through my head, I noticed a rather young man going door-to-door selling plaster figurines that he carried on his head. Knowing that these salesmen made the rounds all over, I asked him if he had ever been to the capital. "We've been in Amiens the past three months," he told me, "and the day after tomorrow, we're leaving for Paris."

"I'd like to go there with you," I told him. On his advice, I got together with his boss and asked him if he would agree to let me sell his figurines during the journey. He was an Italian. He asserted that the French were too proud to lug these artistic pieces door-to-door. There was a certain irony in his words. I answered that I considered myself as capable as an Italian of plying this trade. Next he objected that the weight of these articles, though not very heavy, was nonetheless tiring for someone who was not accustomed to carrying burdens on his head. I reassured him on this point. We agreed that I would leave on Monday with his first assistant. This was the young man who had introduced me to him, a very good fellow about fifteen years old. The boss was from Florence. He had eight youngsters who peddled his wares throughout the provinces. The general rendezvous was in the Rue de la Roquette in Paris. Each would take a different route, but the boss traveled in better conditions.

And so we left on the appointed day at nine o'clock in the morning. My coworker had become my boss. He set my sales prices. I made two sous for each object sold. When I sold something at a higher price, I split the difference with him. "It's customary," he added, "to ask for a piece of bread as part of the deal." I had never failed to do this back in the days when I was buying and selling bones.

My coworker was very surprised to see that I promptly began selling off my merchandise, and at a good profit, while he himself had hardly made his first sale. He handed over half of his load and stayed with me all the same. I had become the salesman, and before we got to Beauvais, we had sold off our entire stock. I made three and a half francs, after expenses.

I wanted to stay over one day in Beauvais to visit the cathedral at my leisure. My coworker tried to talk me out of this plan but resigned himself when I insisted. We then resumed our journey and arrived in Paris on Saturday at noon.

He took me to an inn located at the back of a courtyard. Its clientele consisted of Italians who were masons, chimney builders, and so forth. At dinner, the first assistant ordered a bottle of wine, which we drank with great pleasure. I had not tasted any since the death of my master, Auguste. The Italians were surprised to see a Frenchman who peddled plaster figurines just like themselves.

The next day, I set about finding my father. Only chance could make our paths cross. Meanwhile, I had to look for work. I had heard that there were mills that made woolen cloth in the Rue Saint-Maur. I put on my First Communion outfit and entrusted the package of rags that I had taken off to the woman who ran the inn, who made a face but then agreed to keep them for me. In the Rue Saint-Maur, I asked someone to point out a place to stay in the neighborhood, saying that I had just arrived from Amiens. He suggested that I speak directly to the concierge of the nearby factory.[19] When I heard this, I remembered that a worker whom I had known in Amiens was employed in that factory. The concierge, whom I asked for

19. A concierge lived permanently in a residential apartment house or occasionally, as here, in a commercial building, as caretaker and supervisor (see chapter 2, n. 23).

news of my acquaintance, gave me a very poor reception, saying that he was not being paid to page workers. Nonetheless, at my repeated request, he went to tell the worker's foreman. This foreman happened to come precisely from my village of Rozières. I informed him that I had come to join my father and asked if he had news of him. He told me he had not heard any for twenty-five years.

I seized the opportunity to ask him for work. They were in the process of setting up some new combing machines. He urged me to come back on Monday and gave me the worker's address I had asked for, which turned out to be in the Rue Saint-Martin. I went there immediately, but as it was Sunday, the worker was out for a walk. I mounted guard in front of his doorway until nine that evening.

All I had eaten that entire day was one sou's worth of apples. At last I saw my man approaching, accompanied by his wife. He did not recognize me right away, since the only clothes he had ever seen me in were rags and tatters. Also, he probably suspected that I was going to be a bother for him. He was about to leave without offering me hospitality. I plucked up my courage and told him that I had not come to inconvenience him but only in the hope that he would direct me to some place for me to stay. He commented that it was not easy to find a place at ten o'clock at night, but he recalled that there was a rooming house for masons in a small street nearby. He took me there. There just happened to be an unoccupied bed, which he paid for. I then announced to him my intention of going to present myself at the factory. "That's good. So we'll see you at the factory," he added. I understood that he was not anxious for me to disturb him again.

The next day at eight o'clock I was at the factory. They told me to come back the following Monday, giving me some hope that I would be hired. I had an enormous appetite, which I satisfied by buying four sous' worth of bread and two sous' worth of fried potatoes. When the workers left for the day, one of them told me about a rooming house at 8 Boulevard des Amandiers. The only available bed was in a dormitory and cost seven francs a month, payable in advance. When this was paid, I had twenty-four sous left to make it through the week. That evening, I spent four on my dinner and then went to take possession of my bed.

The dormitory to which I belonged had been nicknamed the Academy. It contained nine beds. Among the guests in this rooming house were three noblemen; a captain who had served during the wars in Spain and had his commission revoked, I don't know for what offense; a former notary who had been convicted of some crime (these personages were traveling book salesmen); an artist who sold his drawings in the *cabarets* during the evening shows; an old drunk nicknamed Raphael who was a stage-scene painter; and a former soldier of the Empire who had a job turning the grinding wheel to sharpen tools in a wood-carving shop. I filled out the group of nine.

That evening, one of the nobles, Mr. de Villeneuve, came to pay me his compliments, expressing his satisfaction at having a dormitory mate such as myself. As he questioned me, he learned that I was going to have a job but that I had been put off for a week. He assumed a tone of importance to announce to me that he had found me work that started immediately and was much better paid. The next day, when Mr. de Villeneuve saw that I was on my way out, he told me that he happened to be going my way. When we reached the customs gate in the Rue des Amandiers, he suddenly cried out, "Oh, damn! I've forgotten my purse. If you would be so kind as to give me twenty sous, I will return them to you this evening."

"But sir," I told him, "that's all I have, and I can only lend you half that amount." I was convinced that he would pay me back, and so I risked buying three sous' worth of bread and two sous' worth of cod. That evening, Mr. de Villeneuve came home drunk, but I asked him for my ten sous on Wednesday morning. "I'll give them to you shortly," he said, and then he left. Seeing that I had been tricked, I resolved to make the best of it, which meant that I had to economize. That day I ate just two sous' worth of bread, and the next day the same. But on Friday I spent my last sou. I was going to have to wait until the following Monday to eat, and then only if they gave me work.

V. FURTHER TRIBULATIONS; A SOLDIER'S STORY; THE FEBRUARY DAYS; DISBANDING OF THE NATIONAL WORKSHOPS

I spent the days I was without work visiting Paris, but by Sunday I no longer had any strength. I was unable to walk. I stayed in bed until nightfall with the intention of letting myself starve to death. I thought about going to see the worker in the Rue Saint-Martin. The welcome he had given me was not such as to encourage me to pay him a visit, but I forced myself to make one last effort before giving up altogether. I got up and, with great difficulty, headed for the Rue Saint-Martin. Mr. Pierre was out again. When he arrived, around ten o'clock, *I told him that I had not eaten anything for three days.* He loaned me twenty sous. I immediately used two of them to buy bread. I could easily have devoured four times as much, but I had no job and I knew how to curb my appetite.

The next morning, when I went to the company office, they made me wait for more than an hour. My heart was beating hard enough to burst my chest, for I was wondering what would become of me with eighteen sous in my pocket if I were not hired. My imagination provided me with no way of escaping this terrible situation. At last the director appeared. He looked me over from head to foot and, after asking the usual questions, ordered me to come to work the next morning at five o'clock. I was to be paid one franc twenty centimes a day. When I went back out in the street, I bought four sous' worth of bread and one sou's worth of apples. That was not much, for I could have swallowed the tradeswoman's basket.

Now I had to make my thirteen sous last until payday on Saturday. You can imagine that, given what I was eating, I was not exactly bursting with energy. What is more, the other street urchins, who thought I was weak, would make fun of me. The worker who ran the combing machine to which I was assigned would constantly tell me, "Work faster, will you!" I was afraid of being fired. On payday, I received five francs fifty centimes, which seemed like a fortune to me. That evening I feasted on a pound of bread, two sous' worth of cod, and one sou's worth of apples, that I went and ate next to my bed. I offered some to my dormitory mate on the left, the former soldier, who thanked me but said that apples were lousy food and gave him a stomachache. On his advice, we went to a restaurant in the Rue Ménilmontant where we each bought ten sous' worth of meat scraps. That made a whole handkerchief full. The soldier was laying in his stock for the coming week. We ate like kings.

My companion told me his adventures. He had survived the campaign in Russia.[20] A prisoner of the Russians in 1813, he had escaped, only to be recaptured by the Austrians. The latter wanted to force him to join their army, but when he and his countrymen refused, they were locked up in prison without food for four days. Hunger made him decide to accept the offer he had been made, but he secretly promised himself he would desert at the first opportunity. This opportunity occurred during the Hundred Days.[21] He returned to France and was wounded at Waterloo. After he had recovered, he found work as a common laborer. In 1830 he took up arms against the Bourbons, was wounded again, and was recommended for a decoration. But since he had served in the Austrian army, he received

20. The reference is to Napoléon's disastrous attempt to invade Russia. Unable to win a decisive victory in the field, the French Army was forced to retreat. Napoléon's forces suffered so acutely from the early winter cold and harassment by Russian troops that, of his original complement of 100,000 soldiers, barely 1,000 were fit for action by the time the army left Russian territory on December 14, 1812.
21. The Hundred Days was the brief period of Napoléon's return to power before his final defeat at Waterloo in June 1815 (see chapter 3, n. 9).

neither a medal nor any compensation.[22] Then he told me about current affairs. The bigshots were stirring about an awful lot, he told me. He said we were on the eve of a revolution, and he advised me not to get involved, because *it was always the people who had to pay the piper.* "That's just what we saw in 1830," he added. *"We got our heads bashed in for the sake of those bigshots who, once they were in power, gave us a kick in the behind."* He also told me that in 1833 he had gone back to his village in the Artois region, where he owned a little property. His sister and her husband welcomed him warmly and persuaded him to turn his property over to them for a payment of twenty sous a day plus board. He let himself be caught in the trap. He received his annuity regularly for a month, then they made him wait. He went for a year without receiving anything but insults. The children called him an old beast, while his sister accused him of ingratitude for wanting to force them to make him payments when they themselves were without a cent. His brother-in-law added that if he were not happy, he could leave. He was even refused the food they had agreed upon. In the end, when he could stand it no longer, he returned to Paris, begging for food along the way.

At that time he was earning two francs a day turning a grinding wheel in a wood-carving shop. The former soldier was not exactly enchanted with his dormitory mates. One day he told me, "Do you see those folks? *They have some education, and yet it would be hard to find a more worthless or dissolute crowd.* Watch out for them. They often steal the food I keep in my handkerchief."

And indeed, a few days later, I caught Mr. de Villeneuve taking some meat from the packet that I had hung above my bed. "Hey, buddy, leave my meat alone!"

"Everyone has to live," he replied, not the least bit disconcerted.

As for the captain, he had found his way into a family of masons. First he got them to do his laundry, then he ate with them for five months, letting those good folks hope that he would reimburse them four times over from an inheritance that he was supposed to receive.

One morning, the mason's wife came looking for the ex-captain in our dormitory. He had disappeared the previous week. This poor woman had a six-month-old child in her arms. "Who would have thought," she cried, as she addressed Mr. de Villeneuve, "that such a well-bred man could have

22. The medal that Truquin is speaking of was the cross awarded to those who had distinguished themselves in what were known as the "three glorious days of July," the insurrection that chased the Bourbon dynasty from the throne of France forever and that set in place the monarchy of Louis-Philippe.

been so dishonorable as to take the bread from our children's mouths for so long?"

"You're right," he replied with an embarrassed look, "it's shameful!" [. . .]

Since first arriving in Paris, I had not ceased visiting the sights of the capital. In the evening I would sometimes pay fifteen centimes for a ticket to the Little Lazari.[23] If I was able to visit the principal buildings, museums, and public gardens, I owe it all to my frock coat, for they would not let people in workers' dress enter. For this reason, many young people grow old without ever getting to know Paris.

In the museums, what interested me most were the paintings. I tried to guess their subject and I would often pester visitors with questions. Some would turn their heads away with scorn. Others, on the contrary, quite willingly responded to my request for explanations. That is when I began to observe people. I noticed that those who wore a full beard and had straight noses rarely refused me information, while I could get nothing from those whose noses were flattened or in the form of a parrot's beak. After the February Revolution, I had the opportunity to confirm the accuracy of my predictions. I was consumed by the desire to learn and, since I did not know how to read, I used every means of getting to know a little history.

During the day of 22 February, the factory remained calm. No one breathed a word. But toward seven o'clock that evening, a muffled rumor circulated among the workers. Then they were suddenly seized as if by an electric shock. A foreman came to give the order to stop work. The workers poured out into the streets. As I made my way in the direction of the boulevards, I saw kids throwing stones at the gas lanterns, crying "Long live reform!" I returned to the dormitory. *The six distinguished members of the Academy had disappeared.* The only ones left were Raphael and the former soldier. I was all excited. The soldier advised me not to get involved with the movement.

That night, I dreamed that I was hunted by the police. But this did not prevent me, the next morning, from going wherever I saw unrest. Toward ten o'clock, I found myself on the Place de la Bastille where the crowd was taunting the Municipal Guards, who were armed.[24] *Not one of these provocateurs was from the working class.* They were, in general, well-

23. The Little Lazari was presumably a popular theater.
24. The Municipal Guards were, roughly speaking, the Parisian police force. This was the only group that remained loyal to Louis-Philippe's government throughout the February Days.

284 / *Norbert Truquin*

dressed young men. It may just have been the effect of the situation, but I found them swarthy skinned and harsh voiced. You would have sworn they had just gotten out of Jesuit seminaries or prisons.

The Municipal Guards seemed to be getting ready for battle. Their attitude was feverish, their faces pale. This spectacle was distressing to see. I withdrew along the Boulevard Beaumarchais, heading toward the Faubourg du Temple. The entrance to the Rue Ménilmontant was occupied by a squadron of dragoons, their sabers drawn, but the crowd did not seem to be concerned.[25] The boulevards were full of gawkers. Some women were selling fruit on the corner. All of a sudden, the dragoons began to charge the crowd. The result was a general stampede. People fled in all directions. Those trying to escape would jostle one another, fall to the pavement, get back up, and clear out as fast as they could. The fruit sellers were knocked over. I picked up a dozen apples that I stowed inside my shirt, without thinking what I was doing. I took refuge behind a tree and from there I attacked the dragoons by throwing apples. I threw one with such force that the horseman whom I hit on the helmet was shaken and nearly fell to the ground. No one was wounded. The dragoons did not strike out. They went back to their position, all lined up in formation, and the crowd also returned to the street, crying "Long live reform!"

Next I went over by the Tuileries.[26] The boulevards were chock-full of soldiers. On the left bank, about twenty young men were constructing a barricade at the corner of the Rue de l'Echaudé. I set to work alongside them.

Toward noon, a battalion of infantrymen advanced and came to a halt twenty-five yards from our barricade. Four or five young men, armed with old rifles, were sitting on top of the paving stones. They began shouting, "Long live reform! Long live the infantry!" A moment later, the troops fired a volley of shots in the air! The insurgents did the same. These detonations lasted a quarter of an hour. It was terrible to hear the sound of rifle fire in those narrow streets. Then the troops withdrew, still accompanied by the same shouts of "Long live reform! Long live the troops!" From there, I headed toward the Boulevard Saint-Martin. On the boulevards, the guard posts occupied by the Municipal Guard had been set on fire. People were shouting, "Down with the bearskins!"[27] It seemed more

25. Dragoons (*dragons*) were mounted troops.
26. The Tuileries palace was the seat of the French government (see chapter 4, n. 24).
27. The reference is to the tall, furry hats (similar to those worn by the Guards at Buckingham Palace) that distinguished members of the elite companies of the National Guard. One of the reforms instituted in the wake of the February

like a celebration than a revolution. Bourgeois and workers seemed all mixed together, helter-skelter, like brothers. *But from the physical appearance of the bourgeois, you could tell that there was something false in their effusive gestures and that they were experiencing a poorly disguised aversion for their comrades-in-arms.*

By the end of the day, a new cry was being heard, that of "Long live the Republic!"

The next day, 24 February, all Paris was out and about. The agitation that had stirred this immense population to life was impressive to observe. I went off to the Tuileries very early that morning. I had great difficulty getting inside. I was carried by that tide of humanity to the great stairway of the central pavilion. Certain individuals were urging the crowd to throw the furniture from the palace down into the Carrousel courtyard, but a very tall man who appeared to exercise a great deal of influence over the masses shouted that these agitators had to be stopped. "These are agents of the Prefecture of Police," he added. "They're not hard to recognize; there's one." And these individuals would immediately disperse into the crowd.

After visiting the royal suite, I left the palace. In the street, a crowd had gathered around a young man, eighteen to twenty years old, who was about to be shot for having been found carrying a roll of tricolor ribbon and six francs in small change that he had stolen. They had tied a sign to his back on which they had written, "Shot for stealing."

An old man who had a long white beard wanted to stop the execution. "Are you going to let this young man be shot?" he said. "It's not a crime he's committed, but a simple act of childishness." Several onlookers, myself among them, shared this opinion. But the executioners called us accomplices in the theft, adding that we should suffer the same punishment as the thief. The kind old man made further desperate efforts to snatch the victim from his executioners. He shouted with all his strength that such an execution was a crime, a foul deed, an act of barbarism, and that responsibility rested with the law and not the people. All this was in vain. When the deed was done, the executioners dispersed to cries of "Long live the Republic!"

The old man approached the body to note down its description. The face was untouched by the bullets. With this information, he told us, the parents would be able to identify their child.

Those poor workers who had let themselves be drawn into committing

---

Revolution, partly in response to demonstrations like the one that Truquin describes, was the democratization of the National Guard by opening its ranks to all adult males.

this murder on the pretext of respecting property would soon be massacred themselves by the same individuals who had incited them to commit this error. If the people knew history, it would not let itself be duped in this way.

As I made my way home, I saw the throne being carried to the Place de la Bastille to be burned. The city was celebrating, the ranks were all mixed together. Workers chatted fraternally with bourgeois. You could also see the students of the Ecole Polytechnique marching through the streets, surrounded by groups of varying size, consisting in large part of the purest "hooliganocracy."[28] These inexperienced youngsters tried to ape Bonaparte on the Bridge of Arcola.[29] [. . .]

As of 25 February, uneasiness began to take hold among workers who no longer had either work or any prospects of obtaining an advance against their wages. To meet the most pressing needs, the government installed relief committees in each quarter. Vouchers for bread of very inferior quality were distributed to the heads of households, but all that unmarried people could do was to tighten their belts or sell the few belongings that they possessed. Following its victory, the people had to endure all kinds of privations with courage, right up to the time that it was treated with such savagery by its former comrades-in-arms during and after the June Days.[30]

On 26 February, my last sous were exhausted. I tried in vain to find work, but all the factories were closed. Fortunately, that evening I managed

28. The Ecole Polytechnique, a famous military engineering school, was located in the central districts of the capital. Its students had played a prominent role in Parisian insurrections since the Revolution of 1830.

29. The battle of Arcola occurred in 1796 as part of the Italian campaign of the French Army, led by Napoléon, against the Austrian Army. The French army had fought without spirit on the first day of the engagement, but on the second and third days, the rank and file were roused to victory by their commander. He devised the ruse of sending a few trumpeters to the rear of the Austrian Army to sound the charge and convince the enemy that they were being surrounded. At a key juncture, Napoléon personally led the charge that stormed the Bridge of Arcola, carrying a flag in his hand. This victory over an opposing force nearly twice the size of his own army was largely due to Napoléon's personal prowess and command over his men; it has thus come to symbolize the decisive role sometimes played by the military hero.

30. Truquin refers to the insurrection of 23 to 26 June which pitted members of the working class against the army and the Parisian militia. Participants were protesting the policies of France's newly elected Constituent Assembly and specifically the government's decision to disband the National Workshops, the sole source of livelihood available to the many unemployed workers residing in the capital in that time of economic crisis. The June insurrection was repressed after four days of fighting, resulting in heavy casualties on both sides. It led to a political reaction against the social reforms introduced by the Revolution of 1848.

to get hired by some pavers for two francs fifty centimes a day. The streets were in disorder. More than a thousand barricades had been built. I was swollen with joy. At noon, I spent a franc dining with the pavers, but as I had my rent to pay and had no idea how many days I would be employed, I cautiously placed myself on a diet of bread and fried potatoes. This job lasted twelve days. After my rent was paid, I had fifteen francs left, and considered myself as rich as Rothschild. [. . .]

The National Workshops had been organized, and I enrolled.[31] All those who signed up, without distinction, were given eight francs a week. For me this was a great windfall. Instead of having us work, they sent us twice a week to march around in the plain of Saint-Maur. I took advantage of this opportunity to visit the countryside. I used the five other days of the week to loiter in front of bookshops.

My landlady in the Boulevard des Amandiers complained that I came home too late at night. I explained to her that when I found myself at the opposite end of the city, it was impossible for me to get home any earlier. She called me a rascal, and I gave her notice.

I rented a little room in the Rue Saint-Ambroise, also at number eight. It actually was a closet without windows, for which I paid seven francs a month. In this house I became friendly with a young man who had four other brothers, of which he was the oldest. This boy was very small for his age. He often took me to his parents' home. In my friend's earlier years, his father had been an administrative clerk but was, at that moment, reduced to poverty. One day when I was there, Mrs. Lamartine brought presents to this man, who gave her in exchange a list of indigent sick people in the quarter.[32] Mrs. Lamartine, armed with a fat purse that she held in her hand, distributed to each indigent from five to ten francs of aid. She also gave vouchers for clothing and medicine. Another time she came in the

31. The National Workshops originated as a public assistance program designed to alleviate the misery caused by the massive wave of unemployment that intensified in the capital in the wake of the February Revolution. Workers unable to find a job could enroll and draw an initial daily compensation of one franc fifty centimes, approximately as much as the wage earned in normal times by an unskilled laborer. But whereas the new government anticipated a peak enrollment of 10,000 workers, by May more than ten times that number had signed on. The administration of the National Workshops had no useful way to occupy such vast numbers of unemployed, and the institution soon developed into an enormous make-work program. The expense and potential political volatility of such an assembly of workers generated increasing political opposition. It was the announcement on 22 June that the government intended to disband the National Workshops that precipitated the June insurrection.

32. Truquin refers to the wife of Alphonse de Lamartine, the celebrated poet and author who was a minister in the provisional government that ruled France immediately after the February Revolution.

company of another woman who was said to be Mrs. Marie and who was making the charity rounds with her.[33] The same operation was repeated in all the needy quarters. This policy earned great popularity for Lamartine and Marie. *It was worth hundreds of thousands of votes in the elections.*

The worker is kind and grateful to the point of stupidity. To give thanks for some kindness, he will sacrifice his freedom. When, after the fighting of the June Days, the victorious reaction tore fathers away from their children, these families found themselves in a situation that was far more lamentable, yet Mrs. Lamartine and Mrs. Marie did not reappear in their garrets.[34]

[Truquin goes on to recount his experience of the June Days of 1848, which ended in the declaration of martial law and the bloody repression of the insurgent workers. In the aftermath of the fighting, many rebels were arrested and sent into exile.]

Until 23 June, my heart had been cheerful. I would gladly stroll through the various quarters of the city and would go to the Little Lazari whenever I had three sous in my pocket. But since the shootings and the deportations had taken place, I never thought about those things. I would ask myself how men could be so barbarous as to treat their fellow creatures with such cruelty. My only thought was to run off to a desert or some island and live far away from those who pretended to be civilized but had hearts blacker than the feathers of a raven.

Work had started up at the factory again. They were setting up some new combing machines, and the foreman had promised to assign one to me at a salary of three francs fifty centimes per day. But all that could not make me abandon my plans to emigrate.

[There follows a long chapter that details Truquin's reunion with his father and his first trip abroad, in his father's company, as a colonial settler in Algeria. It includes a lengthy yarn that he made up, memorized, and would tell to acquaintances. Because he was illiterate, this oral form of communication was the only means available to him for conveying the new system of social organization he had devised. Seven years later, discouraged at his inability to wring a decent living from the soil, Truquin resolved to return to France, having recently turned twenty-one.]

33. This would be the wife of Pierre Marie, who was Minister of Public Works in the provisional government and was responsible for the administration of the National Workshops in Paris.
34. Truquin refers to the families of men sent into exile for having participated in the unsuccessful June insurrection.

VIII. MY RETURN TO FRANCE; MARSEILLE

Disgusted with farming and with Algeria, I decided to return to France to learn a trade. To scrape together enough money for the journey, I took a job in the salt works. [. . .]

After two months of this back-breaking work, I embarked for France. The steamship took us first to Algiers, where I stayed a week visiting the city and its environs. The region of Algiers is more fertile than the area around Oran, and food was very cheap there at that time.

I then took a second steamship which, after a calm crossing, landed us at Marseille toward the end of August 1855. My first concern upon arrival was to check my purse, which contained seventy francs. I was itching with the desire to visit Toulon, but, seeing the state of my finances, I resisted the temptation. [. . .]

I met a very old man who walked all bent over, supporting himself with a cane. When I asked him the way to Aigues-Mortes, he asked me questions and we got to know one another. I told him about my situation. He invited me to eat at his house, and he did everything he could to be kind to me. After having made me describe in detail the February Revolution and the June Insurrection, the memory of which was still fresh in my mind, he told me his story. During the Revolution of 1789, he had taken part in the march of the Marseillais and had been wounded in Paris, where his injury kept him for some time.[35] A partisan of Marat and Robespierre, he felt that the latter would have better served the Revolution if he had been older. *"The lifetime of a man is not enough to resolve all questions.* Robespierre's ideas had not had time to ripen, and he upheld them with the ardor of youth, without having studied them in enough depth."

"Marat," he would say, "was the most accomplished revolutionary of that era. He fought his adversaries openly, and it was this openness that destroyed him. Those who are rich have an interest in sacrificing part of their wealth to get the people to commit crimes that will bring disgrace upon their cause. The king's treasury paid the bribes responsible for many a scene of disorder. So you don't know history?" he interrupted himself to ask me.

"Why, no," I answered, "I don't know how to read." When he heard those words, he let his arms fall and exclaimed, "Oh! That's a pity!"

35. Truquin's host was one of the provincial volunteers from the region of Marseille who had marched to the capital in support of the revolution and taken a prominent role in the storming of the Tuileries in August 1792, an event which helped bring down the French monarchy. The patriotic tune that these volunteers adopted as their marching song later became the French national anthem, *La Marseillaise.*

Next we talked about the current situation. *The February Revolution, in his opinion, had been concocted by the Jesuits in alliance with the Bonapartists.* "It's a giant step backward for France. The peasants have become Bonapartists. All they think about is their own self-interest; all they hope for is one day to be stockholders. No one cares about politics any more. A veritable reign of terror has taken hold of the country since 2 December."[36] [. . .]

When I arrived in Lyon, I had six francs left. After buying a ticket to the Grand Opera, all I had was one franc twenty-five centimes. It was therefore impossible for me to continue on my way to Paris.

IX. SUCCESSIVE JOBS AS WELL DIGGER, NAVVY, AND WEAVER

While taking a tour of the lawcourts, I recognized an artilleryman who had served with me in Algeria. He had gotten married eighteen months before. He was delighted to run into me, and took me home with him. He was a journeyman weaver. The next day I went with him to visit the Grand Camp parade ground. We went to have a snack in a *cabaret* whose owner was a former soldier and quite an engaging fellow. He knew a well digger who happened to pass by just as we were talking about him. When I assured him that I had dug a well at my father's place and that I had experience with explosives, he hired me, starting the next morning.

So there I was, a well digger. A few days later, my boss told me that this trade did not suit me. "Almost all well diggers," he told me, "are fools and drunkards. It's the job that does it. I have a brother who is president of the butchers' association and very well respected in the city. He'll find you a job." I then had to confess to him that I did not know how to read or write. "What?" he said. "A young man like yourself! How is that possible?"

"There are circumstances," I replied, "in which it is not easy to learn." [. . .]

The wells that I dug were as much as one hundred thirty feet deep. By the time this job was completed, it was the end of November and there was little hope of finding another before the following spring. Just as I was about to resume my journey to Paris, I ran across my artilleryman, who began telling me about his wife's illness and ended up borrowing twenty-five francs that I never saw again. All I had left was ten francs.

36. On 2 December 1851, Louis-Napoléon, nephew of Napoléon Bonaparte, overthrew the constitution under which he had been elected president of France in 1848, and declared himself emperor. Armed resistance to this coup d'état broke out in many parts of France but was quickly repressed. The early years of the Second Empire saw the institution of an authoritarian regime which imposed rigid controls on political activities.

I then found work on the railroad tunnel at Loyasse at a wage of three francs a day. We worked in shifts from six in the evening to midnight, and from six to eleven o'clock in the morning. Beneath this vault, the water seeped through the rock and penetrated us to the bone. I made the mistake of buying huge, covered wooden shoes into which I inserted fur-lined slippers. I was not used to this footwear which, despite the winter cold, made my feet sweat. In the evening, I would return, completely soaked, to a navvies' boarding house located two kilometers from the tunnel on the Saint-Just plateau. And what a boarding house! A freezing room in which there was never a fire, it was furnished with twelve beds, each consisting of a straw mattress and sheets made of coarse fabric that were washed just twice a year. I had to go to bed soaking wet, in this mean and foul-smelling litter, alongside a bedmate who was just as drenched as I. He was also in the habit of drinking a shot before going to bed and thus gave off a strong odor of spirits and tobacco, which I found suffocating. But what was most revolting of all was to feel at my side the contact of another man. This was the first time that I had had a bedmate. In Algeria I had long slept on the ground, it is true, but at least I slept alone. In France, the climate does not permit this.

Given the kind of life I was leading, I inevitably ended up falling sick. I came down with pneumonia at the end of January but kept on working all the same, in the damp, which was hardly the way to get better. Soon I was forced to stay in bed for four days. From time to time someone would bring me a bowl of broth, which turned my stomach. I was consumed by a fever that only got worse in that icy room. I was no longer aware of my condition. I got up and went out on a walk that took me through the city. I arrived at the stone bridge over the Saône River. The desire to throw myself into the water overcame me. The bridge was covered with ice. I was wearing my wooden shoes and I slipped so violently that I hit my head on the pavement. The blow caused me to bleed heavily, which made me faint. I was carried by some passersby into a *cabaret* where they made me drink warm wine, which revived me.

In these earthwork enterprises, they withhold three and a half centimes per day from each worker's pay to cover the cost of medicines when he is sick. But navvies are rarely sick. Their illnesses amount to the occasional pain in the side and pneumonia; and when they are taken to the hospital *they usually leave only to go to the cemetery.*

The workers rarely get the benefit of this insurance, while the entrepreneurs almost all make a fortune. On these jobs, the personnel on the work site is constantly turned over, and when the workers' strength begins to fail, they are fired for being too weak or for no reason at all. The three and a half centimes then remain the property of the management. [. . .]

I did not want to continue working in these unhealthy underground haunts any longer. Once my pneumonia was cured, I went to offer my services to the well digger. That work also has its dangers, but you are not in water until you arrive at the bottom of the well. This subcontractor had no jobs coming up before the month of March. "You're still weak," he told me. "You'd do better to learn another trade. During the winter, well diggers are very miserable. They are almost always unemployed. I know a weaver who could take you on at his place, if you want me to take you there." I consented and he took me to his friend's, where we agreed that I would serve a three-year apprenticeship.

I started out in velvet weaving. I quickly became adept, but seven or eight months later, work ceased completely. My master and his wife, who were about fifty-five years old, had begun to see too poorly to work in the silk trade, and they were very badly off.[37] The baker who supplied them with bread on credit came to demand his overdue payments, and the landlord his back rent, but there was neither money nor work in the household, except for me, for I was still doing a few odd jobs. The poor man, tormented by his creditors, told me that he could no longer feed me and that he would have to work my loom, which was the only one he had left.

This was in the month of October 1857. He issued me a certificate to help me make a living elsewhere, telling me that I could return to his place once work started up again.

The city had started a few relief projects. They were laying out a park called La Tête-d'Or, and I got taken on. Their plan called for draining a large swamp in order to transform it into a park. There is no one clumsier at doing earthwork than a silk worker. More than three thousand of them were employed on this job, and already more than five hundred had had to go to the hospital. Most of these unfortunates had hurt themselves or gotten hernias while slipping on the mud-covered ground. They were paid one franc a day and barely managed to earn this meager wage. Professional navvies could have earned three francs. Every evening I would bring half of my day's wage to my master. I worked on this project for three weeks, after which I found work with a metalworker, who had me turn the wheel and "strike from in front" for two francs and twenty-five centimes a day.[38] This

37. Lyon was the center of the silk-weaving trade in Europe. The more skillful silk weavers managed to earn a decent living, but the rate of pay in other branches of the trade was less attractive.
38. Apparently Truquin was employed to turn either a lathe or a sharpening device by hand and to provide assistance striking red-hot metal objects on the metalworker's anvil.

was a little more than at the Tête-d'Or work site, but it was far from sufficient. The cost of living was very high that year, and so I had to ration myself.

In the month of March, I returned to the well digger's. He gave me work paid at three francs a day. With this sum I could meet my needs. At the end of nine months, I became foreman and was sent to Oullins, to the home of a landowner, to negotiate the construction of an underground gallery. I knew this bourgeois. He had them serve me dinner in the kitchen, where he sent a bottle of old wine for me to drink before going off to dine in his own quarters. It was then the month of September. The bourgeois took his meal in the company of his family under an arbor of greenery. There were ten people at the table. From the kitchen where I sat, I could see everything that was served at their table. After the meal, we agreed upon the work to be carried out, and the gallery was begun.

This bourgeois was a philanthropist who enjoyed the company of workers and liked to chat with them. Among us there was a former soldier who had completed three tours of duty in Algeria. He was an old joker who knew how to laugh with one eye and cry with the other. He was shrewd enough to wheedle a few old clothes out of the owner. These consisted of a few pants and overcoats that he immediately turned around and sold. He always knew how to win people over. He was blessed with Herculean strength, which earned him the respect of the boss. But he worked three months of the year at the very most. This time as well, he had shown up only to take advantage of the owner.

One day, the owner expressed amazement that the navvies were so badly dressed. "It's because of their occupation," I told him.

"I'm well aware," he replied, "that they can't wear fancy clothes while they work, but they should at least have some clean clothes for Sundays."

"Well," I told him, "let me acquaint you with our budget and you can judge for yourself. When there's work to be had, we earn three francs a day, Sundays and holidays excepted. In wintertime, work is scarce. When we finish a job, we often have to wait several days to find a new one. And when we change work sites, we have to carry our tools on our shoulders or in a wheelbarrow, though we don't get paid for that work.

"When the worker starts to lose his strength, no one wants to hire him any more. If he should get hired, it's only for as long as it takes to find someone stronger. That's how it is that the worker who brought water to your ornamental ponds and made your fountains spurt is reduced to begging, condemned as a vagabond, and sent to the poorhouse."

"And yet, if they really wanted to . . . !" he interrupted, without finishing his sentence.

"But they don't really want to!" I told him. He then glanced at me in a way that was half troubled and half scoffing.

During our conversation, he had had a bottle of old wine and some crackers brought out. I would eat one from time to time, and I felt at ease in his company. "Allow me," I said, "to make an observation. The day when you invited me to dinner, there were ten of you at the table. Well, if forty well diggers had that meal to share, they would think they had been sent to heaven. And yet . . . and yet . . . " I repeated, imitating his interruption of a moment ago.

"You're quite the sly one, aren't you?" he said.

We worked at his place for three months. He would often come and invite me to have a glass of wine and a chat, but I never spoke to him about having public affairs run by veteran workers, for I would surely have had a falling out with him.[39] Of his two sons, one was destined for the bar, the other for medicine.

Once again I left the trade of well digger to resume that of weaver. I had some difficulty in getting myself hired, because my clothes and my general appearance made me look like a navvy. At last I managed to find a job. Though it involved making a kind of article I was completely unfamiliar with, I nonetheless succeeded with it right from the very start.

This workshop specialized in novelties, and this required that I constantly switch from one article to another. As a result, I had become fairly skilled by the end of a year. This workshop was located in the Rue Sainte-Catherine, in the Croix-Rousse district, on the fourth floor. It was six meters long and was mainly occupied by young women weaving satin. In summer, these young working girls would be at it from three-thirty in the morning until sundown. In winter, their day ran from five in the morning until eleven at night.

I asked my boss, with whom I had become friendly, why these young women had such yellow complexions and such tired faces. *He confessed that nearly all of those who left that shop were on their way to the cemetery.* When I insisted, he willingly explained further. "In all Lyon," he told me, "there are perhaps seven thousand workshops like this one. Almost all their owners are zealous churchgoers. They go to regions like Dauphiné, Bugey, and Savoy to recruit their apprentices, carrying certificates issued by their own parish priests. Armed with these documents, they approach the rural priests, who indicate the houses from which they can make a

---

39. Truquin is referring to his personal plan for social reorganization as outlined in the fable recounted in a previous chapter of his memoirs, not included in these excerpts.

choice. Assisted by a recommendation from the priest, they gain access and are naturally well received. They come laden with pocket watches and a whole supply of trinkets, not forgetting to stuff their pockets with big, fat coins. As they chat, they are careful to let a little of the scrap metal they have laid in stock fall to the ground, as if by accident. The children rush to pick it up to return it to these gentlemen who, in their generosity, give it to their helpers. They claim that their working girls have put hundreds of francs in the savings bank and that, if certain of them did not indulge in luxuries, they could save a good deal more. The rumors spread throughout the commune and soon a swarm of young girls sign up for Lyon. *They agree to an apprenticeship of four years, though four months would be sufficient to learn how to make satin or taffeta.*

"They almost always hire girls about fifteen years old. For the first six months, all they have them do is housework and winding the spools on shuttles. On Sunday mornings, the girls are taken to six o'clock mass, then returned to the workshop for the rest of the day, because they might otherwise meet someone and get married, which wouldn't serve the boss's interests. He uses every means at his disposal to keep them for a long time and to extract from them the greatest possible profit. Because they work *seventeen hours a day,* often in unhealthy workshops where the beneficial rays of the sun never enter, half these young women become consumptive before their apprenticeship is completed. When they complain, they are accused of putting on airs. The boss urges them to work harder by always flattering the most skillful. Finally, when they are no longer able to work, they are told that they have perhaps committed indiscretions. Those whose relatives live in the countryside are sent home to their families to recover, but it's often too late. The boss's greed has kept them from getting care too long. As for those who have no relatives or who are too poor, they're sent to the hospital. *They rarely leave there alive* or, if they do escape, they're likely to be sick for the rest of their lives. Their bedroom is generally a dirty garret that's infested with vermin, into which dust from the looms continually rises. All kinds of chemical ingredients are used to make the silk more glossy: mercury, arsenic, and even mercury chloride. These young women breathe these unhealthy fumes night and day, and that's what makes them lose their color and develop consumption.

"As his reward for all these crimes, the boss sometimes manages to scrape together ten or twelve thousand francs. Of seven or eight thousand bosses, five hundred at the very most may achieve this result, and the ones who obtain this minor affluence rarely live to a ripe old age, for they have also worked too much and breathed the lethal fumes."

When I asked why doctors, who know what goes on in the hospitals, have not tried to combat more effectively the spread of this evil, my employer did not know how to respond. "How can it be," I asked myself, "that the appointed guardians of public health are not addressing indignant reports to the administration? These young working women are not dying of natural causes; *they are the victims of premeditated murder!*" I did not dare believe that the doctors were taking their lead from the bosses, content to make a small profit by caring for these young women! On reflection, I understood that medicine was their livelihood and that, to bring in a good income and maintain their families in affluence, they had to turn a blind eye to these horrors so as not to harm their own interests.

These are the ideas I had been putting forth to my employer for over a quarter of an hour before I realized that he had fallen asleep. I was annoyed, and all the more so because I believed that what I had been saying was worth listening to. He woke up yawning like someone who has just been bored to death.

In Lyon, among weavers, there are two sorts of workers. Those who make plain, solid-colored material are generally bigots, but so as not to expose themselves to too much ridicule, they call themselves *conservative republicans*. Those who weave fancy novelty goods are more likely to be *progressive republicans*. There is a very definite hierarchy among them. Those who own two or three looms are considered to be ordinary employers. Those who have four or more constitute the aristocracy of the trade. They have their own separate cafés where they gather and hold their assemblies. Their wives are incredibly arrogant and are careful not to say hello to the wife of a man who owns only two looms.

An analogous hierarchy exists among the workers employed by these small-time workshop owners. In all the vast number of workers who swarm through the streets of Lyon, there can hardly be twelve to fifteen hundred who earn enough to be properly dressed. These are the ones who carry a cane and wear high hats. They sometimes even wear a monocle. But since it is rare for the novelty-goods sector to go more than eighteen months without a wave of unemployment, during every slack season they are forced to take their fancy clothes to the pawn shop, usually never to see them again. Still, once the employment situation improves, they start all over again.

The workshop owner must provide the shop itself, heating, and the various tools necessary for making silk goods. The manufacturer furnishes the warp already set up on the frame and the woof in skeins. The workshop owner returns the finished material. All the worker needs to supply is his productive labor and to share the wage it earns him with his employer.

The year 1859 was coming to a close, and work ground to a complete halt. Fortunately, I was not entirely without resources. Of the forty francs of savings that I possessed, I gave fourteen to my landlord and four to my laundrywoman. Because it was cold out, I bought a heating stove for six francs, a hundred kilos of coal for the same price, and one franc's worth of oil. I then had nine francs left, and I lived on that for six weeks. My food consisted of bread, cooked in water, with garlic.

At last, at the end of six weeks, I found work with someone who taught the theory of silk manufacture. On Thursday of the week when I started working again, I found myself absolutely without a cent. I would not be paid until Saturday. Fortunately, a fifty-centime coin that I found in the stairway of my rooming house allowed me to make do.

Three months after I was hired by this enterprise, the instructor assigned me a sample-making loom located in a room next to the one in which he gave his classes. He would come visit me several times a day, either to examine the designs or to take a rest from his lessons. On my side, I had a lot of free time. Once a sample had been prepared, I had to wait for orders from the manufacturers before getting back to work. I sometimes had to waste the entire day.

One day, the boss came and told me, "Today is the anniversary of the battle of Leipzig.[40] It was lost because Napoléon the First had caught such a violent head cold that he was nearly delirious." From then on, my employer became my history instructor and, every time he came to see me, he would teach me a little bit.

I had been working there for a year when an unemployment crisis occurred, depriving the shop's employees of work. I was practically the only one who was not laid off. I mentioned this to the instructor. "The situation is bad for the workers of Lyon," I told him. "We have a slack season about every eighteen months. It must be due to some selfish design on the part of the manufacturers."

"When the economy's flat," he answered, "the manufacturers are more to be pitied than the workers. Their honor is at stake. They have a fancy lifestyle to maintain. They have to see to their sons' education. They have to think about their daughters' dowries. The workers don't have these worries."

"You don't know the working class very well," I told him. "You can't imagine the worry and melancholy a worker with a family goes through

40. Leipzig, a city in east-central Germany, was the site of "The Battle of the Nations." There, in October 1813, Napoleon won an early victory over a numerically superior force of Austrians, Russians, and Prussians, but was eventually forced to retreat to the Rhine River, thus completing the liberation of Germany from French occupation.

when he is without a job and without money! And what about the poor mother who has no bread to give to her children when they're begging for more, no clean clothes for them to change into, and no soap to wash their miserable rags? Don't you think the proletarian has to worry about the landlord's agent, who is sure to come claim the quarterly rent and who has the right to seize all the household belongings? And how is this proletarian to pay for housing if he hasn't a cent, or find a new place to live if he doesn't have a receipt to show that he left the old one on good terms?"

"Workers are less sensitive," he replied. "Their wives suffer less from lying on a slag heap than a lady is troubled by a feather that moves out of place in her bed. And anyway, manufacturers are not responsible for unemployment."

"Why, then, do they go and set up factories in the countryside wherever they can find cheap labor?"

"Competition forces them to."

"How is it that the English manage to pay their journeymen as much as we pay our masters? Most manufacturers who install huge factories in the countryside are former salesmen who got rich by starting their own companies or by entering into partnerships. These factories cost them millions, so it's not competition that forces them to set them up but just a desire for more profit, which plunges city workers and country workers alike into poverty."

"What! You say it keeps country workers in poverty, but my experience, on the contrary, is that it does them a great service by providing them with a way to earn money!"

"You're wrong. You have to know the countryside before you can discuss it intelligently. It's true that this new industry dispenses a certain amount of money in rural areas, but the young folks of both sexes who go to work in the factory lose their taste for farming. The result is that the father and mother are the only ones left to tend the fields, and they're unable to improve their property. When unemployment hits, instead of producing foodstuffs for their family, they're forced to buy them. When the children go back home, the father's forced to sell off a corner of his lands to buy wheat, and the family, which had previously done so well, begins to break up little by little. That's the benefit the rural areas get from factories. While it's true that wages bring in a certain amount of money, the other side is that all the labor power that abandons farming represents a loss for general production. Just as you say, that's what drives trade. We go and buy wheat on foreign markets, and sell them our silk goods in exchange. *But while this trade builds the fortunes of a few, it also brings ruin to France as a whole.*"

My boss had nothing to reply. At that time, he had thirty-four students studying theory. I do not know whether they overheard our discussion or whether the instructor reported it to them. Until then, they would come to the room where I worked to look at samples without getting involved in things that were none of their business. But after this discussion, one of them came to pick a fight, telling me that if the workers were so badly off, it was their own fault, for they were mostly drunkards who would celebrate Holy Monday and even Holy Tuesday and would go get drunk in *cabarets* where they paid much too much attention to politics and liberty.[41] "If we were governed by those folks, things would really be a mess." Several of his fellow students who came in at that point agreed with what he was saying.

"There are, no doubt, some workers like that, but they're the tiniest minority."

"More like the majority."

"How could the majority lead such disorderly lives when they earn such low wages?"

"They're not so much to be pitied. There are some who earn four francs a day."

"Well now! Your calculations are off. Almost all of you have been shop clerks. Check your books and you'll see that on average they earn perhaps less than one franc fifty centimes a day. Then tell me what conduct you expect from workers?"

"They might be more polite and not spend so much time in the *cabarets*."

"Gentlemen, workers can't do without their outings to the *cabaret*. Take me for example. I live on the eighth floor in a room that has a single dormer window for light. It's freezing in winter, and in the summer it bakes. What would you do if you were in my place?"

"Oh! We weren't talking about you."

"Yes, but all workers are housed in more or less the same way, whether they live in cellars or in garrets."

"They could read, they could educate themselves."

"There are some who don't know how to read, and I'm one of them. And anyway, if the worker remains cooped up in his room, how will he manage to find work and see to the matters that concern him?"

"Oh! Politics is none of the workers' business."

"Let's leave politics aside. A man can't live his life shut up in his room.

41. To celebrate Holy Monday was to stay home from work after spending Sunday drinking and carousing.

The worker has to find distractions, interact with his fellow workers, drink his bottle and sing his songs."

"Yes, and if the government hadn't straightened things out, all those drunkards would do would be to bawl about the administration and religion."

Nearly every evening, these young men would come engage me in discussions, but never in a friendly way. [. . .]

X. I START A FAMILY

I met my wife at the home of a friend I had known in Africa. She was a weaver like myself. There are two categories of female silk workers: those who are given housing by their employers and those who live on their own. The former are considered more respectable. I was given approval, as custom required, to court my fiancée. Her employer was a jobber who had saved up a little nest egg with the help of seven or eight working women.[42] His wife was a good housekeeper. He was not a very hard worker, but he was clever and admitted that it was not work that paid the best return. With his wife's dowry of six thousand francs, he had continually played the stock market with success.[43] [. . .]

My express intention was for my marriage to be a civil ceremony. I had so informed the fellow workers who were supposed to serve as my witnesses, but I had to struggle against their objections. They argued that I should overcome my personal distaste for religion so as not to offend the relatives and friends of my fiancée. They were unanimous in portraying a civil ceremony as a poor way to start off married life. In short, they indoctrinated me so well that, instead of doing as I wanted, I gave in to their entreaties. This did not prevent my fellow workers from being very revolutionary, but only up to the point where it came to taking action.

I had moved into a small place that could hold two looms. I owned a typical bachelor's selection of home furnishings, plus about fifty francs. My wife, on her side, had two hundred francs in a savings account. I paid

42. In the silk-weaving trade, the jobber (*chef d'atelier*) served as middleman for other weavers as well as himself. Usually a male head of household, the jobber subcontracted with a manufacturer for the completion of a "lot" or agreed-upon quantity of work. He would then organize other workers—typically other family members, along with an occasional hired hand—to assist him in carrying out the work, usually at home.

43. The Paris stock exchange had been in operation since the early eighteenth century; by the year 1869, some 380 issues were listed. During the second half of the nineteenth century, public awareness of the stock exchange became more widespread, but it would still have been exceptional for a Lyon jobber, even one with several thousand francs of capital, to engage regularly in market transactions.

six hundred francs for all the equipment necessary to set up my two looms, but I put just two hundred francs down and took out four notes, payable at intervals of three months, for the remainder.

Two months after our marriage, the economy ground to a halt. We went six months without finding work. When the first note came due, I did not have a cent to pay it off. Three months later, I had two notes to pay, plus one hundred francs of quarterly rent. We were still without work. Fortunately, the baker supplied us with bread on the cuff, and the grocer also gave us credit. For our first six months of honeymoon, we practically lived on boiled potatoes. My wife would buy a quarter liter of wine for dinner. I tried to put an end to this wine ration, but my wife held firm, alleging that without this drop of wine, we would completely lose our strength for when work started back up.

It did indeed start back up, but mainly in novelty materials that used fancy designs. I needed to spend one hundred francs to set my loom up for making such goods. I managed to get a tool merchant, who was a specialist in that branch of the trade, to extend me credit for this sum. I was assigned to weave a piece of cloth fifty meters long, for which I was supposed to be paid one franc fifty centimes per meter. It was the manufacturer's prerogative to write on our order books: *expenses not guaranteed.* That way, if the manufacturer ordered just a single piece, then after having obliged us to spend a hundred francs to set it up, not counting the loss of several days devoted to this work, he did not have to pay the jobber any compensation for these costs. Furthermore, the jobber had no right to present a claim before the conciliation board. If he maintained that he had not been consulted before the notation "expenses not guaranteed" was written in, he would be told that all he had to do was to insist on the removal of those conditions that seemed against his interests.

That was the situation in which I found myself. Had I made a claim, the manufacturer would have cut off my supplies, and I would have found myself in the most abject poverty. That is why the worker remains silent. As a result, these manufacturers make colossal fortunes in a few years. Their arrogance is extreme. *They say you have to have as firm a hand as Napoléon's to rein in the workers,* yet most of them are nothing more than upstarts themselves. But it's well known what men become as soon as they think they have some privilege to protect.

My wife had also found work, and so we both were working night and day so we could pay off our creditors. I turned in my piece in the hope of promptly being given another. After a few days' wait, I was assigned another hundred meters, but as the woof was not ready, I had to wait, from one day to the next, for a week. When I got hold of it, I took it to a woman who did winding, and she gave me back the wound silk the next day.[44] I had to lose another day going to get the pattern, carrying it back on my shoulders, and getting it set up and running. Sometimes, when the pattern is new, there are corrections to be made; and if it is old, there are cards to be repaired.[45] All that is just so much time lost. Other times, the woof is so bad that the silk winder refuses to take it, and you have to go and find another. From this you can appreciate the hell into which the worker is plunged, especially when his creditors can say, "But you have a job. If you're not paying me back, it's a sign of bad faith."

When the third note came due, I gave a little money to each of my creditors, but none of them was satisfied. "I can't give you more," I told my landlord. "Yet we're saving every way we can. My wife is about to have a child and we don't have a cent."

The vulture then turned to my wife and told her: "Madame, when one is so poor, one either doesn't get married or else goes to the hospital. Myself, I had two wives, and they both went to the hospital to give birth."

My wife could not hold back her indignation and replied: "*If you weren't such a miserable wretch, you wouldn't have needlessly sent them to the hospital. That's why they're dead, and you'll die there too, in misery.*" This prediction did in fact come to pass a few years later.

The landlord withdrew, furious. He soon returned with a mason whom he told to remove the doors and brickwork. So my wife was forced to have our child at the hospital. But we were unable either to feed the child or to pay the monthly fees of a wet nurse, so I decided to go ask the manufacturer for money.

The cashier, who was a decent sort, informed one of the partners that I was asking for an advance of fifty francs. The partner replied that the company did not give advances and turned his back on me. But I was in a state of excitation brought on by my financial distress. I marched alongside him in lockstep and set about following him wherever he went. I was so provoked that, if he had asked me why I was following him, I would have punched him in the face. He probably understood that my intentions were hardly peaceful, for, after a few trips from room to room, he returned to his office and, without a word, saw that I was handed the fifty francs I had asked for.

44. A silk winder or rewinder (*dévideuse*) would unravel skeins, or sometimes the silk cocoons themselves, making the strands into bobbins that could be inserted into shuttles and used in the weaving process.
45. The cards (*cartons*) are the perforated cardboard rectangles which, on the Jacquard hand loom, determine which strands of the warp are to be raised in sequence in order to produce a specific woven design.

He did not hold a grudge for what I had done, and I worked for his company for some time after that. He would probably have made me pay dearly for the punch that I was thinking of giving him, for he had no obligation to give me an advance or to get involved in the details of my unfortunate situation. There were thousands of workers like me in Lyon. Yet the critical situation of journeyman weavers was the result of some kind of business scheme. As I have already said, it is speculation that causes factories to be set up in every rural area where there are poor devils to exploit.

There is no one more timid than the pauper, who trembles when the rent falls due, who is afraid of seeing the landlord's agent and the process servers appear, and of having his belongings sold at auction on his front doorstep.

Speculation in housing has grown pitiless in the nineteenth century. The landlord no longer wants to have any contact with his tenant, for often he cannot hold out against the latter's entreaties. He is then obliged to make concessions and wait for his money. Sometimes he loses the overdue rent as a result of the bad faith or the extreme poverty of his debtors. There are even some who would rather renounce what is owed them than sue a tenant.

To avoid all these difficulties, landlords have turned to using agents. These agents, always recruited from the working class and affiliated with businessmen, are mostly shameless people who are ready to do whatever it takes.

This system is essentially destructive of the family, but what does that matter to speculators? All they care about is that their business prosper. The government has served their interests rather well. It has frequently taken loans that brought these people enormous profits, while at the same time making it harder for workers to feed themselves, by levying indirect taxes.

All these reflections caused me great irritation. I had gotten married in order to raise a family and I told myself that if I had sacrificed myself by delivering that punch, my wife and children would have lost nothing, since I was unable to feed them anyway. Perhaps on the witness stand I would have been able to explain the circumstances that had pushed me to this act of violence. Vain illusion! *For don't the judges also belong to the caste that exploits us?* They would have condemned me, like so many others, as a common criminal, and I would have been dishonored and smeared with mud by the overblown rhetoric of some plodding lawyer!

Moreover, it could not be otherwise. Those folks are well paid and well housed. When they come to sit at court, their stomachs are full of delicious meat and they are slightly overstimulated with good wine. Given these circumstances, they inevitably act harshly toward the poor.

If judges are to represent true justice, they must be treated like soldiers. Given them their morning ration of coffee that's been made with grounds already used three or four times. Bring them their bowl of broth right there in court, just as it is brought to the guardhouse. This would, moreover, mark a return to the principles of true justice, for the defenders of the country are worth every bit as much as the defenders of the law, and both should be treated on an equal footing.

My landlord, after having my door and an interior wall demolished, had me called before the justice of the peace and had me sign promissory notes for the back rent. Despite the embarrassment that this eviction caused us at the time, he nonetheless rendered us a great service. Our lodging was in a courtyard, facing north, and was never heated by the rays of the sun. We had both fallen ill and would have worked ourselves to death if the landlord had not forced us to vacate the premises.

I was having considerable difficulty finding a new place to live, since I could not provide a deposit, until a friend who came to see me loaned me twenty francs, making it possible for me to rent a pretty place in the Rue des Chartreux opposite Saint Joseph's Convent. [. . .]

After a stay of a few years in the Rue des Chartreux, we went to live on the fifth floor of a house in the Rue Lebrun, where we enjoyed a view of the Rhone River. What made me decide to move is that my children had begun to grow up, and the Rez Park, where they could play, was right in front of our new house. Nothing is sadder than the life that the children of weavers lead in those vast barracks that are sometimes seven stories high. They cannot play, for their movement might break a thread or upset the weaver.

Workers in the luxury trades are slaves from the moment they are born. They go right from school to the workshop and then remain shut up inside until they die. It would be better if they were never born or if the luxury items they make did not exist. But let us continue the enumeration of the joys shared by these pariahs.

I worked for the Schulz firm, which was the biggest manufacturer of novelty items in Lyon and perhaps in all Europe. Schulz was a Prussian. For his company I made articles of rare beauty that were destined for the court of Austria, but for which I was paid low wages. Some of these dresses were fourteen meters long.

As I was working on an item on approval, I was obliged to prepare a bunch of samples that I carried to the store. I would wait for the response, and the designs and colors would then be changed, one after another. I have on occasion had to use up to thirty colors to make up a single sample.

When I asked the first assistant why I was only being given dresses fourteen meters long, he calmed me down by telling me that, judging by the samples that had been sent to the broker in Paris, they expected substantial orders. For an entire winter, I therefore prepared samples three meters long in the hopes of a big order. In the end, I asked for compensation for all these samples. The first assistant appeared to be completely surprised and said: "But you've already been paid!"

"I've been paid for the fourteen-meter dresses, sure, but that doesn't take into account the samples of from ten to fifty centimeters that I've made up!"

"Well then, we'll pay you for these samples at double the usual rate."

"What! At double the usual rate! I made a number of samples just ten centimeters long, and for that work alone it took me three days to prepare the patterns and to wait for the colors. At double the usual rate, I'll be paid three francs fifty centimes a meter for the article. By that accounting, I'll have earned twelve centimes a day."

"I didn't think you were so clever," he replied. "How much do you think we owe you?"

"I should be paid for these samples at five francs a day."

"Where would we be," he cried, "if we had to pay for samples at that rate? For a start, you should have told me this as soon as you were given the first samples."

"You didn't warn me that you would keep me busy making samples the whole winter. You go about it very shrewdly. First you ask for a sample ten centimeters long, then twenty, then fifty, and the weeks go by without any other work."

"You should have told me all this when you did the first samples!"

"If I didn't, it's because I trusted your company. When one is dealing with an honest merchant, one knows that he's going to pay you."

"Yes, but you're demanding five francs a day, and that's exorbitant. You make up a sample, but then it's two or three days before you prepare another. You're not always busy!"

"My loom is always busy, since your job is sitting on it, and we can't do anything while we're waiting for your orders."

This malicious employee offered me one hundred twenty-five francs in compensation for work that was worth one thousand five hundred at a rate of five francs a day for each loom.

"You'd better think over what you're doing," he told me. "You have three of the company's looms. Think it over carefully and come back tomorrow. If I were you, I'd sleep on it."

It is true that I should have laid down my conditions from the beginning and that I would not have won my case if I had taken the owner before the conciliation board. So I accepted the one hundred twenty-five francs I had been offered. But just to punish me for having dared to make these demands, *he took away my three looms.*

I had nothing to lose in leaving this company, which had plunged me and many other jobbers into poverty. The rumor making the rounds in Lyon was that after having workers from Lyon prepare samples for nothing, this merchant was sending the orders to other factories that he owned in Prussia.

It was now 1867. Poverty was spreading its ravages over Lyon. The commercial class, supported by the courts and by the military, had everything its own way and took every advantage of that fact. When the shawl workers tried to organize a strike, they were severely punished. Some of them were sentenced to five years in prison.

The government understood the gravity of the situation and gave the workers a somewhat freer rein by authorizing assemblies. Several were held in the Rotunda, and each category of silk workers demanded an increase in pay. Many merchants understood the need for this raise, but most of them opposed it.

The weavers designated eleven delegates for *ready-made* goods. I was one of the eleven. Almost all of us were jobbers, with just a single worker.

The jobbers from the Croix-Rousse district (*which is thought, quite incorrectly, to be a hotbed of revolution*) are even more conservative than the merchants, for the simple reason that there would be no luxury trades if there were no aristocracy, and as a result no silk to be woven, or at least very little.

The delegates met every evening in a café. I made a motion to seek the raise demanded by the workers, which involved an increase of 20 percent over the average of the going rates for various items.

The majority protested this increase, which it characterized as exorbitant, saying that if we appeared too hard to please, we would force the merchants to turn down our proposal. They would then take their orders to their factories in the countryside or build new ones.

"It's true," I said, "that twenty percent is a big increase, but everyone working in the silk trades will want to get a raise, and that'll wipe out a good portion of the twenty percent." And that is just what happened. The loom makers raised the price of their machines. The silk winders, the warp winders, and all the others did the same. The landlords took advantage of the situation to increase their rents.

Despite this fact, the majority resisted. *It preferred to economize at the expense of the apprentices, and even of their wives and children, rather than offend the manufacturers.* In a word, it preferred to uphold the latter's interests. On their side, the manufacturers terrified the majority by trying to demonstrate that the raise being demanded would have disastrous results for the members of the trade.

Of eleven delegates, there were only three of us in favor of the raise. Nothing could be decided. I did my best to prove the need for this raise. "Silk work," I said, "is a luxury item. Luxuries can perfectly well stand an increase in price. The cost of raw silk sometimes rises by twenty or even thirty percent without paralyzing sales."

"But when silk goes up in price, its value increases all over the world, whereas the increase we're asking for is entirely local."

"Silk goods," I replied, "are selling at the same prices that were charged before the Revolution of 1848, yet since that period, rents and the cost of food have doubled. This raise is therefore urgent. The manufacturers can easily absorb it. Twenty years ago, if someone referred to a firm that had a million francs in capital, it was mentioned as an exception. Today there exist a swarm of manufacturers who are more than millionaires, and these fortunes have been made in less than ten years."

The fear of offending the manufacturers (for it had at times cost dearly) caused several delegates not to reappear at the meetings. There were only five of us left. From that point on, we were unanimously in favor of the 20 percent raise. There was one among us who never spoke up but who was reporting all our discussions to the manufacturers.

We went to the trade council to discuss our wage rates with the merchants. The latter got on their hobbyhorses about foreign trade. "If we accept your raise," they said, "we'll have to sell homespun cloth as a result."

We could not come to terms, and I saw that some of my colleagues were about to give in. At the third meeting, I asked to speak to defend our general interests.

"Without mentioning names," I said, "there are some manufacturers who were paying one franc ten centimes a meter for a certain item. When they saw that jobbers accepted this price without protest, the manufacturers successively lowered the price of this same item to one franc, then ninety centimes, then eighty centimes."

A manufacturer named Couder cried out that he was being insulted. He was the manufacturer in question and the item whose price had been reduced was mine, but I was not the only one affected.

"You tell us about foreign competition," I continued. "That's wrong. Workers in the factories in Zurich are paid more than jobbers are paid here. It's the same in England. Manufacturers in those two countries have to bear production and tooling costs that don't even apply in the case of our manufacturers in Lyon, and workers in those two countries work fewer hours than we do.

"Apart from this, there's a local factor that must be taken into consideration. The superior quality of goods made in Lyon is much vaunted, but if wages are not increased, we run considerable risk of losing this superiority. The jobber who just barely manages to feed his family even now will soon be unable to take on any apprentices because he lacks the means. Moreover, any man who's poorly nourished loses his mental ability, and mental ability is more necessary than ever to maintain our preeminence.

"There's another way of standing up to foreign competition. Let the manufacturers, who own buildings and coal mines, bring down the cost of rents and coal, and let all taxes on food be abolished.

"We would much prefer that. All the necessities of life have doubled in price over the past twenty years. Wages must therefore be doubled to restore the balance. So you see, gentlemen, our proposal for a raise is very moderate."

The raise was, in fact, accepted by the majority of manufacturers just as we had requested.

The manufacturer who thought he had been insulted asked the chairman for the name of the individual who had made the speech. He took my name and stopped giving me work.

This raise produced a great deal of good in Lyon. It benefited everyone who belonged to the trade. It permitted the weavers to buy new equipment which greatly eased the strain of their day's work. Working women dressed more neatly, and general health improved.

But the successful resolution of this labor dispute did little to improve Truquin's personal situation. The Franco-Prussian War soon intervened. Truquin, a participant in the events that took place in Lyon in conjunction with the Commune of 1871, only narrowly avoided prosecution as a participant in the execution of an officer who had fired upon a National Guardsman sympathetic to the republican cause. All of these circumstances reinforced his resolve to depart from France a second time. At the age of forty, having learned to read a little but still unable to write, Truquin left his wife and children behind and boarded an English steamship bound for Argentina. This trip lasted only one year, but it was followed by another and apparently permanent emigration of his family, first to Buenos Aires and then to Paraguay. Nothing is known of Truquin's history or whereabouts after he finished drafting his memoirs at Villa Encarnación in April 1887.

6 Jean-Baptiste Dumay

Memoirs of a Militant Worker from Le Creusot

The significance of Dumay's autobiography is concisely summarized in its title. The chronicle of his early years is also the history of the industrial city of Le Creusot during the second half of the nineteenth century, and of its economic and political domination by the Schneider enterprises. Known formally as Les Usines du Creusot (and referred to by Dumay as "the industrial penal colony"), this enormous industrial complex was an example of the paternalist and authoritarian form that capitalism assumed in a few outposts of concentrated industrial production in France.

This is the story of a militant in revolt against this factory system of organization. By the time of his adolescence, Dumay, the son of a Schneider employee killed in a coal-mining accident several months before his birth, would define himself in opposition to the experience of large-scale industrial capitalism, which he was the first among these authors to confront. Apprenticed as a machinist at age thirteen, within four years he had already been fired and blacklisted for indiscipline and refractory political opinions. His description of the Tour of France he undertook at age nineteen, partly to escape Le Creusot, underscores the changes that had taken place during the span of a generation that had passed since Perdiguier's earlier journey. Dumay's occupational training was completed during five and a half years of military service. This was, in effect, an extension of his apprenticeship since it was primarily spent (between unauthorized leaves and brief stays in an army jail) as a machinist in the arsenals of the Second Empire. Upon his return to Le Creusot, he became involved in the political agitation of the late 1860s and played an active role in the movement to organize workers in his native region.

Dumay went on to achieve a certain prominence in the political struggles of his day, at both the provincial and the national level. It was only in the relative calm of his retirement from public affairs that he wrote this record of his life. His memoirs were drafted and revised over a period of more than twenty years, from 1902 to 1926, and thus date from as much

*as a half-century after the events which they recount. With the exception
of one chapter not included in these excerpts, they were not intended for
publication. Believing that his life story held no interest for a wider audience, Dumay expected that it would be read only by his children and de-
scendants. It was only fifty years after his death that the manuscript first
appeared in print, thanks to the generosity of his heirs and the very substantial job of editing the unpolished manuscript carried out by Pierre
Ponsot. This translation appears with the kind permission of the Presses
Universitaires de Grenoble and is taken from its 1976 joint edition (with
François Maspero) of* Mémoires d'un militant ouvrier du Creusot, 1841–
1905.

PART I: CHILDHOOD AND YOUTH AS A WORKER'S SON IN LE CREUSOT, 1841–1868

I was born in Le Creusot on 10 September 1841, the posthumous son of
Sébastien Dumay. My father died in a Le Creusot mining accident on
26 February 1841 at the age of thirty-three.

MY FAMILY

Three months before his death, my father had married a young woman
named Forest who was born in Saint-Didier-sur-Arroux in the department
of Nièvre. She was fifteen years younger than he and came from a family
of wooden-shoe makers that had been attracted to Le Creusot, like so many
others, by the then-nascent factory. Peasants from the surrounding regions would come and be swallowed up by this vast enterprise, drawn by
the lure of wages slightly higher than those they could earn making
wooden shoes or putting in a few days here and there working on farms.
But in the factory they had much less freedom than in their forests. My
mother was widowed before she was eighteen years old, and because all she
had to live on were her earnings as a seamstress, she would often leave me
in the care of my maternal grandmother while she went out to work in the
neighborhood for eight sous a day plus meals.

I should not forget to mention that the paternalist administration of Le
Creusot Industries granted me a food allowance in the princely amount of
three francs per month from the time of my birth until I was twelve. My
mother, for her part, received a monthly allowance of eight francs, and it
was with this sum, plus her earnings as a seamstress, that she somehow
raised me until 1847. When I was six years old, she got married again, to a
man named Perrin. He came from somewhere near Le Creusot and was a
stoker on the big forges. My mother and my maternal grandmother had

both been widowed at nearly the same time and had therefore united in misfortune by living under the same roof with one of my mother's sisters, who was four years younger than she and made her living taking in ironing.

Let me tell you about the accident in which my father lost his life. He was employed in the Le Creusot mines as a head miner (in other words, a foreman or what they call an overseer in Belgian mines). He had finished his day's work and was eating his evening meal in the company of my mother and other relatives when a miner came to find him. The miner told my father that the team assigned the job of blocking off a gallery into which poisonous gases had seeped felt it could not continue because it had become too difficult to breathe. My father left his family behind and went straight to the mine, which was near his house. The situation had gotten even worse since the messenger had been sent, and two of the workers had just collapsed, overcome by suffocation, as my father arrived at the work site. He rushed to their assistance, took one of them by the shoulders, and had barely taken a few steps with this burden before he himself keeled over, never to rise again. Four other workers tried, one after another, to save my father, but that just made four more victims. Faced with this situation, the survivors fled, rightly figuring that seven victims was enough.

My mother maintained a sort of cult around my father's memory—as did his brothers and sisters, for that matter—and would often tell me about him when I was a child. This cult derived in large part from the circumstances in which he died, but there was also a respectful appreciation for the man himself. In those days there were no railroads, and people's attitudes about distances were different from those we have today. My father had done his military service in places quite distant from his native region and had been away seven years before returning. That gave the man a certain mark of superiority over his peers, of a sort, moreover, that can still be observed in certain remote areas. My father was, apparently, an extraordinary gymnast. He was, in addition, a fencing master of considerable repute throughout the entire department, and until I was fifteen, I took great pleasure in hearing those who had known him tell stories about the brilliant matches in which he had participated against masters who were passing through. Until I was sixteen, I even kept in the house a mask and two foils as souvenirs of my father's exploits, but this sorry old junk finally fell apart, and with it went the little shred of pride that I derived from being the son of a fencing master.

Neither my stepfather, Perrin, nor my mother knew how to read or write. He was an honest worker whose chief concern in life was to be respected by his bosses in the factory. He did very well in his job as stoker, despite being illiterate, and believed that it was not essential to know how to read and write in order to be a good worker. Even though he treated me just as if I were his own son, the question of providing me with vocational training and education was always the least of his concerns. He was very proud of me the day I became a representative of the Paris district, but the man must have suffered when I was still young and would go around the house fulminating against the exploitation that the serfs of Le Creusot experienced at the hands of the Schneider family, which he defended as best he could against my attacks! He had just one argument to offer against all of mine: that the weak are no match for the strong. He sometimes added the following economic heresy, which the naive still repeat today: "If there were no rich people to give us work, what would become of us?" There was nothing more to say. How often must the poor man have rejoiced in his heart of hearts, as he observed what hateful ideas I possessed, that he was not the one who had brought me into the world?

MY CHILDHOOD

Despite his lack of enthusiasm about the need for people to learn to read, my stepfather sent me to school at the age of six, to a sort of day nursery where I learned my ABCs. Then, at the beginning of 1848, I entered the public elementary school. Its principal was a fine man whom we called Old Nolet, and who is very fondly remembered by my whole generation.

I was therefore six and a half years old when the Republic was proclaimed in February 1848. I still have a very clear recollection of people planting a "liberty tree."[1] Like most others, this was an enormous poplar that had been dug up in the Baraques quarter of Le Creusot, where I was born. But the event that stirred my young imagination more than any other was the arrival of the military to put down an attempted revolutionary movement that was an echo of the June Days in the capital.[2] I still remember it as if it were yesterday. The schoolmaster, without waiting until it was time for school to let out, came to tell us that we had to clear the classroom so soldiers could be quartered there and that we should all go home as quickly as possible by back roads. More curious than many of my young fellow students, I stopped for a moment on the square. I witnessed a

1. It had become customary, in the immediate aftermath of a successful popular insurrection, for proponents of a democratic regime to join in the ritual planting of "liberty trees" on public squares and on sites where heavy fighting had occurred. The trees symbolized the spirit of liberty that had to be tended with vigilance, and at times nourished with the blood of patriots, in order to grow and prosper.
2. On the June Days, see chapter 5, n. 30. The first reports of combat in the capital to reach cities in outlying areas like Le Creusot sparked a number of provincial disturbances.

charge of gendarmes against a group of miners, and I recall that one of them, whose name was Chevenet but who was called Capron, was arrested and "roughed up," as the saying goes, in a big way. This scuffle was followed by a panic, and there was a general stampede that included my diminutive self. In fact, I fled so rapidly that I fell several times along the way, and I truly think that the spectacle of these various incidents played a role in my opposition, from a very early age, to tyranny in all its forms.

Between the ages of seven and ten I was a more or less proper student, but then I began to play hooky in both winter and summer, but especially in the summer. It got so bad that at the end-of-the-year ceremony, Mr. Nolet, the principal, pointed me out as the worst student in all three classes. I had missed school one hundred fifty times during the year. The two worst students after me were the Michalot brothers, my companions in playing hooky. The elder of them had one hundred thirty absences; the younger, one hundred twenty. The elder died in 1870 and the younger, Jérôme, later became one of the leaders of the company union in Le Creusot and president of the mutual aid society.[3] The two of us have definitely gone our separate ways. My poor mother was so strongly affected by having her son singled out in front of everyone that she cried for a week.

This passion for missing school was caused by my love of reading. I liked everything: old newspapers, history, novels, travel literature. I often left my father's house with the quite definite intention of going to school, but all it took was for one of my fellow students to loan me a book of any kind along the way, and right away I wanted to know what was in it and would end up not going to school. And when I had spent the whole day reading in the woods or elsewhere, I wanted to continue all evening at home. But as my parents were not rich—there were three more children younger than myself—we economized on everything, and the little oil lamp that so sadly illuminated the house while we were eating our soup was put out just as we were swallowing the last spoonful. From then on, the only light was what passed through the bars of a little grate behind which burned the coal, mixed with clay, with which we would pack it each evening to make it last the night. I would then kneel on the tiles and, with my forehead a few centimeters from the bars, I would read for another hour or two. Yet, though I am sixty-two years old as I write these lines, I still do not use glasses.

When I was nearly twelve, I began to work a little harder at school, without giving up my reading. In the space of six months, I went from the

3. Concerning mutual aid societies, see introduction, pp. 13–14.

third to the second grade and then from the second to the first.[4] I am ashamed to say that even so, I was never a good enough student to win the least prize, not even an honorable mention.

In this way, I managed to reach my thirteenth year. In those days—and, what is more, it is still the case even now—the management of Le Creusot Industries would recruit all the apprentices for its workshops from the public elementary schools. These were even called "Mr. Schneider's schools," for the simple folk of that region made no distinction between the administration of the company and the administration of the city. The two were in the same hands and fairly often became confused, to the detriment of the taxpayers. (For example, the office of municipal welfare sometimes provided assistance for illnesses that were contracted on the company's work sites.) Whenever possible, future miners were recruited from the families of those already employed in that job category. They were hired at the age of eleven—I recall that at that time there was no child-protection legislation—but those who were destined for the workshops outside the main factory did not begin before the age of twelve. They were taken in groups of six, ten, or twelve, according to need. The principal, Mr. Nolet, would first come to the first-grade class and say to the students: "They need so-many apprentices in the ironworks, so-many in metal fitting or in boiler making! Who wants to go?" And everyone would raise their hands, provided they were at least twelve years old. And they would do this without any advice from their parents, often without any sense of vocation for the jobs available, impelled by a single motive, the pleasure of getting out of school.

Without consulting anyone, I had decided not to leave school until they were looking for students to go into engine fitting, because I had a desire to travel and I hoped to fulfill my aspirations in this regard by going on the road, as so many do, once I became a journeyman. But one fine day they were asking for apprentice turners, and because the schoolmaster had slapped me that morning for one reason or another, I was in a bad mood and got myself signed up.[5] I was accepted, and that is how, though not yet

4. In general, grades in French schools are enumerated in descending order, leading toward a terminal year designated as "first." In Dumay's time, the curriculum was geared toward a youngster completing schooling at about the age of twelve.
5. Metal turners or machinists, like the wood turners discussed in Bédé's autobiography (chapter 1), worked at a lathe. Because they worked with far more resistant materials like iron and brass, their machines were typically power driven and their tools specially adapted. Because of the need for a high degree of precision in measurement and execution, most metal turners were highly skilled and relatively well paid.

thirteen, I began as an apprentice at Le Creusot Industries in the spring of 1854.

I had hardly been in the workshop a month before I took a dislike to my trade, and this dislike was all the more pronounced because the system of apprenticeship in use in this part of the factory was absolutely disastrous for the young people who happened to blunder in, while on the contrary, it was advantageous for the factory. About thirty apprentice turners were grouped together, and each was made to specialize in nuts or bolts that were always more or less identical, for a period of six months, a year, two years, or even more. Through constant repetition, they developed extraordinary dexterity. A young apprentice earning one franc a day might manage to make up to two hundred bolts in that time. Those bolts would have cost at least ten francs, had they been made by journeyman turners; and because that vast factory of eight thousand workers required large quantities in all sizes, they could make them to their hearts' content, for there were never too many.

Though I had begun my apprenticeship, I had not lost the passion for reading that I mentioned above. The more I read, the more the desire to travel took hold of me and the more I took a dislike to a job that I considered absolutely stultifying. This aroused my indignation. What is more, I saw so many injustices and so much arbitrariness in that factory that a violent hatred for its two-faced administration came to be superimposed on the disgust I felt for an apprenticeship that really was nothing of the kind, for I knew just as much at the end of six months as I did after three years. My sense of rebelliousness grew stronger day by day. I vented my anger by constantly posting signs all over the factory, calling upon the workers to revolt. It was a true miracle that the numerous guards who swarmed all over that vast establishment never managed to put their hands on the author of those signs, which so exasperated them, especially since they received such harsh reproaches for their negligence each time my appeals appeared on the walls. At the same time, I did my best to spread my own spirit of rebelliousness around the workshop, and in a fairly open manner. As a result, I had a very bad reputation. This lasted until the end of 1859, a few months after I had turned eighteen.

At the time of the industrial crisis of 1858, the management of Le Creusot Industries informed its workers that in view of the conditions in which the Schneider firm was forced to operate and in order to avoid layoffs, there would be a general wage cutback of 10 percent. At that time I, like all apprentices my age, was earning one franc twenty-five centimes per day. In one fell swoop, our daily wage was reduced to one franc fifteen centimes. This was not exactly encouraging, so I told my parents that I had had enough and wanted to leave the area. Because the little that I earned brought some slight relief to my family, where there were four more children from my mother's second marriage to feed, my parents protested. Then too, the principle of passive obedience that my stepfather professed in his dealings with the management of Le Creusot Industries created a second obstacle to my departure. In the end, I had to bide my time for a few months. But at the end of 1859, I suggested to my fellow apprentices that we should demand our former wage and, with this objective in mind, should direct some collective action at the foreman, a man by the name of Renaud who was a petty tyrant of the worst sort. Renaud was literally frightened out of his wits to see thirty of us protesters arrive together.

He declared that he did not want to receive the delegation, but that each of us should separately explain what he wanted. He asked who wanted to be heard first. I stepped forward resolutely, saying, "Me!" He quickly figured out what was going on and had me step into his office. He called me an agitator and all the other names that go along with that one. He did his best to reprimand me and finally threatened me with dismissal. When he called a second protester, the whole group fled, and I was then called from one office to another to receive a heap of warnings. They even called my mother and my stepfather to threaten him with dismissal if he did not make me be quiet. But I became more and more aggressive and finally spent a fair amount of time with Renaud himself, who had taken the liberty of grabbing me by the collar to make me leave his office. After three or four days of useless negotiations in which they asked me to apologize, I was finally dismissed from the factory.

MY TOUR OF FRANCE

As I was still a minor, the laws in force at that time required my parents' consent before the city hall would approve my labor passport.[6] This was a sort of internal passport without which a worker could not go off and do what was then called the Tour of France. My parents wavered for a few days but finally made up their minds after several squabbles over an affair of the heart which had been superimposed on my dispute with the management of Le Creusot Industries. For just a moment, I even had the terrible idea of enlisting in the army. I still had a certain fondness for the military from hearing the recital of my father's exploits as a fencing master, and in

6. Concerning labor passports, see chapter 1, n. 3.

addition I saw military life as a way to satisfy my taste for travel rather than as a career.

In the end, it was the prospect of a stay in Paris that won me over, and in the first few days of January 1860 I set out for the capital with three five-franc coins in my pocket as my only provisions for the journey, once I had paid for my railroad ticket. I was not rich. Among my fellow apprentices, there was just one who had, like myself, stood up against Mr. Renaud. This was someone named Thomas, who perhaps exercised a certain influence over my destiny, for it was at his instigation that we would later leave Paris after a stay of eight months, though my original intention had been to remain in the capital until it was time for the draft lottery.[7] He had been fired at the same time I was. We arrived in Paris together in the first days of January 1860. We landed in the Grenelle district in a place that rented furnished rooms, where a dozen of our countrymen from Le Creusot were living. They offered us help in finding work. Because I had specialized, as I mentioned earlier, in making bolts, I was not very familiar with the various kinds of jobs my trade involved, and what was more, I was not very strong. But I was energetic and full of goodwill, and I was determined, given my slender financial resources, to do any kind of work to earn my living. Thomas and I first tried to get jobs in our own trade, as turners, but when we had not found any after a week and our money was all spent, we were both forced to hire on as common laborers at Cail Industries.[8] I still remember this beginning of my occupational calamities. Along with another worker, I was assigned to work under the supervision of a sheet-iron layout man who was making beams. The sheets of iron were one to two centimeters thick and very heavy. We had to go find them where they were piled up in the snow, remove the ice they were covered with, and carry them with our bare hands, just the two of us, to the layout man, who would make fun of us when he saw us breathing on our hands.

The result was that when I got home each evening to the garret that I had rented for six francs a month, I would go to bed with my spirit as badly battered as my hands. After two weeks of such an existence, I left that hell to take a job in a big ironworks next door. I was still a common laborer, but doing work that was not so terrible. What's more, I only had to wait a few days, for this ironworks was in the process of setting up a lathe for making

7. On the draft lottery, see chapter 3, n. 5.
8. The Cail metalworking factory was one of the largest in the Paris region. In a period when the majority of the labor force of the capital still worked in small shops, this suburban firm boasted many hundreds of employees, most of them concentrated in a few enormous workshops.

cylinders, and I was supposed to be its operator as soon as the installation was complete. But I ran into some bad luck. There were four puddling furnaces in this ironworks.[9] It happened that one evening the assistant of one of the puddlers did not come to work, and on the ground that, since I came from Le Creusot, I had many a time seen how a puddling furnace operated, the foreman asked me to spend that night working with the puddler as a replacement for his missing assistant. I refused at first, but they gave me to understand that if I did not help them out, they would not give me the lathe that I was waiting for. I had to give in, for I was beginning to get worn out doing common labor. So I went off to find something to eat for the night, and started my shift at seven that evening. I have had to endure some harsh tests in my life, but I have never since spent such a cruel night. That is when I learned from experience a lesson that has, alas, been repeated since: that workers in certain trades are beasts unworthy of being called human. I had indeed watched puddlers' assistants working in Le Creusot, but with different equipment, much better organization, and, moreover, doubled up, two assistants per furnace, instead of alone, as I was in this rudimentary ironworks in the Grenelle district. I had hardly arrived and put my work clothes back on before the head puddler sent me to a furnace a hundred fifty yards away to get a load of pig iron in a wheelbarrow. I began by battering my hands on the rough edges of the blocks, for my boss had not told me that there were leather pads that you fastened at your wrists and that were made just for this work. When I brought the pig iron over next to the furnace, I had to place the pieces on the puddler's shovel, one after another, so they could be heaved into the furnace. I then had to go pull the chain attached to the weight that opened the furnace door. My boss began cussing me out in the foulest of language because I would either lift the door so high that the heat burned his face, or not lift it high enough, in which case he could not see inside the furnace well enough to place his ingots properly. Then I had to remove the slag. I was neither strong enough nor adroit enough to remove the bars from the grate with my arms outstretched, and as I half dragged them along, they would strike heavily against a sheet of iron that ran vertically between me and the ash bin, overturning it onto my legs and causing me injury. The glowing charcoal that I dropped while dragging the bar set fire to my pants. When I saw this, I let go of everything and ran around the factory trying to find a

9. Puddling (*puddlage*) is a method of refining iron ore. Molten, glowing-hot pig iron is mixed with bits of oxidized iron that have been flaked off in the forging process. When the puddler judges the refining process to be complete, he makes the red-hot metal into a "bloom," a spongy mass of wrought iron ready to be forged and rolled.

way out through which I could escape, but the walls were too high to climb. Though I rang the bell for the porter, he refused to open the door for me without an exit pass from the night foreman. Exhausted, burned, and injured, I came back and sat on a heap of pig iron, where I declared to my puddler through my tears that I would not so much as pick up another tool. He was a man of thirty or thirty-five who was built like Hercules. He swore at me even more intensely and said he was going to give me a thrashing if I did not carry on, for, he said, I was going to make him lose his day's pay. I told him that if he hit me, I would defend myself with whatever I could lay my hands on. My reply, delivered in a tone that left no doubt as to my intentions, suddenly calmed him down, and he told me in a gentler tone that I should not pay any attention to his coarse language, that forge workers always spoke that way to their assistants—which is true—and that if I wanted to continue working, he would help me as much as he could. I ended up letting myself be persuaded and went back to work. That proved to be my misfortune.

The puddler had formed the boiling pig iron in the furnace into a ball. The next step was to bring it to the stamping machine so it could be hammered out before being taken to the rolling mill, jobs that in Le Creusot were done by different workers. I was bringing the first ball to the stamping machine in my iron cart, but instead of inverting it onto the anvil, I let it fall alongside. The hammerer, who had to get another worker to help him set it back in place, called me a clumsy, lazy good-for-nothing and paid me other compliments of that sort. Then when the ball was formed into a squared-off bar about fifteen centimeters wide and sixty to eighty centimeters long, I set about taking it to the rolling mill. I managed to pick my route badly, so that a roller who was walking backwards, using his blacksmith's tongs to drag along a bar that had just come out of the cylinder, bumped his back against my cart, which he could not see. Wild with anger, he let go of the bar he was dragging and threw the tongs in my face. Fortunately for me, I had taken a few steps, and he missed his target, but the tongs hit me in my right side. The blow was terrible all the same. I let go of the cart and staggered. People gathered around me and carried me over to a packing crate, where I lay for nearly an hour without being able to speak. At last, at three in the morning, I rang for the porter to tell him that I had been injured and wanted to leave. I had the greatest difficulty persuading him to open the door for me, because he only wanted to do it on orders from the foreman, who still had the gall to tell me to finish my shift. I went straight to bed and was sick for three days, at the end of which I went to the ironworks to collect the few days' wages I was owed, promising myself that I would never again serve as a puddler's assistant.

I next found work in my own trade, as a turner at Kenzi's in the Rue Pierre-Levée. Since I had no money to pay two weeks' rent in advance for a furnished room in the neighborhood, I had to keep the one in the Grenelle district where they would give me credit, and every morning and evening I had to make the trip on foot. It took me a good hour.

One day I left this shop to go work for Lemoine, an axle maker on the road to Choisy in the thirteenth ward. I arrived in that neighborhood with forty-two sous in my pocket. It was a Wednesday. To pay for the three nights of Wednesday, Thursday, and Friday, I gave one and a half francs to the manager of the small rooming house situated just opposite the workshop. I kept twelve sous to live on until Saturday evening, at which time my four days of work would entitle me to a partial payment of ten francs. At each of my four meals from Wednesday evening to Friday noon, I ate two sous' worth of bread and one sou's worth of fried potatoes. But since by Friday evening I no longer had a cent and still had twenty-four hours to go before getting paid, I decided to explain my situation to my landlord, who also ran a cheap restaurant. He offered to feed me on credit, an arrangement I gratefully accepted, for this forced diet had so weakened me that I no longer had the strength to hold my tools at work.

A few days after I was hired, my friend Thomas came to join me. I introduced him to the foreman, who gave him a job. After a three-month stay in this factory, he suggested, as I mentioned earlier, that we leave Paris and head for the provinces in order to continue our Tour of France, as we used to say. I resisted for a few days, because I liked the capital, but in the end I gave in.

We left Paris in the first days of August, taking the train to Auxerre. We stayed in that city two days, looking for work and walking around, and at the end of that time we set off on foot for Tonnerre.

Ah! What a wonderful time, and what pleasure I take in remembering it even as I write these lines. What a cheerful way to travel, with my little bundle tied on the end of a stick! In Tonnerre we did not find any work either, and as the weather was fine we set out at night on foot for Dijon, where we had no better luck. But in Dijon someone told us that a metal-worker from Pommard by the name of Gallo might perhaps hire us both. Because we had stayed a night in a rooming house in Dijon so we could look around the city a bit, we were well rested from our night's journey. Once again we set out after sunset on the road to Pommard, where we arrived around eight in the morning. But the employer only needed one turner, and since my companion had asked first, he was the one who was hired. The workers in that shop welcomed us as if they had known us for years, and the good wine of that region flowed so plentifully that my head was slightly heavy that afternoon, which prevented me from catching the train to Lyon as I had intended.

On what slender threads a man's destiny depends! While all this was going on, Mr. Gallo received a letter from the management of the mines in Epinac, asking him to send a journeyman metal turner if the opportunity arose. At almost the same instant, the carriage from Beaune to Autun, which stops at Epinac, came by. I hopped inside and there I was, off to my new destination. At five o'clock that evening I arrived not in Epinac itself but in a suburb called Le Currier, where the mines, the company railroad station, and the repair shops were located. I went straight to the head office to offer my services and was told that the engineer in charge of hiring was not in and that I would have to come back the next day. I then went to each of the two local inns to ask for a place to stay and was told that they had no beds. I left the village and came across a meadow where there were piles of cut hay. I placed my bundle (or my "kit," as the tramps say)[10] under my head and was just getting ready to surrender to the sleep of the just when a few large drops of rain fell on my face, calling me back to reality. Before stretching out on my rustic bed, I had noticed an old woman and her young daughter, who must have been about twenty, watering flowers in a garden adjoining the meadow where I intended to spend the night. They had watched me prepare my bed and talked about me. I did not understand their conversation, which I could barely hear, but I clearly saw that they took an interest in my situation. I was not rich and had just ten francs in my pocket, but I was rather neatly dressed for a tramp, and it seemed odd to these folks to see me getting ready to sleep out under the stars. I left the meadow and, when I spotted a villager passing by on the road, asked him if he could direct me to a house where someone might offer me the hospitality of a barn. I added that I would pay what it was worth. Just then, the two women whom I mentioned came over. I hastened to tell the villager that I had gone to both the local inns and had been told that there were no

10. Dumay uses the slang term *trimardeur*, which today connotes vagrancy and begging but which in the nineteenth century might designate an itinerant worker who maintained his own sense of dignity and respectability. It is interesting to note a similar evolution in the English word "tramp," which originally designated someone who traveled about on foot, as artisans had done since the middle ages. Dumay's account makes it clear that in his trade, the custom of doing a Tour of France was in sharp decline in the mid–nineteenth century. Despite Dumay's positive experience in Dijon, the itinerant metal turner could no longer be assured of a warm welcome in a strange town and the help of fellow workers in finding employment. Gradually, all connection between respectable trades and the practice of tramping would be lost, and the twentieth-century meaning of "tramp"—a hobo or social outcast—would take hold.

more beds. At that point he turned to the older of the two women and asked her, "How about you, Mrs. Bobin? You might be able to put this young man up in one of your barns." The good woman answered that she had come over to make that very proposal. She led me into a large cattle shed where her cows were housed and showed me the pile of straw in a corner where their shepherd slept. He happened to be absent that evening, and she asked if I wanted to make do with that resting place for one night. I told her I did, but before letting me stretch out on my bed, she wanted to reassure herself that I was not some vagabond, so she asked to see my labor passport, which every tramp had to carry in those days. I showed it to her, and after she had looked it over, she asked me about my family. I was happy to tell her about them. Then she took me to her house and after a good hour of conversation, she offered me a glass of good wine before I went off to take possession of my litter of straw.

The next day, I was hired as a metal turner in the workshop at the mine, and when I returned to tell the news to Mrs. Bobin, I asked if she would be willing to keep me on as a boarder, for her daughter's beautiful eyes had had quite an effect on my young, eighteen-year-old soul. Mrs. Bobin told me that she could not do that and besides, she did not need to in order to get by, but she would put me up for a week until I had established some contacts in the region. That very evening, she gave me a good bed in a small room. Two days after I moved in, my fellow workers in the shop informed me that Miss Bobin was a religious devotee of the first water, that she never left church, and that she was driving her parents to despair by constantly insisting that she wanted to become a nun. It did not surprise me when I noticed that her bedside reading was *The Imitation of Christ*, a book designed expressly to fanaticize naive souls. I undertook to dissuade her from this course and, despite the active surveillance of her mother, found the opportunity over the next week to have a few brief conversations on this subject with this candidate for the cloister. It was not hard for her to see that my feelings about her were at least the equal of those that she professed for her God, and I quickly realized that she was not indifferent to them. But, alas, her mother also noticed and when the week was up, she would not grant me any extension. I had to go find another place to stay and be content with three or four subsequent visits. That was all, for the young woman had understood my arguments against her taking the veil, and six months later she married one of my friends, whose hand she had energetically refused before my arrival. Whenever I would meet her afterward, we would talk about our discussions of religious matters, and she always thanked me for having dissuaded her from her disastrous plans. I left the region a year later, but held onto the precious memory of the good deed that I had accomplished.

When I left Mrs. Bobin's house, I became a boarder in the home of an old Flemish lady by the name of Dégand. She was a fine woman who took a liking to me and who so bewildered me with her advice that at the end of two months I left her house just so I would not have to listen to her. While living in that region, I had a few amorous adventures, like all young folks of that age, adventures that have no place in this narrative. Just for the sake of old times, I will mention the names of the two best friends I made in that region. I have only seen them a few times since then, and two of them, Pouleau and Roiseau, are very dedicated foremen today, one in the Schneider works in Le Creusot and the other in the mining company in Montceau-les-Mines. According to my information, if they ran into me in the street, they might very well not speak to me, but at the age of nineteen we were less concerned with political struggles than with having a good time, and that is what we often did in each other's company.

Although I was quite happy in this little hole, my wanderlust took over again as soon as April arrived, and I headed for Lyon after passing through Le Creusot to see my parents. I stayed just a week in my native region and, once arrived in Lyon, went to the home of one of my cousins, named Genevois, who had been living in that city for about ten years. Thanks to his contacts, I easily found a job. I worked in two firms in Lyon: first at Gabert's, and then, toward the end of my stay, in a workshop in Oullins. There I ran into several men who also came from Le Creusot, among them a certain Gérard with whom I was close friends and about whom I will perhaps have more to say in the course of this narrative, for having met him in Paris thirty years later, I realized that my old comrade from the Tour of France was nothing but a scoundrel. But let us change the subject. My stay at Lyon and Oullins lasted until the month of September 1861. At the restaurant where I ate, I became friends with a Belgian by the name of Georlette who, like me, loved to travel. The two of us decided to make the trip from Lyon to Marseille on foot. We left our trunks with some friends in Lyon and, with a twenty-five franc coin in each of our pockets, lots of good cheer, and boundless enthusiasm, we left behind France's second city with a song on our lips.[11]

We passed in succession through Vienne, Saint-Vallier, Valence, Montélimar, and then Arles, where I met one of my first cousins, Jean-Marie Dumay, a metalworker like myself. He had been working in that city's railroad repair yard for several months. He welcomed my fellow worker Georlette and myself with open arms. After we had rested two days while seeing the city's sights, we set out one fine morning for Nîmes, where we

11. Marseille is today the second largest city in France, but in the period of which Dumay is writing, that honor belonged to Lyon.

arrived toward evening. When we were unable to find work in that city, we left for Alais, but our purses were giving out and we arrived in Uzès the evening of our departure from Nîmes with seventeen sous between us, and with me sick from exhaustion. Purely by chance we found employment in that city with a small-time metalworker who had a contract to install a water main and who hired us to drill holes in flanges and chip off burrs on pipes. When we told him about our financial situation, he took us to a little restaurant and told the proprietors he would guarantee our credit for the cost of food. As soon as we were settled, we both wrote our parents to send us a little money, and a week later we again had sixty francs of capital at our disposal. In those days, people were happy with very little. We decided to bolt for Marseille, and arranged to settle accounts with our employer. Because I had lost three days of work as a result of illness, and also because our employer would only pay us absurdly low wages, it turned out that we owed the restaurant keeper, who was also our landlord, one sou more than we had earned. Since we were not very happy about the way we had been treated, we weren't going to pay him his sou, which made him violently angry. Since the train did not come all the way to Uzès in those days, we took the mail coach to the railroad station in Nîmes. It still brings a smile to my face to remember all the curses that this honest southerner heaped upon us because of his sou. He followed the coach for at least fifty meters, using the local dialect to call us "French scoundrels, thieves, robbers" and so on. What exasperated him the most was that, from high atop the carriage where we were perched, we let him see our hundred-sou coins as if we were as rich as Rothschild.

That evening we arrived in Marseille, where we stayed five or six days, looking for work and visiting with a number of my fellow natives of Le Creusot whom I ran into. Finding no employment, we then took the train to La Ciotat, location of the great naval shipyard which at that time was called the Messageries Impériales. I was hired as a metal turner, but as there was no call for fitters, I handed over all our joint travel funds to my friend Georlette, who continued on to Toulon. I stayed on alone in this beautiful region, where I was destined to remain some fourteen months, until I left for the army. I made some firm friends in that area and still see some of them even today. That is also where I had a love affair, the memory of which is still sweet today, some forty years later. There I met a Parisian named Bouveron who, like me, was not very rich and who today is a great landowner in Charenton. We are still good friends. Along with Bouveron, I had two other friends named Content and Perrin. The first was from Bordeaux, the second from Montélimar. People would call us "the four inseparables." Content, Perrin, and I were going out with the three Planchot sisters, in whose parents' home we were boarders. The one on which I had designs was called Elisa. We were seriously in love with one another and had become engaged. It was understood that our marriage was to take place immediately if the luck of the draw in the draft lottery spared me from military service, which at that time lasted seven years. But luck ran against me, and I had to put on red knee breeches. [12] We promised to be faithful to each other until my discharge, but that was rather chancy, as subsequent events amply proved. My fiancée found complete security by marrying a painting contractor. She seized this opportunity, and she did right. I loved her not only for her personality but also for her beauty, and who knows whether, after seven years, the ravages of time might not have cooled my ardor. The fourteen months during which I lived in that charming region of La Ciotat are one of the sweetest memories of my youth. I loved, I was loved, and I was earning a good living. I was healthy and happy and was the life and soul of every party at which young people my age gathered. Every Sunday, there was either an outing by boat to L'Ile Verte, where we lunched and dined, or a pleasure trip to Marseille or especially to Toulon, where I would meet up with a number of men from Le Creusot and join in noisy parties.

When at last I turned twenty, I returned to Le Creusot for the draft lottery. In those days, there was such a thing as a "good number." If fate smiled upon you, you might not have to be a soldier at all. For a moment I had this hope, but it did not last long, for I drew number 57, and 320 men were conscripted. So there I was, bound in chains for seven years, my life interrupted and almost at a dead end. The warlike spirit I had possessed at the age of seventeen was far behind me, and I hated military life before ever setting foot in the barracks.

I stayed in Le Creusot for a couple of weeks after the draft lottery and then returned to La Ciotat to await the arrival of my marching orders in the month of September. A few weeks after I arrived, my friend Bouveron left the workshop to return to Paris. Content, who had married Geneviève, the eldest of the Planchot sisters, had left La Ciotat to go live in La Seyne near Toulon. Only Perrin and I were still living at the boarding house.

MY MILITARY SERVICE:
THE BARRACKS AT CHERBOURG

The month of September arrived quickly, and I set off to join the eighteenth infantry regiment in Cherbourg. I can't tell you how painful was my first

12. Red knee breeches (*la culotte rouge*) were the uniform of French soldiers in that period.

day of life in the barracks and what dread I felt at the conversations I heard in the first hours of my stay in that hell! I find it impossible to explain: I would hear people speak such nonsense, such smut, such filth, that I thought I was dreaming. But what troubled me later was seeing that young folks, who like me had been disgusted by the disgraceful things they saw and heard in those first days, had become contaminated six months later and behaved exactly like the people they had so strongly disapproved of. It was the influence of the surroundings. During my first year of service, my friends Content, Bouveron, and Perrin sustained my morale by writing long letters every couple of weeks, and my fiancée Elisa Planchot for her part did all she could to console me for the loss of my freedom and my disgust with life in such a setting. But that was not to last.

During the entire time that I spent in the army, it was the day of 15 August 1863—the Emperor's Day celebration—that left the most sickening memory. Early that morning, they brought barrels of a mediocre reddish juice they called wine, giving everyone a liter to last the day, half for the midday meal and half for the evening meal. After that, anyone could have as much over the official ration as he could pay for. People drank so much that most of the men were already tipsy when they sat down to eat around eleven that morning. Proper plates and place settings had been rented for the occasion, and we were served a small extra portion of meat and vegetables, salad and coffee, as well as lots of "cognac" that was more or less pure alcohol made from beets or potatoes. At the end of the meal, the officers came to deliver the obligatory imperialist speech, as they did in every unit. Our captain, a nobleman named d'Espagnet, addressed us in approximately these words: "Today you are eating a meal of meat, vegetables, wine, and coffee—a meal so extraordinary that most of you would surely not do as well if you were home instead of in your barracks. You know as well as I do that it's His Majesty the Emperor Napoléon III who brings you this blessing. So lift your glasses, stand up, and join me in shouting: Long live the Emperor!" Everyone obeyed but me. I was seated at the end of the table near an open window. I pretended to be looking out into the courtyard so that none of the officers could tell whether or not I had opened my mouth. Nonetheless, a second lieutenant named Bousquet set to watching me so long and in such an unfriendly way that I understood that he had realized the meaning of my gesture. And in fact from that day on, he never missed a chance to show his hard feelings toward me, which naturally increased my hatred for military institutions more and more.

THE ARSENAL AT RENNES

[. . .] Because active military service lasted so long in those days, its seven-year term was broken up by a six-month leave that came during the third or fourth year of service. These leaves were distributed on the basis of requests that were handled in the order of the men's matriculation numbers. As I had arrived in the regiment forty-eight hours late, I had one of the highest numbers in my unit, and when I returned to Cherbourg and wanted to put my name in for the next departure, I was informed that those places were already taken and it would have to be the following year, for only six men per company could be gone at once. That meant my request would not be granted, but I still had one hope. [. . .]

I wrote a long letter to my Colonel, begging him to grant me a hearing at which I would explain my mother and father's need to have me with them for six months. I begged him to excuse this departure from military regulations but added that, while I was sure that as a colonel he would feel I was in the wrong, I was also certain that as a father he would forgive me. I was granted a hearing. I confess to my shame that I spouted a series of unconscionable lies to that poor colonel, but I can be excused on grounds of the profound disgust—all too justified, alas—that army life inspired in me. [. . .]

SIX MONTHS IN LE CREUSOT

So there I was, back in Le Creusot. But how was I going to get work at the factory when I had been expelled for all time under the regulations then in effect, which said that any trainee who left the company before his draft lottery was banished for life?[13] Fortunately for me, the vast Le Creusot Industries included a few autonomous departments whose managers sometimes (and for good reason) neglected to observe the factory's general regulations forbidding them to hire a worker who had previously been employed by the firm without written permission from his former department manager. This permission was called a "transfer ticket." One of these autonomous departments was the main ironworks, the part of the factory where the puddling and annealing furnaces and rolling mills were located. It included a repair shop run by a Mr. Léon, who was on good terms with his personnel and was quite open to accepting gifts, or what in polite language are called gratuities.[14] My stepfather got his own foreman to knock on Léon's door, for the foreman and this Léon were friends. The response came back that all I had to do was show up with my transfer ticket, and I would immediately be put to work as a metal turner. I took the bull by

13. The intent of this regulation appears to have been to allow the firm to recoup the investment made in training the apprentice. This was achieved by obliging the apprentice to continue working at a low rate of pay for a predetermined period of time even after his increased skill level might be expected to command a much higher rate in a free labor market.
14. The term that Dumay uses is *pots de vin*, literally "jugs of wine."

the horns, as they say, for I was not terribly keen on staying in Le Creusot anyway and was making a great sacrifice by letting my parents get involved in finding me a job in the region, which I detested. So I went off to find the head of the personnel office and asked him for a copy of my work evaluations so I could show them, or so I told him, to a department head who had asked me for them to see if he could hire me. When they were handed over, this is what I read: "Unruly worker, hot-head, dangerous man, never take him back." That same day I went off to find Mr. Léon and showed him my evaluations. He said that under the circumstances he could not hire me, despite the very strong recommendations I had received. I withdrew, quite satisfied, and notified my parents that I was going to head for Lyon. My stepfather asked me to be patient for just a few days more, and informed me three days later, to my great surprise, that all I had to do was show up at Mr. Léon's workshop at six o'clock the next morning and begin work. That is just what happened, without any explanation offered. I had been working there for about a month, when one day, as I was chatting with my stepfather, he admitted that he had brought Mr. Léon a rabbit and two partridges. I then understood why the regulations had been bypassed. I stayed in the repair shop for about a month before being transferred to a team of turners who made cylinders for iron milling machines. The team's foreman was one of Mr. Léon's subordinates.

My father and mother, seeing that I was not inclined to settle in Le Creusot, decided to make me settle there anyway by getting me married. If it couldn't be managed during my six-month leave, then at least they would find me a serious fiancée, so that the actual marriage could take place as soon as I got my discharge, which was supposed to happen in about two years. This was a risky proposition. There were two unsuccessful attempts, partly because I did not like the young women and also because I was already somewhat involved with the woman who later became my wife and was then Miss Rosier.

Due to these marital negotiations and the relative calm in my work life, my six-month leave seemed to go by very quickly, and I was sick at heart to see the first of April 1865 come around, for that was the date on which I had to rejoin my regiment, which had been transferred from Cherbourg to Lyon. I had become firm friends with all my fellow workers in the shop. For my departure, they arranged a great banquet that took place at the Dauvergne Hotel in the Bois Breton near Monchanin-les-Mines. My closest friends were a certain Faurobert, as great a hunter as God has created, whom the foremen would send off hunting while covering for him at the workshop; and a certain Minard, whose son later became one of the bigwigs at the Schneider factory.

I rejoined my regiment on the prescribed date in Lyon. [. . .]

LIEUTENANT BALOCHE

From the age of fourteen or fifteen to the time of my departure from Le Creusot, I had never missed a single year of going with young folks my age to a rustic celebration held on the Monday after Pentecost on the summit of a mountain called La Certenne in the commune of Saint-Symphorien. There, parenthetically, legend tells us that a female saint cured a variety of illnesses. While I was stationed at Camp Sathonay, it had been two years since I had danced on the summit of the mountain. When my old friends summoned me, I asked for a four-day leave on family business. Because maneuvers were being conducted at that time, I was refused a pass; so I forged one with the stamps, signatures, and all the flourishes necessary to obtain the travel discount, and I set off for Le Creusot. [15] I was happier than ever to cast off my military uniform and head for the celebration in civilian clothes. I was absent without leave from my regiment for six full days, and the gendarmes came to pick me up at my parents' house one hour after my departure. When I arrived at camp, I was put in jail and given a punishment of fifty days' confinement in a cell. I was rather surprised when one day I received a visit from my lieutenant, Baloche. He sat down on my cot and spoke these words, more or less: "I've come to see you, Dumay, because you seem to me to be headed down a very rocky path. I'd like to try to get you to turn back. I understand, as I've already told you, that given your temperament and your previous history as a metalworker, military life is a disagreeable chore. But what I don't understand is your refusal to recognize that by taking off like this you'll end up in one of the disciplinary companies in Africa. [16] What with one disaster after another, you'll soon have not seven years to do, but a good ten or fifteen. It's happened to some, and you're all the more at fault because you'll soon have just two and a half left, which isn't all that much." I quickly realized that this man was speaking the truth. I thanked him for the token of friendship that he had shown me and promised to follow his advice in the future. My cousin Jean-Marie, who lived in Lyon and whom I mentioned above, had written, telling me to be sure to come have dinner at his place the day I got out of prison. I was careful not to forget the invitation, but as I had to be back in camp for the 9 PM roll-call and there simply wasn't enough time to get back from Lyon, I had the nerve to ask Lieutenant Baloche for a ten-hour leave. He reminded me that any soldier who had been punished with time in

15. Military personnel on official business or legitimate leave were given a 75 percent discount on the price of railroad tickets.
16. The reference is to special units (*biribi* in the slang of the period) reserved for repeat offenders against military discipline who were assigned undesirable duties, including hard labor, in France's North African colonies.

prison was denied all leave for a month after his release and consequently he could not go against the regulations. But since I was telling him that it was a matter of some urgency, he would authorize me to be absent for one hour after roll call, but without giving me an official pass. If I wasn't back at ten o'clock precisely, I would be reported absent and considered to have run away from the camp after the nine-o'clock roll call. I gave him my word that I would return by the specified hour. I was punctual, but so was he. Just as ten o'clock was ringing, I arrived at the gate to the barracks where he had been waiting for me for five minutes. He said these simple words—"That's good!"—and walked away. That man always remained an enigma to me. At the same time that he was so tolerant with me, he continued to be tyrannically harsh to all the other soldiers, and what particularly bothered me in my observations of him was that, on the several occasions when I had to enter his quarters to have him sign some document, I would see on the night table that stood near his bed the works of Cabet, Victor Considérant, and especially Proudhon.[17] A short time after this incident, I changed companies; then toward September 1866, the Eighteenth Infantry Regiment was sent off to Saint-Etienne, and I never had the chance to see this rather odd officer again. I later learned that he had been killed at the battle of Sedan on 2 September 1870.

My boring existence in the gloomy city of Saint-Etienne continued until, toward the month of May 1867, there was talk of a possible war between France and Prussia over Luxembourg, which Bismarck had promised to that imbecile Napoléon III in compensation for the considerable territorial expansion from which Prussia had benefited at the expense of Austria after its victory at Sadowa in 1866. In anticipation of that war, they had called up the reserves from the classes of 1863 and 1864, one hundred thousand men who had never had any training and most of whom had never held a rifle. Subsequent experience showed that this crowd wouldn't have been worth much, even had its members been integrated with seasoned troops. Although the Franco-Prussian dispute was settled by a European conference held in London, these hundred thousand men were kept on active duty to be trained while the hundred thousand regulars from the classes of 1861 and 1862 were discharged. The result was that, though

17. These were well-known Socialist writers. For Cabet, see chapter 4, n. 33. For Victor Considérant, see chapter 4, n. 57. Pierre-Joseph Proudhon (1809–65) was a libertarian and antistatist, best remembered for his slogan, "Property is theft." His system drew the criticism of Karl Marx, who considered it "utopian." After universal manhood suffrage was instituted in the early months of the French Second Republic, Proudhon was elected to the Constituent Assembly. He was exiled in 1852.

not due by law to be released until the end of December 1868, I had the good fortune to be discharged as of June 1867 or eighteen months earlier than I had hoped. I could hardly believe my good luck, and it made me wild with joy.

RETURN TO CIVILIAN LIFE; BRIEF JOBS

On my parents' urging, I designated Le Creusot as my place of residence, even though I would have preferred Paris. Despite all the efforts that my relatives and friends made on my behalf, I went nearly a month without finding work. Impossible to obtain a position, even in the foundry repair shop where I had worked during my six-month leave. I decided to leave Le Creusot at all costs and head for either Lyon or Paris. But that required money, and I did not have a cent to pay my way. I begged my parents to borrow about thirty francs from a neighbor on my behalf, so I could leave. They could have done so, but they really wanted me near them and told me to have patience and I would surely end up finding a place at the factory. I wouldn't listen and decided to go earn the money for my trip by signing on as a laborer on the railroad line between Chagny and Nevers, where there was a good deal of work at that time because they were putting in a second track. So I went off to find the station chief of Le Creusot, a man by the name of Mallet, and ask him for a job as a laborer at the station. He asked me where I was from. When I told him I was from Le Creusot, he said he would not hire me even if he had a position available, because I surely had training in some trade. "You're like so many others," he told me, "who come to work here for three or four weeks to get the money to pay your trip out of Le Creusot, and then you'll leave me flat just when you've learned the job." I readily conceded that what he said was true. Then he asked me why I didn't look for work at the factory. No less candidly, I confessed that I had been blacklisted for breaking the rules concerning apprentices who, as I mentioned elsewhere, had to stay until the age of twenty, supposedly to pay for their apprenticeship. My frankness pleased him. He asked me if I wouldn't rather leave metalworking and make my career in the railroad. I answered that I would gladly do so if I thought it was in my interest. Then he asked my name and address and promised to write me in a few days. But because I had only limited faith in this promise, I decided to look elsewhere to earn the money necessary for my trip away from Le Creusot.

RAIL LAYER

Out on the tracks, I approached a foreman who was supervising the unloading of some rails. I asked him whether he needed someone. Because

I was fairly neatly dressed and didn't look like a hobo, one of the workers who had overheard my request said to the foreman in an ironic tone, "Hire him right away. He can help us unload these rails." Thinking he would embarrass me, the supervisor asked if I wanted to start right away. It was five in the afternoon. I set my coat aside and got to work, along with the others. Our job was to load the rails from one railroad car into another. Three men would grab each rail, one on each end and one in the middle. Together, all three would say, "Ready! Heave!" and as they pronounced the last syllable, they would toss the rail. My fellow-workers had "leather hands" for doing this work. These were soles of thick leather that attached to their arms with a strap and that protected their hands from the inevitable cuts resulting from metal burrs on the rails, but they were careful not to give me any. I had been doing this work for barely a quarter-hour before my hands were all bloody. My fellow workers seemed glad to see my hands torn up, for each laughed harder than the next. They would have left me in this state until quitting time if they hadn't been running the risk of paying dearly for their cruel amusement. Because I wasn't very strong and not at all accustomed to this work, I was always letting go of my end either before or after the others, such that two or three times in the quarter-hour, the rail nearly fell and hit our legs. So they called over the foreman and explained the situation to him, laughing heartily. The foreman took pity on me and gave me a shovel and wheelbarrow, ordering me to spread slag onto the new track. I had been there for a week when one day Mr. Mallet, the station chief, passed by and recognized me. He came up and asked what I was doing there. I replied that I was afraid that the position that he had promised me would take too long and that I was working as a laborer until something better came along. It was four in the afternoon. To my great surprise, Mr. Mallet gave this response: "The work you're doing proves to me that you've got heart. I'm taking you with me. As of tomorrow, I'll be the station chief at Autun. Quit this job immediately and go get ready so you can meet me at the station and take the first train for Autun tomorrow morning."

IN AUTUN

I arrived at the rendezvous right on time, and Mr. Mallet temporarily put me in charge of keeping statistics. I was boarding in the home of a Mrs. Laumy, where there were a dozen of my fellow workers from Le Creusot, all of them metalworkers at Mr. Villepigue's, where they made drilling machines for mines and quarries. Since I brought home only three francs a day while they earned an average of six or seven, they would kid me about my low wages. So much so, in fact, that one fine day I notified Mr. Mallet that I had decided to quit. The story of what finally capped my disgust with this job is worth telling.

In those days, certain categories of PLM railroad employees wore a uniform.[18] This consisted of a frock coat, or what is sometimes called a "whistle," cut in the shape of a magpie's tail out of green broadcloth with red piping, along with a cap made of oilcloth—in short, a veritable flunky's outfit. The company tailor had already come twice to take my measurements, and twice I had refused. The third time, Mr. Mallet tried to get me to agree to this sacrifice, stressing that it was just a work uniform and that I was free to come and go to work dressed as I pleased. I wouldn't listen and resolved that I would quit. My decision was all the easier because all I had to do was show up and I could get a job at Villepigue's nearby.

This was surely one of the great mistakes of my life, for Mr. Mallet, who had become my protector, had one day recommended me in a very special way to Mr. de Lataille, the divisional inspector of the PLM, boasting of my intelligence and energy in such laudatory terms that I blushed from my head to my toes. They both promised me a raise as soon as I had completed my six months of mandatory probation, and a brilliant career as a railroad employee. Though I don't want to exaggerate my abilities, I would certainly have become a station chief at some important center and would long since have been retired instead of still working as a steward at the Paris Labor Exchange as I continue writing my memoirs.[19] But there is still one important proviso: who knows if, with my temperament, I would not sooner or later have rebelled against some iniquity of the kind that railroad companies commit so often, and got myself tossed out on the street, without any trade in hand, so to speak, for having cried out too loudly against an injustice of which I had been a witness or a victim. That is not so impossible, for I have seen it happen to several railroad employees after twenty or twenty-five years of solid service.

When I had finished my last day at the Autun station and was due to go

18. The period from the 1830s to the 1870s was the great age of private railroad construction in France. The PLM (Paris-Lyon-Méditerranée) line, which served the southeast region from the capital, was among the earliest and largest of these companies. It continued to exist until 1938, when the French government incorporated the seven surviving private railroads with its own state-operated line into the SNCF (Société Nationale des Chemins de Fer).

19. In 1896, Dumay obtained the post of manager of the Paris Labor Exchange. The position was of some delicacy for a militant and ex-communard because it placed him in the middle of factional socialist politics and at the same time made him a paid bureaucrat ultimately responsible to Eugène René Poubelle, the Prefect of Police. After ten years of service, Dumay resigned, still with no secure source of retirement income.

the next day to Villepigue's, Mr. Mallet called me into his office and asked me one last time to stay. When I once again refused, he told me: "I'm going to confide a secret to you. Will you give me your word of honor never to tell anyone?" I promised. "Well," he told me, "Mr. Villepigue, in whose firm you are going to work, is on the verge of bankruptcy, and in three or four weeks at the most you'll be out of a job if you persist in your resolve to leave the railroad. In every respect, therefore, your interest lies in staying here." I wouldn't listen, and I quit. Just as Mr. Mallet had told me, my new employer's collapse occurred four weeks after I starting working for him, and I had to leave Autun and return to my parents' home in Le Creusot. The day of my departure, Mr. Mallet offered to give me back my job, but I obstinately refused.

IN MONTCHANIN

I remained without work for only a few days in Le Creusot before being hired in the machinery repair shop at the mines in Montchanin around February 1868. The coal mines of Montchanin-les-Mines, which now belong to Le Creusot Industries, were at that time operated by an independent company whose director was Mr. Charles Avril. I worked there for about three months. That's when my future father-in-law informed me that there was a position available for a turner in the blast furnace repair department. I went to ask Mr. Picard, the director of that department, for a job. I quite frankly told him that I had been banished from the factory for having left before reaching the prescribed age and that I had, moreover, had a very heated altercation with Mr. Renaud, the supervisor. I added that despite this banishment, I had been rehired in the main ironworks repair shop whose foreman, Mr. Léon, was one of his friends. I also confessed that the evaluations from my first stint were not exactly positive.

Picard was a very honest man who thanked me for my frankness and said, "Under the circumstances, I won't be the one who messed up by taking you on after you were blacklisted. Bring me your evaluations from Mr. Léon's workshop, and I'll hire you." Because I had not been involved in politics during my six-month leave, my evaluations were very positive with respect to both my technical performance and my conduct. And that is how I returned for the second time to the factory in Le Creusot from which I had been banished. All this happened around the month of June 1868. Right from the start, Mr. Picard liked my work a great deal and gave me proof in many ways of his profound respect. Finding myself firmly settled, with a degree of security for the future, and with the help of love, I got married on 21 November in that year of 1868 to Miss Rosier, whom I had been actively courting for more than a year.

Dumay soon found himself drawn into the renewed labor unrest of the late Second Empire and assumed a prominent role in efforts to organize the working class in Le Creusot. After the fall of Louis-Napoléon, the Gambetta administration appointed the thirty-year-old Dumay provisional mayor of the city. He was the animating spirit behind the Commune of Le Creusot—a faint and short-lived echo of the great Parisian events, which never garnered much working-class support. He managed to flee to Switzerland before being condemned in absentia to deportation and a life sentence of hard labor. The eight years spent abroad make him the third of these seven authors to have experienced the rigors of exile. Thanks to an amnesty, Dumay was able to return to France in 1879, and for the remainder of his career in politics, he would bear with pride what others variously saw as the honor or the stigma of his actions.

In this later period, Dumay resumed his efforts to propagate his Socialist beliefs and promote a workers' party. Stymied in his native region, he moved to the capital in 1882. After several unsuccessful campaigns, he was elected in 1887 to the Municipal Council of Paris, representing Belleville. That same district made him its deputy to the National Assembly for four years, beginning in 1889. Even before his electoral defeat of 1893, a growing distaste for and disillusionment with politics caused him to contemplate semiretirement. During the ten years from 1896 to 1906, he served as manager of the Paris Labor Exchange. He withdrew permanently from public affairs in 1907.

For the last nineteen years of his life, Dumay lived in relative poverty and isolation. This phase of his life was marked by a certain bitterness and disenchantment with the political divisions among French Socialists. It accentuated his pessimism over the future prospects for democracy and for the working class in France. He died in Paris in 1926 at the age of eighty-five.

7   Jeanne Bouvier

*My Memoirs; or, Fifty-nine Years
of Industrial, Social, and Intellectual
Activity by a Working Woman,
1876–1935*

*From the opening paragraphs of her narrative, Bouvier succeeds in estab-
lishing a tone of intimacy that captivates her readers and immediately
draws them into this absorbing account of working-class life in the last
third of the nineteenth century. Her vignettes are sketched with a deceptive
simplicity and possess a remarkable aura of authenticity.*

*Born in 1865 and destined to survive nearly to the age of one hundred,
in many respects Bouvier shares the outlook and sensibility of our own
era. Yet her socializing experiences were those of a nineteenth-century
female worker, obliged to enter a silk-throwing factory at age eleven,
to accept a series of positions in domestic service throughout her teenage
years, and later to acquire on the job the skills of a highly qualified seamstress.[1] Only in sections of her autobiography not included in these excerpts does she explain how she went on to become a Syndicalist, a
feminist, and a historian of the working class.*

*Bouvier's memoirs were published in 1936, in the author's seventy-first
year. In them, she adopts the pose of one looking back on a full life that
is nearing its conclusion, little knowing that it would last almost thirty
years more. At the time it appeared, her book was widely noted and reviewed, but actual sales were disappointing, amounting to just three hundred copies during the first nine years it was in print. The appeal of her
narrative has, however, proved enduring, and a new French edition, prepared by Daniel Armogathe with the collaboration of Maité Albistur, was*

---

1. Throughout her memoir, Bouvier refers to herself as an *ouvrière*, which I have
variously translated as "working woman," "female worker," or "worker" according
to context. In French, the term generally refers to someone working in the manufacture of goods; technically, it perhaps would not apply to Bouvier in the period
she spent in domestic service.

published in 1983 by Editions de la Découverte. It is from that edition that the present translation has been made, with the generous permission of the publisher. Footnotes preceded by the initials "JB" are those which Bouvier included in her original text.

MY LITTLE BROTHER'S BAPTISM

My earliest childhood memory is of my little brother's baptism.[2]

A great commotion reigned in the household. A little brother had just been born. A few days after his birth, the family made ready a baptismal celebration and dressed up his oldest sister, who was to be the godmother. The baby was also decked out in a beautiful dress. All the guests were in fancy dress, and the procession got under way. Bells were ringing.

My own godmother's son and I were still in shirtsleeves and bare feet, our faces unwashed. (And yet a little brother's baptism must really be something magnificent, since everyone dresses up in their Sunday best.) Taking advantage of my godmother's momentary absence, we opened the bedroom door and slipped out into the stairway. Once out in the street, we started running along on our little legs and bare feet. Moments later, we were at the church. Without proper respect for the temple of God, we threaded our way up to the baptismal font and, with eyes wide in wonder, we observed the religious ceremony. No one had noticed the arrival of two brats whose noses were running, whose hair needed combing, whose faces needed washing, whose feet were bare, and whose only clothing consisted of shirts that surely were no longer white, since we had been rolling on the ground all morning.

When the ceremony was over and the procession formed up once again, everyone was full of joy—until they found themselves face to face with the two brats whom they had tried to leave at home. There was a moment of amazement before such a spectacle. We had disturbed the celebration. The eyes of all those people, dressed so well, became threatening. Anger began to color all their faces. Suddenly we realized that by our presence we were running the risk of great danger and we took off at full gallop. Knocking over chairs, we reached the road as fast as we could. This time it was no

---

2. JB: I was born in Salaize-sur-Sanne in the department of Isère on 11 February 1865. My father, Marcel Bouvier, was a member of the work crew at the Paris-Lyon-Méditerranée Railroad (PLM) in Salaize. My mother, Louise Grenouiller, did not work outside the home. My father quit the station at Salaize for the one in Saint-Rambert-d'Albon in Drôme when I was just sixteen months old. As a result, I have no recollection of the village where I was born.

longer the desire to see the baptism that made us run so hard but the certainty of a punishment we could not avoid!

When we arrived home, out of breath, my godmother was looking for us to get us dressed up for the meal.

"Where were you?" she asked us.

"At church for my little brother's baptism."

"At church dressed like that!"

That was not possible, and she did not want to believe us until the procession, which had taken longer to return than we had, burst into the house. The initial amazement had passed, and everyone began to laugh at the incident and at our air of puzzlement. It was the most frolicsome thing that happened all day. We were so happy to have seen my little brother's baptism! What did it matter how we were dressed! Our curiosity was satisfied, and the story made the rounds of the village.[3]

MY LITTLE BROTHER'S DEATH

Sixteen months had passed since my little brother's baptism. A measles epidemic was raging in the village. Nearly all the children caught it. At our house, the three of us slept in the same bed. My sister and I quickly got better, but our little brother had a relapse that carried him off in the space of a few days. My mother cried a great deal, and we cried with her. Total silence prevailed in our household. We had to walk on tiptoe and speak only in whispers. Everyone seemed to be afraid of disturbing our little brother's eternal sleep.

I sensed that something strange was happening. The curtains of the little bed were drawn, a candle burned on a table covered with white linen, a branch of boxwood was soaking in a saucer full of holy water. The women of the neighborhood came to visit my mother. They would spread the curtains of the little bed, say a prayer, and sprinkle a few drops of holy water. Then they would speak a few words of consolation to my mother and her sobs would redouble. This sadness lasted two days. The village bells rang the knell. Then, one day, my sister and I were taken to a friend's house, and when we returned home, the candle had disappeared along with the holy water. I opened the curtains of the little bed: it was empty. This empty bed made me very sad. The house was also empty. My little brother would play with me no more. He was gone forever.

In 1869, my father permanently quit his job with the railroad and returned to the village of Bougé-Chambalud where our entire family lived.

3. JB: I was three years old.

My father was a cooper by trade.[4] He had forsaken his trade because his belongings, house, land, and meadows had all been leased out. He had to wait until the leases had expired before taking possession of what his parents had left him as an inheritance. He intended to practice cooperage at the same time that he farmed his land. [. . .]

PAQUALAIS

When I was little, I did not like soup. It was a major undertaking to get me to eat it. Every evening it was the same old story. All through dinner: "Jeanne, eat your soup! Jeanne, eat your soup!" I heard it so often that when someone asked my name, I would answer, "Jeanne-eat-your-soup."

After the Franco-Prussian War of 1870, my father hired a worker who had served out the entire war after enlisting in an army regiment stationed in a seaport. At the dinner table, he would tell stories about the events he had witnessed. I was so enraptured to hear his fascinating tales that I ate my soup without noticing. This was a great stroke of luck for me, for that way I avoided the usual scoldings. I had great admiration for this worker, whose name was Paqualais. So much admiration that one day when I was about seven years old, I made him an unexpected proposal:

"Say, Paqualais, how would you like to marry me?"

"Sure! I'd be glad to."

Oh, how happy I was! I asked my father if he was willing for me to marry Paqualais, and he answered, "Yes." I asked my mother the same question, and she also answered, "Yes." Everyone was agreed. I was truly happy to think that I was going to marry Paqualais. But, though just a child, I knew that to get married you had to have a house. I asked my father·

"Say, father, when I'm ready to get married, will you really give me a house?"

"Yes," my father answered.

"And then a piece of land? Which one will you give me?"

"The one being worked by the Clavettes family."

"Then I'll need a horse and a cow."

"You'll have everything you need."

I was very happy.

"Say, father, will you also give me a cart?"

"Yes, you'll have a cart." And each time my father granted me one of

4. A cooper (*tonnelier*) is a highly skilled artisan who fashions wooden containers, especially watertight receptacles such as barrels, kegs, casks, buckets, vats, and tubs.

my requests, I would turn to Paqualais and tell him, "You see, my father's providing everything that's necessary." Then one day I said, "Say, father, will you also give me a tipcart?"[5] My father was no doubt in a bad mood, for he got angry and shouted, "And now a tipcart! Well then, I'll give you nothing, nothing!" I was very annoyed at this response. I turned to Paqualais and said, "Since my father doesn't want to give me anything, I'm not going to marry you anymore." And everything was broken off.

Despite this rupture, Paqualais still told me stories, to my great satisfaction, and I continued to eat my soup without it occurring to me that I did not like it. [. . .]

TENDING THE COWS

I would help my mother do all the little farm chores: hoeing, gleaning, and gathering grass for the animals. But my main job was tending the cows, and it kept me busy both morning and afternoon.

My mother made me get up before daybreak. She would call me several times without managing to wake me up. Tired of calling without results, she would take me, still asleep, and stand me up next to the bed. It was such a torment to be forced to get up when I so needed to sleep that I would stagger and sometimes I would cry. Not yet completely awake, I would get dressed with difficulty and leave the house still struggling against a desire to sleep, which I only managed to shake off long after my departure. You cannot imagine how a child suffers from being torn from sleep in this way.

My departure in the afternoon was completely different, especially when I would take my cows to graze in the meadows, once the haymaking season was over. All residents of the village were then allowed to take their cows to pasture, and as a result, a large number of children would gather in those meadows.

When it was time to go and the cows had been untied from their stalls in the cow shed, I would take my whip and whistle to the dog—"Let's go, Labry!"—and we would be on our way. I would crack my whip in the air, and when I passed beneath a walnut tree I would lash at the branches to make the walnuts fall. I would pick them up and put them in my apron, which I would gather up so it would hold a lot. I would eat them when I got to the meadow.

At the foot of a hillside beneath which ran a small river (the Dolon), a great oak was planted, as if to indicate that the path skirted the flank of the hillside. From this spot, you could look out over the whole meadow, and

5. A tipcart is a small, one-axled cart that can be tipped to the rear so as to dump out its contents.

when my friends had got there before me, I would call out to them: "Hey there! Delphine! Louise! Here I am!" I would give my cows a few lashes with the whip: "Get along, Bardella (a spotted cow)! Get along, Savina (a black cow)!" They would continue along in no special hurry. From the moment I had seen my friends in the meadow, I no longer had the patience to follow at their agonizingly slow pace. Leading downward from the foot of the great oak was a nearly vertical little path, a real goat's track, that I started down at a run. That way it took me only a few seconds to reach the bottom of the hillside. I would cross the river without worrying about how I placed my feet on the large stones that served as a ford, as water splashed up onto my legs. And that is how I caught up to my friends. "What are we going to play today?" That was the first question asked. But before playing, I had a chore to take care of. My mother made me knit while I was tending the cows. She would tell me, "You'll do twenty rows on that sock you're working on," and so that I would not cheat, she would make a mark. I would do my chore first so it would be out of the way and I could then play at my leisure.

What wonderful outings we would share in those beautiful meadows, irrigated by the Dolon and the Beige rivers, which partly enclosed them like a little millrace. We would climb the trees to find baby birds in their nests. We would jump over streams, and sometimes I would fall right in, so often and so completely that I developed pains in my legs. I was taken to the doctor's and he prescribed a delicious syrup and silver pills. How beautiful they were, and what a pleasure it was to take them! As for the syrup, I would have liked to drink it all day long!

My mother, who had only limited confidence in the doctor's prescriptions, did what all the good women of that region do. My ailment might well have been a "saint's illness." She therefore took three ivy leaves and put them out to soak overnight in a glass of water. On each leaf she placed a mark so she would know which saint she had to appeal to. One of those leaves represented Our Lady of the Seven Sorrows, another Our Lady of the Willows, and the third Saint Jean-François-Régis. The three leaves were all spotted, which meant that I had to seek the protection of all three saints. But Saint Jean-François-Régis's leaf was the most spotted. I did a novena to all three, and it was understood that I would also make a pilgrimage for each of them. But my mother pledged to Saint Jean-François-Régis that I would wear violet for a year. These remedies pleased me less than the delicious syrup and the superb pills. I was cured without ever being too concerned whether it was the medicines, the novenas, or the violet clothes that caused my recovery, and I never had those pains again. [. . .]

BOARDING SCHOOL

I reached the age of ten. It was time to learn the catechism and make my First Communion. Because the school was too far away for me to attend class regularly, my parents arranged for me to be a boarder at a religious establishment in Epinouze, a few kilometers from my village. There were twenty-five of us who were boarders in addition to the day students. For me, boarding school had a certain attraction. I would be among young girls my age with whom I could play. What is more, I wanted to learn! I have never been lazy. When my mother made me work, which happened frequently, I always did my chores with enthusiasm. I was not afraid to study, but I was in the habit of living and working outdoors, of running as fast as my legs could carry me when my mother sent me on some errand. No longer would I be taking my cows out to the meadow where I would join in such wonderful outings with my friends, often to the detriment of my clothes. School discipline appeared all the more harsh to me, especially at the beginning.

I was fairly well behaved during lessons. I would pay close attention to everything the Sister taught us. But at certain moments, I would feel pins and needles in my legs and ask to be excused. The lavatories were at the other side of a rather large courtyard. I would hop across it on one foot or, when I had my jumprope in my pocket, I would make several circuits of the courtyard with it. I sometimes forgot that I was supposed to return to class right away. The Sister would bang on the window pane very sharply, and I would rush back in. But my escapades would earn me demerits and often some kind of punishment.

One day I was placed in a nearly dark room that was supposed to serve as my dungeon. That was very distressing to me because I was afraid of the dark. Almost as soon as I entered, I noticed several baskets of cherries in a corner. What a windfall! I could eat cherries at my leisure! I put five, six, seven, eight in my mouth, and started over as soon as I had swallowed the first batch. I was careful to even up the tops of the baskets so that no one would notice a thing. When my punishment was over (it had not seemed long to me), the Sister came to let me out. She said, "Have you been eating cherries?" How could she know? So that no one could find any trace of my gluttony, I had even swallowed the pits, something my mother forbade me to do. She would tell me, "If you swallow the pit, the same thing will happen to you that happened to the priest's nephew: they had to get the doctor to clear his bowels, because he had swallowed too many cherry pits!" Fortunately, such terrible incidents hardly ever happen except in parents' imaginations!

I got used to the regimen at school and I was a good learner. The Sister declared to my mother: "She's a very good student. If only she could sit still! But she's restless and moves around all the time!"

I made my First Communion. What made me very happy was being dressed in white muslin and having a handsome crown on my head.

During the time that I was in boarding school, my mother, or someone she sent, would come see me on Sunday and bring me my food for the whole week. This invariably consisted of a rather large loaf of bread that would easily last me a week, some lard, sausage, eggs, goat's cheese or Swiss cheese, and a basket of potatoes. All this food was uncooked. The Sisters prepared the meals and they were eaten in common. I was also brought a little cask of wine that was placed on a shelf in the refectory alongside the other students' bottles. Sometimes, if my mother had made waffles or pancakes, she would bring me a stack. These provisions, along with my clean laundry, were brought in a wagon fitted with benches. We were, in short, well cared for in this boarding school. There was nothing fancy, and that is understandable. The cost of boarding was moderate: twenty-five francs a month for students who were fed by the Sisters, while those whose parents supplied food paid four francs a month and one-quarter franc for the cost of a bed. The total cost to my parents for the entire time that I spent in this boarding school was forty-seven francs and a few centimes.

There was scant concern for cleanliness. We would wash our face and hands every day. In preparation for this washing, a large yellow earthenware pot containing four or five liters of water was placed in the dormitory. Each student took her turn washing face and hands. Imagine the color of water that the last one got. Every month, we would wash our feet, using the very same pot. As for the mouth and the other extremity, that was out of the question. Those were parts of the body which, for a very long time, were not included in personal hygiene.

When vacation arrived, the Sister told my mother, "It's a shame that you can't leave her longer. She's very gifted. She works hard even when it comes to manual tasks." I had in fact learned to crochet in this brief time. I had made myself a pretty shawl of violet wool (because I was pledged to violet). One of my schoolmates had asked her mother to buy her the same wool, not because she was pledged to violet but because a bond of friendship existed between us due to the fact that we were born on the same day of the same year. We were convinced that this coincidence made us twins.

I loved to crochet and had quickly acquired great skill. I knew how to copy patterns, but what I preferred was crewel work. How I loved to make beautiful flowers and handsome fruits of brightly colored wool and silk! I had learned crewel work without the slightest difficulty. I knew how to vary tones. I worked with zeal. I was delighted. Those were the days when crewel-work slippers were in fashion. The Sisters either had lots of presents to make or else they were custom manufacturing crewel work. I don't know why they had so many orders for slippers! What I do know is that I made a lot of them. When they were pleased with me, the Sisters would take away some of my demerits, which overjoyed me.

I had also learned a little sewing, but I found this work monotonous. Endless little white stitches on white linen! This work produced no embossed pattern, no design! Stitches and more stitches, that was all! I definitely did not like sewing. I liked crocheting and crewel work best of all.

My stay in this boarding school did not exceed eight months. The store of knowledge that I took away with me, though slim, was enough that I could enter the factory immediately.

THE DISASTER

This disaster was provoked by the phylloxera infestation.[6] My father was a cooper, and his trade fell into a slump. For us this spelled complete ruin.

My parents, who until then had lived in relative comfort, were forced to sell everything: house, meadow, vineyard, and even furniture and various belongings. Someone carried off this, someone else bought that; it was a disaster. I was about to leave the house where I had played so hard, the trees in which I had climbed so often. Never again would I see the cherry trees, plum trees, and peach trees which had made me so happy. Indeed, everything that had represented childhood for me was about to be taken from me.

It was over; nothing was left. The house was empty and we were leaving. As we passed in front of my Aunt Marie-Anne's house, my mother stopped to say farewell. I took advantage of this stop to return one last time to the house in which my childhood had slipped by. I can see it still: the shutters and doors were closed, and it all looked so sad. No more clucking hens, no more barking dogs, no more playing children. There was no more life in that house, which had once been so noisy. It resembled a

6. Phylloxera is a type of plant louse, similar to an aphid, that originated in the New World. It attacks the leaves and roots of plants, including grapevines. The introduction of phylloxera in Europe caused widespread losses and devastated the wine-growing industry until the practice of grafting the traditional grape varieties onto phylloxera-resistant root stocks imported from America brought the infestation under control. For a time, however, the demand for barrels and casks was drastically reduced.

tomb. Seeing this, my heart constricted, and I left it behind, sobbing as I turned away.

We left our little village to go to Saint-Symphorien-d'Ozon, which is fifty kilometers away.

A WORKING GIRL AT THE AGE OF ELEVEN[7]

The first thing my mother did after we arrived at our new home was to go to the silk-throwing factory to ask if they wanted to hire me.[8] The foreman said yes, and I became a working girl. I was eleven years old. The working day began at five in the morning and did not end until eight at night. There were two hours of rest at mealtimes, from eight to nine in the morning to eat our breakfast, and from noon to one o'clock for lunch.

Before sending me off on my first day of work, my mother gave me a thousand bits of advice: "Pay close attention to what they show you, be very well behaved," and so forth. I was so afraid of being late that I was at the factory door early! The five o'clock bell finally rang, and the doors opened. The workers swept into the shop. I followed them, my heart beating with emotion. I was upset by all these changes, coming one after another: yesterday still living in the house where I had spent my childhood, then the departure from our little village, and now the arrival in this one, so full of unknowns for me. I was in a new world. There I was in a workshop with some fifty other working women.

As I entered, my eyes were drawn to everything that surrounded me: the noise of the machines and the sound of the *tavelles* (reels on which the skeins of silk were wound). The forewoman placed me under the supervision of a woman worker who was to show me the different operations involved in reeling silk. I listened to her very attentively. From time to time, I would turn around to see what was going on behind me. When eight o'clock finally rang, the women hurried out of the workshop, and I followed them.

As soon as I got outside, I set off on the double for my mother's house. She was anxious to know what impression I was going to bring back of my first shift in that factory. As soon as she saw me, she said, "So how did it go this morning?"

"It went well."

"Is it difficult, what they had you do?"

7. JB: September 1876.
8. Silk throwing is the doubling and twisting of raw silk into thread. In the period of which Bouvier writes, this process was performed by power-driven machines.

"Oh, it's as easy as pie. You just go like this to find the end, then when you have it, you have to add it to what's been rolled onto the *roquet*, the large reel. You have to make a knot like this. . . . (I was showing her with gestures.) Then you have to carefully even out the spooled raw silk with more strands, so the skein can be unreeled without breaking the thread."

That first morning's impression was favorable. I went running off as soon as I had eaten my breakfast and once again arrived well before the doors opened. That is how my life as a working girl began. I did not complain. I knew that poverty had entered our lives and that my thirteen-hour day at the workshop would earn me fifty centimes.

A law had been passed in 1840 making it illegal to have children under the age of twelve work more than eight hours, but it was never enforced. That is why I was working thirteen hours, or five too many.

When the first two weeks had passed, I received my first six francs in pay. I squeezed it in my hand for fear of losing it. I was proud to bring my mother the fruits of my labor.

The terrible part was winter, when I had to leave the house at quarter to five. It was so dark going out in the streets in the cold, the rain, and the snow! How I suffered, and oh how afraid I was of the dark!

Our household was desperately poor. My father was often out of work. Money was scarce in our home. My father could not pay his rent. Landlords are everywhere alike: they are hard on the poor. Ours simply had what was left of our furniture attached. When the sheriff's officer came for our belongings, I felt I was forever disgraced. It seemed to me that the local residents would all be pointing me out with their fingers. I was deeply upset, as if we were criminals, though we had committed no crime. We were simply poor, very poor.

I told my mother: "I'd never dare return to the factory. I'm too ashamed. I'd rather go drown myself than always be so miserable. And what's more, everyone will know we've had our property attached!" I was wearing an apron that was none too clean. I wanted my mother to give me another so that, when they fished me out of the river, they could not say that I was wearing a dirty apron. I had firmly resolved to end it all. I could not reconcile myself to living in such anguish. I was then twelve and a half years old. My mother refused to give me a clean apron. It is to this refusal that I owe not having done away with myself.

But I could not stand everyone knowing in what poverty we lived. I resolved to escape and go to my godmother's house. I informed my mother, and she gave me her approval. She said that she would follow me. I waited until nighttime to escape, so as not to be seen by the local people who knew that the sheriff's officer had come to our home.

When night fell, I set out. After I had walked for a while, I found myself on a plain. It was the middle of the night, but a night illuminated by a moon that seemed unusually large and so bright that it frightened me. In the distance was a forest whose trees were gigantic and whose silence was awful. It seemed that I was alone in the world, and I was so terrified that I hardly dared breathe. I felt so small before that moon and that forest. I was seized by a dread that is impossible to describe. I kept looking at the moon and the vast forest. It seemed to me that the trees were becoming bigger and bigger and that the moon itself was continuing to grow.

Abandoning the plan to go to my godmother's house, I retraced my steps. I turned my back on the moon, so I would not have to keep looking at it. But my tiny little body made an enormous shadow on the road. This shadow was a new cause of dread, and I began to run. I do not know if my fear was caused by the moon, the forest, my loneliness, or my shadow. All I know is that I was trembling with fright.

I continued on in this state for some time before I met my mother and my two younger brothers. One was seven and the other two. She was following me in order to avoid the shame of the sheriff's officer's visit. When I told her what had frightened me, we turned back, but instead of returning to the house that had been attached, we sought refuge in an old hovel that my father had rented and to which we were supposed to move as soon as the attachment of our furniture had been lifted. We spent the night there, sleeping on boards.

The next day we did not have anything to eat. My absence was noted at the factory and my fellow workers came to see me. They gave me some chestnuts, which calmed my hunger a bit, and persuaded me to return to the factory. I resumed my work.

Once we were settled into this hovel, poverty did not loosen its grip. I was forced to work outside the factory once my thirteen-hour day was over. I did crochet work and often stayed up all night. I worked night after night so there would be bread in the house. Despite these sleepless nights, often there was no bread.

I remember one such time when I went nearly two days without eating. That evening, when I came home from the factory, I started to work. My mother spent the night with me, shaking me whenever, in spite of myself, I began to fall asleep. She would tell me, "Don't fall asleep. You know very well that you mustn't sleep. Tomorrow we won't have any bread." I made superhuman efforts to stay awake. It was very cold. Snow was falling against the window panes. Despite all these tortures, I continued to work until four-thirty in the morning, at which time I got ready to return to the factory.

When I left the house, it was terribly cold. There was snow up to my knees. I had to cross the whole village in this snow and the dark of night. I was shivering from cold, from fright, and because I was so hungry and so tired! My eyelids burned like hot coals. These were the circumstances in which I began my thirteen-hour workday.

At eight o'clock, the factory let out for breakfast. I rushed home to finish my work. There were a few details to finish up before quickly going to deliver it and get the pay that would permit the whole household to eat. My brother accompanied me to the lady's house. He waited at the door. The lady paid me seven francs, just as she had promised. Because it was very cold, she offered me a cup of coffee with milk to warm me up. The coffee was served in a beautiful white cup and saucer. This cup had a gilt garland—what a pretty cup!—and the coffee was delicious and hot. I did not really like coffee and milk, but I certainly liked it that time, served in such a beautiful cup! I left this lady's house in raptures.

I handed my brother the seven francs I held in my hand. I kept five centimes to buy myself a roll. The cup of coffee had not satisfied my hunger. I had not eaten for nearly forty-eight hours. My brother brought the seven francs to my mother, who made a good soup to satisfy everyone.

I lived through many other bad days. I was a good worker at the factory, but I almost never got a raise. My mother, who was always short of money, would get angry to the point of beating me. She thought that I was not working hard enough and she would call me lazy. I could not stand this insult, but though I told her how hard I worked, she would not believe me. One payday, when I had received no raise and, as usual, the foreman told me that he would give me one in two weeks, I set to thinking about how my mother would take the news. Tired of always being beaten and never getting a raise, I resolved to go look for a job in another factory. I showed up and was hired with a raise of six francs every two weeks.

I got home a little late. As soon as I arrived, my mother asked if I had gotten a raise. I told her no. She immediately began to shout, and I was about to get hit when I explained to her that I was going to work in another factory where they would give me six francs more than in the one I was leaving. This happy news calmed her down, and she did not beat me.

The following Monday, my absence was noticed by the foreman, and he was told that I had left the factory because he never gave me a raise. He sent someone to find me and tell me that he would give me a raise of six francs every two weeks. The explanation behind all this was the following: the foreman would ask the owner for raises. The owner would grant them, but the foreman would keep them for himself as a way of getting rich. While poor little unfortunates like myself endured poverty and received beatings, he kept the money. The proof is that if he had not already arranged the raise, he would have had to ask permission from the owner before offering me one.

During the entire time that we spent in that region, poverty never left us. Tired of suffering, my mother left one fine morning, taking all three of us with her and leaving my father, who never paid us any attention after that.

We returned to my grandfather's house, though he was not very happy to see all these new arrivals. It was the season when there was lots of work in the fields, and I was employed there as a laborer.

When winter came and the work in the fields was over, I took a job in a silk factory in Saint-Rambert-d'Albon, a few kilometers from my grandfather's house. I would leave my grandfather's on Sunday evening and return the following Saturday evening. I would bring food to eat for the whole week.

At the factory, they served soup in the morning and evening, but what soup! It was so bad that the dogs refused to eat it. We were also given a place to sleep, but in deplorable conditions. The beds were made of four planks nailed together, a sack of wood shavings as a mattress, barely any bedspread, and sheets that were almost never washed. The dormitory was an attic without a ceiling. The roof tiles were directly above our heads, and if we sat on our beds, our heads would touch them.

DOMESTIC SERVICE

I was so unhappy in this factory that I went off to Vienne. There a cousin found me a job in the home of some truck farmers. These truck farmers had two small children. I was to serve as nursemaid, cowherd, and truck farmer. I was, in short, to do whatever they wanted. They lived in an isolated house, and when they went to town to sell their vegetables and milk I stayed behind, alone with the children.

I was bored as I have never been before or since. This solitude was oppressive. I cried all day long, to the point where I could not eat because my throat was so constricted. My eyes were constantly full of tears. I was thirteen and a half. You cannot imagine what kind of sadness sometimes enters the heart of a young girl of that age. When evening came, I would go to bed in a sort of nook made up in a corner of the attic out of poorly joined planks. The wind would blow through the roof and make the strings of onions that were hanging in a corner of the attic move around. This scared me, the more so because I was still afraid of ghosts. Still, I preferred to be in bed rather than up and about, because I could cry as much as I liked. My mistress had surely noticed how sad I was. Fortunately she never said anything to me! If she had mistreated me a bit or simply scolded me, I don't know what I would have done.

Sometimes I wanted to get the children to play. I would force myself to be cheerful, to laugh, but right away a torrent of tears would flood down my cheeks. What was I to do to chase away my sadness? Complain? I never complained; I suffered in silence. I suffered a great deal. How was I to get out of there? I could not just leave, for I needed to work. And then if I complained of boredom, they would perhaps think that I was unwilling to work, and I would be taken for a lazybones! I could not stand such an insult.

I saw only one way to escape this melancholy. In the garden there was a basin that was used for washing vegetables before they were taken to town. All I had to do was let myself fall in, and people would think it was an accident. I knew how much suffering it takes to drown, but that did not frighten me as long as I would no longer have to experience such boredom. And then I would no longer be obliged to sleep in my nook of poorly joined planks, in that awful bed, where I was so terrified!

The truck farmers must have mentioned my sadness and lack of appetite to my cousin. The following Sunday, my mistress told me to go visit her, that it would change my mood. It was with a certain joy that, my tears dried, I set off in the direction of town. It was several kilometers away. I did not know the way, having traveled there just once, when I initially arrived. I set off all the same. I remembered having seen, when I first came, a little house surrounded by red dahlias. When I sighted this house, I would be saved. I had already been walking for a good while. I would take a left and then a right and would go on walking. I was not really sure where I was. I was in a sunken road with nothing on the horizon to guide me except the sun. Could I have been getting farther away from town rather than closer? I continued walking, on and on, when at last I saw the little house with the red dahlias. As I passed by, I looked at it with gratitude, as if it had rendered me a great service. I was saved. With a light heart and a light step, I began to run toward town. At last I arrived at my cousin's. She immediately asked if I was happy in my job and if I would get used to it. The only way I could answer was to shake my head, because my throat tightened up so much whenever I thought of that house where I was so miserable.

When I was ready to leave, my cousin told me, "Stay a while!" I said to myself, "But later it'll be dark and I won't dare return, for I'll be too afraid and I won't be able to find my way again. I nearly got lost on my way here. I did kilometer after kilometer in daylight, but at night I won't see the little house with red dahlias. I mustn't wait any longer to be on my way." My cousin must have let my godmother know, because my godmother came to my cousin's house. She too asked if I was happy in my job. I did not dare to say no. "If you're miserable," she said, "you must tell me, and I won't let you go back." My godmother had always shown me the warmest friendship, and I was not surprised that she would speak to me in this way. So, crying all the while, I poured out to her all my unhappiness. It was decided that I would not return to the truck farmers'.

The next day, my godmother took me to a silk factory. The director gave me a job. Once again I took up the factory life that was familiar to me.

In that factory, as in so many in the region of Lyon, the female workers are provided with lodging. In this one we were well housed. The beds were well made and clean, the sheets were changed every month. I was happy to sleep in a comfortable and clean bed, as I had at my mother's. The dormitory was well lighted, heated in the winter, and had a cupboard for each worker. The refectory was also well lighted and heated, and each of us had her own wall cupboard there as well. The workers prepared their own food in an enormous kitchen. All the cupboards locked with keys. I thought this arrangement was wonderful.

I breathed more freely in this factory where I was better off, with wages of one franc twenty-five centimes a day. I managed to meet my needs, buying everything I required to feed myself except my soup. One of the women from the factory sold soup. She would serve me soup twice a day for ten centimes. Good or bad, I ate it all the same. The bad times, when there had been no bread, had gotten me in the habit of eating everything I was given. On Sundays, this woman did not make soup. I took advantage of this opportunity to spoil myself a bit: a ten-centime square of chocolate and five centimes' worth of milk, and I would make myself a good cup of chocolate.

On Sunday, I would wash and iron my laundry. We had as much hot water as we wanted, which made our task easier, and a drying room was set up in a shed. This shed was only available to the workers on Sunday, for it was used for something else during the week. When I was not washing my laundry, I would go see my cousin and play with her two children. I was happy in comparison with all the misfortunes I had endured.

There was, however, one problem with that factory: the workday was too long. The bell would ring at four-thirty in the morning. I would curse it when I heard it. The workday ran, as in my first factory, from five in the morning until eight at night, with two one-hour rest periods for meals.

I was content, living in this gentle calm, when I received a letter from my mother telling me to leave the silk factory and come with her to Paris. What prompted her to make me move from that region? What new trials would this change bring? No, really, I could not bring myself to accept the idea of changing jobs. Paris held no attraction for me. I was broken-hearted, for I had made a life for myself, and now I was supposed to change yet again! And then too, would I get chocolate on Sundays in Paris? Maybe not!

I went to see my godfather and godmother. I told them about my mother's letter and informed them of how little I looked forward to this new change. My godfather told me, "If you didn't have parents, you wouldn't leave Vienne. But if your mother wants to take you to Paris, you have to go."

I left Vienne with a heavy heart and full of worries about the future. When I joined my mother, she explained that she had found a job in Paris with some people who manufactured shaving brushes. She would be a maid and I would be an apprentice. These new employers had sent money to pay for our trip, for otherwise we would never have come to Paris, for lack of money.

A MAID IN PARIS

One fine morning—25 February 1879—we arrived in the capital, before proceeding on to Montreuil-sous-Bois, where the brush factory was located.

My mother went right to work, but service in a Parisian household was completely different from service in a country household. Things just did not work out at all. I got started with brushes, using a knife dipped in some kind of substance to dye the bristles. This was boring work, and I did it without enthusiasm. What I liked best about that house was the soft white bread. It was so good, I could have eaten two kilos a day. One evening, the master and mistress adopted a mysterious manner to talk with my mother. They made me wait in one room while they chatted in another. Whatever was going on had to be rather odd for them to have made me wait alone. When they were done, my mother came out, and we headed for our room. When the two of us were alone, my mother explained that the master and mistress were not satisfied with her service and could not keep us. We had hardly been there a week, and they were letting us go. But as we owed them the eighty francs they had paid for our travel, we could not take our belongings with us. We were to leave the next day, as early as possible. If we could pay back the eighty francs within a year, they would return our belongings. After my mother had told me all this, I said to myself, "Just my luck. So why did you make me leave Vienne? If I'd been older, I wouldn't have come."

The next day, we dressed by putting on as many clothes as possible. I wore two shirts, two pairs of pants, and two skirts so I would later have a change of clothes, for we were supposed to leave that house with empty hands. My mother and I were about to find ourselves without money, without jobs, without clothes, and without belongings.

We left Montreuil to go to Belleville, where my sister worked as a maid. My mother left me at her place while she went on to some cousins' in Versailles, hoping to find a job.

My sister found me a position in Meudon with some storekeepers.[9] I was supposed to do the shopping, the housework, the cooking, the dishes, and the laundry. There were three children (sons who were fifteen, seven, and two) as well as the husband and wife. The seven-year-old, who was especially spoiled, was very mean. He hit me all the time, and if I ever complained, he was always right. One day he hit me in the back with a brush, and it hurt me so much that I cried for a good part of the day. They all made fun of me when they saw me cry.

The mistress, a small woman with red hair and pinched lips, was known for her spitefulness. My life was no picnic in that house. I was not strong enough for all the work I had to do. I was supposed to do the laundry for five people, plus my own. I even washed the sheets. Washing was very difficult. I had to carry the water I needed down into a garden that was located on a lower level.

My mother found a job as soon as she arrived in Versailles, then another, and then still others. She could not hold any of them. Seeing how little luck she was having, she decided to go home to the countryside. For that, she needed money. She came to ask me to get an advance on my pay. I gave her the fifteen francs I had earned as my first month's wages, though I really needed those fifteen francs, as I had nothing to wear, neither clothes nor underwear. The two shirts that I owned were five or six years old, too small, and badly worn. I kept that job through the month of July, getting hit by the seven-year-old boy and enduring the mistress's fits of anger.

For the Fourteenth of July, a number of friends were supposed to come visit, and for this occasion we had to do a major housecleaning which involved washing the curtains and bedspreads so that everything would be irreproachably clean.[10] From the seventh to the fourteenth, I cleaned all day long and then did two loads of washing. I don't know how many

9. Bouvier describes her employers as *marchands de couleurs,* sellers of paints and dyestuffs.

10. The Fourteenth of July, French Independence Day, celebrates the fall of the Bastille prison in 1789, an event which is seen as the beginning of the French Revolution. It is roughly the equivalent of the Fourth of July in the United States. Bouvier is recounting the events of 1879, the year in which the official and public celebration of the Revolution was resumed for the first time since the Paris Commune of 1871.

buckets of water I had to carry down to the garden! These buckets weighed more than I did, and I had to carry them two at a time. My poor arms were worn out.

One morning, I was finishing the laundry and hurrying to spread the clothes out in the garden to dry. I had strung up a number of ropes to hold this great quantity of laundry. When I had almost finished, one rope broke. When it broke, it made the other ropes go slack. Suddenly, all the laundry had fallen into the vegetable beds and gotten dirty! After all the difficulty I had experienced washing all those clothes, I was going to have to start over! I was utterly disheartened.

When Madame noticed my misfortune, she started calling me an imbecile, an idiot: "How dumb you are, my poor girl! You foolish peasant! For your punishment, you won't eat until it all has been rewashed! And on the Fourteenth of July, you won't go see the illuminations or the fireworks![11] That will teach you not to be so dumb in the future!" I listened to all this without responding. I was very annoyed. The rope had broken because it was too old, and that was all there was to it. It was not my fault. I had to carry down more buckets of water, bending beneath their weight. I bemoaned my lot for all I was worth while they, meanwhile, were up there eating lunch. I went on doing the washing. I was hungry but I did not ask for anything to eat. I just went on crying as I carried my buckets of water. A woman who sold them wine was making her way to the cellar and saw me crying during the lunch hour. She asked me, "Aren't you going to eat, little one?"

"No," I answered, "I have to finish all my laundry before I can eat."

I then went on to tell her of the misfortune that had befallen me, the scene that Madame had made, and how upset I was. I finished at five-thirty, too late for lunch. I had to wait for dinner. I was so humiliated by this whole episode that I told Madame I did not want to remain in her service any longer. She taunted me, saying that I would not easily find as good a job as the one in her house—not a girl as dumb as I was, who owned no clothes and no wardrobe—and that no one would want me.

The next day, when I went to the wine merchant's shop to fetch a bottle of mineral water, I told the woman that I was quitting, for I could not stay any longer in a job where I was so badly treated.

"Do you have another job?" the wine merchant asked me.

"No, madame. I'll go to an employment bureau in Paris, and they'll surely find me one."

11. Illuminations involved the lighting of public buildings and monuments on the occasion of popular celebrations or commemorations. When accompanied by the reading of texts or dramatizations based on historical events, illuminations become the "sound and light" displays (*son et lumière*) still much in use in France.

"But, my poor child, you don't know what Paris is like. Do you have any money?"

"I'll have the month's wages that I'll be paid when I leave."

"But, my dear, you should ask the local tradespeople. Ask the fruit seller, for example. She often has jobs."

"But I don't know the fruit seller and I wouldn't have the courage to ask her . . ."

With that, I left the wine merchant's. The next day was the Fourteenth of July. Many friends came to the house to spend the day and take part in the national celebration. They were all in high spirits, talking about the illuminations and the fireworks. When evening came, they all went off in a joyful mood to see them. I had never seen a celebration like it and would have liked to join them. I was left alone at the house and, to make sure I could not escape, I was locked in. The house was big and had little nooks and corners everywhere. When I saw that I was alone, I was overcome with fear and went to take refuge in the bathroom, which opened onto the passageway alongside the house. The bathroom window looked out on this passageway, but heavy iron bars closed it off. I put my face against the bars like a prisoner at the window of her cell. From this window I could make out the courtyard. I could hear the rockets and see the blue and red colors reflected in the courtyard. That is all that I saw of that Fourteenth of July, 1879!

At a certain point, I heard footsteps in the courtyard. It was the wine merchant. I called out to her. For a moment she tried to make out who it was. When she had recognized my voice, she came over to where I was and, seeing me peering out through the bars, said, "What are you doing here, little one?" I explained. She asked me if I had found a job. "I don't dare ask the local tradespeople," I told her. "I'll ask for you," she replied.

The next day, I had to start over, doing the laundry that had gotten dirty since my last washing. Since I would be leaving, they had to take full advantage of me so that everything would be clean! While I was carrying down my buckets of water, the wine merchant called me over:

"There's a lady at the fruit seller's who needs a maid, but this lady wants a girl twenty-five years old. How old are you?"

"I'm fourteen and a half."

"You're too young, but go ahead and tell her you're eighteen. Perhaps she'll take you anyway."

I went to the fruit seller's to see the lady, who immediately asked, "How old are you?"

"Eighteen, madame."

"Eighteen, but that's too young. Are you responsible for an eighteen-year-old?"

"Oh yes, madame, I'm very responsible."

"Do you know how to cook?"

"Yes, madame."

"Do you know how to do housework?"

"Yes, madame."

"Do you know how to do laundry?"

"Yes, madame."

"Do you know how to iron?"

"Yes, madame."

"You seem rather young to me. I would have liked a girl of twenty-five or thirty, but if you assure me that you're very responsible, I'll hire you."

"Madame, I am very responsible."

I said this in a way that conveyed that I could not possibly be more responsible. "Now here's what needs to be done in my home. We're merchants. Our business is in Paris. I have two young girls who are at boarding school at the moment. In a few days, they'll be on vacation. I've rented a house in Meudon so they can spend their vacation in the countryside. That's where I'm going to take them. My older girl is fifteen, the other eleven. The three of you will be all alone during the week because my business requires that I stay in Paris. On Saturday evening, my husband and I will come spend Sunday in Meudon, but during the rest of the week I'll be entrusting my girls to you. I'm counting on you to take good care of them. You will care for them as if they were your own children."

"Yes, madame."

"Since you assure me that you're responsible, I'll pay you twenty-five francs a month. I'm only hiring you for the two months of vacation, but if you're responsible and if I'm pleased with your work, I'll find you a job at the end of the vacation."

When we had reached this agreement, she gave me two francs to seal the arrangement. This lady had come to Meudon with the firm intention of hiring a young woman twenty-five or thirty years of age. She hired one she thought was eighteen but who in reality was just fourteen and a half.

I was pleased with the way it had worked out. I had a job and could leave the one I was in. The day of my departure arrived, and with it also the moment for settling accounts. That disagreeable redhead kept back twelve francs and sixty centimes for breakage, making me pay five francs for a bowl that was already cracked when I arrived and was not broken when I left. The crack had grown no larger during my stay at the house, and this bowl was not worth more than ninety-five centimes new. In much the same way, she inflated the price of all the objects, broken or not, that she made me pay for. So instead of fifteen francs, I was paid just two francs forty centimes. I do not know what would have become of me with my two francs and forty centimes if I had not had a job. She continued making fun of me because I did not have a trunk for my belongings. I had no clothes or wardrobe. A kerchief with its four corners tied together was all I needed to carry everything I owned.

When I mentioned the money she had withheld from my pay, the wine merchant said, "What a scoundrel that woman is!" She told me to go to the justice of the peace to seek redress. I told her that I would never dare. When you are fourteen, it's impossible for you to obtain justice. That is why poor young girls get cheated! Once I had left, I heaved a sigh of relief. I was happy to get out of that house where one child hit me and the mistress had robbed me.

On the agreed-upon day, I showed up for my new job with my little bundle of clothes under my arm. I presented myself at the door of an unpretentious little house and said, "I didn't bring my trunk. I left it at my sister's." I was ashamed of having so few clothes and I was afraid they would not take me because I was poor.

The house consisted of a dining room, a living room, and two bedrooms, along with the kitchen and my bedroom. My room was bright and clean. During the week, I slept in the mistress's room so as to be closer to the young girls. They were not afraid, nor was I. These two young girls were very nice.

The household equipment was extremely simple, consisting of no more than what was strictly necessary. Because the furniture was rented, it received only enough care to keep it up, which left me free time and allowed me to play with my young mistresses. The garden was fairly large and had a lawn and fruit trees. I had not forgotten how I used to climb trees in my native region. I gave my two charges a demonstration of my skills and they followed suit; soon all three of us were climbing around, which we enjoyed immensely. I relived my childhood in that garden.

We did the shopping together and the cooking too, but sometimes, in the heat of play, the food would burn and I would not know what to do. I would say, "I'm not going to play anymore. The food burned while I was playing, and Madame's going to scold me." The girls would quickly answer, "We won't tell mother and we'll eat it all up before she comes. She'll never know." And we'd start playing all over again.

I had been ordered to make them play the piano for an hour each day, but I would forget about the piano, and so would they. I would not say anything about it either. On Sunday, Madame would ask me if they were each playing for an hour. I would tell her, "Not every day. When they're having fun, I leave them alone."

"You're right," their mother would say. "As long as they're enjoying themselves, I'm happy."

One day there was a celebration somewhere. Madame took her two girls. I stayed home all alone, all day and all night. How frightened I was in that isolated house, practically surrounded by the forest of Meudon! I could not sleep all night. All sorts of ideas went through my mind. I imagined that someone was breaking down the door and that the furniture was shaking. By the time morning arrived, my face was all distorted with fright and the effects of a sleepless night.

When the ladies of the house arrived, I heaved a sigh of relief. Madame noticed my ravaged face: "What happened to you?" I told her that I had been upset when I saw they were not coming home. I was afraid that they might have had an accident and could not sleep all night. I said I had been expecting them from one moment to the next and then they never came. I told her I had been extremely uneasy all night long but that now that I saw that they were fine, I was reassured. I did not want to let on that I was frightened for myself. I was afraid she would find out how old I was. I preferred to say that I was uneasy over what had become of them. That made me appear more responsible. Since I was supposed to be responsible, I did my best to be just that.

When vacation was over, we returned to Paris. Madame told me, "I've found you a job. You'll start there as soon as my girls have gone back to boarding school." Everything was going fine, when suddenly I managed to destroy all the respect that I had earned during those two months of vacation.

I was supposed to accompany the two girls to their grandfather's house. To get there, we were to take the omnibus. I was overjoyed at the prospect, as I had never taken an omnibus. This omnibus passed right in front of my employers' shop, and it was from there that the three of us were to depart. Madame was watching us. When the omnibus arrived, I rushed forward first and climbed aboard, and as there was just one seat free, I took it, leaving the two young girls to follow in my wake. They got on after me and had to remain standing on the platform. Madame, who was watching us, was outraged that a maid should permit herself to get on before her mistresses. I understood nothing of these niceties, but that evening, when we got home, I was given a sound scolding. I was called an ill-bred person, someone improperly trained who must have previously served only with louts with no sense of manners. I struggled to give as my excuse that I had got there first and that naturally the first to get there was supposed to sit down. The more I gave the explanation that I thought logical, the more I exasperated Madame, who ended up calling me an idiot and an imbecile.

"When I think that I entrusted my girls to someone as stupid as you, I shiver to think of the dangers they must have risked in your care." But in my heart of hearts I was telling myself, "It's very simple: the first one to get there gets on first!" It was an obsession. I could not reconcile myself to getting on last when I had been the first to get there.

The girls returned to their boarding school, and I left my job with an explicit warning never to set foot in that house again: I was too badly brought up, for I got into the omnibus before my mistresses!

I started the job that this last employer had found me in the home of some people who owned a hardware store. My pay was twenty francs a month for doing all the work: housekeeping, cooking, laundry. My employers were young people, but they were old young people who never seemed to be cheerful. They never did anything fun, for fear of spending money. Their business took up all their time. The house was in poor condition. The walls and ceiling of the kitchen were black.[12] This kitchen, where I spent part of my day, was located behind the store. The only daylight it received came through a transom window, so it was badly lit. There was never any sun and the walls oozed damp and filth. As for my bedroom, it was a sort of dark, windowless cell that opened onto the passageway alongside the house. In front of the door was an open gutter in which the household waste water flowed. The health laws had not yet forbidden this arrangement. I did not have to endure the unpleasant odors that it must have given off in the summertime, for I stayed with the hardware merchants only through the terrible winter of 1879–80. That job was the epitome of dreariness. I spent my days working alone, always alone, between a kitchen that resembled a tomb and a bedroom that was a real dungeon. My employers were boring beyond all comparison. All they talked about was nails and cookware.

At the end of 1879, there was a political affair—the earliest I can remember—that caused a stir. First the Senate and the Chamber of Deputies resumed meeting in Paris.[13] They had previously decreed an amnesty

12. Most cooking was done over open fires or wood-burning stoves that deposited layers of soot and grease on every exposed surface. The usual remedy was to clean and whitewash the kitchen periodically, but where this was not done, the result was the dark and dingy environment that Bouvier describes.
13. The National Assembly had moved to Bordeaux as a result of the Franco-Prussian War. After an armistice was signed with the victorious Prussians, the Assembly moved to Versailles rather than Paris, which had refused to accept defeat and was besieged for four months before capitulating in January 1871. Parisians refused to recognize the authority of the National Assembly that had negotiated unfavorable terms of peace with the Prussians, leading to a period of civil war known as the Paris Commune, lasting from March to May of 1871. Wary of Paris, which as a capital city had spawned so many insurrections and overthrown so many

for those exiled in 1871. This produced two opposite reactions within the population of Paris: some were pleased at the exiles' return, while others were terrified at seeing them come back. My employers were among those who were terrified. They therefore took all necessary steps to secure everything they owned of value. They carried it all off to the countryside, to Madame's parents' house. They stocked up on rice and other staple foods to avoid the famine which would not be long in returning to Paris along with such individuals. I wondered just how terrible these people must be to make the Parisian population tremble so. My employers would tell stories about the war and the siege during the Commune. At least it made for a change from their usual conversation, which always had to do with bits of hardware. Madame would say to me, "Imagine how terrible it was! We were dying of hunger during the siege. I was sick, and my husband had to pay seventy-five francs for a chicken. This cost so much, and that cost such and such," always prices that were exorbitant. I would say to myself, "It must truly have been a horrible period if these people, who are such misers, spent that much money!" When I heard them list all these horrors, I would tremble just like them. "They'd have done better," I said to myself, "to toss all those folks in the sea instead of bringing them back. And then there are the women! There's the great incendiary, Louise Michel, who fired the machine gun in the Rue Turbigo![14] A woman like that is a monster!"

When the day and hour of their arrival had been determined, my employers closed their shop, or rather they did not open it that day. They had left for the countryside the previous evening. I stayed behind alone. I had told them, "I want to go see the Communards at the station." I wanted to examine at close quarters those horrible men and that terrible woman, Louise Michel. "You poor wretch!" Madame told me. "If you go there, you won't return. You don't know what those people are like. And there'll be police and soldiers there too!" I was going to get myself crushed in the crowd, perhaps taken along to the police station. Fear of the police and the police station alone made me abandon my plan. I stayed home alone and continually went out on the doorstep to see if I could catch sight of a Communard. I did not have the pleasure of seeing a single one.

---

previous regimes, the National Assembly remained in Versailles until the stabilization of the fledgling Third Republic made it possible for it to return to its traditional seat in 1879.

14. At the final defeat of the Paris Commune, some of its supporters set fire to a number of buildings in the capital. Exaggerated stories made the rounds, describing atrocities committed by the insurgents, including women incendiaries (*pétroleuses*) who were supposed to have used lamp oil to spread fires. Louise Michel (1830–1905) was the most famous of this group.

New Year's Day arrived and, since my employers were such misers, all they gave me as a New Year's present was a half-dozen pocket hand-kerchiefs with violet and white checks, which cost one franc ninety-five centimes a dozen. That amounted to a New Year's gift of some ninety-five centimes. This annoyed me and I resolved to find another job. I was sure I would not miss that dreary house.

In the year that I had been in Paris, this made the fourth job I had left: the brush makers, the storekeepers, the grain and fodder merchants, and the owners of the hardware store.

I found another job. This time it was not with tradespeople but in the home of a doctor. The husband did not practice medicine but worked in a laboratory at the Collège de France. My new employers were young. They had a little girl who was fifteen or eighteen months old. They lived in a stylish, sunny, and well-ventilated apartment. The kitchen had a window that looked out over several courtyards, onto which the kitchens of other houses also opened. It all seemed quite cheerful to me. My bedroom, on the seventh floor, had a skylight window, but by climbing on a chair I could see the Saint-Jacques tower and Notre Dame, as well as the chimneys of Paris. That was an improvement. I was happy to have left behind the hardware sellers' dark cell. I continued to represent myself as older than I was, as I had done ever since leaving the storekeepers' employ. With my "borrowed" nineteen years, I made a proper maid for a middle-class house-hold. In this job, I had to do everything: cooking, housekeeping, washing, ironing. With a small child, there was lots of washing and ironing. I would also go out with Madame, to carry the little girl.

I therefore took up my new duties with enthusiasm. I admired the living room and all the objects it contained. I found all this very beautiful. In the husband's study, there were books everywhere, nothing but books. I would read the titles and the names of the authors, but did not dare open them for fear of being scolded. There were also wide-mouthed jars containing all kinds and all sizes of snakes, and when I had to dust I was afraid to touch them. It seemed that these snakes were going to move about. I performed my duties well enough. I earned only minor reprimands. I would hurry to finish my work so I could play with the little girl, who was very cute. I really had fun with her. She had some pretty playthings. I had never had such beautiful ones when I had been little, and these toys delighted me. When one is fifteen years old, one likes to have fun, even when one is forced to earn a living.

My new employers did not talk business like those I had left. I learned from their conversations that Madame was the daughter of someone who had been a National Representative in 1848 and had been exiled in 1852.[15] Her father had written many books. After everything that my previous employers had told me about the exiles, I listened to what was said about them with a curiosity mixed with fear. And when I would go out with Madame to the homes of former exiles of 1852, I would look at them with an extraordinary curiosity. After such visits, I would ask Madame for information, which she would graciously provide. I would say to myself, "They don't seem so mischievous, all these people. I don't tremble before them. So what was wrong with my former employers that they spoke so badly of them?" I regretted not having gone to see those who had returned from Nouméa.[16] I surely would not have been killed if I had gone to the station. And then too, it seemed to me that when someone is called a "representative of the people," that person is a great man. I was not quite sure just what "representative of the people" meant. I would also see their names in the newspapers and in Monsieur's library. Many of the names I would hear were also among those I read on the spines of books.

One day, as we were sitting at the table, Madame said, "Today, I'm going to visit Victor Hugo, the great Victor Hugo."[17] I said to myself, "Victor Hugo! The one whose name is in the newspapers nearly every day, the one who has so many books in Monsieur's library. I'll ask if that's the one. Madame will surely tell me on our way." She asked me to hurry and I rushed off to get dressed. I put on my prettiest dress and my beautiful, red Scottish shawl, the one that could be seen from so far off. I wore my most beautiful white bonnet, decorated with a pretty, bright-green ribbon. I was very happy to make the acquaintance of a man who had been a representative of the people and who wrote books! On the way, I questioned Madame, who told me many things about Victor Hugo and also about his great attachment to the Republic. She also said that if her father were not dead, he would have been happy to live in a Republic. I did not understand the significance of what she was telling me, because I was preoccupied with the thought that I was going to see such a man. When we arrived, he kept us

15. Bouvier indicates in a footnote that the individual in question was Pierre-Joseph Proudhon (see chapter 6, n. 17). Bouvier's employer is likely to have been Proudhon's elder daughter, Catherine (1850–1947).
16. Nouméa is the capital of New Caledonia, an island in the South Pacific. It had been a French possession since 1853; until the end of the nineteenth century, it was a penal colony. Today it is an overseas French territory.
17. Victor Hugo (1802–85) was among the most celebrated poets and writers of his age and a prominent figure in the Romantic movement. He was also a deeply committed republican who was elected to the Constituent Assembly in 1848 and went into exile after Louis-Napoléon's coup in 1851. He returned to France and to public life at the end of the Second Empire in 1870.

waiting for just a moment and could only stay with us for a few minutes, as he was expected at a meeting. But when he entered, I looked him over carefully. I saw his venerable white-haired head. I watched him continually and saw only him, though he was accompanied by his granddaughter, to whom I paid no attention. I did not even notice the room in which he had received us. As we left, I said to Madame, "I'm happy to have met this gentleman who writes so many books!"

While working in that household, I was well fed and properly, even kindly, treated. And the little girl was a great attraction, too. I liked her very much. She would never leave me, and I would go on wonderful outings with her. Summer arrived, and with summer, the holidays. We all went off to the department of Oise. The husband's grandmother lived on a beautiful estate there. That is where, during the vacation, the family got together. The assembled group consisted of the husband's father and mother, his two sisters, himself, his wife, and his daughter, along with three maids. Each maid was supposed to take care of the private service of her employers. All three of us joined in general service and cooking. But I, who fortunately had a little girl to take care of, would take her for walks in the great garden and push the doll's carriage. What wonderful outings the two of us would have. At times, I was as happy as a six-year-old. Madame, who would watch us play, would say of me, "She enjoys herself as if she were the same age as the child!" In the morning, before anyone was awake, I would go run under the great, covered walkways, and that would remind me of my time in the meadows of my native district.

On this estate, there was a very large kitchen garden with a large plot of red currants, heavy with fruit. The family had given us permission to eat as many currants as we liked. But one day it was decided that, since the currants were ripe enough to make preserves, the next day everyone would start picking them. I was saddened at the thought that I would no longer be able to eat them. I told myself, "Tomorrow, when I wake up, I'll go eat an enormous quantity for the last day." I got up very early. All the shutters were closed, or so I believed. I headed for the plot of red currants, sat down against a bush, and picked ruby-red bunches that the morning air made even more beautiful. I ate a lot of them, and then, when it was time for everyone to get up, I headed for the kitchen to do my work. Our sole preoccupation was making preserves, and to accomplish this, all the rest of the household duties were put off. Soon everyone took up baskets and headed for the currant patch. When we started picking bunches, I managed to eat a few, but really I had had enough! The husband's father came to help. As he passed right by me, he said, "So you're eating some?"

I answered, "Yes, sir, I'm eating a few."

"A few?" he told me. "You're eating a few? I don't know how you can eat any more. I watched you this morning from my bedroom window." I was gripped by fear. I thought all the shutters were closed, but obviously those of the husband's father were not. "Yes, this morning you looked like a child of fifteen. In what year were you born?" The fact that I had been observed had taken my breath away, and besides, it had never occurred to me to figure out in what year I was supposed to have been born. I answered, "Sir, I was born in 1865."

"In 1865? Then you are fifteen?"

"Yes, sir." I did not know what to say. I was confused and angry for having been so stupid. I should have said that I was born in 1861, which worked out to the nineteen years that I had claimed. He said, "Follow me," and I hastened to do so. Where was he taking me? Was he going to put me in a cell?

He went back into the house and up the stairs to the third floor. I was still following him, wondering what was going to happen to me. My face was as red as a beet, and I walked like a convict on her way to the gallows. He knocked on Madame's door. "Come in," she answered. Because Madame was feeling a little ill that day, she had stayed in bed. I followed him in. He told me, "Stand there, at the foot of your mistress's bed and tell her how old you are." How I suffered just at the thought of it! To confess that I had lied was distressing to me, but there was no way to escape! I said, all atremble, "I'm fifteen and a half."

"What do you mean? You told me nineteen just a few months ago, and now you're fifteen and a half?" She was as surprised as I was embarrassed.

"You lied to me when you told me you were nineteen?"

"Yes, madame." I was forced to acknowledge my lie. Did the grandfather, who was watching this scene being played out, understand how disagreeable it was to have to pretend to be older because of the need for a job? Or was he touched by my expression of embarrassment? He told Madame, "Don't scold her, the poor child!" These words, "poor child," were the first terms of compassion that I heard directed my way. I was so touched by them that I began to sob. I ran out of Madame's bedroom, leaving the two of them to talk.

When I was alone, I grasped the situation in which I found myself. Now everyone knew I was a liar. I was terribly humiliated. Fifteen years old? They would no longer have any confidence in me. And whenever I said something, they would no longer believe me because I had once lied! The grandfather, who was an exceedingly kind and very sensitive man, must have told Madame to treat me like a child. At times he would say to me, "There now, little girl!" I felt hurt at the thought that I was no longer considered responsible and that their confidence in me had declined to the level of my true age. I could no longer stand the thought of living in that house where I was too young and a liar besides. I decided to leave. When the family returned to Paris at the end of vacation, I quit my job. I went to Versailles, where my sister was working.

A few days later, I began work in the home of a retired general. This general had three children: one son was a soldier, one daughter was in a convent, and another daughter lived at home. I served four people: the general, his wife, his daughter, and the wife's mother. The daughter was twenty-six years old. Until the age of eight, she had lived with her grandparents, but when she lost her grandfather at the age of eight, she and her grandmother had come to live with the general and his wife. The daughter was hated by her parents, or I should say by her mother. For this reason, the life she led was terribly unfair. She had to live in a tiny little bedroom. She was only rarely allowed to go out. She never ate at the dining table. Her meals were served in her room, and all she got were dishes that she hated. These practices resulted in frequent quarrels. This young woman had arrived at a high degree of nervous excitement. Claiming she was disturbed by the quarrels that the daughter picked with her, her mother would say, "I hope we'll soon be able to have her put away at last!" This young girl would come find me in the kitchen. It's true that she would often annoy me, but I took pity on her. I understood, despite my youth, that she must have really suffered at being treated in this way by her parents. I endured her all the same, though often Madame would tell me, "Chase her out of your kitchen! Let her go to her room." The grandmother would come and thank me for putting up with her and tell me how much she suffered for all the injustices done to this young woman, while the general's other children were coddled.

Sometimes I would agree to take her out as a way of pleasing and entertaining her a bit, but in the street she would make me uncomfortable. With her, I never knew which way to turn.

One day there was a terrific row, and to punish the daughter, the general's wife forbade her to set foot in the kitchen. She told me that I had to choose between chasing the daughter out of the kitchen or being fired. I replied that I would rather quit than chase her away, and I left.

A WORKING GIRL ONCE AGAIN

When I quit that job, I returned to Paris. I had learned the addresses of some cousins and went to see them, thinking that they might help me find a good job. My arrival was a surprise for them.

The woman of this couple was my father's niece. They had a twenty-two-year-old daughter. The husband worked in a business firm. The wife sewed ready-made clothes.[18] Their daughter was employed in a firm that did machine pleating.

When I informed them of my intention to find a job, these relatives told me that I would do better to look for work in some trade rather than remain in domestic service. I adopted this perspective all the more readily since I had thus far been unable to hold onto any job and because this unstable lifestyle—spending one day here and the next somewhere else—gave me no satisfaction. I therefore accepted their proposal that I look for something other than a job as a maid.

It was decided that until I had found something, I would do sewing with my cousin. I began this work with enthusiasm and quickly picked it up. But a friend of my cousins' came to visit them. She said, "I could get her hired where I work. It doesn't take long to learn the trade." She was a hatmaker.[19] A few days later, she came and got me so she could introduce me at the hat factory. I was accepted and put to work. I continued boarding at my cousin's, where I paid fifteen francs a week toward my room and board. I was responsible for my own living and laundry expenses.

That's how I became part of that hatmaking shop. I was happy to find myself in the company of so many fellow workers. The working day was less boring than at my cousin's, for all she talked about were serials, suicides, murders, or the neighborhood gossip.[20] The exploits of the dog and cat were prominent among her preoccupations.

At the workshop, I found many young women of my age. I immediately became close friends with one of them, and we hardly paid attention to what the other working women did or said. All I earned for the first two

18. During the eighteenth century, most peasant and many working-class households made their own clothing; in urban areas, the middle and upper classes purchased garments that were made to order. In the course of the nineteenth century, a market in ready-made clothing—mass-produced garments that sold at relatively modest prices—gradually developed, thanks to the introduction of standardized sizes, labor-saving machines, and the reorganization of the production process itself. Among the consequences of these changes was an influx of female labor and a decline in skill and wage levels in the garment sector.

19. The profession of hatmaker (*chapelière*) was highly varied and might involve working in such materials as leathers, felts, feathers, and fabrics. Skill levels and wages were high, especially for a trade in which women worked in substantial numbers.

20. Serialized stories (*feuilletons*) were published in newspapers on a daily or weekly basis. While many literary classics, including the novels of Balzac, Dumas, Sue, and Zola, were originally published in this form, the quality of this popular literature was often mediocre, in part because authors were paid by the line. Bouvier's cousin's reading habits reflect the rapid spread of popular literacy toward the end of the century.

weeks was room and board, but at the end of that time I was placed on a piece rate, for this trade was conducted in part on a piece-rate basis.

I picked it up quickly and began to earn a reasonable livelihood. In the busy season, I would bring home from thirty to forty francs a week, and sometimes as much as forty-five. This dropped as low as twelve or fifteen francs in the slow season. This specialty within the garment trades had been very good, and working women had easily earned their living at it, but a crisis was threatening at the time I became a worker.

My cousins were fine people, but their inability to manage their family budget was their downfall. They liked to set a fancy table and eat like very rich people. They always served the choicest tidbits at their table and all the money they earned was spent on feasts, without any concern for the future. I was paying a fixed sum for my board, but every Sunday I had to offer this or that as a gift. When my weekly wages were high, I spent everything, and when the slow season came, I did not earn enough to pay for my room and board and went into debt, to the point where I could not manage to dress properly. What is more, we never went out and never took part in any entertainment; nothing but fancy food! I was growing anxious over this state of affairs when one day, following an argument for some reason or another, I parted with my cousins with nothing but the clothes I was wearing and a tiny bit of money in my pocket.

I went off to rent a small furnished room in a residential hotel.[21] This room was filthy, but I wanted to spend very little money. My rent was three francs per week. That was all I could pay, for I needed to buy underwear every week in order to get to the point where I had enough to change into. Every Saturday, for three or four weeks, I would buy myself a shirt for Fr 1.55, a handkerchief for Fr 0.20, a pair of pants for Fr 1.75, and a pair of socks for Fr 0.55, or Fr 3.75 in all, which with my rent made Fr 6.75.[22]

I had arranged my food as follows: In the morning I would have a five-centime loaf of bread and five centimes' worth of milk—milk cost twenty centimes a liter—or ten centimes for my breakfast. At midday I would take my meal with the other women from my shop, and there I did not want to seem to be scrimping, for fear that my cousins would hear of my hardships

21. A residential hotel offered rooms, usually furnished, on a weekly or monthly basis. It differed from a boarding house in that it typically rented individual rooms rather than dormitory-style beds, did not serve meals, and attracted fewer transients, though the lines between these two forms of lower-class housing were often blurred.
22. A small error has crept into Bouvier's calculations; her weekly expenditures on clothing actually total Fr 4.05, not 3.75. Her subsequent totals are all slightly off as a consequence.

and make fun of me. So I ate the usual fifty-centime bill of fare, consisting of boiled beef and vegetables in broth. I would eat the broth, in which I put a lot of bread, then the vegetables, but I kept the beef for the evening meal. I finished off this lunch with a portion of cheese. My expenses broke down as follows: Fr 0.50 for the broth and beef; Fr 0.20 for wine; Fr 0.15 for bread; Fr 0.15 for cheese; or Fr 1.00 in all. In the evenings, I would buy ten centimes' worth of bread to eat with my beef. My daily food cost me Fr 1.20 in all. My weekly expense for food came to Fr 8.40, which, when added to the cost of clothing and lodging, made a total of Fr 15.15. I earned more than Fr 15.15, but I wanted to save so I could set myself up in a place of my own, with my own bed. I did not want to stay in that residential hotel.

The hotel disgusted me all the more because it was filthy and was frequented by undesirables. I could not clean that small room as I would have done if I had been in my own place. On Sundays, I would do my laundry. I could not stand dirty clothes. I could stand to do without treats or entertainment, but to do without cleanliness was intolerable to me. I would suffer any sacrifice to be able to buy what I needed to set myself up in a place all my own. But to buy a bed and everything necessary to outfit it constitutes a considerable expense for a working woman who does not have a cent to spare and who is, moreover, without clothes or underwear. What little I owned when I had shown up at my cousins' house had been worn out, and I had never been able to buy myself anything to wear. I was worse off than when I had arrived at their place. When I moved away, I left behind the little that I owned to serve as a guaranty of a small debt I had contracted as a result of the excessive expenditures they forced me to make.

I put myself on a regimen of hardship in order to escape this situation. I saved as much as I could. Thanks to these daily restrictions, I was able, after a while, to buy myself a bandy-legged bed and a straw mattress, for which I paid ten francs; a bedspread bought on credit for ten francs; and two chairs, a table, and a very old, small sideboard, which together cost twenty-five francs. I had bought myself a half-dozen dishcloths and towels for three and a half francs, and two pairs of sheets for fourteen francs. Then I rented a small room. I paid thirty francs rent in advance, including the tip for the concierge. This room was a horrible little hovel, but it had one virtue that I appreciated enormously: it was clean. The walls were whitewashed. It was not comfortable, but it was home. I also had bought a few kitchen utensils and some dishes, which allowed me to eat at home and to realize some savings on my food.

I had been working in hatmaking for several years when that trade was threatened with a severe crisis by the manufacture of hats made of wool rather than felt.[23] These hats of wool felt sold for Fr 3.60. Because these goods came from England, they were ruining the French hatmaking industry, and the earnings of workers were in decline. Unemployment was getting steadily worse and poverty was on the increase.

Some time earlier, I had moved. I was a little better situated, though I did not have what, in the circumstances, was strictly necessary, namely a fireplace. Rooms with fireplaces were not within my budget. I was still living in a garret, lit by a skylight window, for poor folk have no right to heating. For someone like me, heating was a luxury item, and in wintertime, with no fire, those who live in garrets suffer a great deal. But there is one thing the poor cannot do without, and that is to eat. When you live in a room without a fireplace, the preparation of food is difficult. You have to buy it all prepared, which raises the cost.

On that seventh floor, there were a number of us living in rooms without fireplaces. We had found a way of cooking our food on a little charcoal stove placed in the corridor so we would not be asphyxiated by the gases that it gave off. To get the water we needed, we had to go down and fetch it in the courtyard. All the renters on the seventh floor were honest and sober workers, and we lived in perfect harmony.

Thanks to an installment company, I had replaced my bandy-legged bed with a brand new one, equipped with a box-spring and mattress, for the sum of seventy francs.[24] With this iron bed, which represented a great luxury for me, I could give my narrow room a somewhat stylish appearance. I covered my bed with my red Scottish shawl. I had nailed planks to the wall so as to simulate a fireplace. These planks were covered in and surrounded by red cotton cloth. Beneath this drapery, I would store my few dishes and kitchen utensils. The old sideboard that I had bought had not survived the move. It fell to pieces, and I did not even have the option of burning it, as I had no fireplace.

The poverty of the renters on that seventh floor made them stick together. We did each other favors. Many of the others were too busy or lacked the skills to do mending. I had never really learned to sew, but despite that I managed fairly well and was able to make aprons, skirts, simple women's blouses and morning jackets, as well as to do some mending. I earned a little money doing these jobs after my workday of hatmak-

23. Felt was originally made from animal fur that was pressed or bound together, but much the same effect could be achieved more cheaply by mechanically processing wool fibers. In time, wool felt would itself be replaced with straw as a raw material for hats, thus exacerbating the crisis in the trade.
24. Installment companies allowed individuals to purchase goods on credit by making payments over time.

ing, a workday that was becoming more and more uncertain. So I did my best to carry out these sewing jobs, and very often my customers would ask me, "Why don't you try to get a job in a dressmaking shop? You already know how to do good work and you could improve your skills." Oh, sure! I would have liked to with all my heart, but I didn't know of any dressmaking shops.

Life was very pleasant on that seventh floor, thanks to the good relations shared among all the renters. It was like a big family, and when one of them was ill, the others hastened to take care of her.

We had little in the way of entertainment except for our companionship. We would sometimes go out together, and when we did, you might have thought it was a regiment that was trooping down the stairway. We would go to the neighborhood traveling carnival and all ride the merry-go-round. Our celebration was rounded out by ten centimes' worth of fried potatoes that we would eat as we walked among the carnival booths. We would have a wonderful evening, one we would talk about for a long time! This expenditure was not often repeated, for it would have ruined us.

I lived on that seventh floor for several years. I had to leave because the renter who was subletting me my room needed it and gave me notice.

Hatmaking was getting worse and worse. Finally the inevitable occurred: I was out of work. What was I to do without a trade, without education, and without money? I prepared to go out looking for something. I made the rounds of places where little help-wanted signs were posted.

One read, "Wanted: corset-fan makers."[25] A neighbor and I went off to try to get this job. They explained to us what we had to do. It was not difficult, and we brought home a fairly large quantity of work, which we set about executing with a certain enthusiasm. We got up early and went to bed late. When the work was done, we went to return it to the woman who had employed us. She told us that our work had earned us eleven and a half francs and that, when the cost of the braid was deducted, that left us four francs in pay. Four francs! And the two of us had worked for two days, from five in the morning until ten at night! Deeming this work to be too poorly paid, we did not take on any more.

I went back to look at the help-wanted notices. Outside the shop of a feather merchant I read, "Wanted: young girl for easy work." I went in and asked what work they had. The employer showed me. I had to mount the eyes and beaks on birds used to decorate hats. After a moment's trial, the

25. These were women who did the embroidery stitching that held in place the whalebone stays of women's corsets.

boss told me, "I see that you'll do. I'll pay you one and a half francs for an eleven-hour day." The work was so simple that I could not hope to earn more. I turned the job down.

So there I was, still looking for a job. I rushed back to the help-wanted notices. I was lamenting my situation, standing with another woman before the notices that had been stuck to the walls of Saint Eustache Church, when a lady came up to us and asked, "Are you seamstresses?"

"Yes, madame," the other worker answered.

"Well, then," the lady said, "you're hired."

I was just saying to myself, "She's lucky she's a seamstress; she got herself a job," when the lady turned to me.

"And you, miss; are you a seamstress?"

"No madame, I would very much like to be a seamstress. I can sew well, but I'm not a seamstress."

"Well," she replied, "come along just the same."

I could not believe my ears. I was going to work in a dressmaking firm, I who had been hoping for just that for so long.

I showed up the next morning, at the agreed-upon time. They gave me an easy job, then another. They decided that I sewed well and that I readily understood instructions. I worked as hard as I could, but all week I tormented myself with this thought: "What is she going to pay me for the work I'm doing?" I was anxious. I told myself, "If she only pays me an apprentice's rate of half a franc a day, I can't keep coming to work. I can't live without earning money. I'm quite willing to bear some hardships (I knew what hardships were, for I had almost always imposed a certain number on myself), but there's a limit one can't go beyond. I have to live, and live by working."[26] I was determined to endure hardships in order to learn the trade of seamstress. Every day, I wished it were Saturday. At last Saturday arrived, and all day long I was feverish at the thought of the wages my employer would pay me. That evening she took me aside. She told me that I sewed well and that she believed I would pick it up quickly, but that I was not an accomplished worker. Her words pierced my heart like a thousand arrows. What would be the outcome of this conversation? Would I become a seamstress or not? That was what was riding on all this. "In short," she told me, "I can only pay you two and a half francs a day, but

26. The phrase *vivre en travaillant,* "to live by working," had special resonance in the nineteenth century, when it signified both the need and the right to earn a decent livelihood through one's labor. It had been very much in vogue in 1848, when the new republican government responded to a severe economic crisis by declaring the "right to work" and creating the National Workshops, in which unemployed workers could enroll as an alternative source of livelihood.

if you work hard, I'll give you a raise." These two and a half francs a day seemed like a lifesaver to me, like a rescue performed right in the midst of a storm, and I clung to this buoy. She was saving me from poverty. I had to struggle long and hard, for two and a half francs in wages is little enough, too little to allow a woman to live from her labor. But though I had to bear so many hardships, I at least had some hope of escaping my financial straits.

In the evening, when I got home to the seventh floor, I told everyone the happy news: I would be able to become a seamstress. This delighted my neighbors. The neighbor ladies were pleased that I would be able to make them beautiful dresses. I got orders for the day when I would be a full-fledged seamstress. I would describe to them the dresses that were made at the workshop, and they would tell me, "How beautiful they must be, all those ladies with their gorgeous dresses!"

I continued to take in mending and make simple dresses as I had done before entering the dressmaking shop. These jobs brought a certain comfort to my life, but they were a kind of overwork. I had already been working in that shop for a year. Contrary to what I had been promised, I received no raise, even though I had made enormous progress. I decided to change firms.

I went to look for another job in the Opéra quarter and was hired for five francs a day. I was delighted to be earning such a salary, but less so with the work to be performed. It was difficult. I was not equal to the task that had been entrusted to me. I really had to struggle to face all the difficulties that this work presented. How many sleepless nights I spent, thinking about the dress that I was to make the next day! But the five francs a day gave me the courage to overcome all these difficulties. That lasted for about a year.

One day I was hired by a firm in the Rue Caumartin. I was still earning five francs a day. It was the practice in this firm to make us work very late, without allowing time to eat dinner. During the season that I spent in that workshop, these late nights lasted until two in the morning nearly every day, and without our having eaten, except for a small loaf of bread and a bit of chocolate at four o'clock. They made us remain absolutely silent. And why were they having the seamstresses work late? You might think that there were lots of orders and that they required late hours to fill them. Not at all. We worked late so that the competitor across the street would think that our firm was overflowing with work and so that its good reputation would be known throughout Paris. It was simply hateful to make us work late in this manner, and in a terribly harsh winter, what is more!

The Seine was full of enormous blocks of ice, and great piles of snow swept along the quays. It took me three-quarters of an hour to make my way home, and this was at two in the morning, without having eaten dinner. When I got home, I did not have the energy to eat. After a season like that, I had to take to my bed and go to the hospital to have myself cared for. All the women working there were annoyed about this regimen, but they had hopes that soon the owners would no longer be able to make them work late. The law of 1892 was about to go into effect.[27] It would be a relief, they said, because, after all, there were evenings when we had nothing to do and still had to stay until two in the morning. The longest day that I worked was from eight in the morning until five o'clock the following evening, or thirty-three hours on my stool. That is why I shared the seamstresses' joy at the thought that the law of 1892 would free us.

I continued to live very frugally and was still doing extra work to keep myself afloat. I wanted to move, for I wanted a room with a fireplace. Yes, I wanted to offer myself the luxury of a fireplace, and then I wanted to buy myself some underwear and some clothes. The moment arrived when I was at last able to move. I had a fireplace in my room and even a little cupboard in which to put away the few dishes that I owned. There was also a storage space beneath the eaves. All my kitchen implements and other things could remain hidden. To have all these conveniences, I had to climb an extra story. I was living on the eighth floor. There was water on the landing. What a convenience, instead of having to go all the way down to the courtyard! For that reason, I would squander water. You cannot imagine how often I was capable of washing up, with water there on the landing!

When I had moved in, the concierge told me, "I have a little sideboard in your room. If it's not in your way, I'll leave it." I was delighted: a sideboard, a fireplace, a cupboard, a storage space, and water; it was really too much. I could not believe I had so much luxury. And then, to complete my happiness, my room looked out over the street. I was opposite a church that had a clock. That way, I always knew what time it was. It was all the more convenient as my old watch was no longer working, and I could not consider buying myself another.

With time I had succeeded in becoming a good seamstress. I no longer had difficulty executing the work that was entrusted to me. But I continued taking on extra work. I needed so many things: underwear and clothes, and then I harbored hopes of owning a wardrobe with a mirror!

When I had gotten used to that house, I familiarized myself with my new neighborhood, which was diverse. This was not the same world I had

27. The law of 1892 regulated the length of the working day for women and children. It would have limited Bouvier's day to eleven hours and forbidden night work altogether; however, it was not consistently enforced.

known in the house I had left behind. The eighth floor of this middle-class house was occupied almost exclusively by women. The rents were low, but the rooms and studios were moderately comfortable. I had the prettiest room, even though it had no proper window. Like the little place I had just left, it had a skylight window. In the midst of all those women's financial distress, I was the best off. I was considered a rich girl. All those women lived on a miserable income. There were twelve renters on that landing. I would leave in the morning and not come home until late at night. The working day ended at eight, but late nights were still common, and as a consequence, many of these women spent three to six months in the house without my ever getting to know them.

Among the renters who made the biggest impression on me, I recall a woman who made fine linen goods.[28] She had been raised in a religious orphanage, and from the age of four she had worked doing laundry and embroidery. She worked for a big firm in the Rue de la Paix. Despite the delicacy of her work, she could not live decently, eating a small loaf of bread at Fr 0.05 and Fr 0.10 worth of milk. One day she could not pay her rent. She moved out. She went to live in a nearby house and, tired of living in such poverty, threw herself into the street from the eighth floor. She was twenty-two years old. She preferred to kill herself than to die of hunger.

Another strung pearls and spangles on fancy braidwork. She earned next to nothing and, when evening came, would go down into the street and seek through prostitution what she could not earn in a ten- to twelve-hour workday.

How many young girls have I seen fall, because they earned such miserable wages. I have seen them go down into the streets. Poverty is an insufferable situation, and those who do not escape into suicide escape into prostitution. All that any of them needed in order to remain honest women and become worthy mothers with families of their own was a reasonable wage.

After my mother had left Paris and I stayed behind alone, I changed jobs, as we have seen, several times. I had been in Paris ten months when, on the occasion of the first of the year, I sent my mother a money order for fifteen francs as a New Year's gift. A few days later, my sister quit her job. She sent her trunk to my address. This trunk was not locked. I was curious enough to look inside and there I found letters written by my mother. I pursued my indiscretion to the point of reading them. They were post-

---

28. A linen-goods worker (*lingère*) made women's undergarments and fine lingerie and adorned them with embroidery, lace, and other embellishments.

marked from the region where I had started my career as a worker and where I had endured such poverty! I read them. One of them began like this: "My dear little girl, you're just like me: you have a generous nature, unlike your sister. She earns sixteen francs every two weeks, gives me ten, and when I have no bread to eat, she hangs on to her money. She is a heartless child." What! I was a heartless child? My own mother would write that to my sister? I was dumbfounded. But here is the explanation behind this letter:

You know all that I suffered because the foreman of the factory would not give me a raise, and what means I employed to get one. At the time I got my raise, my father and mother had found some work. I was hoping for a lull in our distress and I said to my mother, "Since you and father are both working, I would really appreciate it if you would leave me the six francs of my raise so that I can have some ankle boots. And besides, I don't have any more dresses!" But this proposal always remained a dream. No one ever bought me a dress. The only new dress that I had in all the time I lived in that region was given to me by my godmother. This was a dress made of the kind of linen they make in Vichy. My godmother also gave me the material to have a frock made, but I had to wait a long time before I had saved Fr 1.75 to pay to have it sewn.

And here I was reading how my mother insulted me to my sister. She dared to write such a thing! I was a heartless child! And this letter had been sent from a region where I had suffered so much and where I had spent my nights earning bread for my little brothers! I could not believe my eyes! I reread the letter: "Yes, yes, that's right, that's what it says. I am a heartless child." I was seized by rage mixed with sadness. This letter hurt me so much that I cried and stamped my foot in anger. And I repeated to myself: "What do you mean, I am a heartless child? I, who just sent a money order for fifteen francs even though I lack clothes and underwear?" Reading this produced a deep wound in my affection for my mother and in my pride. In my fury I told myself, "It doesn't surprise me that she could write such a thing about me: she doesn't love me. That's why she always punished me so harshly."

All the dignity and conscientiousness that I possessed rebelled against such treatment. I firmly resolved not to write to my mother anymore. "From now on, I'll ask no one's advice, I'll complain to no one, and when I'm hungry or cold, no one will know. I'll live alone in the world without a roof to shelter me when I'm out of work, without a heart to warm me or a conscience to guide me. I'll make my way alone in Paris. In this steaming hell, I'll remain unknown, and no one will know that I'm a heartless child."

You have seen the daily struggle I had to undertake in order to be able to live, and live by working. But I did not want to fall like so many others and I did not want them to be able to say one day, "She lacked courage," or "She didn't know how to make her way; she is indeed a heartless child."

I did not hear news of my mother directly for more than ten years. My sister would give me some now and then. Thanks to the extra work I was doing and my five-franc wage for a ten-hour workday, my situation was fairly good. From time to time I would treat myself to an evening at the theater. My favorite was the Opéra-comique. A one-franc ticket was all I needed to keep me entertained. I would remember a few bits of songs and hum them for weeks. For a long time I had cherished the desire to go see a performance of *Carmen*. One day, as I left my workshop, I had, by way of dinner, a ten-centime cup of coffee and a large croissant for the same price. Thus fortified, I rushed off to the Opéra-comique, where I was at last to see *Carmen*.

But Don José and Michaela's duet had a profound and unexpected effect on me. Michaela sings the message that Don José's mother has asked her to deliver:

> Tell him his mother
> Thinks of him night and day;
> That she misses him and that she hopes,
> That she forgives and that she waits.

On hearing these words, my thoughts immediately turned to my mother. She also was waiting for me and hoped that I would write her, that I would come see her. She forgave my silence.

Don José replies:

> My mother, I see her; I see my village once again!
> Memories of bygone times! Memories of my native region!
> You fill my heart with strength and courage,
>   Oh cherished memories!
> Memories of bygone times! Memories of my native region![29]

By the time Don José had finished singing, I was sobbing at the memory of my mother and my native region. I pictured the little village in Dauphiné where I had spent my childhood. I could see the fields and meadows that I had so much enjoyed, the trees in which I climbed with such agility. All these memories stirred up my deepest emotions, and when I hummed those lines my eyes would grow moist with tears. I wanted at all costs to see my mother and my village once again.

29. Bouvier's version differs in several minor respects from the standard French libretto.

I was seized by homesickness. I remembered the letter that had been the cause of so much sorrow, but perhaps I had overdramatized and been harsh and cruel toward my mother. I wanted to convince myself that I was wrong. I would tell myself, "Mothers are always right." I could not hope to make the trip that year. I had been sick, and my illness had confined me to a hospital bed for two months. During that time, I had not earned a cent but had to pay my rent all the same. It was impossible to pay the cost of such an expensive trip!

But I was going to make arrangements for the following year. I would take on extra work. I would spend part of my nights at it. I would get up at four in the morning and go to bed at midnight. In this way I would surely scrape together the money I needed to go see my mother. And back there in that region where I had been raised, where my childhood friends were, what a surprise my return would be! No one had heard a word from me, and one fine day, there I'd be. They'd all be surprised. Perhaps they would not recognize me, I'd been away so long!

I spent the whole year figuring out and drawing a map of my journey. By buying a tourist ticket, I could make stops along the way. I would also go see my father. I knew that he was working in Tarare and I would go surprise him. I also decided to take my niece. She would be happy to visit her grandmother. The fresh air would do her a lot of good. Everything was settled, I was saving up, and the late nights were piling up. I was getting little sleep. I constantly thought about my trip, which I had scheduled for the slow season so as not to lose my job. I was going to bring my mother a dress and alter it to fit her once I was there. She would be happy to have a dress made by a Parisian seamstress. All I thought about was my trip.

FIRST RETURN TO MY NATIVE REGION

At last the day arrived. I had my tourist ticket in my hand. All my preparations were complete, and the straps on my trunk were buckled. I was off to my native region!

My first stop was Tarare. I went to see my father. I asked for him at the place where he worked, and when he saw me he said, "Good morning, madame, what would you like?" This "Good morning, madame" froze me. Absence had erased me from his memory and perhaps from his heart. I asked him:

"Don't you recognize me?"

"No, madame."

"What! You don't recognize your own daughter?"

"My daughter? Which one? Jeanne?"

"Yes," I answered.

I did not feel his heart thrill. The bond of blood relatedness had died out. "Oh, it's you, Jeanne? Fine, fine, I'll ask permission to get off work and I'll step out with you." He came back after an instant and took me off to his boarding house. When I told him that I was going to see my mother, he began to pour out a torrent of curses upon her. I was broken-hearted. It was as if I were reliving the household quarrels I had witnessed in my childhood. I left the next day. He made me promise to come back to see him on my return trip. I promised him but I did not keep my word. The memory of this visit that I took away with me was too unpleasant. I got back on the train. During the trip, I was seized by an extraordinary anxiety. I sighed, I could not breathe, and it seemed that my heart would burst. What an awful feeling I experienced! What was going to happen to me? I did not know. When the train stopped, I could not believe my eyes. I thought I was dreaming, and my anxiety redoubled. Surely I would never be able to make it to the end of the road that I had to travel to get to the little village where my mother lived.

It was seven in the evening, a beautiful summer's evening, and scorching hot in the valley that I had to cross. The wheat was ripe and the crickets were chirping. Their song made the earth tremble beneath the golden wheat. The sun was about to disappear behind the Cévennes mountains, but its torrid rays still flooded the valley, and my heart was still beating too hard. I had seven kilometers to cover and my niece, a child of four, did not want to walk. I was forced to carry her. How she made me suffer! I would have been happy to be alone to contemplate all this, without having a four-year-old child on my hands! From time to time, I would set her down on the ground and tell her to walk. She would say yes and then refuse, which tormented me all over again.

I was afraid I would not be able to find the road that leads to the hamlet. I asked directions of every country person I met. They would tell me, "It's about forty-five minutes more. When you get to such-and-such a place, turn left, then right, and you'll find the such-and-such district." They told me the names of all these places in French, but I only knew their names in the local dialect.[30] I could not get my bearings. Once up on the hillside, I kept on walking. I seemed to remember that house. Yes, yes, I recognized

30. This detail is revealing. During the approximately twenty years—Bouvier does not specify the precise moment at which this incident took place—that had elapsed since 1876, when she left the village where she grew up, the use of French had spread. Bouvier found herself in the paradoxical position of one whose knowledge of the local scene had been overtaken by the progress of the national language and culture which, to the inhabitants of this isolated village, she must have appeared to represent.

the house, but I no longer remembered the name of the people who lived there. A little further on, I noticed a vineyard that belonged to one of my uncles. And then another vineyard that was part of the farm that my uncle had worked for nearly thirty years. I found the field of pink clover where I had made such beautiful wreaths with my cousins.

When I was closer to the farm, I saw people coming and going with lanterns. It had grown completely dark. I said to myself, "They don't suspect that I'm here, that I'm watching them," for these farmers were my uncle and aunt and cousins. "That's them down there, rubbing down the livestock after a hard day's work. And when the livestock has been groomed, they'll go sit around the big table on which they have set an enormous soup pot in which an excellent soup is steaming. I almost want to go see them first, they're so nearby, and then I'll go find my mother." An idea went through my head. "Suppose I went to ask them for their hospitality without telling who I am? I'll tell them that I got lost in the countryside, that I'm worn out from carrying this little girl, and afraid to walk in the dark. If they don't recognize me, maybe they'll let me sleep in their barn. But no, I can't try that; my heart is beating too hard, and besides I'm too tired. I'd rather go straight to my mother's house. But it's so dark, and I have to pass through a little wood! How frightened and tired I am!"

At last I arrived at the hamlet! In another moment, I would be at my mother's. Now I was in the courtyard. It's about time that I arrived, I thought. My arms are weary from carrying this child, and my heart is beating harder and harder. No light whatever. Is she already in bed?

I knocked. From the rear room, a voice cried out to me, "Come in." I entered and found myself in total darkness. I asked if anyone was home and I heard someone get up. It was my oldest brother. He came toward me and I asked him, "Don't you recognize me?"

"No." I told him that I was his sister, and he immediately went off to find my mother, who was at a neighbor's house. When she saw me with my sister's child, she started to cry. I could not breathe any more. It seemed to me that I was going to collapse from so much emotion and fatigue. I was asked a thousand questions that I answered only briefly. I could not eat a thing and went straight to bed. The next morning, after getting up quite early, I began by telling my mother that I had visited my father. That displeased her a great deal. She told me, "You shouldn't have gone to see him. He's not worth the trouble." She began by pouring out a torrent of curses against him. I said to myself, "My God, how sad it is to have parents who hate each other so!"

The neighbors, emboldened by curiosity, would come see me and speak in the local dialect. I had forgotten it, but I listened carefully: I did not want the local residents to think that I was putting on airs by pretending not to understand them. Next came visits to the family. Everyone was surprised to see me. First I went to the house of my uncle, aunt, and cousins, who were living in perfect harmony. One of my cousins was married; her husband lived there along with their two children. What a beautiful harmony reigned in that family! What a difference from my own family in which some were here, others elsewhere, and in which the father and mother called each other names from a distance! My heart constricted to think that I had struggled so hard to live and so as not to fall, and that meanwhile my cousins were living happily! How harsh fate had been for me! How sad it is to have parents who could not get along!

Every day I returned to that farm. I was so happy to be back with my cousins and to sit down at that great table around which all the members of that close-knit family would gather. My month of vacation passed by very quickly. I had to get ready to leave, but in leaving I carried away the firm conviction that absence and distance diminish feelings between mother and daughter. This observation saddened me a great deal.

I returned to Paris, satisfied at having made the trip, at having seen my family and childhood friends again. Upon my arrival in Paris, I had to start work and put some order in my finances, which were not in the best of shape. I took up my needle with renewed enthusiasm. I went back to my dressmaking shop, where I got back together with my fellow workers. I had fun with them. Women who work as seamstresses are pleasant comrades. You have to see them, working so hard to correct the slightest flaw that might make them seem vulgar, trying always to appear distinguished. The only songs they would sing were the sentimental ones. Songs with coarse lyrics were excluded from their repertoire. And how they would scrimp and save so they could buy gloves, perfume, and a thousand other accessories. The midday meal was often reduced to its simplest expression, and the slab of chocolate at teatime was often done without, in order to get together the sum needed to buy some cosmetic. They would subject themselves to a severe diet just to be beautiful. This love of finery comes from the fact that all they make are luxury items. Most of them enter the trade between the ages of twelve and fifteen. They grow up within this specialized branch of the clothing industry, one of the glories of our national economy. How could they not end up loving finery, beautiful dresses, handsome hats, and all those elements that constitute the elegant dress of a lady, when these children, who have grown into young women, spend their entire day making dresses that will adorn other women! If these young dressmakers earned better wages, they could dress up properly without having to skimp on their food. On their diet of privation, many become anemic and tubercular.[31] That is the cause of such a high rate of mortality in this trade. These consequences are not significant only for the working women; they can also affect the clientele.

For some time I had had clients who would have me work at their homes during the off-season. I would thus escape the period of unemployment, which provided me with a certain comfort. In this way, I was never without work. But during the busy season, these clients brought me more work than I could handle. In addition to the days spent at the workshop, I always had a few orders to do at home to satisfy my personal clientele. After my workday, I therefore had to take on long late-night vigils. My time was divided up as follows: wake up at four o'clock; work at home until eight; then get dressed and have breakfast in the space of a half-hour; at eight-thirty, leave for the workshop, where I arrived at nine o'clock and got out only at eight or nine in the evening. I would rush home, eat dinner in a hurry, and go back to work until midnight, which is when I finally got to bed; then I would sleep until four o'clock the next morning.

I forced myself to take on all this work because I cherished a sweet dream, which I have not been able to realize. I remembered the sad days of my childhood, the days when I was hungry. I did not want to go hungry in my old age. I wanted my old age to be better than my childhood. It was this prospect that gave me the courage to work. My ambition was to put together a life annuity and save enough to buy myself a little house in the country. Yes, I dreamed of a house with a garden where I would grow vegetables and flowers, where I would raise chickens and rabbits. That way I would spend my old age in sweet peace. I remembered my childhood friends in my beloved Dauphiné. I wanted to end my days there. To realize this dream, I had to sew my heart out, and so I sewed with fervor.

When my young fellow workers in the shop would say, "I want a beautiful dress, a handsome hat," I would tell them, "Me, I want a little house in the country with chickens and rabbits." They would laugh and tell me, "You'll get bored in the country."

"Oh no, my dear little ones, I'll never get bored as long as I'm sure that I'll never go hungry and as long as I have a garden filled with flowers, chickens, and rabbits!"

---

31. Though tuberculosis has been largely controlled in industrialized nations thanks to the introduction of antibiotic medications since the Second World War, it was responsible for approximately 150,000 deaths per year in late nineteenth-century France, or nearly one death for every three hundred persons.

Jeanne Bouvier never managed to realize her dream of retiring to the countryside, but she went on to live a long and rewarding life. In part 2 of her autobiography, she details how she became a member of the Syndicalist movement; lived through the First World War; assumed a leadership role in the French federation of garment workers; traveled to the United States as a delegate to the International Congress of Working Women, of which she was elected vice-president; and became a significant participant in the political struggles of the working class. Part 3 is devoted to her new career as author, launched after she became involved in a large-scale collaborative project of research under the direction of the historian Georges Renard. Bouvier wrote the volume on linen-goods workers in the resulting series on French trades. In the course of this work, she also became interested in the parallels between the economic resurgence of France at the end of the sixteenth century and that of the 1920s, and she eventually published a book on the subject. With Renard's encouragement, she also wrote a treatise on female employees of the French National Post and Telegraph Office; another on the role of women in the French Revolution; and the autobiography from which these excerpts have been taken. This last work was completed in the 1930s, while Bouvier was living in a retirement home that offered her something of the "sweet peace" she had hoped to find in her later years. It was there that she died in 1964 at the age of ninety-nine.

Compositor: Keystone Typesetting, Inc.
Text: 10/13 Aldus
Display: Aldus
Printer: BookCrafters
Binder: BookCrafters